2495

D0031407

CALIFORNIA NATURAL HISTORY GUIDES

SIERRA NEVADA
NATURAL HISTORY

California Natural History Guides

Phyllis M. Faber and Bruce M. Pavlik, General Editors

SIERRA NEVADA NATURAL HISTORY

REVISED EDITION

Tracy I. Storer
Robert L. Usinger
David Lukas

UNIVERSITY OF CALIFORNIA PRESS

Berkeley   Los Angeles   London

California Natural History Guide Series No. 73

University of California Press
Berkeley and Los Angeles, California

University of California Press, Ltd.
London, England

Library of Congress Cataloging-in-Publication Data

Storer, Tracy Irwin, 1889–1973
  Sierra Nevada natural history / Tracy I. Storer, Robert L. Usinger, and David Lukas—
Rev. ed.
      p. cm.— (California natural history guides)
    Rev. ed. of: Sierra Nevada natural history / by Tracy I. Storer and Robert L. Usinger. 1963.
    ISBN 0-520-23277-1 (case)—ISBN 0-520-24096-0 (pbk.)
      1. Natural history—Sierra Nevada (Calif. and Nev.)   I. Usinger, Robert L. (Robert
Leslie), 1912–1968.   II. Lukas, David, 1964-   III. Title.   IV. Series.

  QH105.C2S8 2004
  508.794'4—dc22

                                                                        2003061287

Manufactured in China
10   09   08   07   06   05   04
10   9   8   7   6   5   4   3   2   1

The paper used in this publication meets the minimum requirements of ANSI/NISO
Z39.48-1992 (R 1997) (*Permanence of Paper*).

Cover photograph: Marsh Lake in the John Muir Wilderness, © Dennis Flaherty.

The publisher gratefully acknowledges the generous contributions
to this book provided by

the Gordon and Betty Moore Fund in Environmental Studies
Richard & Rhoda Goldman Fund
and
the General Endowment Fund of the
University of California Press Associates.

Grateful acknowledgment is also made to
the California Academy of Sciences.

CALIFORNIA
ACADEMY OF
SCIENCES

CONTENTS

Plates follow pages 16, 96, 208, and 320.

PREFACE

This guide, first published in 1963 by Tracy I. Storer and Robert L. Usinger, is one of the most enduring natural history classics of all time. For over 40 years it has been a definitive handbook for countless visitors to the Sierra Nevada, many of whom were introduced to the mountain range for the first time through these pages. Numerous field biologists, naturalists, and students could pay homage to this book for its influence on their lives and careers. This is a book that has withstood the test of time as well as the rigors of field use by people who have hiked, driven, climbed, surveyed, and studied every corner of the Sierra Nevada with this guide in hand. It goes without saying, therefore, that this classic guide is a gem, and with the addition of new knowledge, updated scientific names, and brand new illustrations it is hoped that it will shine again as a polished gem.

This guide is a comprehensive introduction to many common plants and animals of the Sierra Nevada. Stretching from the Central Valley to the Great Basin desert, and with elevations over 14,000 ft, the Sierra Nevada is one of California's dominant natural features and home to a large proportion of the state's plants and animals. This book's Introduction provides essential background on the Sierra—its physical features, climate, waters, geological history, and the ways in which the mountain areas are affected by human occupancy. The bulk of the book, however, comprises species accounts grouped into taxonomic sections.

The plant accounts include a selection of fungi, lichens, ferns, wildflowers (including grasses, sedges, and rushes), many shrubs, and most of the trees found in the Sierra. The sections on animals omit various small creatures that are rarely seen, most of the waterbirds that are merely migratory visitants, and a few lesser known mammals. Due to the immense variety of species, the bulk of the insect accounts deal only with the order or family, but for the butterflies and dragonflies a larger selection of representative species are described. The book contains descriptions of more than 750 species or groups, most of which are illustrated.

Because of space limitations it is impossible to deal with every plant or animal known in the Sierra Nevada. Those of common occurrence that are readily identified are included. Where a group is represented by several kinds that cannot be distinguished from one another except by a trained person using a technical book, a single account is provided (examples being willows, shrews, and bats). In other cases the commonest and most widely distributed species is described, with brief mention of others. Using this book to identify a species requires comparing the plant or animal in question to the illustrations and then turning to the species account. Species accounts highlight some diagnostic features and provide additional details on distribution and life history features that are of interest or that help in identifying a species. Aspects of the life history of many of the vertebrate species are covered in greater detail.

The common and scientific names used in this book are based on taxonomic authorities acknowledged at the beginning of each section, but in some cases there is little published literature to draw from and the names were developed with feedback from specialists. Common names are especially problematic because in many groups no standard names have been chosen or agreed upon, so that each expert disagrees slightly on what should be put into print. Scientific names, however, follow strict rules and are almost universally accepted, although new interpretations of genetic or morphological evidence lead to frequent changes. Species names are composed of two parts: the genus name and a species epithet. Thus the Common Loon has the scientific name *Gavia immer,* the first part being the genus of loons and the second being the unique name for this species. In this book the convention of providing scientific names varies in the invertebrate section where order, superfamily, or family are mostly used in lieu of lower level names.

Over the past 40 years there has been an immense body of scientific studies and advances published that improve our understanding of the Sierra Nevada landscape and its plants and animals. On top of this, a massive four-volume compendium of the "state of the knowledge" on the Sierra Nevada was published in 1996, pulling together for the first time a sweeping summary of how the region is faring. The "Sierra Nevada Ecosystem Project Report" (or SNEP as it is popularly known) paints a complex yet troubling picture that is detailed more fully in the Introduction under the heading The Changing Landscape.

Since the original publication of *Sierra Nevada Natural History,* populations of numerous species have declined sharply and new information has pinpointed declines that were already ongoing. A handful of these species have been accorded special status, even as many other species slowly dwindle with no official status. The status of species officially acknowledged as being at risk are noted in individual species accounts. Categories of risk fall into two groups—those recognized at the Federal level, and those recognized at the State level—sometimes these two tiers are in agreement, other times not. The categories of Endangered or Threatened indicate populations in need of immediate attention; while the category Species of Special Concern is akin to a red warning flag raised before immediate action becomes necessary. Furthermore, some species are more at risk during certain seasons or in certain parts of their range. Therefore the notation— Federal Species of Special Concern (nesting)—signifies, in the case of a bird, that this species is recognized at the Federal level as being at risk on its nesting grounds.

Despite the abundance of information and knowledge, the shelves of new field guides, and the tireless labors of countless biologists and naturalists, what stands out is how much remains to be learned about Sierra Nevada ecosystems. Even the most basic details on status and distribution are entirely lacking for a good number of Sierra species; not to mention the plants, insects, and salamanders being discovered that are totally unknown to science. The field has never been more wide open for new students, new questions, and new discoveries!

David Lukas

ACKNOWLEDGMENTS
FOR THIS EDITION

Just as the first edition of this guide was the work of many people, so too this revised edition is the reflection of many naturalists, biologists, and other specialists who generously donated their time and expertise in reviewing and reshaping the text. This was not in every case an easy task because some fields of study have grown immensely in complexity since Storer and Usinger first published their book in 1963. Even more astonishing, some groups of plants and animals have received so little attention that it's nearly impossible to gather information for a book of this nature. Lichens and quite a number of invertebrates come to mind, but it's surprising how little is known about the status and distribution of charismatic groups like amphibians, reptiles, birds, and mammals.

I wish to thank the folks who helped bring this text up-to-date, taking time to offer feedback and enduring countless questions because, in many cases, they wanted to contribute to a book that affected each of their own lives in some way.

INTRODUCTION: Michael Barbour (Plant and Animal Distribution), Steve Beckwitt (The Changing Landscape), Bob Erickson (The Changing Landscape), Mary Hill (Geological History), King Huber (Geological History), and Randall Osterhuber (Climate).

FUNGI: Dennis E. Desjardin, Daniel A. Nicholson, Margriet Wetherwax, and Michael Wood.

LICHENS: Charis Bratt and Stephen Sharnoff.

MOSSES: Brent Mishler and Jim Shevock.

FERNS: Alan R. Smith and Margriet Wetherwax.

FLOWERING PLANTS: Julie Stauffer Carville, Carolyn Chainey-Davis, and Margriet Wetherwax.

SHRUBS: Hugh N. Mozingo, John Stuart, and Margriet Wetherwax.

TREES: Ronald M. Lanner, Bruce M. Pavlik, and Margriet Wetherwax.

MISCELLANEOUS ANIMALS: Elizabeth Kools (overall review), D. Christopher Rogers (overall review), Darrell Ubick (spiders and relatives), Leonard S. Vincent (overall review), and Gary C. Williams (overall review).

INSECTS: Lawrence A. Baptiste (overall review), Kathy R. Biggs (dragonflies and damselflies), Michael M. Collins (moths and overall review), Steve Heydon (overall review), Tim Manolis (dragonflies and damselflies), Paul A. Opler (butterflies), Jerry A. Powell (overall review), D. Christopher Rogers (overall review), and Arthur Shapiro (butterflies).

FISH: Peter B. Moyle.

AMPHIBIANS AND REPTILES: Sean Barry, Gary M. Fellers, Robert Hansen, and Mark R. Jennings.

BIRDS: Edward C. Beedy, David F. DeSante, Ned K. Johnson, and Mac McCormick.

MAMMALS: Peter E. Busher, John H. Harris, E. W. Jameson, Jr., and James L. Patton.

Special thanks to Bruce M. Pavlik and Joseph L. Medeiros for extensive comments on the original Storer and Usinger text, and to Simone Whitecloud for assistance in reviewing drafts of the revised text.

David Lukas also thanks the many people who have joined him in exploring the Sierra, with deep gratitude to Eric Beckwitt, Tavia Cathcart, the late Chuck Dockham, Bob Erickson, Liese Greensfelder, Sara Greensfelder, Maya Hill, Theo Killigrew, Carole Koda, Erin Noel, Gary Snyder, and Jerry Tecklin for their unique and instructive ways of making the Sierra Nevada home. Thanks also go to Brett Hall Jones (Squaw Valley Community of Writers), Jack Hicks (Art of the Wild), Bartshe Miller (Mono Lake Committee), and Jim Steele (Sierra Nevada Field Campus), for each providing a special place to teach Sierra Nevada natural history.

This revision would not have been possible without the hard work of the folks at University of California Press, especially Laura Cerruti, who got the ball rolling. Laurel Anderson, Cindy Wathen, and Stephanie Rubin did a tremendous job in art research; Joanne Bowser at TechBooks carefully fine-tuned the manuscript; and Scott Norton skillfully and graciously brought all the pieces together.

David Lukas

ACKNOWLEDGMENTS
FOR THE FIRST EDITION

The authors are grateful to many persons and several organizations for much generous cooperation in producing this handbook—selecting lists of species to include, reviewing the manuscript, and lending or permitting use of illustrations.

GEOLOGICAL HISTORY: C. G. Higgins (review).

WEATHER DATA ON PLANT BELTS: P. A. Munz and D. D. Keck.

FUNGI: R. T. Orr (list, review, photographs); and University of California Herbarium, Berkeley (Elizabeth Morse negatives).

LICHENS: J. W. Thomson and Isabelle Tavares (identifications).

FERNS: Figures from Leroy Abrams. 1926–1960. *Illustrated Flora of the Pacific States.* Stanford, CA: Stanford University Press.

WILDFLOWERS AND SHRUBS: J. T. Howell (lists); J. M. Tucker (review); June McCaskill (identifications); figures from L. Abrams and R. S. Ferris. 1926–1960. *Flora;* a few from N. L. Britton and Addison Brown. 1913. *An Illustrated Flora of the Northern United States and Canada.* 2d ed. By permission of New York Botanical Garden; color slides (besides those of the authors): California Academy of Sciences (Charles Webber collection); Sierra Club; Yosemite National Park Museum; E. O. Essig; and T. H. Jukes.

TREES: Figures from W. L. Jepson. 1923. *Trees of California.* Berkeley, CA: Sather Gate Bookshop; G. B. Sudworth. 1908. *Forest Trees of the Pacific Slope.* Washington, DC: USDA Forest Service; and L. Abrams and R. S. Ferris. 1926–1960. *Flora.*

MISCELLANEOUS ANIMALS: Some figures from T. I. Storer and R. L. Usinger. 1957. *General Zoology.* 3d ed. New York: McGraw-Hill Book Co. By permission of the publishers.

MOLLUSKS: Allyn G. Smith (list, review, specimens for figures).

INSECTS: Arthur C. Smith and Jerry Powell (review); Frieda L. Abernathy, Celeste Green, and other persons in Department. of Entomology, University of California, Berkeley; T. I. Storer and R. L. Usinger, 1957. *General Zoology;* and R. L. Usinger. 1956. *Aquatic Insects of California.* Berkeley and Los Angeles: University of California Press; some photos of insect work from Pacific Southwest Forest and Range Experiment Station, Berkeley.

FISHES: W. I. Follett (list, distributional data, review); California Department of Fish and Game (three color plates); other figures from scientific papers.

AMPHIBIANS AND REPTILES: R. C. Stebbins (list, review, figures from his *Amphibians and Reptiles of Western North America.* 1954. New York: McGraw-Hill Book Co. By permission of the publishers.

BIRDS: R.T. Orr (list); L. H. Miller (review); Yonekichi Makino (line figures); Museum of Vertebrate Zoology, University of California, Berkeley; owl figures and color plates from J. Grinnell and T. I. Storer. 1924. *Animal Life in the Yosemite.* Berkeley: University of California Press; and Edward Spaulding color plate of red finches and *Leucosticte* used in Ralph Hoffman. 1927. *Birds of the Pacific States.* Boston: Houghton Mifflin Co. By permission.

MAMMALS: R. T. Orr (list); L. P. Tevis, Jr. (review); Museum of Vertebrate Zoology, University of California, Berkeley (color plate of chipmunks); plate of mammal tracks adapted in part from W. H. Burt and R. P. Grossenheider. 1964. *A Field Guide to the Mammals.* 2d ed. By permission of W. H. Burt; and Emily E. Reid, Don G. Kelley, and Julia P. Iltis (line figures).

Other drawings made by Emily E. Reid, Julia P. Iltis, Barbara Daly, Paul Catts, and Petr Wygodzinsky.

Tracy I. Storer
Robert L. Usinger

INTRODUCTION

THE SIERRA NEVADA, with its rugged topography, varied resources, and superb flora and fauna, is a dominant feature of California. For countless centuries, Native Americans wintered on its lower flanks, foraged in its higher parts during summer, and even crossed it to trade with tribes beyond. Spanish occupants of the coastal hills and valleys thought of it as a *terra incognita*, distant and foreboding, and considered it a barrier to invasion from the east—although later that proved otherwise.

Discovery of gold in the western foothills of the Sierra, in what became known as the Mother Lode, stimulated a spectacular invasion of California by new peoples in the mid–nineteenth century. This commanding range, with its feed, water, and game, was a haven of refuge to westbound pioneers after the rigors of parched deserts in Utah and Nevada. Crossing the Sierra with wagons, however, before roads were built, was a herculean task for both humans and animals.

For several decades after the gold rush, the major enterprises in the Sierra were mining, timber production, and livestock grazing. Meanwhile, discovery of Yosemite Valley in 1851 and of the giant sequoias the following year by white settlers gave hints of the recreation values present. The building of a railroad across the range and a connecting narrow-gauge line from Truckee to Lake Tahoe led to the establishment of early resorts and summer homes in that area. Mountain climbers and campers pushed into various parts of the range to scale the peaks, to enjoy the rugged scenery, and to hunt and fish. Throughout the "horse and wagon" days an outing in the mountains demanded time, effort, and perseverance, but brought rich rewards (fig. 1). The automobile and improved roads have spread

Figure 1. By the 1920s visitors to the Sierra Nevada were leaving their imprint.

opportunities for outdoor enjoyment so that now millions of people use the mountains for a wide variety of reasons and many portions are accessible at all seasons.

Because of its geographic position and topographic features, the Sierra Nevada has a wide variety of climatic conditions and biological features—equivalent to a spread from northern Mexico to the fringe of the American Arctic. A trip on any cross-mountain highway between the Central Valley and the Great Basin reveals a diversity of plant and animal life scarcely equaled by a journey of similar length anywhere else. In two or three hours during summer you go from the hot grasslands of the Sacramento–San Joaquin plains to cool elevations under pines and firs, then on to alpine meadows. There are changes in the flora and fauna every few miles (figs. 2 and 3). From the lowland valleys that never experience snow, the roads cross summit passes where winter drifts may exceed 20 or 40 ft in depth. Each elevation and each season has its sequence of change in weather and floral pattern. The lower western flats and slopes become green with winter rains and colorful with wildflowers in spring, but by midsummer their ground cover is parched, tinder-dry, and yellow. The mountain valleys and slopes, by contrast, are snow blanketed for months during winter, but from May or June to August they are green parks bright with wildflowers.

Recorded history of these mountains began precisely on April 2, 1772. The missionary Pedro Font, while at the western edge of the San Joaquin Valley, saw, about 120 miles to the east, a great snowy range. In his diary, he sketched the mountains and termed them *una gran sierra nevada*—a great snowy range; today we use this name. The lower reaches of the larger rivers—Sacramento, San Joaquin, Feather (Las Plumas), Merced, and Kings—were visited and named in the early 1800s, but neither the Spaniards nor the Mexicans went farther. First white men to cross the range, from the west, were Jedediah Smith and two companions in October 1827, through snow, probably over Ebbetts Pass. In October 1831, Joseph Walker and a party of 50 struggled up the east slope and descended, presumably between the Merced and Tuolumne Rivers, making them the first nonnatives to glimpse Yosemite Valley and perhaps the giant sequoias. The explorer John C. Fremont and his party, with Kit Carson as guide, saw Lake Tahoe on February 14, 1844, and in the ensuing month forced their way over what is now Carson Pass and on to Sutter's Fort. A few years later, with the discovery of gold, crossings became common.

The California State Geological Survey in 1863–1864 made the first scientific studies in the Yosemite region and southward, and in 1875 members of the federal Wheeler Survey examined the Lake Tahoe region. The intrepid John Muir began his visits to the mountains in 1869, and his enthusiastic accounts of the scenery, geology, plants, and animals did much to inform the public about the wonders of the Sierra Nevada. Before 1900, professional and amateur naturalists had started to collect, study, and describe the native plants and animals. Such work has proceeded with increasing tempo until there is now a fairly large literature on the subject, both technical and popular.

There are many subjects of interest in the natural features and denizens of the Sierra Nevada. These include the rocks and minerals and the evidence

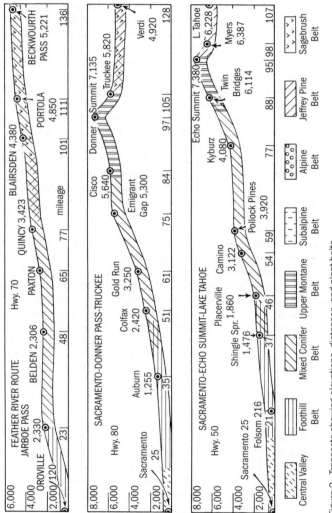

Figure 2. Transects showing elevations, distances, and plant belts.

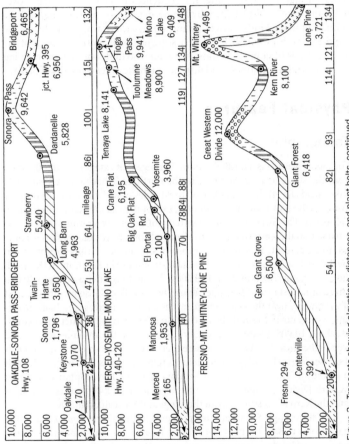

Figure 3. Transects showing elevations, distances, and plant belts, continued.

of many geological processes, including much on the work of glaciers; the differing types of weather at various elevations and in the many unlike parts of the range; the work of water in modifying the landscape, the varied kinds of lakes and streams, and the water cycles of snow, ice, and rain; the diverse belts of plant cover, and the many adjustments made by plants with different requirements for temperature, moisture, soil, sunlight, and shade; the responses of plants to natural environmental changes by erosion, landslides, drought, or lake filling; the sequences of changes in plant cover following human disturbances by lumbering, fire, or overgrazing; and the animals of many kinds, both large and small, each of which has distinctive requirements for food, shelter, and nesting places. The varied aspects of the Sierra Nevada offer much to those like Muir who find "books in the running brooks, sermons in stones," and inspiration in the other elements of nature.

Physical Features

Topography

The Sierra Nevada is a unified mountain range that extends about 400 miles from the shore of Lake Almanor in the north, to Tehachapi Pass, south of Bakersfield (fig. 4). It varies from 60 to 80 miles in width and trends roughly from northwest to southeast. All of it, except the Carson Range, lies within California. The Sierra consists essentially of a massive granite block that is tilted so that the western side, 50 to 65 miles broad, has a gradual slope of only two to six percent. The spectacular eastern side, however, rises abruptly from the flattish bordering valleys that are 4,000 ft or more in elevation. At the north the escarpment rises only 2,000 to 3,000 ft, but at the south it ascends 7,000 ft in a horizontal distance of five miles along Owens Valley. Consequently, the crest of the range is near the eastern border. The summits increase gradually in elevation from north to south, being 6,000 to 8,000 ft in the Feather River country, about 10,000 ft west of Lake Tahoe, 13,000 ft in the Yosemite region, and even higher near Mt. Whitney, where there are 13 peaks more than 14,000 ft above sea level. The entire range includes fully 500 peaks that exceed 12,000 ft in elevation. The central part of Sequoia National Park contains the Great Western Divide, a huge north–south ridge, with 14,000-ft peaks, that separates the Kern River system from the Kings and Kaweah drainages.

The term High Sierra applies properly to the alpine region above the main forest (~8,000+ ft), where peaks, lake basins, and other rock structures carved by glaciation are conspicuous. It extends about 150 miles from north of Yosemite south to Cottonwood Pass and spreads on both sides of the crest, with an average width of about 20 miles. Between the peaks there are extensive highlands that are relatively flat and open. This is the land of the hiker and the pack train, accessible only in summer.

Many deep stream valleys with steep slopes dissect the west slopes of the range. The lower foothills, however, grade imperceptibly into the Central Valley, where the flat agricultural lands on both sides of the Sacramento

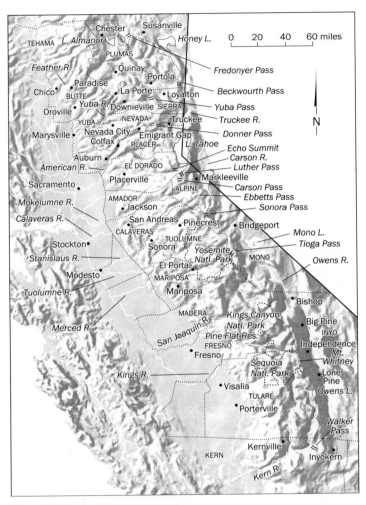

Figure 4. Relief map of the Sierra Nevada.

and San Joaquin Rivers are only 50 to 500 ft above sea level. East of the range the vast plateau of the Great Basin extends across Nevada to western Utah and the first ranges of the Rocky Mountains.

The crest is broached by a succession of passes, earlier used by Native Americans and pioneers and now crossed by motor highways in the northern and central parts of the range. Fredonyer Pass (5,748 ft) west of Susanville marks the northern limit of the Sierra Nevada. Next, in turn, the chief routes are Beckwourth Pass (5,221 ft); Yuba Pass (6,701 ft); Donner Pass (7,135 ft); Echo Summit (7,380 ft); Carson Pass (8,573 ft); Ebbetts Pass (8,730 ft); Sonora Pass (9,642 ft); Tioga Pass (9,941 ft); and Walker Pass

(5,250 ft). Several of these are crossed by highways that are kept open through winter. Other passes between Tioga and Walker, where there are no roads, are usable only in summer by hikers and horses, mules, or burros.

The topography and rock formations of the Sierra Nevada are too diverse and grand for description. They must be experienced—visited and explored repeatedly, especially on foot—to obtain an appreciation of their grandeur. Tapered peaks, jagged crests, and massive mountains surround valleys and rock basins, wide and narrow, of every shape and kind. The High Sierra has the most spectacular panoramas, but there are many other places with notable scenery, including some on highways and lesser roads. The Carson Pass highway is especially attractive because much of it is on the summit of a ridge, affording wide vistas of the surrounding mountains.

Waters

High in aesthetic appeal are various Sierra waters—streams, falls, lakes, snow, ice, and glaciers. In their many and varied forms they add immeasurably to the pictorial beauty. Less evident but important is their role as erosive forces that gradually modify the landscape. These actions vary from the slight expansion of seepage freezing in a rock crevice, to the powerful transport of a fast stream or the colossal forces in a slow-moving glacier.

The most conspicuous waters are those of the major river systems. On the precipitous eastern flank there are a few short but turbulent rivers such as the Truckee, Carson, Walker, and Owens, as well as some lesser creeks. After leaving the mountains they all flow into the Great Basin desert, often forming large alkaline lakes.

On the broad west slope, where most of the rain and snow fall, the situation is quite different. Twelve large river systems have cut deep canyons there. From north to south these master streams, each with many tributaries, are the Feather, Yuba, American, Cosumnes, Mokelumne, Stanislaus, Tuolumne, Merced, San Joaquin, Kings, Kaweah, and Kern. Their general trend is southwesterly, but the Kern River system flows southward out of the southern Sierra, then westward. The waters of the first nine join the Sacramento–San Joaquin system in the Great Valley and discharge into San Francisco Bay. The output of the Kern formerly fed the Buena Vista Lakes west of Bakersfield, and that of the Kings and Kaweah formed Tulare Lake, all in the San Joaquin Valley. The lakes are gone because the supplying waters are now mostly tapped for agricultural purposes.

The upper valleys of some of the big rivers rival Arizona's Grand Canyon in depth. Yosemite Valley (Merced River) is 3,000 ft deep; the "grand canyon" of the Tuolumne is 4,000 to 5,000 ft deep; Kern Canyon is 6,000 ft deep; and part of Kings Canyon is a stupendous 7,000 to 8,000 ft from stream to summit. In general, these canyons are deeply V-shaped where carved by rivers and U-shaped where carved by glaciers.

Sierra streams fluctuate widely in volume. Late spring rains and snowmelt yield maximum runoff, often with heavy flooding of bordering meadows and some normally dry areas. Formerly, when these waters reached the Central Valley, they covered vast areas and did much damage to crops and towns. Control by dams in the mountains and by levees in the lower elevations now moderate this hazard. Further protection results from dams that impound water for hydroelectric power and irrigation, making many artificial lakes at middle elevations (resulting in significant ecological consequences). By fall many mountain streams carry little water. Besides seasonal variations there are lesser daily fluctuations because of the alternate freezing and thawing of sources at high elevations. Not all the streams flow throughout the year. On both east and west slopes many of the smaller ones are intermittent, flowing during periods of rain or snowmelt and then declining. Some become entirely dry in late summer, and others flow then only near their sources.

Cascading and falling waters are never-ending attractions, and the several high falls of Yosemite Valley are the most famed in the Sierra. The narrow Nevada Fall (594 ft) and the broad Vernal Fall (317 ft) flow over huge steps of massive granite planed bare by glaciers on the upper Merced River. The Bridalveil Fall (620 ft), the majestic three-part Yosemite Falls (total 2,565 ft), and some lesser ones pour from high, hanging side valleys where the former hillslopes and streambeds were stripped away during the Ice Age. Other falls, less renowned, occur in Tenaya Canyon and the Hetch Hetchy Valley (both in Yosemite National Park), and on the upper San Joaquin River near the Devils Postpile. Cascades of turbulent whitewater are present on the upper reaches of many rivers and creeks.

There are well over 4,000 lakes in the Sierra, varying from rock pools of 20 ft to the great "lake of the sky," Lake Tahoe. Scouring by ice and accumulations of rock debris has made the high country a land of lakes. The scooping by glaciers near their origins left many shallow basins (tarns) that became lakes with narrow sandy beaches. Their waters freeze and thaw repeatedly throughout the year. After ice forms, a sharp drop in temperature causes it to contract and split. The crevices in the ice fill with water that freezes and expands, forcing the margins of the ice out on the shores. Rocks and sand from the bottom and sides are gradually pushed out to form a surrounding beach ridge or rampart. The sandy and rocky shores are relatively barren. The "pure" water of these lakes lacks the minerals essential for growth of algae, diatoms, and the minute animals in the food chains for fish; thus, few of them contain trout. High-elevation lakes are cachement basins for rain and snowmelt, which overflow to cascading brooks; these join to form upper tributaries of the large rivers.

Below the high country there are fewer lakes. Some in and below the Upper Montane Belt are of water dammed behind glacial moraines; Fallen Leaf Lake of the Tahoe region is an example. The level floor of Yosemite Valley resulted from the filling of a postglacial lake basin. Best known and largest of all is Lake Tahoe, 21 by 11 miles in extent. Because of its great depth (1,685 ft), the surface waters never cool to 32 degrees F, and so it remains ice free at all seasons.

Rocks

The rocks of mountain ranges in other regions are often hidden under forest or lesser vegetation. In much of the Sierra, however, rock masses can dominate the landscape. The topography, coloration, and other features of a mountain range result from the kinds of rock and the ways they have been altered by erosion and other geological agencies. Rocks in the Sierra Nevada are of three major groups: granitic, volcanic, and metamorphic (see Geological History, below).

Sparkling white granite is exposed over much of the range. Granite is a crystalline mixture composed chiefly of two light-colored minerals, quartz (silica or SiO_2) and feldspar (aluminum silicates), with lesser amounts of dark-colored hornblende and biotite (a mica). Some varieties of granite have higher proportions of the latter materials that make them darker in overall color. The granitic domes of the Sierra (pls. 1 and 2) are an outstanding feature, seldom found as well developed elsewhere in the world. These are of unjointed massive rock with smoothly rounded contours. In size and shape they vary from low eminences that rise only slightly above their surroundings to the enormous Half Dome dominating the eastern end of Yosemite Valley. They are most numerous in the Yosemite region, but some occur to the north and south. Domes owe their form to slow loss (exfoliation) of curving shells or scales, somewhat akin to the peeling of the layers of an onion. The shells vary in thickness on the different domes from 1 ft or so to many feet (pl. 3). Their formation is caused by expansion toward the earth's surface due to pressure released within the granite body as overlying material is removed by erosion.

On either side of the Sierra block there are somber red, brown, green, gray, and black metamorphic rocks, derived from earlier sedimentary and volcanic rocks. For example, Dana, east of Tioga Pass in the Yosemite region, is composed of both metasedimentary and metavolcanic rocks. Ancient slates (such as the nearly upright "Mariposa gravestones") and other nongranitic rocks are exposed at many places on the lower western slopes.

Another type of rock is rough brown or blackish basalt and andesite from relatively recent lava flows. Basalt occurs from Plumas County to Tulare County. One flow, at the outlet of Lake Tahoe, slightly raised the lake level and that of its drainage, the lower Truckee River. Later this obstruction was broached, and exposures of the lava can be seen on the highway to Truckee. Devils Postpile, about 300 ft long and 100 ft high, near Mammoth Lakes, comprises five- or six-sided huge basaltic columns of volcanic origin; the tops are cut off and scored where overridden by glacial ice. From Mammoth Mountain to Mono Lake there is a line of postglacial volcanic craters, some 2,000 ft high, that showered out pumice (vesicular lava) to deeply cover areas in the Mono and Long Valley region. Volcanic rocks—pinkish, reddish, dark gray—cover areas west and southwest of Lake Tahoe and parts of the east slope near the origin of Owens River. Hot springs, indicative of subsurface heat, are common along the eastern base of the Carson Range and in the Devils Postpile area.

Over much of the Sierra, joints or fractures in one or more planes mark rocks of all three types. These permit water to seep in, freeze, and expand. This action contributes to breakage and disintegration and ultimately produces sand and soil. Rock crevices are the places where many rock-dwelling plants—from herbs to trees—get started. Growth of their roots later aids fracture and disintegration. As the crevices become enlarged they serve as daytime and winter retreats for various animals.

Limestone (calcium carbonate or $CaCO_3$) is rare in the crest region but is present at lower elevations on the west slope. As a result of water action caves have developed, principally in two areas. In the Mother Lode are Bower Cave, east of Coulterville, and Moaning and Mercer Caves near Murphys. The Sequoia–Kings Canyon region includes Church, Crystal, and Soldiers Caves; Boyden Cave in Kings Canyon is fully 800 ft long. Marble (metamorphosed limestone) is quarried at several places, notably near San Andreas, for manufacturing cement.

From the lower parts of the conifer forest down into the foothills, flat upland surfaces are covered by a deep, powdery red soil. Travel there in the dry season on unimproved routes envelops humans, beasts, or vehicles in suffocating dust, which blankets the roadside vegetation. This is the Mother Lode—from Plumas County to Mariposa County—where the "forty-niners" found gold-bearing quartz in modern and ancient streambeds and recovered $500 million in gold. Gravels and sands in the beds of west slope streams still sparingly yield small nuggets to amateur prospectors who work river gravels with vacuum dredges.

Climate

The pattern of weather in the Sierra Nevada results from the physical form and the geographic position of the range in relation to the Central Valley, Coast Ranges, and Pacific Ocean. Oriented perpendicularly to prevailing westerlies, the range receives the full force of storms and winds (especially at higher elevations where peaks intercept upper airflows, see pl. 4), while at the same time the height and size of Sierra peaks exert a tremendous influence on airflow and precipitation patterns in the western United States. There are many local climates in the Sierra because of its diverse topography and wide span in latitude and elevation. The exact weather at a particular place and time is not easy to predict, but for the entire range there is an overall seasonal characteristic that makes the Sierra an ideal recreation area. The dry, relatively cool summers provide a pleasant change from the hot lowlands on either side and from the foggy coast, and the mild winters with record snowpacks at middle elevations are ideal for winter sports. Such a combination is rare among mountain ranges elsewhere in the world.

The climate affects the economy and well-being of people living in the Sierra and of all who dwell in adjacent parts of California and Nevada. Water from Sierra storms accumulates in the winter snowpack then melts slowly to fill streams and reservoirs that sustain the enormous needs of lowland agriculture and communities. These waters, when they reach the valleys, refill underground water storage spaces (or at least they did formerly, before the era of dams and water diversions). A wet year means prosperity, but a series of dry years is disastrous. A summer cold spell in the mountains drives out visitors and causes resort owners to lose money, but an early snowfall followed by well-spaced storms brings profits to ski resorts.

Weather records in the Sierra began in 1870 with completion of the first through railroad (now the Union Pacific) with stations at Folsom, Auburn, Colfax, and Truckee. This transect, paralleled by Interstate 80, is fairly central. Climatic records for the southern Sierra, where elevations are higher and the few passes are closed in winter, are scarce. Throughout the range there are not many weather stations above 8,000 ft and so the record is far from complete.

The annual cycle of seasons follows the familiar pattern of the Northern Hemisphere, but the position of the Sierra near the western coast of the continent determines the type of climate for both summer and winter. Ordinarily, there is a low-pressure area over the northern Pacific Ocean throughout winter and a high-pressure area there in summer. The reasons for this shift are complex, involving the alternate cooling and warming of Arctic landmasses and the rise of warm, moisture-laden air over the ocean in winter. The rotation of the earth pushes the prevailing winds from west to east and carries storms across California. The Coast Ranges catch some of the resulting rain, especially in the north, but there is less of a barrier at the Golden Gate, and the heaviest precipitation occurs to the northeast of that gap as the air ascends the gradual west slope of the Sierra (in the Donner Pass region). Often a high-pressure area sets in over central California in winter and deflects storms northward, so that the weather turns pleasant. An average storm lasts five to six days, during which the temperatures are moderate because of the incoming maritime air. Temperatures drop again after a storm passes and the night skies are clear.

In general, temperature decreases 1 degree F for each 300 ft of rise in elevation, and the air, thus cooled, drops its moisture as rain or snow. Precipitation increases 2 to 4 in. for each 300-ft rise, reaching a maximum at about 5,000 to 6,000 ft elevation in the central part of the range. Above that elevation the amount of precipitation declines because much of the moisture in the air has already fallen. The east slope of the Sierra is definitely in a "rainshadow" where little rain or snow falls and desert conditions prevail.

Temperature

Sierra temperatures are generally warm in summer with maxima of 80 to 100 degrees F and minima of 15 to 37 degrees F, depending on elevation. In winter maximum temperatures range from 55 to 70 degrees F and the minima from about 0 degrees F to more than −30 degrees F. Some examples of extremes are Folsom (elevation 216 ft), 119 degrees F in July and 22 degrees F in January; Yosemite Valley (3,960 ft), 90 degrees F in July and 22 degrees

F in January; and Lake Tahoe on the east side (6,239 ft), 93 degrees F in July and –15 degrees F in January.

Temperatures at middle elevations on the west slope (Cisco, 5,939 ft) and east side (Truckee, 5,820 ft) are similar, the mean being about 62 degrees F in July and 30 degrees F in winter. The extremes, however, are much greater at Truckee (–30 to 100 degrees F) than at Cisco (–6 to 94 degrees F). Alpine temperatures doubtless will show the widest extremes when data become available. On the summit of Mt. Whitney, during a brief period in September, the daily maxima averaged 62.5 degrees F and the minima 22.5 degrees F. The coldest part of the day was 3 to 6 a.m. Alpine temperatures in the Sierra are significantly milder than in other alpine zones of North America.

Precipitation

The total precipitation includes both rain and snow. In the Sierra, 95 percent of the precipitation falls between October and May, with more than half falling in January, February, and March. Precipitation decreases steadily from north to south—thus, at 5,000 ft, it is 90 in. in Plumas County but only 55 in. in Mariposa County. In general, a map showing precipitation, like a map showing temperature, conforms to elevational contours. However, the contrast in rainfall between the west slope (75 in.) and east slope (20 in.) at 5,500 ft elevation is striking.

The frequency of summer showers increases at higher elevations, and correspondingly there are more cloudy days. This trend is typical of high mountains and results from local increases in humidity and movements of air (winds) up the slopes and canyons during the day and downward at night. As air moves up the slope, it cools, and moisture condenses to form rain, often with hail, thunder, and lightning. Such thundershowers are usually of short duration, most less than an hour, and make little impression on the predominantly dry summer season, although lightning causes many forest fires. From July to August as many as 70 percent of all days may be sunny—rare for other mountain ranges in the world.

Snowfall

Snow is one of the most spectacular features of the Sierra (the second snowiest mountain range on the continent). Increasing with elevation in much the same pattern as rainfall, it starts with an ill-defined "snowline" at about 2,000 to 3,000 ft on the west slope, precipitation below 2,000 ft being mostly in the form of rain, and above 6,000 ft being mostly snow. In the central Sierra the annual average increases steadily from about 2 ft of snow at Colfax to 34 ft at Norden, near Donner Summit. At the latter station 86 percent of the total precipitation falls as snow. The total seasonal fall there, however, varies within wide limits, from 13 ft in 1880–1881 to 66 ft in 1938. The greatest annual fall ever recorded in the Sierra was at Tamarack, Alpine County (8,000 ft): an amazing 73.5 ft during the winter of 1906–1907.

Such heavy snowfall and the resulting snowpack are equaled only in a few places in the Pacific Northwest. Yet the winter climate in the Sierra is comparatively mild, and all but about 500 glaciers and glacierets in northern exposures at high elevations evaporate or melt by midsummer. At Donner Summit melting proceeds at about 4 in. per day in mid-May. The snow naturally persists longer at high elevations or during unusually cool summers. The ground is again usually blanketed with snow by late November. Snowmelt during warmer spells in winter results in waterlogged snow—a 14-ft pack at Donner Summit, for example, increases in weight from 10 pounds per cubic foot at the surface to 28 pounds at the bottom. A special feature of the Sierra snowpack is its persistence in spite of warm air temperatures (40 to 60 degrees F) during the day and only moderately low temperatures (20 to 32 degrees F) at night. The reasons for this involve both reflection of sunlight from the surface of the snow and the capture of much of the sun's heat by the coniferous forest canopy. In one year at Tahoe City all snow had melted on a treeless meadow by April 10, but at the same elevation 1.3 in. remained in a pine-fir forest and 7.1 in. in a fir forest on April 20.

Snow falls as flaky crystals that have innumerable surfaces reflecting (rather than absorbing) heat from the sun, but alternate daytime melting and nighttime refreezing changes this characteristic. Melt water trickles down and freezes to form hard-packed granules. A new crust forms most nights on the surface. Early storms build the snowpack, the later layers protecting those beneath from melting. As winter ends the character of the surface changes: it becomes granular and receives a scattering of needles and other plant debris. By mid-March the once crystalline top has become an irregular, heat-absorbing surface. Melting increases, and three-fourths of the total pack progressively disappears in April, May, and June. In spring, therefore, waterfalls are at their best, rivers are at peak levels, and snowmelt streams and pools pass through their ephemeral existence. The runoff, in wet years, is sufficient to fill all reservoirs and also send much water down in lowland streams.

Typical winter temperatures in the High Sierra (mostly above 9,500 ft), from Cottonwood Pass in the south to Yosemite in the north, are nighttime lows between –14 degrees F and 12 degrees F, though many nights can be significantly milder (mid-20s) due to cloud cover. Daytime highs can reach 50 degrees F during periods of sunny, stable weather, and the high teens during periods with airflow from the north. Many high summits along the Sierra crest may be blown free of snow because of the great wind speeds there.

Streams and Lakes

Sierra streams usually flow throughout winter but are impeded during freezing weather. Yearlong records for Sagehen Creek (at 6,337 ft, 12 miles north of Truckee) show average water temperatures of 45 to 67 degrees F in July and 32 to 40 degrees F in January. Winter snow usually covers part of the stream. Each night in the coldest period, small masses of white anchor ice form on the bottom and on immersed objects. This slows the flow, causing pools along the stream to rise in level. Anchor ice melts by day, and normal flow is resumed. If the night temperature drops to 32 degrees F, small crystals of frazil ice form a slushy layer on the surface of the stream water.

The situation is different in lakes. Some of the smallest freeze solid. Those of moderate size become ice covered; Lower Echo Lake (at 7,450 ft, near Hwy. 50) is an example. The water freezes to a depth of about 8 in., and a 7-ft surface blanket of snow persists for about six months. The bottom water in winter is about 40 degrees F (roughly the temperature where water has the highest density), and that close under the ice is 32 degrees F. After the spring melt, wind-driven waves circulate the entire water mass, which becomes uniform in temperature by mid-June. As summer sun heats the surface portion, a stratification results, with warmer, lighter water above and colder, heavier water (45 degrees F) below, there being an abrupt change (thermocline) about 40 ft down. In fall, the surface waters cool and circulate until the whole lake again is of uniform temperature.

Lake Tahoe never freezes, being large and deep (1,685 ft). Sierra winters are not long or cold enough to lower the entire water mass to 40 degrees F. Hence cooling and lightening of surface water to 32 degrees F does not occur. The bottom water is always near 40 degrees F; the surface varies from 40 degrees F in March to over 68 degrees F in August.

Unlike waters in lower elevations, few Sierra lakes are comfortable for bathing. The surface portion in a protected cove may reach 70 degrees F on a sunny afternoon, and then quickly chill as a breeze causes upwelling of colder, deeper water.

Geological History

The area now occupied by the Sierra Nevada has had a long and complex history—too complex to cover in much detail in this volume. For our purposes we will focus on geological aspects that produced the landscape against which the bulk of this volume is framed, the biological world of today. Our understanding of this landscape continues to evolve, but summaries can be found in Hill (1975), and, for the Yosemite region, in Huber (1987).

The oldest rocks in the Sierra block are metamorphic rocks that extend in a belt along the western foothills from the San Joaquin River north to the end of the range near Lake Almanor. Discontinuous bodies of metamorphic rocks are also scattered throughout the central and southern parts of the range. As noted above, metamorphic rocks are derived from preexisting sedimentary and volcanic rocks by mineralogic and structural changes in response to increases in temperature, pressure, and shearing stress deep within the earth's crust. Those rocks now exposed in the Foothill Belt include quartzite, slate, crystalline limestone, greenstone, and serpentine, and are derived from rocks ranging in age from late Paleozoic to mid-Mesozoic, ~250 to 150 million years old.

Beginning in the Triassic period (~210 million years ago), and culminating in the Cretaceous period (120 to 85 million years ago), vast amounts of molten granite (magma) were injected, as many small intrusions, into the overlying preexisting crustal strata. This molten granite originated as the eastward edge of the Pacific plate (which was being overridden by the westward-advancing North American plate) was pushed down to a depth where it melted from intense heat near the earth's core. Over time this material recrystallized beneath the surface as a huge mass of solid granite that we know as the Sierra Nevada batholith. Along with these intrusions, rocks of the central Sierra and foothills received their content of minerals such as gold, copper, and tungsten. Subsequent erosion (beginning in the late Cretaceous) began to expose the granite and reduced the landscape to one of broadly rolling form, covered by deep residual clay soil.

During the early Cenozoic era (~50 million years ago) the Sierra Nevada region was relatively stable, and it continued to be worn down. Then beginning perhaps as many as 25 million years ago, the continental crust east of the Sierra began to expand in an east–west direction, and the thick, lightweight Sierra crust began to rise. The exact mechanism of this uplift is not understood, but the results are there to see. In the Yosemite area, the Sierra is clearly an uplifted block of the earth's crust, with a long slope westward to the Central Valley and a steep escarpment separating it from the country to the east.

Meanwhile, much of the northern Sierra, from south of the Stanislaus River north, was blanketed by a flood of volcanic rock, much of it consisting of rubbly deposits of fragmented material known as lahars (volcanic mudflows). The bulk of this material was erupted about 15 to 5 million years ago. It buried many of the stream channels draining toward the Central Valley, and rivers were forced to cut new canyons down through the volcanic deposits.

François Matthes (1950) inferred from his Yosemite studies that the Cenozoic uplift occurred in a series of three pulses, interrupted by pauses in uplift. In his view, each pulse initiated a new cycle of erosion and thus produced multiple stages of landscape incision characterized by successively greater relief. More recent studies conclude that uplift, once initiated, was more nearly continuous than Matthes envisioned. As the Sierra mass began to rise and tilt to the west, the gradients of streams flowing southwesterly down the slope was increased. As a result, their erosive power was increased and they cut deep canyons into the western slope.

Throughout the last million years or so, a significant process was at work that produced much of the spectacular scenery of today. The high country, pushed above the snow line, and with a cooling climate, acquired glaciers and was sculptured by them. To this day, glaciers form in high latitudes or elevations where the climate is such that the annual total of snow received exceeds that lost by melting and evaporation. (A decrease in average annual temperature of only a few degrees probably would result in large new Sierra glaciers.) Snow intercepted and accumulated on a high mountain gradually compacts into ice. Because of its weight, the ice mass wants to flow outward and thus

Plate 1. Fin Dome, atop the glacially carved ridge between Rae Lakes and Sixty Lakes Basins in Kings Canyon National Park

Plate 2. North Dome with exfoliating layers of granite, in early morning light

Plate 3. Foliated pattern on weathered granite rock

Plate 4. Mountain-induced wave (lenticular) cloud

Plate 5. Glacier-carved valley

Plate 6. Glacial polish with chatter marks from pressure of ice

Plate 7. Glacial erratics at edge of lake

Plate 8. Summer cumulonimbus cloud east of Mt. Humphreys, seen from ca. 11,000 ft

Plate 9. Mt. Humphreys reflected in a glacial tarn, Humphreys Basin

Plate 10. Whitebark pines at timberline (11,000 ft) encased in rime ice

Plate 11. Principal trees and shrubs of the Sagebrush Belt

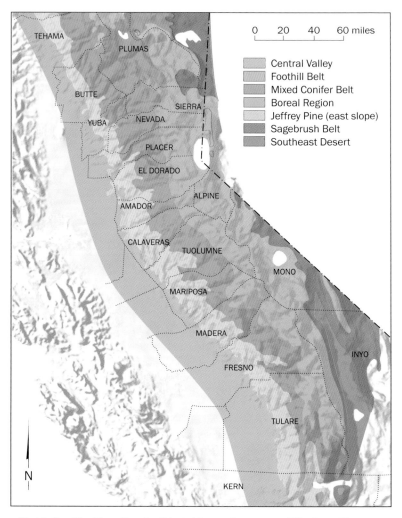

Plant belts of the Sierra Nevada. (Adapted from various sources.) The Upper Montane, Subalpine, and Alpine Belts are grouped as the "Boreal Region" here, but are shown separately on the Sierra transects (figs. 2 and 3).

becomes a glacier moving slowly downslope, normally in a preexisting stream valley. At some lower elevation, where the temperature is more moderate, melting at the front of the glacier may equal or exceed the glacier's forward motion and it will come to a halt. From the sides and floor of its path the great forces of the huge, slowly flowing ice mass pluck rocks. Additional debris from above (talus) falls onto the glacier as the valley walls are undercut. As these rock materials are carried along, they cut and scour the surfaces over which the glacier moves. Lateral tributaries to the trunk valley, whose lower portions are removed by a glacier, become hanging valleys that end high on the walls of the broadened and deepened gorge. After the ice disappears these waters descend as cascades or falls. The area below a peak, where a glacier starts, becomes scooped out as a bowl-like depression, or cirque (pl. 5). At the lower end of a glacier, where the ice finally melts, the rocks and soil that it carried are deposited in a transverse ridge of debris, or terminal moraine. As a glacier recedes it may form a succession of these moraines. Debris deposited by the glacier along the side of the valley produces a lateral moraine.

During the so-called Ice Age (Pleistocene epoch), there were many individual episodes of glaciation. In the Sierra, however, instead of one huge, undivided ice cap—such as covered much of northeastern North America—glaciers and ice fields were discontinuous, and we do not have a clear record of how many occurred. Some parts of the range had none. At the northern end (elevation ~7,000 ft) there were only small cirque glaciers nestled in declivities on the taller peaks. But from Donner Pass south to the upper Kern River Canyon there were, in different stages, individual ice fields of a few to many square miles. From each of these there were trunk glaciers that flowed down valleys, both east and west from the Sierra crest, and south down the Kern Canyon.

The region between Lake Tahoe and Yosemite, with peaks up to 13,000 ft, received great supplies of moisture-laden air through the gap in the Coast Ranges where the Golden Gate Bridge now stands. A true ice cap developed, up to 275 miles long by 40 miles wide, above which only a few peaks projected. From it, among others, came the Tuolumne Glacier that descended Hetch Hetchy Valley and was at one time up to 60 miles long. The Yosemite Glacier, formed of an ice flow from the upper Merced drainage, supplemented by one from Tenaya Canyon, reached slightly below the community of El Portal, some 10 miles downstream from Yosemite Valley. The San Joaquin River drainage also had an ice field and glaciers, as did the Kings and Kaweah basins. Southernmost of the trunk glaciers was one in Kern Canyon.

The earliest Yosemite Glacier submerged much of Half Dome (but the now absent front section, actually not quite "half," disappeared because of erosion along a joint plane). This glaciation, known as the Sherwin, produced a glacier that was 3,000 ft deep opposite Glacier Point, and this was the glacier that excavated Yosemite Valley. Later glaciers were nowhere near as thick and none filled the valley to its rim. A terminal moraine of the last glacier lies across the valley just east of Bridal Meadow, and a recessional moraine lies near El Capitan. As the ice melted back, this latter moraine served as a dam to impound waters that formed a "Lake Yosemite" of prehistoric times. Now the moraine is breached by the Merced River near the south valley wall. François Matthes provided a series of sketches that depict stages in the evolution of Yosemite Valley, and these continue to be useful illustrations (fig. 5). As noted above, however, these should be viewed as snapshots in a continuing process rather than as the separate stages he originally envisioned.

The Ice Age ended perhaps 10,000 years ago, being followed by a warming climate when there were no glaciers in the Sierra. Today, however, there are about 99 glaciers and 398 glacierets thought to have formed within the past 1,000 years, products of what is called the Little Ice Age. The largest are on Mt. Lyell and Mt. Maclure in the Yosemite region, and on the Palisades farther south. None is a mile long; most of them are half this size, and some are even smaller. These little glaciers can be distinguished from snowfields by the presence of crevasses on the upper surface; a "bergschrund," or pull-away gap, at their heads; and the whitish "glacial milk" water emerging below them. Modern increases in temperature are once again melting these glaciers, and several have disappeared in recent decades.

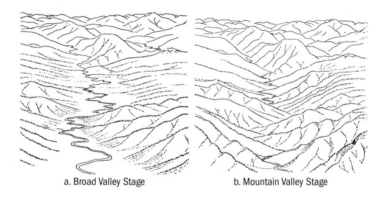

a. Broad Valley Stage   b. Mountain Valley Stage

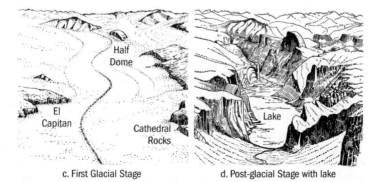

c. First Glacial Stage   d. Post-glacial Stage with lake

Figure 5. Four stages in the geological evolution of Yosemite Valley. (After François Matthes, 1950.)

The Sierra Nevada shows much evidence of glacial action. There are moraines of various sizes and ages and scattered hanging valleys. Many massive rock surfaces were planed and polished (pl. 6), some to mirror-brilliance by sand particles, or scored with parallel grooves by harder materials carried in the ice. Boulders weighing hundreds or thousands of pounds were transported from higher regions by glaciers and later stranded where the ice melted; they are the "glacial erratics," now resting on surfaces commonly of different rock composition (pl. 7).

The scenic features and biological environments of today are products of various geological processes. Angular peaks derive from "rock plucking" by glaciers once under their summits (pl. 8). Many cirques and other rock basins scooped out by moving ice became lakes, with little or no organic debris, and they are thus biologically poor (pl. 9). A stream entering a glacial lake carries gravel, sand, and soil that will accumulate at its mouth or outlet. With gradual filling, plants begin to grow on the surface and the area in turn becomes a marsh, a meadow, and ultimately land invaded by forest. Many mountain meadows are filled lake basins. At each stage in the succession, from wet to dry environment, various species of plants and animals occupy the area in turn, according to the kind of habitat each requires.

From steep-sided canyon walls scoured by glaciers other environments evolve. Exposed rocks develop cracks into which water seeps, freezes, and expands, eventually loosening the outer portions. Angular pieces, small and large, later slide or fall down the slope, aided by avalanches and frost action, to accumulate below as jumbles of steep talus rock. Spaces within talus cones and aprons serve as shelters for many kinds of animals, from insects and small reptiles or mice to bigger carnivores. In time, plants of successively larger size colonize the slides. The great talus slopes of Yosemite Valley now support a forest of canyon live oaks, affording acorns for Band-tailed Pigeons, woodpeckers, and squirrels, together with food for many insectivorous birds.

Other geological processes yield soil where forest trees grow; gravelly slopes, which are the sites for certain kinds of flowering plants and shrubs; and exposed masses of partly fractured granite that support Jeffrey pines, junipers, and other "rock-loving" plants. The segregation of animals by habitats is related to the types of plant cover that can grow on different kinds of substrate, or ground surface, and these in turn result from the kinds of rock present and the ways in which they have been weathered through time. Geological materials and processes, together with climate, are therefore the ultimate bases for plant and animal distribution.

Plant and Animal Distribution

Plants and animals are not of uniform occurrence. Instead, each species is limited to a definite geographic area, within which it is further restricted to a type of environment where its essential needs for life are available (its habitat or niche). Many kinds of animals can live only in certain kinds of plant cover so that their occurrence depends in part on conditions that regulate plant distribution. In general, plant and animal distribution is controlled by annual and seasonal patterns of temperature, precipitation, and other climatic factors and by the type of ground surface (substrate). The distribution of plants and animals, however, is not infinitely varied. Some kinds of both are so often found together that it becomes possible to group them in larger and smaller units, each with certain member species. Several schemes have been developed for describing distributional assemblages—biotic provinces, life zones, plant-animal communities or associations, and others. These systems, however, are not altogether in agreement, because factors affecting distribution are not fully understood or are classified differently.

Geographic Distribution

Plants and animals are distributed in a series of belts that roughly follow elevational contours along the length of the Sierra Nevada (see color map following pl. 11). The boundaries of each belt are higher in elevation at the southern end of the range than at the northern end, and comparable belts occur at relatively higher elevations on the east slope than on the west.

The boundary between two belts is seldom sharp or straight; instead the belts interlace broadly or narrowly. This blurring of vegetation types in the transition zones between belts makes the process of delineating or describing the belts rather challenging. In addition, lower belts extend upward on warm south-facing slopes, whereas higher ones descend on cooler or moister sites, as in shaded river canyons. For example, sun-facing hillsides of gray pines and associated plants in a canyon may stand opposite shadier slopes with ponderosa pines and Douglas-firs; one will have Western Scrub-Jays, the other Steller's Jays.

Among both plants and animals, some species are restricted to a single belt, others occupy two or three belts (although not always in equal numbers), and a few are present in any belt where particular habitat needs are available. The scheme of belts used in this book is herein described with two caveats: First, this scheme, an updated version of the one used by Storer and Usinger in the first edition of this book, is not entirely consistent because two belt names are based on plants (Mixed Conifer and Sagebrush) while the others are based on ecological zones. These two names were retained because they will be more familiar to most readers than alternate choices (one possibility being Lower Montane for Mixed Conifer and Cold Desert for Sagebrush). Second, it must be remembered that belts represent only one layer of understanding of the diversity of habitats available in the Sierra Nevada. Within each belt are an immense variety of specialized niches that transcend elevation, including streamside riparian zones, ponds or lakes, and rock outcrops.

Foothill Belt

Occurs on lowest portions of the west slope at 500 to 3,000 ft (north), 800 to 4,000 ft (center), or about 1,250 to 5,000 ft (south). Summer rainless and hot, average maximum temperatures 75 to 96 degrees F; winter moderate, average minimum temperatures 29 to 42 degrees F; rainfall 15 to 40 in., little fog; growing season 6 to 10 months.

The Foothill Belt is a low-elevation mosaic of grassland, oak woodland, and oak savanna. Characteristic trees include blue oak, gray pine, interior live oak, and California buckeye. Dense shrub assemblages (chaparral) dominate rocky soils with low fertility, or occupy recently burned areas until overtaken and shaded out by a new crop of young trees. Foothill chaparral is a complex mix that includes in various combinations: chamise, scrub oak, manzanitas, ceanothus, toyon, yerba santa, California buckeye, and localized patches of Brewer's oak.

At its upper limits, the Foothill Belt trends into a vegetation type dominated by ponderosa pine and black oak. This type has been variously considered part of the Foothill Belt, combined with Mixed Conifer to form a Lower Montane Belt, or given its own status as a separate belt.

Mixed Conifer Belt

Main timber region. Along west slope at 900 to 5,500 ft (north) or 3,600 to 6,300 ft (south). Summer warm, dry, average maximum temperatures 80 to 93 degrees F; winter cool, average minimum temperatures 22 to 34 degrees F; precipitation 25 to 80 in., some snow, little summer rain; growing season 4 to 7 months.

Although Mixed Conifer is more properly a single vegetation type among many that comprise the zone sometimes named Lower Montane Belt, it is a popular and familiar label that accurately reflects the diverse mix of conifers found at middle elevations in the Sierra Nevada. This is a broad belt that dominates the west slope of the Sierra Nevada. At its lower limits, ponderosa pine is the major species, while at its upper limits this belt is comprised mainly of white fir and some sugar pine, with Jeffrey pine replacing ponderosa pine. Common associates include sugar pine, incense-cedar, Douglas-fir, black oak, and canyon live oak. Less common associates include pacific madrone, tan oak, and giant sequoia.

In the northern Sierra, Mixed Conifer forests also occupy a band on the east slope, but this band is fragmentary south of Lake Tahoe, where the zone between the lower elevation Sagebrush Belt and higher elevation Upper Montane Belt is mainly occupied by a single species, Jeffrey pine.

Very widespread in the upper Mixed Conifer belt and the next higher belt is a montane chaparral that differs greatly from the foothill form. As at lower elevations, chaparral in the higher mountains is a mix of species: greenleaf manzanita (at lower elevations), pinemat manzanita (at higher elevations), snow brush or mountain whitethorn, bitter cherry, bush chinquapin, and huckleberry oak.

Upper Montane Belt

Lower part of high mountain forests, at 5,500 to 7,500 ft (north), 6,500 to 8,000 ft (central), and 8,000 to 10,000 ft (south); on both slopes, but at higher elevations on east slope. Summer cool, average maximum temperatures 73 to 85 degrees F; winter cold, average minimum temperatures 16 to

26 degrees F; precipitation (total water) 35 to 65 inches, heavy persistent snow (hence winter sports area), some summer showers; growing season 3 to 4.5 months (40 to 70 frost-free days).

This zone is best characterized by its dark somber red fir stands with chartreuse wolf lichen growing thickly on the fir trunks. These stands are open and nearly shrub free. Common associates include white fir, lodgepole pine, western white pine, Jeffrey pine, and quaking aspen. White fir co-dominates with red fir at the lowest edge of this belt but drops out at the elevation where winter precipitation becomes solely snow. Lodgepole pine grows in pockets within red fir stands, and also dominates higher slopes above red fir, where it is extremely successful at invading meadows and moist sites.

For the east slope, biologists often combine the Upper Montane Belt with the Subalpine Belt to designate the confusing mix of red fir, lodgepole pine, and other conifers that grow above sagebrush-covered slopes and Jeffrey pine stands.

Subalpine Belt

Includes the sparsely forested High Sierra on both slopes near the summit of the range. Found on only a few northern peaks, but of widespread occurrence farther south; at 7,200 to 9,150 ft (north and central) and 8,700 to 11,000 ft (south). Summer days warm, nights cold; winter minimum temperatures poorly documented; precipitation 30 to 50 in. (15 in. on east slope); heavy persistent winter snow, some summer rain; growing season 7 to 9 weeks (killing frosts in any month).

Mountain hemlock is the most common indicator of the Subalpine Belt in the Sierra Nevada, growing in extensive groves north of Yosemite National Park. To the south, this species occurs more sparingly and mixes with lodgepole pine, western white pine, foxtail pine, and red fir. At the upper edge of the Subalpine Belt or on rocky sites, whitebark pine is the primary conifer (foxtail pine in the southern Sierra). Many trees in the Subalpine Belt grow in contorted or stunted shapes due to the extreme growing conditions at these elevation (pl. 10).

Alpine Belt

This is the zone above timberline (although some summits are treeless due to scant soil and the extreme wind). Only the highest mountain peaks and ridges greater than 9,000 ft (north) to 11,000 ft (south) reach this zone. Extreme sunlight exposure at all seasons, cool or cold in summer because of upmountain winds, lightning strikes common, precipitation scant, some summer thundershowers, much of winter snow evaporated by wind. Few climatic records exist for this zone.

At these elevations where trees can no longer grow, the dominant vegetation is first a low shrub layer, then at higher elevations, communities of densely matted cushion plants in rocky crevices. Plants of this zone include mosses, lichens, grasses, diverse herbaceous plants, and a few dwarf shrubs, typically growing in patterns that reflect the distribution of late-lying snowbanks.

Sagebrush Belt

On east slope at 4,200 to 5,600 ft (north) and 6,000 to 7,000 ft (south). Summer dry, hot, average maximum temperatures 82 to 89 degrees F; winter cold, average minimum temperatures 10 to 20 degrees F; precipitation 10 to 30 in., mostly as snow; growing season 2 to 5 months.

Along the eastern base of the Sierra Nevada and ascending onto its lower flanks are parts of a Cold Desert Belt characterized by extensive stands of sagebrush. This familiar plant is often used as the catchall name for this zone, even though other vegetation types also characterize the region. Bitterbrush is another abundant shrub of the east slope, especially in the presence of pines.

While generally treeless, the upper edges of this belt may have thinly scattered to dense stands of juniper and pinyon pine (pl. 11). Pure stands of Jeffrey pine (sometimes referred to as the East Side Pine Belt) occupy large areas above the Sagebrush Belt on the east slope south of Lake Tahoe.

Beyond the general limitations of geographic range and habitat, each species of plant or animal is further restricted to a small local environment called its *ecological niche.* A pine tree, for example, offers a variety of niches for different kinds of animals—the trunk, twigs, or needles; low or high; against the trunk or on the outer periphery of the foliage. Other sorts of niches are the rockslides used by Pikas, the deadwood used by termites, or the spaces amid rocks in a stream used by caddisfly larvae. The distinctive requirements of each animal for its food, shelter, and breeding places are to be found in its niche.

All the plants and animals at any one spot are interacting members of a *biological community,* as may be seen in a fallen log, willow thicket, or meadow. The members are specialized for various "jobs": producers, consumers, or scavengers. Plants are the *producers.* From soil minerals, water, and sunlight they manufacture the complex substances of their roots, stems, leaves, flowers, and fruits. These are the ultimate source of food for animals, which have diverse diets. Some, like bears or ground squirrels, eat a variety of foods, but others take only certain kinds—hummingbirds drink the nectar of flowers, termites eat only wood, beavers eat the inner bark of softwood trees, and so on. Many kinds of animals prey and feed solely on other animals. The plant eaters are *primary consumers,* the predators are *secondary* (or higher level) *consumers,* and any that eat dead plants or animals are *scavengers.* Thus in any community the organic materials move along in a *food chain* or *food web:* plants ⇒ plant eaters (insects, rodents, deer) ⇒ predaceous insects or flesh eaters (snakes, foxes), and so on. Viewed in another way the member animals form a *pyramid of numbers* in which those at the base are abundant but small and those at the top are few but large. For example, in deciduous woods the aphids and other minute plant-feeding insects may be enormously abundant, spiders and insect-eating beetles that prey on them fairly common, insectivorous birds that eat spiders or beetles fewer, and hawks or weasels that capture the birds rather scarce.

Here, then, is the basis for differences in numbers among the various kinds. The shifting fortunes, and thereby the populations of some member species in a community, may rise or fall, and such change can affect other parts of the community. These and other factors bring about the alterations in local populations and distribution of plants or animals from year to year. A conspicuous case is that of the population of California Tortoiseshell Butterflies, which periodically "erupts," producing huge numbers of caterpillars that strip the leaves of tobacco brush. Thus other animals are deprived of using that shrub for food or cover, but birds of several species from other habitats concentrate there to feed on the resulting abnormal food supply—the larvae and later the butterflies—at the same time that various parasitic insects such as Ichneumon Wasps and others multiply and destroy many caterpillars, thereby helping to restore the usual balance.

The web of life in nature is complex and only partly known; much further study is needed for better understanding. Interested amateurs can contribute usefully to the subject by making careful observations and keeping records in natural history.

The Changing Landscape

Despite its formidable, rock-hewn profile the Sierra Nevada is a ceaselessly changing landscape. Our human perspective makes human-wrought changes seem paramount, but in fact the mountains creep and shift on timescales we scarcely comprehend. Even the forests and plant communities we accept as part of the landscape are only a few thousand years old, having moved and sorted in response to two million years of dramatic Ice Age fluctuations. Then above it all—above the rocks, the plants, the rivers, and the humans—the very nature of the atmosphere and its weather systems is shifting in profoundly important and unforeseen ways. Not only has the human drama of the past 150 years been played out in a strange climatic blip—a brief yet beguiling window of warm, wet years after millennia of drought and chill—but also global warming poses another set of changing parameters.

Humans have been an integral part of the landscape for at least 10,000 years. It is estimated that at one time 100,000 Native Americans representing 13 tribes inhabited the Sierra Nevada region. Perhaps because of their small numbers and their way of using the land, these peoples had little permanent effect on Sierra flora or fauna. They used fire to clear brushlands and grasslands so that food plants like brodiaeas would grow more luxuriously, and they set fire to chaparral as a means of forcing out rabbits and other small animals to capture them for their flesh and pelts. Certain flat forest areas were fired at intervals to destroy small trees and brush and leave open stands of the larger trees. This may have been to lessen the chance of surprise attacks by enemy tribes. The well-spaced forest on the floor of Yosemite Valley, which was seen until the early 1900s, resulted from this practice.

With the discovery of gold and launching of the gold rush in 1849, there began a 150-year transformation of the Sierra Nevada that falls into three phases: A period of intense settlement and resource use that began in the mid-1800s; a period of restraint starting in the 1920s when resource use became increasingly regulated and forest and range protection codified; and a new period of growth and expanding demand following World War II. These are useful but not strict categories; for instance, the regulation of resources began even while gold mining was in full force.

Gold mining and the sudden influx of new peoples into the region from 1849 onward made the first changes in the Sierra landscape. Early hydraulic mining used high-pressure streams of water from hoses to sluice apart hillsides and expose gold-bearing quartz. Scars of this destructive practice still show along Interstate 80 near Gold Run and in places bordering California Hwy. 49. More than 1.5 billion tons of debris had been washed from the Sierra foothills by the time a court order in 1884 shut down hydraulic mining because of the devastation it was wreaking. Many west slope streams and rivers have been irreversibly altered from the massive infusion of mining sediment and rock, and studies are only beginning to reveal that potentially lethal concentrations of mercury (used to separate gold from crushed ore) remain in river and lake sediments as a legacy of the gold-mining era.

The new settlers also had a tremendous impact on Sierra woodlands and forests. Miners needed timber to construct buildings, to reinforce mining shafts, and to use as fuel, and they often started forest fires as a means of exposing prospecting sites. The needs of ever-growing towns and cities in turn fostered a fledgling lumber industry. The latter has evolved from much hand effort in felling trees and transporting logs by ox teams to cutting trees with mobile tractors and transporting logs by helicopter and log truck. This has led to an exponential increase in the capacity for removing trees from the landscape.

The most accessible coniferous forests on the lower western slopes were logged a century ago, but roads and helicopters have since permitted cutting almost wherever there are suitable lumber trees. Much of the present forest cover consists of second- (or third-) growth timber. Old forests that have never been cut are scarce in the Sierra, with the vast majority of these stands restricted to national park lands or steep river canyons. Areas denuded of forest, when few or no "seed" trees were left, sometimes revert to seemingly permanent chaparral where conifer seedlings fare poorly. Efforts at reforestation by planting seeds or seedlings are not always successful. Rodents of several kinds dig up and eat the seeds, and young trees are damaged or destroyed by these animals and by rabbits, deer, and insects. Moisture conditions—the amount and timing of rain or snowmelt—may be such that new trees can start and survive only in occasional favorable years.

Much logging on state or federal lands (less so on private lands) now is by selective cutting, in which some mature trees are left behind, leaving space and sunlight for smaller conifers to grow. Clearcutting is used less often, in part because it is aesthetically unappealing, but the main harm of logging derives from the impact of large, heavy machinery compacting forest soils, and from erosion resulting from road building and other disturbances. Despite this long history of logging, however, the forests of the Sierra Nevada have proven resilient. Trees in many places grow back rapidly, and in fact there are probably more trees today than ever before, even though these trees are younger and large diameter logs and snags are scarce in areas managed for logging.

The original cover of oaks on the western foothills and stream valleys was far greater and more extensive than today. For more than 100 years, oaks have been cut for firewood and, in many areas, removed to increase range and pasture lands. Nearly 800,000 acres of oak woodlands in the Sierra Nevada have been lost since 1950 alone. Young trees sprouting from naturally planted acorns are relished by livestock, and thus oak woodlands that are heavily grazed contain few or no replacement trees. Some foothills now covered entirely by grassland formerly supported oak woodlands.

In California's Mediterranean climate of hot, dry summers, fire plays a dominant role in shaping ecosystems, and a great many plant species are uniquely adapted for a fire regime. The influence of fire decreases in the Subalpine and Alpine Belts but is important in all other belts. Plants survive fires through various adaptations, including having seeds, flowers, or sprouts that are stimulated by fires; having fire-resistant bark or buds; and, in the case of some conifers, having cones that release seeds after a hot fire. Fires are critical, therefore, in the life cycles of many species, because they set the stage for growth and regeneration.

Much vegetation in the main timber belt and foothills becomes tinder dry in the long, hot rainless summer. Fires start easily, burn fiercely over large areas, and are difficult and costly to extinguish. In the prehistoric period some fires resulted from lightning, and Native Americans set others. Such fires burned until ended by natural barriers or rain. Early white travelers in the mountains saw much evidence of fire in scars on trees, charred trunks, and areas denuded of forest. As settlers began to occupy the Sierra, damage increased from other causes—sparks from untended campfires or wood-burning locomotives, slash burns that went out of control, and malicious efforts of "firebugs." In the late 1800s, sheepherders were notorious for starting late fall fires as they left the mountains, trying to clear off forests and brush to improve the next spring's grazing.

Fear of wildfires and the perception that they are solely negative in their impacts have led to efforts at fire prevention and control by state and federal agencies during the past century. The fire suppression program, however, has resulted in accumulation of much ground litter, seedlings, brush, and dense stands of young trees, so that when fires do start they often burn extremely hot, are increasingly difficult to stop, and may end up destroying entire stands of trees. Controlled (or prescribed) burning has become a common practice to clear out forests and reduce the summer fire hazard. Under appropriate weather conditions, trained personnel can start, guide, and extinguish wildfires. If a severe fire destroys the entire forest cover of an area, it soon becomes densely clothed with brush that may persist for several decades before trees can get reestablished. A century or more may pass before the area is again well forested.

Grazing resources in the Sierra were early recognized and used without restraint. Great herds and flocks were moved upslope in spring to successively higher levels as feed became available and were brought down only when forage was far reduced or at the first hint of winter. Mountain roads became ankle-deep with dust created by hooves of migrating livestock. Mountain meadows and slopes were stripped of vegetation almost as soon as the snows cleared, and were visited repeatedly until snows returned. A forest surveyor complained in 1900 that not a single day's feed could be found for his pack animals while traveling over three million acres of the Sierra Nevada.

For years there was no regulation, resulting in many areas being seriously or irrevocably harmed, especially in areas where nonnative grasses and forbs took over. Even national park lands were grazed for years. Then grazing came under regulation by the U.S. Forest Service, and permittees were limited as to numbers of livestock and the season of use. Reduction, however, was slow, and further injury to vegetation resulted. Currently, most or all of the cattle and sheep are transported by trucks—to lessen herding labor and also the losses in weight of livestock on the long migrations. The number of animals now permitted is a small fraction of those in the mountains in earlier years.

Mountain plants and grasses, because of the short growing season, are easily damaged and slow to recover. Evidence of early abuse is still seen. Severe overgrazing by sheep in parts of the southern High Sierra denuded some areas of vegetation, and the damage is all but permanent. At all elevations, stream banks of fine gravelly soil erode badly where stripped of vegetation by overgrazing, resulting in the downcutting of stream channels and the lowering of water tables, drying out formerly wet meadows.

Humans have significantly altered the populations of many wild animals. Although some animals have been negatively impacted, it is also true that other species have benefited. Introduced species with no natural predators (like Bullfrogs) and species that thrive in disturbed ecosystems have done particularly well. Logging, for instance, can create favorable conditions for shrub-loving birds and rodents, whose populations increase locally. Even roads have proven beneficial to at least one species: Ravens find food by following roads and feeding on animal carcasses, and their populations have grown tremendously. One addition to the Sierra mammals has been the introduction of the Beaver into several streams having growths of willows and aspen. The Beavers have built ponds and harvested trees, but it is uncertain whether tree replacement growths will be adequate for their needs. Because the landscape is forever changing, the very conditions for life are in flux, and depending on a given change some species benefit, others suffer, and still others are unaffected (but perhaps affected by another change later).

Species heavily impacted by humans include Grizzly Bears, once native to the west slope, which were relentlessly hunted and eliminated from California by 1924. Mountain sheep were originally common on much of the High Sierra but early on dwindled to very small numbers due to overhunting, then were further imperiled by diseases transmitted from domestic sheep. The Wolverine, Fisher, and Marten have been greatly diminished by trapping. Mountain Lions were hunted for many decades; then, as public opinion changed in the late 20th century and they were protected, their numbers quickly climbed. In past years ground squirrels and even pocket gophers were poisoned on mountain meadows in a misguided effort to enhance the amount of forage for domestic livestock, but there was no lasting effect on the rodents.

Perhaps more than any other group of Sierra animals, fish have suffered the most from human intervention, especially because so many human activities and needs center around water. Unfortunately, fish are merely emblematic of a much larger and far more devastating transformation of the Sierra landscape. The construction of dams (with associated impacts on water volume, peak flows, sediment supply, water temperature, and more), the introduction of 30 species of nonnative fish (10 of which are now widespread and very abundant), and watershed disturbances from various human activities have had a tremendous, crippling impact on native aquatic ecosystems. Chinook Salmon are one prominent example: Once numbering over a million fish, Chinook Salmon are now nearly extinct in the Sierra Nevada due to dams that block access to 90 percent of their former spawning grounds. One recent study called this a "curtain of dams [drawn] across the Sierra Nevada rivers" that lets nothing pass.

At one time fish were essentially absent above 6,000 ft in the Sierra Nevada, leaving amphibians and invertebrates to dominate hundreds of miles of streams and almost all of the 4,000+ natural lakes in the range. The widespread introduction of nonnative fish, mostly trout, into this formerly fish-free zone profoundly altered these natural ecosystems. These big, aggressive predators largely eliminated amphibians and many invertebrates from countless sites where they formerly abounded, with cascading effects throughout entire aquatic ecosystems. Tadpoles, for instance, are important because they feed on algae and control algal outbreaks that alter lake nutrient cycles.

Of 40 native fish species in the Sierra Nevada, 20 have declining populations, with six of those already listed as threatened or endangered and another 12 species candidates for listing. Half of the 29 native amphibian species are now at risk of extinction. The situation with aquatic invertebrates is perhaps even more alarming because the Sierra Nevada has a high proportion of endemic species that are restricted to single sites and these are almost completely overlooked by resource agencies who could help protect them. Very little is known about aquatic insects in the Sierra Nevada, and only a handful of specialists currently work the field.

A century and more of increasing use and occupancy of the Sierra by modern humans has led to various changes from primeval conditions. It takes a skilled eye, however, to see the full scope of these changes when the landscape looks perfectly "normal" and healthy. Waters of nearly all streams and rivers in the middle and lower elevations have been diverted or stored in reservoirs for power, irrigation, or domestic use. The forests are far different in extent and size of trees, although still beautiful and inspiring over much of the range. Some ferns and other attractive plants, in demand for home gardens, have been taken in such quantities that they now are scarce in well-visited places. Many alien grasses and weeds have invaded the mountains, frequently along roads, and become established members of the flora. Some of the larger mammals have declined and populations of smaller birds and animals have been affected by alterations in tree and shrub cover.

The most pronounced change of all, however, is the invasion of humans and their structures at an alarming rate. From 1970 to 1990 the human population in the Sierra Nevada doubled, and it is expected to further triple, quadruple, or even quintuple by the year 2040. Most of this population growth takes place in the Foothill Belt, placing a disproportionate burden on foothill plants and animals. Only one percent of foothill oak woodlands are protected; most of the remaining oak woodlands are privately owned and have no safeguards against development or conversion.

In 1996 the most comprehensive survey of the Sierra Nevada ever undertaken was published. The four-volume SNEP (Sierra Nevada Ecosystem Project) report evaluated in great detail the state of ecological and human health in the region and found reasons for serious concern. Not only are some systems (e.g., aquatic habitats and watershed health) highly degraded or rapidly deteriorating, but support and funding for agencies in charge of protecting these resources is waning. This report further asserts that many ecosystem declines in the Sierra Nevada can be attributed to "institutional incapacities" resulting from fragmented jurisdictions, absence of cooperation or exchange mechanisms between agencies, detachment between agencies and communities, and inflexibility in response to rapid change. It will take a substantial and concerted effort by all interested parties to address these challenges. Only by careful and intelligent planning and management will some features in these mountains remain attractive in the face of continuing modification. Students of natural history can be of great help by serving as eyes on the ground and by using their knowledge of ecosystems, plants, and animals to document changes over time. Our understanding of the status and distribution of many, even very common, species is sorely lacking, and the observations of naturalists will be a critical contribution to identifying and protecting these species and their habitats.

Ownership and Management in the Sierra

Anyone may travel freely over much of the Sierra Nevada, but there are some restrictions that must be kept in mind. These limitations result from the varied pattern of ownership and management of the lands, forests, and waters. About two-thirds of the Sierra's roughly 13 million acres is publicly owned, but there are many private holdings. These were acquired long ago for timber, mineral, or water rights or as homesteads for ranches or homes.

Other portions belong to the state of California or to counties or cities. Ownership and use privileges are therefore complex and sometimes controversial.

Yosemite Valley and the Mariposa (Wawona) Big Tree Grove were transferred from federal to state jurisdiction in 1864 but were returned in 1906. Federal forest reserves were set aside in the 1890s and became national forests in 1907, with some subsequent additions. San Francisco acquired Hetch Hetchy Valley in 1909 as a source of water, and Oakland obtained rights to Mokelumne River water in 1929. Los Angeles did similarly with many waters on the east slope south of Mono Lake from 1913 onward. Irrigation districts and electric power companies have been granted rights to gather water of many west slope streams and have built numerous storage reservoirs—the artificial lakes now at various elevations. State and federal agencies have constructed dams to impound waters as a measure of flood control and to conserve water supplies for power generation, irrigation, and other purposes.

National parks were established to conserve and maintain, for public enjoyment, the natural scenery, fauna, and flora of certain outstanding areas. Sequoia National Park (established 1890; 406,426 acres) features magnificent groves of giant sequoias as well as Mt. Whitney (14,495 ft), the highest U.S. peak outside of Alaska. Kings Canyon National Park (1940; 458,832 acres) includes two great canyons of the Kings River, many High Sierra summits, and the former General Grant National Park with sequoias. Yosemite National Park (1890; 747,956 acres) has Yosemite Valley with spectacular waterfalls, much High Sierra, and three sequoia groves: Wawona, Merced, and Tuolumne. In national parks *no flowers, plants, or animals may be taken* (except under permit for scientific use). Camping, the making of fires, and the speed of automobile travel are regulated. Visitors are advised of other regulations upon entering a national park.

Each national park has a museum with exhibits of plants, animals, geology, Native American materials, and local history. Trained naturalists give frequent lectures on these subjects, answer questions, and conduct field trips for interested persons to learn about the flora and fauna and other natural features. An independent Natural History Association, associated with each park, publishes special booklets on birds, wildflowers, and other special interest topics.

The Devils Postpile National Monument near Mammoth Lakes includes a display of 60-ft vertical basaltic columns. Calaveras Big Trees State Park includes two groves of sequoias on the Ebbetts Pass road (Hwy. 4). Other state parks, especially at Lake Tahoe, allow public recreation and access in other areas of unique interest.

The national forests include practically all tree-producing lands (and some that have no trees) in the Sierra Nevada except those in private ownership or in national parks—about 40 percent of the Sierra Nevada is national forest land. The nine forests from north to south are Lassen, Plumas, Tahoe, Eldorado, Toiyabe, Stanislaus, Sierra, Inyo, and Sequoia. Each has an administrative staff, rangers on patrol, foresters, and resource specialists. Many public campgrounds are maintained in the forests, each with a piped water supply, fireplaces and tables, garbage disposal, and toilets. Visitors are urged to use these facilities for their convenience and to lessen the hazard from campfires elsewhere. Permits are required to build campfires in the forests. Grazing and timber cutting in national forests are regulated by the U.S. Forest Service.

Parts of some Sierra national forests have been designated as wilderness areas where roads, motorized vehicles, buildings, and other forms of permanent occupancy are prohibited. These areas include Bucks Lake Wilderness (21,000 acres), Granite Chief Wilderness (25,700 acres), Desolation Wilderness (63,500 acres), Mokelumne Wilderness (105,000 acres), Carson-Iceberg Wilderness (160,000 acres), Emigrant Wilderness (113,000 acres), Hoover Wilderness (48,000 acres), Ansel Adams Wilderness (228,500 acres), John Muir Wilderness (581,000 acres), Golden Trout Wilderness (303,000 acres), South Sierra Wilderness (62,700 acres), Kaiser Wilderness (22,700 acres), Dinkey Lakes Wilderness (30,000 acres), Monarch Wilderness (45,000 acres), and Jennie Lakes Wilderness (11,000 acres).

Hunting is permitted in national forests but not in national parks. It may be prohibited when the fire hazard is excessive. Fishing is allowed in both national forests and parks. In general, the laws of the California Game Code and regulations of the California Department of Fish and Game apply to all lands and waters in the Sierra Nevada. On all state and county roadsides (rights of way) it is illegal—a misdemeanor—to pick or remove flowers, ferns, plants, trees, or shrubs. The same applies to plant materials on private land except with written permission of the owner.

Good Conduct in the Sierra

It is a privilege to enjoy the natural features of our great mountains. Visitors in the Sierra should be well behaved and not abuse the scenery, plants, or animals but leave them for others to enjoy. Because the Sierra Nevada is visited by millions of people each year the cumulative impact of even simple actions can be immense. Hikers, for instance, have a tremendous impact on fragile mountain meadows. Pioneer travelers and early residents had a simple unwritten code of good manners that should be followed by all who now find pleasure in the mountains.

Streams

Keep them clean. Never use them for laundry, garbage, or human bodily wastes. Wash and rinse dishes well away from streamsides—all soaps pollute. Pack out *all* garbage. When no toilet is available, take to the woods, well away from streams or lakes.

Fires

Build fires only when and where permitted, in an open place where there is no dry grass or ground litter. Dead and downed wood is a scarce resource in many mountain areas so cook on a portable stove whenever possible. Do not start an open fire if there is strong wind. Never leave a fire unattended. Always quench a fire thoroughly with water—then add one more bucket of water for safety. Do not discard burning matches or cigarettes on the roadside. If you see a fire, report it to the nearest forest ranger or office.

Trees

Leave them as they are. Initials cut in the bark remain as scars for years and serve no useful purpose.

Trails

Stay on the trail, wandering off-trail can quickly scar the landscape and create new routes that other hikers follow later. Do not create or follow shortcuts.

Picnic Sites

After enjoying an outdoor meal at a picnic area or in the woods, pick up all papers, cans, and other debris and carry it until you find a trash can into which you can discard it. The pleasant place you enjoyed will remain attractive for the next visitors.

Camps

Set up camp at least 100 ft from trails, streams, and the edges of lakes. Wherever you stop, even overnight, leave the site clean. *Do not add trash to the landscape; pack out everything!* Do not build structures.

Livestock

If you meet riding or pack animals on a trail, step aside (preferably to the downhill side) far enough to let them pass easily.

Wild Animals

It is dangerous to offer food to deer or bears that seem "tame." Deer can strike quickly and severely with their front feet, and a bear's paw, with its claws, delivers a powerful stroke. Many persons have been severely injured by animals that frequent roadsides or camps for gifts of food. Squirrels, chipmunks, and raccoons carry diseases transmissible to man. Do not feed them.

Always store food safely to avoid tempting bears, who will readily break into cars, tents, or other structures in search of food. This is such a serious problem in national parks that bear-proof storage canisters are provided in campgrounds and lightweight ones are required for backpackers.

Personal Safety

Be alert to your own abilities, condition, and skill level; do not attempt hikes, climbs, or other activities that exceed your own abilities and potentially endanger yourself or others. Maintain and carry clothes and equipment in preparation for changing weather conditions in the mountain environment.

FUNGI

FUNGI, UNLIKE HIGHER plants, lack green chlorophyll and feed on complex substances drawn from living or dead plants and animals. Some kinds cause serious diseases in live plants, animals, and humans. Others, such as baker's yeast and the molds used to produce antibiotics, are highly beneficial. The fungi (phyla Ascomycota and Basidiomycota) described here include some that damage live or dead trees and lumber. In nature their role is to decompose woody materials and to serve as mycorrhizal associates of forest trees without which those trees grow slowly if at all. In other words, along with many sorts of bacteria, molds, and insects, they are "sanitary agents" that consume and thereby dispose of dead organic matter.

The fungus starts as a microscopic spore that develops a network of threadlike parts (*hyphae*). These penetrate dead plant tissue in or above the ground to obtain nutriment. Later growth yields the larger and exposed spore-producing stage (*sporophore*). In mushrooms this comprises an upright stalk (*stipe*) covered by a cap (*pileus*) that is either dome shaped or flat. Under the cap are many thin, platelike, radiating vertical gills that carry the spore-producing organs. One group, called bracket fungi, lacks gills, the spores coming instead from many small tubes opening as pores on the undersurface of the bracket-shaped cap or fruiting body. Spores differ in color, size, and form according to the species of fungus. They are produced by the millions and distributed by wind, water, or animals.

Some mushrooms and other fungi are edible and tasty. A few kinds, however, are dangerously poisonous, causing severe illness and even death if eaten. There is no quick, easy, and certain way to distinguish a presumably safe and edible "mushroom" from an unpalatable or dangerous "toadstool" or other fungus. Accurate identification requires some experience and careful study of fresh entire specimens using descriptions and figures in a reliable reference book. *The brief accounts given here must not be depended upon for this purpose.* There are thousands of fungi species in the Sierra Nevada when one includes the molds, slime molds, wood rot, underground truffles and their allies, cup fungi, and our classic mushrooms. Several of the commonly encountered species are detailed here. The taxonomy used follows *Mushrooms Demystified* (Arora 1986).

SHORT-STEMMED RUSSULA   *Russula brevipes*

Cap 3 to 8 in., circular, deeply depressed in center, margin rounded, white, aging to dingy buff or brown. Stem 1 to 3 in. long, .75 to 1 in. thick, stout, dull white aging to brown, can be snapped cleanly like a piece of chalk.

DISTRIBUTION: Common in Mixed Conifer Belt, on ground under needles in conifer woods.

COCCORA   *Amanita calyptrata*
Pl. 12

Cap 6 to 8 in., round to flat topped, varying from yellow to light brown, often with a cottony patch on top in a single piece, fine vertical lines rim the cap; gills and spores white to light yellow. Stem white, hollow, with slight ring halfway from base, sits in thick egglike cup (volva) at base.

DISTRIBUTION: Common in fall under madrones and oaks, fruits in smaller numbers until spring when numbers increase again.

REMARKS: While edible, this species is closely related to the similar death cap (*A. phalloides*) that is deadly if consumed.

OYSTER MUSHROOM   *Pleurotus ostreatus*
Pl. 13

Cap to 12 in., shelflike, white to gray or varying shades of brown; gills white, running down stem (if present). Stem short and thick or absent.

DISTRIBUTION: Grows at all but very high elevations, found early fall to late spring on most hardwood species; on decaying wood.

REMARKS: A very tasty mushroom that is widely grown commercially.

GIANT LENTINUS   *Neolentinus ponderosus*
Pl. 14

Cap to over 16 in. (one of the largest mushrooms in the Sierra), white and robust, with brownish scaling; gills white and serrated (toothed like a saw edge).

DISTRIBUTION: On dead conifers, especially near high mountain lakes or in lodgepole pine forests, late spring to early fall.

REMARKS: The tough flesh of this mushroom can remain intact for many months after fruiting.

HONEY MUSHROOMS   Genus *Armillaria*
Pl. 15

Cap 1 to 6 in., convex or spread, often with fine tufts of brown or black hairs, pale to dark brown, edge finely furrowed with age; flesh whitish, browning with age; gills attached to stem, white, browning with age; spores white. Stem 1 to 6 in. by .25 to .75 in., of variable diameter, tough and fibrous, often with a prominent ring above middle, upper part pale, lower part honey-colored to brown, darkening with age.

DISTRIBUTION: Common in woods or cleared land, on ground or decayed wood, summer and fall.

REMARKS: Dense clusters of this mushroom appear on stumps, logs, and buried roots (rhizomorphs) of both conifers and deciduous trees in fall. Within the wood are the shining brown hyphae. Research shows that honey mushrooms may encompass as many as 14 slightly differing species; apparently all are edible.

DEER MUSHROOM   *Pluteus cervinus*
Pl. 16

Cap 2 to 4 in., convex or flat, smooth margined, top glabrous and moist, yellowish, grayish, or blackish brown; gills free of stem, broad, whitish to pink; spores pink; odor usually radishlike. Stem 2 to 6 in. high, diameter .25 to .5 in., solid, white, smooth or black-haired.

DISTRIBUTION: Common on decaying wood, especially on hardwoods in riparian areas.

COBWEB-GILLED FUNGUS   *Cortinarius glaucopus*
Pl. 17

Cap 2 to 5 in., thin or thick, dryish to sticky surfaced, bright yellow to reddish; flesh yellowish to white; gills thin, slightly purple, aging to dull yellow or brown; spores rust-colored. Stem 1 to 6 in. long, diameter to .75 in., often hollow, whitish to brownish, bulbous at base.

DISTRIBUTION: In woods or partly cleared areas.

REMARKS: There are many species in this genus, but few are readily identifiable. The genus, however, is readily recognized by the presence of a cobwebby veil (cortina) that covers the gills and runs halfway down the stem in young mushrooms.

SULFUR TUFT MUSHROOM   *Hypholoma fasiculare*
Pl. 18

Cap to 3 in., bluntly conical to flat, thin, smooth surfaced, above orangish tan aging to brown, margin yellow; flesh yellow; gills many, narrow, pale yellow, later gray to purple; spores purplish brown. Stem 2 to 4.5 in. high, diameter to .4 in., hollow, sulfur yellow, darkening later.

DISTRIBUTION: In clusters on decaying logs, spring or fall.

REMARKS: Serious poisoning can occur if this species is eaten.

KING BOLETE or PORCINI   *Boletus edulis*
Pl. 19

Cap 4 to 6 in., convex to flat, smooth, moist, reddish or brownish red, or yellowish brown, margin paler, pores on underside are white. Stem 4 to 7 in. high, diameter 1 to 2.25 in., stout, often bulbous, surface finely net veined, white to brownish.

DISTRIBUTION: On ground in woods, summer and fall.

REMARKS: Boletes are in a distinctive order of fungi that do not have gills, but instead they have hundreds of small tubes that discharge spores. The pored undersurface of the cap on this species is colored white in young specimens, becoming yellow then brown or olive with age. Another key feature for identifying this species is the lack of blue staining when the tissue is cut or bruised. This famous edible grows across the Northern Hemisphere with many coniferous and deciduous hosts.

WHITE-POUCH FUNGUS   *Cryptoporus volvatus*
Pl. 20

Cap small, about 2 in. across, hoof shaped, smooth, light yellow brown, later white, interior corky or hard; undersurface hidden by thick leathery skin, the pink spores escaping through a hole; produces superficial gray rot on dead timber.

DISTRIBUTION: On conifers, except junipers and giant sequoias, often peppering the trunks of recently dead trees.

RED-BELTED CONK   *Fomitopsis pinicola*
Pl. 21

Form variable; on standing trees cap often hoof shaped, to 8 in. wide, margin rounded, surface often resinous; underside flat, blackish above, creamy below, with reddish band above lower pale-colored edge; pores minute, white to yellow; flesh layered, corky to woody, light brown.

DISTRIBUTION: Common on dead conifers except incense-cedars, junipers, and giant sequoias.

REMARKS: This common polypore produces a red rot in heartwood of fallen logs and some live trees. On the underside of downed logs the cap may be knoblike, and on the upper side the fungus may be a stemless toadstool.

TURKEY TAIL   *Trametes versicolor*
Pl. 22

Cap .75 to 4 in. wide, thin, many in shelflike layers above one another, velvety or leathery surfaced, strikingly zoned in various colors; pores small, round, white to gray or yellowish. Stem short.

DISTRIBUTION: Common on dead or sometimes living hardwoods, rarely on conifers.

SULFUR SHELF or CHICKEN OF THE WOODS   *Laetiporus*
Pl. 23   *gilbertsonii*

Cap to 24 in. wide, .5 to 1.5 in. thick, of several fanlike layers, flattish, wavy edged; upper surface smooth to woolly, lemon yellow to orange; undersurface flat, silky surfaced, pores minute, light sulfur yellow; flesh spongy textured, juicy, yellow, later white, splitting but not hardening with age; spores white. Usually no stem (or a short lateral one).

DISTRIBUTION: On decaying wood and living tree trunks, mostly oaks.

REMARKS: Shelflike caps of this large, brilliant fungus often overlap one another in clusters. When mature they become dry and crumbling, and in early decay they are phosphorescent. While a popular edible, allergic reactions can occur in some people.

YELLOW CORAL MUSHROOM   *Ramaria rasilispora*
Pl. 24

Comprised of upright corallike branches, pale to orange yellow but lower branches usually white.

DISTRIBUTION: Common and widespread, often found half-buried in soil.

REMARKS: There are many coral mushroom varieties and at least four yellow species in the Sierra so identification can be difficult (based on microscopic features).

CHANTERELLE   *Cantharellus cibarius*
Pl. 25

Cap 2 to 6 in., concave with margin raised so overall form is vase shaped, bright orange; gills well spaced and fairly stout, running down stem.

DISTRIBUTION: Middle to lower elevations in association with both conifers and hardwoods.

REMARKS: A popular edible mushroom with a fruity fragrance.

WITCH'S BUTTER   *Dacrymyces palmatus*
Pl. 26

Cap .5 to 2 in., bright orange, a lobed, convoluted, gelatinous mass of tissue (firmer when young, then turning jellylike).

DISTRIBUTION: Widespread and common in moist forests, mostly grows on conifers.

SIERRA PUFFBALL   *Calvatia sculpta*

Fruiting body (cap) to 6 in. diameter, spiny topped when young, becoming a flattened globe, the surface with both raised and depressed triangular patterns, white. Stem short, stout.

DISTRIBUTION: Common in coniferous forests on both slopes of the Sierra above 2,500 ft.

REMARKS: When young, puffballs have firm white interiors that later dry out and turn powdery with spores. If touched, puffballs may emit clouds of spores at this stage. Insects and rodents eat puffballs and probably carry spores on their bodies or hair by which they become distributed. The decorative Sierra puffball has become scarce in areas where summer visitors have picked and removed it. Smoother puffballs of other species occur in the Foothill Belt.

BLACK MOREL
Morchella elata

Pl. 27

Cap 2 to 4 in. tall, to 1 in. diameter; bluntly conical, whole surface with large dull brown pits, ridges darker, brown to black. Stem 2 to 4 in. long, .75 to 1.25 in. wide, tapered or cylindrical, often furrowed at base, dingy cream to buff.

DISTRIBUTION: Under conifers in many habitats, often common after a fire. Highly prized edible mushroom.

SADDLE FUNGUS
Helvella lacunosa

Pl. 28

Cap 1 to 2 in., shape irregular, lobed, and inflated, lobes bending outward and somewhat saddle shaped, grayish black. Stem 1.5 to 4 in. high, .75 to 1.5 in. diameter, usually tapering upward, deeply ribbed and pitted, hollow, white at first, graying with age.

DISTRIBUTION: Occur in many forest types and on bare or disturbed soil, usually under or near conifers, in spring and fall.

LICHENS

LICHENS ARE fungi that have combined with either single-celled green algae or with blue-green algae (now considered to be a bacteria) to form a new organism—the lichen. Photosynthetic activity by the algae and bacteria provides carbohydrates for the dual organism. Most scientists today feel that the relationship is a controlled parasitism by the fungus rather than a mutualistic symbiosis. Lichens grow on the surfaces of rocks, trees, or soil, often making colorful and decorative patterns. They provide food, nesting material, or habitat for many animals and invertebrates. Those containing blue-green algae are able to fix nitrogen and are important components of a healthy forest. Soil lichens are important soil stabilizers.

The main structural body of lichens is called the *thallus,* which often consists of many lobes. The surface, or *cortex,* consists of tightly compacted hyphal (fungal) cells. Underneath this sits a layer of algal cells and then a thicker layer of loose hyphal cells called the *medulla.* There may be a lower cortex and hairlike attachment structures (*rhizines*). Crustose lichens lack this lower cortex and instead grow directly on and within the surface of the substrate.

Lichens are highly resistant to cold, drought, and strong sunlight. Their growth is often exceedingly slow. Reproduction can be vegetative, by specialized structures such as *soredia* (a powderlike substance) or *isidia* (tiny fingerlike projections), each containing both fungal and algal cells. The fungal portion of some lichens produces spores in either disks (*apothecia*) on the surface of lichens or special internal structures called *perithecia.* These spores must be dispersed by water, wind, or insects and find the proper algae or bacteria to produce a new thallus. Broken pieces of lichens can also begin growth if they fall on a suitable surface.

The lichens of California are poorly known with many species yet to be discovered or described. There has never been a full-time academic lichenologist hired in California even though one-third of North America's species occur in the state and a tremendous amount of work remains to be done. The taxonomy used here is drawn from *Lichens of North America* (Brody et al. 2001).

Fruticose Lichens

In general, these are the lichens that grow from a single attachment point on trees, rocks, or soil. Their shrubby thalli can be either erect and tufted or pendant. They can have either round or flat lobes or branches.

WITCH'S HAIR *Alectoria sarmentosa*
Pl. 29
Pale yellow green, hanging in loose flexible tufts up to 12 in. long; branches of thalli generally round in cross section. This common lichen is associated with conifer limbs and is prevalent in older forest stands. Occurs below 5,000 ft on west slope of Sierra Nevada from Madera County north.

TREE-HAIR LICHEN   *Bryoria fremontii*

Pl. 30

Dark brown, hanging in dense tufts 5 to15 in. long; main branches .06 in. wide, coarsely dimpled and twisting at base, smaller branches less than .03 in. wide and shiny. In some locations this lichen is extremely conspicuous because it heavily festoons conifer and oak branches. Widespread on west slope of Sierra Nevada up to 8,000 ft.

CLADONIA   Genus *Cladonia*

Pl. 31

These lichens have a unique thallus consisting of two forms. The primary thallus is comprised of flattened fleshy scales called *squamules* and arising from this mat is a secondary thallus of fruiting stalks called *podetia*. This diverse and widespread genus is readily recognized by its growth form. Below 7,000 ft in the Sierra Nevada, *Cladonia fimbriata* (trumpet lichen) is commonly found growing amid mosses on the ground in forests and woodlands. In this species the podetia resemble 1-in.-high golf tees dusted with pale green flour.

OAKMOSS LICHEN   *Evernia prunastri*

Pl. 32

Grows in pale yellow green tufts less than 4 in. in diameter, thallus branches flattened and white on the lower surface. This species is characterized by its soft, limber feel (unlike the stiff, brittle texture of the very similar *ramalina* species). Found on bark or branches of oaks and conifers below 5,500 ft on the west slope of the Sierra Nevada. Typically rebranches each year so that the age of individual lichens can be estimated by counting the forks along a single lobe.

WOLF LICHEN   Genus *Letharia*

Pl. 33

Thickly covering the branches and trunks of many mountain conifers, especially red firs, this fluorescent yellow green or chartreuse lichen is without a doubt the most conspicuous and familiar of all Sierra lichens. Two species are present, both growing as bushy tufts 4 to 6 in. in diameter that are formed of wrinkled, irregularly rounded branches. One species (*L. columbiana*) has prominent brown spore-producing disks (apothecia), while the other species (*L. vulpina*) reproduces by means of powdery soredia on its surfaces. Both are common in Mixed Conifer and Subalpine Belts throughout the Sierra Nevada. Where they grow most abundantly they serve as a rough indication of average winter snowpack levels since they don't grow under snow. The yellow pigment (vulpinic acid) is somewhat poisonous but it is also an excellent dye for fabrics.

Crustose Lichens

These lichens grow as crusts that tightly adhere to surfaces. On the underside they lack a lower cortex and their hyphal cells grow into the top surface of rock or bark. In some species the thallus lives completely below the surface and only the apothecia or fruiting bodies are seen. Growth is very slow in this group, .5 to 2 mm per year (just millimeters per century in some parts of the world).

FLAME FIREDOT   *Caloplaca ignea*
Pl. 34

An easily recognized lichen due to its deep orange color. This species has distinct marginal lobes crowding together and creating a brainlike surface pattern, at times fusing with adjacent colonies and covering large areas of rock. Often grows in response to the presence of nitrogen where birds or small mammals defecate regularly on rock faces. Found on exposed rock outcrops below 7,500 ft in the central and southern Sierra Nevada, especially prevalent in the Foothill Belt. Very similar is the foliose lichen *Xanthoria elegans,* which is also orange red in color but with a lower cortex that adheres to rock faces by only a few attachment points.

STONEWALL RIM-LICHEN   *Lecanora muralis*

Grows as a greenish to pale yellow crust in irregularly shaped 2-in.-wide colonies, but readily fuses with other colonies to cover much larger areas of rock. Spore-bearing disks are tan or brownish. One of the most abundant and widespread crustose lichens in California, found on sheltered rocks below 9,000 ft.

BROWN TILE LICHEN   *Lecidea atrobrunnea*
Pl. 35

A very common lichen on rocks, often covering large areas, it is one of the main reasons Sierra granite looks gray from a distance. Forms a dark brown crust with numerous black apothecia, each with a rim that is also black. Occurs throughout the range at all elevations. The name probably applies to a whole group of similar-looking species whose taxonomy has yet to be worked out.

YELLOW MAP LICHEN   *Rhizocarpon geographicum*
Pl. 36

This brilliant, sharply contrasting yellow-and-black lichen is a conspicuous feature on rock surfaces in the High Sierra. Older portions of the yellow thallus crack into segments (*areoles*) that become rimmed in black, forming patterns that give the lichen its common name. With a growth rate of about .44 in. each century, map lichen colonies have helped scientists date moraines and provide information on the movements of glaciers. *Rhizocarpon* is an arctic tundra genus that ranges southward along high mountain ranges (though it may occur at low-elevation sites elsewhere in California); in the Sierra it is found on exposed granite and other acidic rocks as high as 11,000 ft. There are several other species of *Rhizocarpon* with a similar appearance.

Foliose Lichens

These are lichens with flattened leafy lobes loosely attached to surfaces by dark rootlike rhizines. Unlike crustose lichens, foliose lichens have a lower cortex giving them a distinct upper and lower surface.

WATERFAN   *Hydrothyria venosa*
Known in California from only a few sites in the Sierra Nevada, this unique and very rare aquatic lichen looks like a dark, ruffled piece of seaweed. Small spring-fed streams that have little seasonal fluctuation in their water levels are its favored haunts and here it grows submerged or partially submerged on underwater gravels. The tufted thallus is brown when wet and under 3 in. in diameter. Rare from Madera County to Calaveras County on the west slope of the Sierra Nevada, from 5,000 to 7,000 ft; should not be collected.

FORKED TUBE LICHEN   *Hypogymnia imshaugii*
Pl. 37
Thallus consists of narrow lobes that are pale gray above with tiny black dots. On the underside the lobes are black and bare (lacking rhizines that characterize other foliose lichens). Lobes are somewhat inflated and hollow inside, and if one is sliced open it shows white on its interior surfaces. Many lobes end in rich brown spore-producing disks (apothecia). This species grows as discrete tufts up to 4 in. in diameter on oak and conifer branches and trunks. Found on the west slope of the Sierra Nevada below 8,000 ft.

CALIFORNIA CAMOUFLAGE LICHEN   *Melanelia glabra*
Thallus olive to dark green above, black with many rhizines below, up to 2 in. across with individual lobes .1 in. wide and closely adhering to bark. This is one of the commonest lichens in oak woodlands, being found on the branches and trunks of many oaks and some conifers below 6,000 ft on the west slope. In addition to this dark lichen, a number of pale bluish gray-green lichens can be common to abundant on oaks. *Parmelina quercina* is one conspicuous species associated with black oaks.

EMERY ROCK TRIPE   *Umbilicaria phaea*
Thallus a smooth brown ruffle, irregularly circular in outline and under 2 in. in diameter, growing on rock outcrops. Its upper surface is well marked

with dark brown apothecia, often in the shape of stars; lower surface is dark brown to black and covered with fine warts. Found throughout California below 8,000 ft.

CUMBERLAND ROCK-SHIELD   *Xanthoparmelia cumberlandia*
Pl. 38

Lichens in this genus are a dominant feature of granite and other noncalcareous rocks in the Sierra Nevada. Identification to species is challenging but *X. cumberlandia* is the most common and widespread species below 6,000 ft. Rock-shields have a roughly circular yellow green thallus, are lobed at the margins, and closely adhere to rock surfaces.

MOSSES

MOSSES, LIVERWORTS, and hornworts (collectively called bryophytes) are the largest group of land plants after the flowering plants. Of these three groups, the mosses are the more conspicuous group in the Sierra. Upward of 300 species of mosses are currently documented for the Sierra Nevada out of the 600 species recorded for the state. Identification to the species level generally requires a compound microscope, but many common species can be identified with a hand lens. Mosses are always leafy and can be readily separated from leafy liverworts by the presence of a midrib on the leaf. The midrib may be at the base of the leaf, extend the entire length of the leaf, or even extend beyond the tip of the leaf to form a spiky point (*awn*). Hornworts and the thallose liverworts lack leaves altogether and appear as a flat sheet of green tissue (the *thallus*).

Mosses are primitive green plants, small but conspicuous and attractive, that grow on wet stream banks as well as on rocks, trees, and buildings. A moss begins as a microscopic spore. On a damp surface it germinates and grows into a branching chain of cells (*protonema*) from which buds develop into shoots bearing small spirally arranged green leaves. These make the familiar moss plant. In time the tops of the shoots produce organs bearing egg cells and others bearing sperm cells. In wet weather (or under melting snow) the motile sperm swim and fertilize the egg cells. From each union a spore-bearing plant grows up from the leafy shoot. It consists of a wiry upright stalk (*seta*) topped by a cup-shaped capsule in which thousands of spores are grown and later scattered by wind.

Bryophytes occur on numerous substrates. Some species prefer soil or decomposing logs while others prefer rock walls and boulders. The type of rock (rock chemistry) can also influence which species is most likely to occur. Like many of the flowering plants, bryophytes have distribution and habitat preferences, so the bryophytes of foothill woodlands are generally different from those of coniferous forests and alpine zones. Mosses are among the most desiccation-tolerant of all plants. They can be completely dried at the cellular level and recover completely. When moistened after months or years of being dry, they begin photosynthesis within five minutes!

STAR MOSS   *Syntrichia ruralis*
Pl. 39

Grows in loose clumps, the leaves twisted around the stem when dry, but open, recurved and "starlike" when wet and viewed from the top. Each leaf has a long, clear hairpoint, and two kinds of leaf cells: large, clear, windowlike ones below, and small, green, bumpy ones above. The end of the capsule has a set of long twisted teeth (*peristome*) arising from a basal membrane that looks like delicate basketwork. Very common at all elevations on soil and rock.

DARK ROCK MOSSES   Genera *Grimmia, Orthotrichum*
Pl. 40

These two unrelated moss genera are similarly dark green to blackish when dry, and grow in loose to dense tufts. Both contain many species that are difficult to distinguish in the field, yet together are so common that they are certain to be noticed. *Grimmia* grows on rocks and usually has a white hair-point at the end of the leaf, while *Orthotrichum* grows on rocks or trees and has the midrib ending at the apex.

FOUNTAIN MOSS   Genus *Fontinalis*

Grows underwater in long, wavy strands, dark in color, often three-angled. These are the largest mosses in the Sierra, growing completely submerged in unpolluted streams, creeks, and rivers throughout the Sierra and reaching up to 3 ft in length (the smallest bryophytes in the Sierra are fractions of an inch in length).

PEAT MOSS   Genus *Sphagnum*
Pl. 41

Grows along lake margins and in boggy meadows in the Subalpine and Alpine Belts in the Sierra. Stems are upright and whitish green, with a capit-ulum (a round cluster of crowded branches at the top of the stem). There are six species of *Sphagnum* in the Sierra.

COMMON LIVERWORT   *Marchantia polymorpha*
Pl. 42

Commonly observed along springs, seeps, and stream banks. The thallus has a chambered appearance when viewed from above and bears raised cups containing spindle-shaped gemmae (asexual structures that propa-gate vegetatively). The sexual structures are raised on umbrella-like stalks above the thallus but are insubstantial and only persist a few days.

FERNS

THE FERNS (phylum Pterophyta) are green plants that lack flowers and seeds and have a life cycle that consists of two distinct phases. The first, larger phase (*sporophyte*) is the familiar fern. It has a creeping stem or rootstock (*rhizome*) with roots and one to many upright leaves or *fronds*. Each frond starts from the rootstock on a short *stalk* that continues upward as the central support or *rachis* of the frond (fig. 6). A young frond is tightly spiraled like a fiddleneck and uncoils as it grows. The full-sized frond is sometimes cut almost or entirely to the rachis. The divisions are called *pinnae,* and the frond is termed *pinnate.* If a pinna is divided again, the frond is two-pinnate (further subdivision results in three-pinnate, even four-pinnate fronds); the final subdivision is a *segment.* The under-surfaces of all or some segments bear small "fruit dots" (*sori*). Each sorus includes many stalked spore cases (*sporangia*) that produce microscopic spores. The sori may have special coverings (*indusia*), sometimes formed of the curved margin of the frond segment. When spores are mature they shower out as fine dust if a frond is touched. In moist ground a spore grows into the inconspicuous second phase (*gametophyte* or *prothallium*), less than .25 in. wide. In turn this produces male and female sex cells that join and grow to become a new fern.

The taxonomy here follows *The Jepson Manual* (Hickman 1993) in consultation with Alan R. Smith. One notable, and unexpected, exception is the inclusion of horsetails along with ferns. As this revision was being written a new study was published that used molecular and morphological evidence to reveal that horsetails are actually ferns. This conclusion may be controversial but it is followed here.

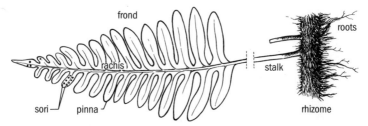

Figure 6. Structure of a fern.

FIVE-FINGER FERN   *Adiantum aleuticum*
Pl. 43

Rhizome thick, short; stalks erect, shiny black or brown, thin, forked at top, bearing 3 to 8 pinnae arrayed palmately like a hand; fronds to 30 in. high, pinnae delicate, to 9 in. long; segments with upper edge lobed, lower edge straight, entire; 4 to 6 sori per segment.

DISTRIBUTION: At 1,500 to 11,000 ft, in moist, cool sites.

REMARKS: The five-finger lives only in cool, damp, and protected rock crevices having much moisture. Originally it abounded near waterfalls in Yosemite Valley, but so many of the plants were removed that it became scarce by the early 1900s—a fate this fern has suffered in other parts of the Sierra. This fern has the appearance of a flat fan spread out to face the sky.

CALIFORNIA MAIDEN-HAIR FERN   *Adiantum jordanii*

Pl. 44

Rhizome slender, creeping; stalks fine, blackish, shiny, pinnately branched at top; fronds to 24 in. high; segments thin, to 1 in. wide, on delicate stalks, fan shaped, lower margins straight, upper edges toothed or lobed; sori near upper curved edge of some segments.

DISTRIBUTION: Local in central Sierra south to Fresno County, 1,000 to 4,000 ft, in moist sites.

REMARKS: The maiden-hair is common in damp situations of the Coast Ranges, but rather rare in canyons of the Sierra foothills, where it may be in evidence from February to June. Another maiden-hair (*A. capillus-veneris*) of the Sierra is distinguished in having its segments deeply lobed with their lower margins forming an acute angle at their bases.

INDIAN'S DREAM   *Aspidotis densa*

Rhizome short with dark scales; stalks shiny, chestnut brown; fronds leathery, 3 to 12 in. long, three-pinnate, segments narrow, linear with rolled margins; sori continuous along margin.

DISTRIBUTION: At 1,200 to 11,000 ft on open slopes in crevices of rocky outcrops.

REMARKS: Growing in dense clumps in rock crevices, this fern superficially resembles the parsley fern except that all its leaves are similar (not occurring in two distinct types) and its stalks are shiny brown.

LADY FERN   *Athyrium filix-femina*

Pl. 45

Rhizome stout, short creeping to suberect, with thin, dark brown scales; fronds to 48+ in. long by 18 in. broad, diamond shaped (tapering at each end), mostly erect, thin, and soft, two- or three-pinnate, segments angled on midrib; fronds and segments varied in form; sori at angle to midrib; indusia flaplike, attached along one side.

DISTRIBUTION: Primarily found in Mixed Conifer and Upper Montane Belts to 10,500 ft; along creeks, ravines, or other moist shaded locations.

REMARKS: Vaselike clumps of this fern inhabit rich soil that is moist throughout the growing season. Another species (*A. alpestre*), of lesser height, narrower fronds, and rounded sori that lack indusia, reaches subalpine forest areas at 7,000 to 12,000 ft, where it favors wet cliff-faces or talus slopes.

LEATHERY GRAPE FERN   *Botrychium multifidum*
Pl. 46

To 18 in. high; rhizome short, with many corrugated roots; fronds stout, to 12 in. wide, two- or three-pinnate; spore-bearing stalk stout, erect, with large green sporangia clustered like grapes.

DISTRIBUTION: Mixed Conifer and Upper Montane Belts, 3,000 to 10,000 ft, on moist meadows or shorelines of marshes and lakes among willows.

REMARKS: Five species occur in the Sierra, all with characteristic spore-bearing stalks quite unlike the infertile leaves. Several species bear the name moonwort, a plant that appeared in old English folklore. Grape fern is a long-lived perennial that may live over 100 years.

BEAD FERN   *Cheilanthes covillei*

Rhizome short, creeping; fronds 3 to 12 in. long by 1 to 2 in. wide; blade three- or four-pinnate, upper surface smooth and green, undersurface and rachis with scales; segments many, crowded, beadlike; sori on margins of segments, nearly hidden by scales.

DISTRIBUTION: At 2,000 to 7,000 ft, on dry slopes, ridges, and peaks.

REMARKS: The densely grouped, bead-shaped segments make this species unlike any other Sierra fern. The related lace and lip ferns have narrow or rounded frond segments. In time of drought the fronds of these and some others roll up and become dry, but open up when moisture again is available. Six species occur in the Sierra, with the common lace fern (*C. gracillima*) having narrow pale scales on the underside of the midribs of the blades and pinnae, as well as dense woolly hairs on the underside of each segment.

AMERICAN PARSLEY FERN   *Cryptogramma acrostichoides*
Pl. 47

Rhizomes in chaffy clumps; stalks densely clustered, strawlike; fronds 2 to 10 in. long, two- or three-pinnate, and of two kinds: sterile fronds (no sori) shorter and broader, segments leafy, rachis with narrow ridge on each side; and fertile fronds (with sori) taller, segments slender, podlike, with rolled margins (sori close together on veins, covering back of segment).

DISTRIBUTION: Upper coniferous forest, at 4,000 to 12,000 ft; in crevices of granite.

REMARKS: With two kinds of fronds, this fern has a distinctive appearance. The sterile fronds look like parsley leaves, giving the fern its name. After the leaves dry and wither in midsummer, this plant is scarcely noticeable.

FRAGILE FERN   *Cystopteris fragilis*

Rhizome slender, creeping; stalks clustered, fragile, reddish at their base; thin fronds break off easily, broadly lance shaped, 2 to 12 in. long, bright green but often turning yellowish by summer, two- or three-pinnate, segments round edged, varying in shape; sori on smaller veins, small and black when young, later brown; indusia hoodlike.

DISTRIBUTION: At 1,000 to 13,000 ft on stony stream banks or in sheltered moist woods.

REMARKS: This delicate fern is widespread throughout the Northern Hemisphere. Resembles the woodsias, but larger, paler, and more delicate. Could also be confused with a young lady fern, which has scales on its leaf stalks.

WOOD FERN   *Dryopteris arguta*

Rhizome stout, woody, with bright chestnut scales and many persistent frond bases; fronds several, close, erect, 12 to 50 in. high by 10 in. wide at base, tapered to tip, mostly two-pinnate, segments with spiny teeth, evergreen; sori large in two rows, indusia kidney shaped.

DISTRIBUTION: Foothill and Mixed Conifer Belts from Nevada County south, 1,000 to 7,000 ft, often under shelter of logs or overhanging rocks.

COMMON HORSETAIL   *Equisetum arvense*
Pl. 48

Stems erect, rigid, jointed, hollow; leaves reduced and united as a six- to 14-toothed sheath at nodes; sterile stems 12 to 18 in. high, green, with many horizontal branches in whorls at stem nodes; fertile stems 4 to 7 in. high, whitish to yellow brown, lacking branches, producing a conelike spore-producing body in early spring then soon withering.

DISTRIBUTION: Up to 8,000 ft in open, sandy wet soil or swamps.

REMARKS: The rushlike horsetail (traditionally classified as a fern relative but with new evidence suggesting they are true ferns) occurs over much of the Northern Hemisphere. The common horsetail is one of the most widespread plants in the world and is considered in many places a weed. Related species formerly served for scouring pots and kettles because of the abrasive silica present in parts of the stem. Horsetails have spores wrapped in appendages that curl when wet and uncurl when dry, helping move the spores deeper into the soil. Two other species occur in the Sierra Nevada, both lacking whorled branches. The common scouring rush (*E. hyemale*) has 22 to 50 teeth on the sheath, while the smooth scouring rush (*E. laevigatum*) has 10 to 26 teeth.

BIRD'S-FOOT FERN   *Pellaea mucronata*
Pl. 49

Rhizome thick, short, woody; stalks clustered, stout, rigid, shiny dark brown; fronds tapered 10 to 16 in. high, two- or three-pinnate near base; segments to .19 in. long, sharp tipped, edges rolled, often in threes suggesting a bird's track; sori near ends of veins under rolled edge of segment.

DISTRIBUTION: At 400 to 9,000 ft, in dry gravelly or rocky sites.

REMARKS: Miwok Indians used the rachis for brown fibers in their baskets. When sheep or goats eat the wiry stalks these may break into sharp pieces that pierce the intestinal wall and result in death (hence nicknamed poison fern). The bird's-foot is one of five species of cliff brakes in the Sierra noted for their tendency to grow in dense clumps on rocks or cliffs exposed to the glaring summer sun. One species (*P. bridgesii*), 3 to 6 in. high with simple rounded segments, occurs among rocks at 4,000 to 10,000 ft.

GOLDBACK FERN   *Pentagramma triangularis*
Pl. 50

Rhizome short, creeping, scales brownish to blackish; fronds clustered, up to 12 in. long, triangular in shape, mixed pinnate and two-pinnate, upper surface dark green, lower surface covered with yellow or white powder; sori oblong, covering most of undersurface along veins at maturity.

DISTRIBUTION: Foothill and Mixed Conifer Belts, to 5,000 ft, in sun or shade on soil or in crevices of rocks.

REMARKS: These beautiful little ferns, with shiny reddish brown stalks and gold-powdered leaves, are common in places. During dry weather the leaves curl up, prominently exposing their gold undersides. Another species (*P. pallida*) has whitish powder on the upper surface of its leaves.

POLYPODY   *Polypodium calirhiza*
Pl. 51

Rhizome to about .25 in. thick, covered with short brownish papery scales; fronds 4 to 8 in. long, arising singly on longish stalks, segments round tipped, cut almost to stem, edges smooth or slightly toothed; sori about .13 in. diameter, near midribs of segments, yellow, turning dark brown.

DISTRIBUTION: Foothill Belt, to 3,500 ft on canyon banks or in rock crevices with seepage, often growing from mossy clumps.

REMARKS: This genus includes licorice fern (*P. glycyrrhiza*), and all four species that occur in the Sierra have a strong acrid to sweet licorice taste in the rhizome. Polypodiums contain methyl salicylate, a compound with some aspirin-like effects including acting as a mild antiinflammatory.

WESTERN SWORD FERN   *Polystichum munitum*
Pl. 52

Rhizome stout, woody, with brown scales; fronds many, in dense clumps, dark green, shiny, 12 to 48 in. high, gently tapered; segments to 5 in. long, tapered, edges toothed; sori many, round, in rows along margins of segments, indusia round, centrally attached.

DISTRIBUTION: From upper foothills into Mixed Conifer Belt, on wooded hillsides and shaded slopes mostly below 5,000 ft.

REMARKS: The seven species of sword fern in the Sierra hybridize where their ranges overlap, even producing fertile forms that are given their own names (three of the seven are such hybrids). Except for *P. munitum,* the other species are smaller and generally favor rocky sites at higher elevations.

BRACKEN FERN   *Pteridium aquilinum* var. *pubescens*

Pl. 53

Rhizomes deep in soil, long, much branched, hairy; stalks scattered, erect, rigid, grooved on upper side; fronds solitary, 2 to 5 ft long, triangular in outline, two- to four-pinnate, basal pinnae large, hairy beneath; sori on veins along margins of segments; indusium continuous along margin.

DISTRIBUTION: Foothill and Mixed Conifer Belts, in pastures, meadows, or hillsides, especially on acid soils; sometimes ranges up to Upper Montane Belt (10,000 ft or higher).

REMARKS: The bracken (or brake) is one of the most widespread ferns in the world and commonest of all ferns in the Sierra where it sometimes covers whole hillsides or valley bottoms with its large fronds. It may grow abundantly after fire or human disturbance has destroyed other ground cover, growing readily from long, spreading, underground rhizomes. Native Americans used the rootstock and young tender fronds for food, and they wove baskets and textiles from the slender rhizomes. Early white settlers thatched summer shelters with the fronds.

CLIFF FERN   *Woodsia scopulina*

Rhizome erect, short, with thin pale brown scales; stalks densely clustered, strawlike, 1 to 5 in. long; fronds many, 5 to 10 in. high, lance shaped, dark green, one- or two-pinnate, with numerous glands and whitish hairs; sori on back of veins, indusia cuplike and broken into tiny fingerlike filaments.

DISTRIBUTION: At 4,000 to 12,000 ft in rocky places from Lake Tahoe south; not common.

REMARKS: A similar woodsia (*W. oregana*), rare in the Sierra Nevada, lacks hairs on its leaf blades.

GIANT CHAIN FERN   *Woodwardia fimbriata*

Pl. 54

Rhizome stout, woody, glossy, reddish brown with scales; fronds to 6 ft or more, almost erect; pinnae to 15 in. long, lance shaped, cut almost to midrib; edges of segments minutely toothed, slightly scalloped; sori oblong in a "chain" on each side of midvein on segment.

DISTRIBUTION: Mainly near lower border of Mixed Conifer Belt, as high as 7,000 ft locally where continuing seepage is present.

REMARKS: This is the largest and most spectacular of our ferns, common among coastal redwoods but restricted in the Sierra to areas of constant wet soil bordering some of the larger rivers. Native Americans used fibers of the rachis dyed red by juice from elderberry bark in weaving baskets and textiles.

FLOWERING PLANTS

WITH ITS VARIED topography and climate, the Sierra Nevada has a large flora of about 3,500 species of ferns and flowering plants. Within Yosemite National Park alone, 1,338 species have been recorded. In general, however, the flora of the Sierra Nevada is poorly documented and species new to science are still being found. This handbook includes about 275 of the more common species known in the Sierra Nevada.

The flowering plants here are divided into three groups according to growth form: wildflowers with little or no woody tissues; shrubs with several woody stems; and trees with a single (though sometimes multiple) woody trunk. The popular term "wildflower" as used here is somewhat erroneous because shrubs and trees also produce "wildflowers," but it is a useful and familiar convention for referring to the herbaceous, showy-flowered plants. Grasses, sedges, and rushes are flowering plants with small blossoms of special form, difficult to identify. Examples of these and a few other types are described on page 65, in the subsection on Miscellaneous Plants.

The sequence and scientific names throughout are from *The Jepson Manual* (Hickman, 1993); common names are derived from *Jepson*, other books, and standard usage by field botanists. In many cases, there are no widely accepted common names even though scientific names are well established.

Individual plants of a species vary in size and form depending on the soil, the seasonal amounts of moisture and sunlight, the degree of shading, and other factors. Structural details about leaf shape, manner of branching, numbers of flower parts, etc., are more constant. Learning some common terms used in describing plants, leaves, and blossoms (figs. 7 and 8) will help when seeking to identify a specimen by comparing it with descriptions and pictures.

A leaf comprises a flat blade, a stalk (or *petiole*), and often two small, leafy *stipules* where the petiole joins the plant stem. Leaves are *simple* when of one blade. *Compound leaves,* consisting of two or more *leaflets,* are *pinnate* when the leaflets are along the sides of the petiole but *palmate* if all leaflets fan out from the end of the petiole.

Flowering plants (angiosperms) and cone-bearing trees (gymnosperms) reproduce by means of seeds, whereas the lower plants (fungi, lichens, mosses, ferns) do so by spores. Seeds of cone-bearing trees (pines, firs, etc.) at first are naked and exposed to the air but later are tightly enclosed by the cone and scales. In flowering plants the seeds develop within an ovary, which ripens to become the fruit.

Typically a flower has four circular rows of parts: *sepals* (being outermost or lowermost), *petals, stamens,* and *pistils;* at its base is the *receptacle,* or enlarged end, of a stem. The sepals together form the *calyx,* and the petals the *corolla;* one or the other is lacking in some plants. In many flowers all sepals and petals are separate; in others they are partly or completely joined or united, often in some kind of tube. The stamen (or male part) has a slender base or *filament* topped by an expanded pollen-producing *anther.* Filaments usually attach to the receptacle but sometimes to the corolla, and occasionally they are united into a tube. The pistil (or female part) has the

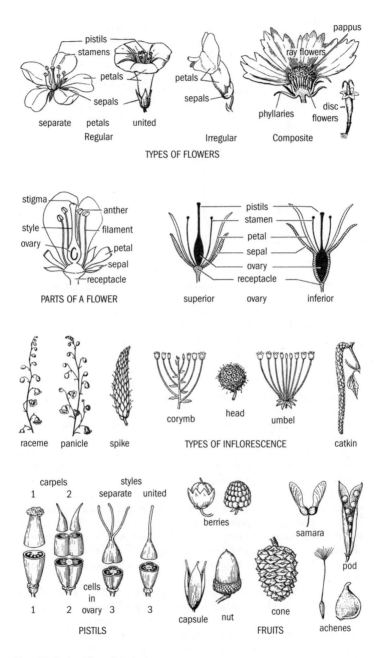

Figure 7. Parts of flowering plants.

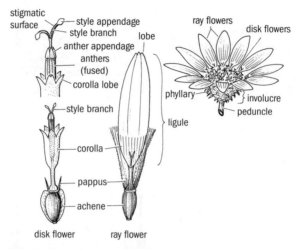

Figure 8. Parts of composite flowers.

egg-producing *ovary* at its base and a slender vertical *style* supporting the *stigma,* which receives pollen brought by wind or insects from other blossoms to fertilize the eggs. Some flowers have one pistil; others (roses, buttercups) have many separate pistils. More commonly, however, the pistils are somewhat joined; when completely united, a *compound pistil* results (each element is a *carpel*); a cross section of the ovary usually will show two or more compartments indicating the number of carpels of which the pistil is composed. Willows and a few other *dioecious* plants have male and female (staminate, pistillate) flowers on separate plants.

A flower is *regular* when the parts are in a circular pattern (radially symmetrical) and each petal or sepal is of the same size and shape; otherwise it is *irregular* (pea, etc.). The ovary is *superior* when above and free from the calyx but *inferior* if somewhat below and joined to the calyx. If a single flower is at the top of a stem it is *solitary* and *terminal,* but if at the base of a leaf it is *axillary.*

When flowers grow in clusters, each usually is borne on a short stemlike *pedicel.* Clusters are named as follows: *raceme* (flowers along an axis, pedicels of about equal length); *panicle* (a branched raceme); *spike* (like a raceme but flowers lack pedicels); *corymb* (like a raceme but lower pedicels are longer so cluster is flat topped); *umbel* (all pedicels arise from one point, like ribs of an umbrella, and cluster is flat topped); *catkin* (a hanging spike with or without a leaflike bract at each flower); and *head* (flowers without pedicels, on a spherical receptacle).

In the sunflower family (Asteraceae) the individual flowers are grouped into a *composite head* that can be mistaken for an individual blossom. Actually the flowers are of two types: in the outermost, or *ray,* flowers the upper part of the united corolla is flared out on one side to resemble a "petal," whereas, the central or *disk flowers* are small and tubular; some sunflowers lack ray flowers. Many sunflowers have circular rows of bracts (*phyllaries*) under the flower head. Sunflowers have one-seeded fruits known as *achenes* and typically have a row of bristles or hairs (*pappus*) arising from the top of the ovary.

Dry fruits are of several kinds: *achene* (small, hard, one-seeded, non-splitting; as in buttercups); *capsule* (splitting, of more than one carpel; ceanothus); *follicle* (pod formed from one carpel, splitting on one edge; delphinium); *pod* (thin, flat, splitting on two seams; pea); *samara* (one or two wings, nonsplitting; maple); *nut* or *acorn* (like achene but larger; oak). Fleshy fruits include: *drupe* (one central seed; cherry); *single berry* (pulp contains one or more seeds; currant, grape); *aggregate berry* (from many carpels on one receptacle; blackberry).

Miscellaneous Plants

Besides wildflowers there are other types of flowering plants that are common and widespread but have inconspicuous flower parts. Examples are included in this section. There are many species of grasses, sedges, and rushes, but to identify them correctly requires complete specimens with flowers and seeds, a magnifier, a technical manual, and some experience.

BROAD-LEAF CATTAIL
Typha latifolia

Pl. 55

Rootstock creeping in mud below water or in wet soil; stem 3.5 to 6 ft high, round, solid, jointless. **LEAVES** are long, linear, to 1 in. wide, sheathing the stem at base. **FLOWERS** are minute in dense, cylindrical, hairy, brown spike, 7 to 13 in. long, at top of stem; male flowers above becoming a withered spike after pollination, female flowers below.

DISTRIBUTION: Common in marshes.

REMARKS: Cattails fill many quiet backwaters and marshes at low to middle elevations. Muskrats eat the rootstocks. Red-winged Blackbirds and Marsh Wrens build their nests between the stems. Various other marsh dwellers find shelter and food among the leaves and stems.

PONDWEEDS
Genus *Potamogeton*

Water plants with stems simple or branched, round or flattened. **LEAVES** are often of two kinds: floating leaves broad, oval; submerged ones grasslike. **FLOWER** parts are small, all in fours—calyx, corolla, stamens, and ovaries.

DISTRIBUTION: In fresh or brackish ponds and slow creeks.

REMARKS: Fifteen species of pondweeds grow from low elevations to 9,000 ft in quiet Sierra Nevada waters. The submerged leaves and stems afford shelter for aquatic insect larvae and other small animals. The pea-sized tubers and leaves of many pondweeds are eaten by some ducks.

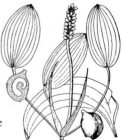

WATER PLANTAIN   *Alisma plantago-aquatica*
Pl. 56

Height 2 to 4 ft. **LEAVES** are erect on long petioles from rootstock, oval, pointed, 2 to 6 in. long. **FLOWER** cluster is a panicle of branches each with umbel of flowers; petals three, minute, white; stamens six.

DISTRIBUTION: Margins of rivers, lakes, and ponds, in shallow water or damp ground, to 5,000 ft.

REMARKS: This plant often grows solitarily. Waterfowl eat the seeds.

ARROWHEAD   *Sagittaria latifolia*

Rootstock with tubers, fibrous roots, and milky juice. **LEAVES** are variable in outline, the blade resembling an arrow point, 2 to 12 in. long. **FLOWERS** are on the stalk (scape), 3 in. to 3 ft high, white flowers near the top in threes; fruit head spherical, diameter to 1 in.

DISTRIBUTION: Stream margins, marshes, and wet meadows up to 7,000 ft.

REMARKS: The tubers, called *wapato,* were food for Native Americans. Later the Chinese on islands of the Sacramento–San Joaquin delta cultivated the plants and ate the tubers under the name of tule potato. Also a favorite food of many ducks and geese.

GRASSES   **Family Poaceae**
Pl. 57

Usually with round, hollow stems, closed at nodes. **LEAVES** are parallel veined, in two rows; each leaf has two parts, a sheath around the stem and a narrow

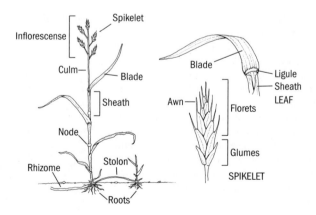

linear blade; junction of sheath and blade with soft tissue (ligule) is usually around the stem. **FLOWERS** are minute, in groups or spikelets; the base of each spikelet has two leaflike bracts (glumes) that often enclose the flowers.

REMARKS: Grasses are the commonest of flowering plants. There are dozens of genera and thousands of species that vary in structure, growth form, and distribution. Identification of grasses is rather difficult and requires practice. Some kinds cover flatlands of the Central Valley and rolling western foothills, and other assemblages carpet the pleasant, green mountain meadows. Still others grow sparingly in the big conifer forests, in gravelly or rocky places, above timberline, or among east slope junipers and sagebrush.

Grasses and grasslands (with some associated herbaceous plants) serve many roles in the complexities of nature. Grasses are the staple foods for grasshoppers and many other insects, ground squirrels, marmots, meadow mice, and rabbits. The seeds are eaten by various insects, doves, sparrows, chipmunks, and other animals. Horned Larks, Western Meadowlarks, Savannah Sparrows, and other birds find both food and cover in grasslands. Carnivorous animals that prey on grass- and seed-eaters are supported indirectly by the grasses. Grasslands afford pasturage for domestic animals, and aesthetically they contribute to many scenic views. Live or dead grasses and their roots serve as soil binders to lessen erosion by wind or water. Many alien grasses have spread widely in California, and some native species have become extinct.

Sedges (Family Cyperaceae)

Pl. 58

Grasslike; roots fibrous, often on long rootstock; stem solid (rarely hollow), often triangular (some round, four-sided, or flat). **LEAVES** are in threes, mostly basal, narrow, with closed sheath around stem. **FLOWERS** are in spikes, solitary or densely clustered; calyx and corolla are of bristles or absent; stamens generally three, ovary one-chambered; fruit a three-sided achene.

REMARKS: Different kinds of sedges (*Carex, Cyperus, Scirpus,* etc.) grow in various sorts of soil, fertile or alkaline and soggy to dry, from the Central Valley lowlands to Sierra peaks. Some occur widely, and others are distributed locally. The achenes are sought by seed-eating birds and mammals. While sedges can be distinguished from rushes by the old adage "sedges have edges and rushes are round," a better bet is to look at the stem (which is filled with spongy pith in rushes) or the fruit (a three-parted capsule in rushes). Sedges differ from grasses in having solid stems and leaves in threes.

COMMON TULE or BULRUSH   *Scirpus acutus*

Rootstock creeping; stem round, 3 to 9 ft high. **LEAVES** are short, basal, or absent. **FLOWERS** are in heads 1 to 5 in. long with stout, short bract at base, spikelets .25 to .5 in. long.

DISTRIBUTION: Marshes and lakes up into Mixed Conifer Belt; widespread.

REMARKS: Lowlands along the major Central Valley rivers originally had huge tule swamps (perhaps 250,000 acres), now mostly reclaimed for agriculture. The stems were used by Native Americans to build small rafts bound together with stems of wild grape. For settlers they served to pack nursery stock or to thatch haystacks. There are nine species of *Scirpus* in the Sierra Nevada, with *S. acutus* being one of the tallest and most conspicuous. All species are very important as food and shelter for wildlife.

RUSHES   Family Juncaceae

Herbaceous, grasslike, often in clumps; stem 3 in. to 4 ft tall; simple, round, with spongy pith or hollow, leafy or leafless. **LEAVES** are stiff, narrow, sheathing at base. **FLOWERS** are in heads, spikes, or panicles; minute, green or brown with six similar narrow segments (three forming an inner ring and three forming an outer ring); stamens six (or three); ovary three (or one)-celled, fruit a three-valved capsule.

REMARKS: The round wiry stems of rushes formerly served as binding material. Different species live in wet places from the lowlands to mountain flats at 11,000 ft. Most species are in the genus *Juncus* or *Luzula*. Their three-valved fruit readily separates them from the grasses that have grains or sedges that have achenes.

Wildflowers

This section includes the more common herbaceous plants that have showy, attractive blossoms. Usually only one species of a genus is described. Related forms often can be recognized from the description of the more common one. Where many species are present, as with the lupines, the account is of the genus, with mention of only a few conspicuous species. Characteristics given under the plant families are usually not repeated in species accounts. The blossoming period is indicated by months: January to April, for example.

In general, wildflowers should be enjoyed in their natural setting and not picked (*never* picked in national parks). For careful identification, blossoms must be examined closely; sometimes a flower must be cut vertically to show whether sepals or petals are partly united or separate, how the stamens are attached, and whether the ovary is superior or inferior. When a specimen must be picked and carried for later identification, it should be wrapped in paper with damp, soft paper around the stem. Botanists take plants as records and for later study, pressing them to dry in half-folded sheets of newspaper between blotters. The pairs of blotters are separated by layers of corrugated cardboard and cinched tightly in a plant press with wooden frames and straps. Full data on locality, habitat, elevation, height of plant, date, and name of collector are written on the margin of the paper. Specimens so prepared are later mounted on stiff white paper and filed in a school or museum herbarium.

Carrots (Family Apiaceae)

Leaves compound; stems hollow; flowers in umbels; calyx usually five-lobed; petals and stamens five, stamens alternating with petals; ovary inferior, two-celled; styles two; fruit of two carpels, each with five ribs or ridges and small oil tubes in the fruit wall.

COW PARSNIP
Heracleum lanatum

Pl. 59

Stems stout, 4 to 5 ft. **LEAVES** are palmately compound, petioles 4 to 16 in. long, three leaflets 3 to 6 in. across, broadly heart shaped, lobed, and toothed. **FLOWERS** are small, white, in compound umbel 6 to 10 in. in diameter; fruit .33 to .5 in. long, flat, rounded, with thin lateral ribs; April to July. **DISTRIBUTION:** Mixed Conifer and Upper Montane Belts below 9,000 ft in meadows or moist, shady places.

WESTERN SWEET CICELY
Osmorhiza occidentalis

Stems 1 to 3 in. **LEAVES** are two-pinnate, oblong with irregularly toothed edges. **FLOWERS** are small and inconspicuous, in loose heads, pale yellow; .5 in. long, slender seeds; May to July. **DISTRIBUTION:** Open or shaded forest slopes, 2,500 to 9,000 ft, Fresno and Mono Counties north. **REMARKS:** The more delicate and white-flowered *O. chilensis* is found in moist, shaded woods. Both species have a sweet licorice smell in their stems and roots.

YAMPAH
Perideridia bolanderi

Stems 6 in. to 3 ft, nearly naked. **LEAVES** are 2 to 6 in. long, triangular, pinnately divided in threes, with lobes linear. **FLOWERS** are small, white, many, lacy in appearance, in compound umbels, peduncles long; fruit oblong, ribbed; June to August. **DISTRIBUTION:** Mixed Conifer Belt to Subalpine Belt, 3,000 to 10,500 ft in dry meadows or open rocky slopes. **REMARKS:** The roots of Yampah have a pleasant starchy flavor and were a staple food item of many Native American groups. The very similar Gray's lovage (*Ligusticum grayi*) is likewise edible. Its leaves are even more finely divided and lacy, while its flower heads have a slightly more flat-topped appearance.

RANGER'S BUTTONS
Sphenosciadium capitellatum

Pl. 60

Stems stout, 3 to 5 ft. **LEAVES** are 4 to 16 in. long, pinnately compound, leaflets .5 to 5 in. by .33 to 2 in., narrowly ovate to lance shaped, toothed. **FLOWERS** are white (rarely purplish), in highly compact balls on 1 to 4 in. long stalks; fruit tapering to tip, flattened, ribbed, and winged; July to August. **DISTRIBUTION:** Mixed Conifer Belt to Subalpine Belt at 3,000 to 9,000 ft in wet meadows and moist areas, but also on open gravelly slopes at higher elevations.

Dogbane (Family Apocynaceae)

Leaves opposite; sepals, petals, and stamens five; pistils two; juice milky.

SPREADING DOGBANE
Apocynum androsaemifolium

Pl. 61

Stems 5 to 15 in., diffusely branched. **LEAVES** are .75 to 1.5 in. long, ovate with round to heart-shaped base, dark green above with pale veins, petioles short. **FLOWERS** are mostly in short clusters; calyx short, deeply five-cleft; corolla nearly .25 in. long, tubular, with five broadly oblong lobes, red purple to pinkish white; June to August. **DISTRIBUTION:** Mixed Conifer Belt to Subalpine Belt at 5,000 to 9,500 ft on dry flats and slopes.

Pipevine (Family Aristolochiaceae)

Calyx bell shaped, three-lobed; no petals; stamens 12; styles six; ovary inferior.

WILD GINGER
Asarum hartwegii

Flowers and leaves rise directly from fragrant, creeping rootstock. **LEAVES** are 2 to 5 in. wide, mottled, heart shaped, on petioles 3 to 7 in. long. **FLOWERS** are close to the ground, on a short stalk; sepals to 1.25 in. long, brownish purple, spreading, hairy, tips long and tapered; May to June. **DISTRIBUTION:** Mixed Conifer and Upper Montane Belts, at 2,500 to 7,000 ft, in shaded places.

Milkweeds (Family Asclepiadaceae)

Leaves opposite or whorled; calyx and corolla five-lobed; stamens five, united as tube on base of corolla; juice milky.

PURPLE MILKWEED
Asclepias cordifolia

Pl. 62

Stems 1.5 to 2.5 ft, erect, branching only at base, reddish purple. **LEAVES** are 2.5 to 6 in. by 1.5 to 4 in., mostly opposite, ovate to lance shaped, with heart-shaped base clasping stem. **FLOWERS** are many in loose umbels; corolla with five lobes bent backward, lobes .25 to .33 in. long, dark reddish purple; filaments united in a circle of five pinkish white hoods; pods 2 to 5 in. long, tapering, splitting to reveal silky-haired seeds; May to July.

DISTRIBUTION: Foothill and Mixed Conifer Belts, 500 to 6,300 ft on open or wooded slopes.

REMARKS: Milkweeds have a milky juice and most are poisonous to livestock. Stems of the showy milkweed (*A. speciosa*), another common species in the Sierra, yield a strong white fiber called "hook-ken" by the Native Americans, who also boiled down the milky juice to make a chewing gum. Insects of the milkweed may share the poisonous properties of the plant, for they advertise their presence to birds and other enemies by red, orange, and blue colors; the conspicuous Monarch Butterfly is "mimicked" in some regions by the presumably tasty Viceroy.

Sunflowers (Family Asteraceae)

Leaves mostly alternate; flowers grouped in heads, on enlarged receptacle, surrounded by bracts; corolla tubular and five-lobed (disk flowers), or strap shaped and toothed at tips (ray flowers), rays appearing like petals of other flowers; calyx united, highly modified (pappus), the segments awnlike, hairlike, scalelike, or absent; stamens five, filaments free; ovary inferior, one-celled, one-ovuled, maturing into an achene crowned by the pappus. Flowers in this family are commonly referred to as "composites" from their old family name Compositae. (See fig. 8.)

Rosy everlasting

YARROW   *Achillea millefolium*

Pl. 63

Stems 1.25 to 3 ft, simple, erect; herbage white hairy. **LEAVES** are 2 to 4 in. by .6 in. or less, three-pinnate, dissected into linear lobes. **FLOWER** heads are in flat-topped or convex terminal cluster; rays three to eight, rounded, white; disk flowers tiny, 15 to 40, white or yellow; achenes linear, no pappus; June to August.

DISTRIBUTION: Mixed Conifer Belt to Alpine Belt, 3,000 to 10,000 ft in open habitats.

ROSY EVERLASTING   *Antennaria rosea*

Stems 2 to 12 in. erect, from branching stolons with leaf tufts that form mats; herbage woolly. **LEAVES** are .5 to 1.13 in. long, to .13 in. wide, basal ones ovate, upper leaves linear to broadly lance shaped. **FLOWERS** are in dense clusters, with several heads, small, .2 in. high, no rays, bracts papery, overlapping, rose-colored or white; achenes smooth; dioecious (although male flowers are scarcely represented): male flowers with threadlike corolla and scanty pappus, female flowers with tubular five-toothed corolla and much pappus; June to August.

DISTRIBUTION: Mixed Conifer Belt to Alpine Belt at 4,500 to 12,000 ft in forest openings and rocky ridges.

HEART-LEAF ARNICA   *Arnica cordifolia*
Pl. 64

Stems .5 to 2 ft, erect; herbage hairy. **LEAVES** are 1 to 3 in. long, opposite, heart shaped or ovate, edges toothed; upper leaves smaller, broadly lance shaped, mostly without petioles. **FLOWER** heads few, in loose cyme with long peduncles, or single and .75 in. high; ray flowers 10 to 15, .75 to 1 in. long, yellow, three-toothed at tips; achenes slender, spindle shaped; pappus in one row of white bristles; May to August.

DISTRIBUTION: Moist, shaded forests from Mixed Conifer Belt to Subalpine Belt at 3,500 to 10,000 ft.

REMARKS: Of 12 species of arnica in the Sierra, heart-leaf arnica may be the easiest to identify based on its readily familiar leaf shape. All species have a characteristic fragrance, and large, buttery, yellow flowers that brighten forest floors in various habitats. Arnicas have been used for centuries for their healing properties, especially in cases of bruises, sprains, or inflammations.

ALPINE ASTER   *Aster alpigenus* var. *andersonii*
Pl. 65

Stems 4 to 16 in., several arising from taproot, first prostrate then elevating as plant matures, hairy on upper half. **LEAVES** are mostly arising from base of stem; sessile, linear. **FLOWERS** grow one flower head per stem, about 1 in. wide; ray flowers white to lavender, many yellow disk flowers; June to September.

DISTRIBUTION: Most common in moist subalpine meadows but ranges from 6,000 to 10,000 ft; south to Tulare County.

REMARKS: Not only are there 12 species of asters in the Sierra but also they are frustratingly similar to the 30 species of daisies (*Erigeron*). In general, asters have many flower heads with the disk flowers bunched in a narrow cluster and the phyllaries arranged in three to four unequal rows with their tips bending out. Daisies have fewer flower heads, wide buttonlike displays of disk flowers, and one to two rows of equal phyllaries in obvious rows. Asters generally bloom later in summer than daisies.

ANDERSON'S THISTLE   *Cirsium andersonii*
Pl. 66

Stems 2 to 3 ft, single or several, simple or branched, slender, purplish-red. **LEAVES** are green above, white hairy below, lanceolate but deeply lobed and spined, middle stem leaves clasping, upper leaves smaller. **FLOWER** heads are cylindrical, rose red; sometimes sessile; phyllaries long, lanceolate, spiny tipped; April to October.

DISTRIBUTION: Dry open areas, 3,500 to 10,000 ft.

REMARKS: Of 11 thistle species in the Sierra, four are invasive or noxious weeds, with new species possibly entering the region in the future.

WANDERING DAISY   *Erigeron peregrinus*

Pl. 67

Stems 3 to 18 in. **LEAVES** are from near the stem base, oblanceolate, to 8 in. long. **FLOWERS** are in one to four heads; ray flowers pale purple, narrow and overlapping, many (30 to 100); disk flowers bright yellow in broad button-like cluster; phyllaries long, narrowly tapered, and glandular; June to August.

DISTRIBUTION: Moist mountain meadows and forest openings, 4,000 to 10,000 ft.

REMARKS: The similar Coulter's daisy (*E. coulteri*) has bright white ray flowers that don't overlap; it occurs in meadows and on stream banks from 6,000 to 10,000 ft.

WOOLLY SUNFLOWER   *Eriophyllum lanatum*

Pl. 68

Stems 5 to 30 in., many, becoming shorter at higher elevations; herbage white-woolly. **LEAVES** are .75 to 1.25 in. long, ovate to linear, sometimes toothed or lobed, narrowed at base. **FLOWERS** are in heads .5 to .83 in. in diameter, single, on long, naked peduncles; ray flowers eight to 13, yellow, each with three small teeth at the tip; disk flowers 20 to 300; achenes .1 to .17 in. long, four angled; May to August.

DISTRIBUTION: Foothill Belt to Subalpine Belt below 10,000 ft in generally dry, open places.

BIGELOW'S SNEEZEWEED   *Helenium bigelovii*

Pl. 69

Stems 2 to 4 ft. **LEAVES** are 4 to 10 in. long, narrow, lance shaped, leaf base clasping and running shortly down stem. **FLOWER** heads occur mostly one per plant, on 4 to 12 in. stalk; ray flowers 14 to 20, yellow, 1 in. long, drooping, three-lobed at tips; disk flowers in 1 to 1.5 in. hemispheric ball, greenish yellow drying to dark brown; achenes .08 in. long, hairy on ribs; pappus chafflike, each scale tapering to a slender awn; June to August.

DISTRIBUTION: From Foothill Belt to Subalpine Belt at 1,500 to 10,000 ft in open habitats.

WHITE-FLOWERED HAWKWEED   *Hieracium albiflorum*

Pl. 70

Stems .75 to 3 ft, several, erect. **LEAVES** are 2 to 6 in. (or 12 in.) long, with pale bristly hairs; basal leaves are oblong, tapering, narrowed basally to a winged petiole; upper leaves are few, small, linear. **FLOWER** heads occur in a panicle; all flowers are small, white, raylike (no disk flowers); achenes .13 in. long, reddish brown, 10-ribbed; pappus longer, dull white; June to August.

DISTRIBUTION: Abundant and widespread in dry, open woods below 9,700 ft.

COMMON MADIA   *Madia elegans*
Pl. 71

Stems 9 to 36 in., erect, simple below, branching above; herbage sticky, hairy, and pungent. **LEAVES** are 3 to 5 in. long on lower stem, linear, edges scarcely toothed or entire; upper leaves reduced. **FLOWER** heads are .33 to .67 in. long, in a flat-topped panicle, with few to many on long peduncles; rays five to 20, three-lobed at tip, yellow, usually with red spot at base; achenes flat; no pappus; June to August.

DISTRIBUTION: Mixed Conifer and Upper Montane Belts at 3,000 to 8,000 ft on grassy hillsides and damp forest openings.

ARROWHEAD-LEAVED GROUNDSEL   *Senecio triangularis*
Stems 2 to 6 ft, several, erect. **LEAVES** are 1.25 to 5.5 in. long, triangular, with

edges minutely toothed. **FLOWER** heads are .33 in. high, with 10 to 30 in a flat-topped terminal cluster with each flower head on a long stalk; yellow; ray flowers eight, .2 to .33 in. long; disk flowers less than 40; achenes cylindrical; pappus of many soft, white hairs; July to September.

DISTRIBUTION: Mixed Conifer Belt to Alpine Belt at 4,000 to 11,150 ft in wet meadows and along stream banks.

REMARKS: Twenty-seven other species of groundsel grow at various elevations. Single-stemmed groundsel (*S. integerrimus*) has leaves that are progressively smaller upward on the stem and 13 ray flowers.

CANADA GOLDENROD   *Solidago canadensis* subsp. *elongata*
Pl. 72

Stems 1 to 4 ft, simple, erect, leafy. **LEAVES** are 2 to 4 in. long, mostly three-veined, oblong to lance shaped, often toothed at edges, and broadest at mid-stem. **FLOWER** heads are yellow, in a dense spike forming a mass 3 to 7 in. long; heads small, scarcely .25 in. high; bracts thin, linear; rays 10 to 13, narrow; disk flowers usually fewer; achenes cylindrical, five- to 10-nerved; pappus of many white bristles; May to September.

DISTRIBUTION: Mixed Conifer Belt to Upper Montane Belt below 8,500 ft in meadows.

MULES EARS   *Wyethia mollis*
Pl. 73

Stems 1.5 to 3 ft, simple, with one or few flower heads; young herbage white-woolly. **LEAVES** are 7 to 10 in. by 2 to 9 in. at base of stem, oblong-ovate, petioles long; upper leaves few, small, short-petioled. **FLOWER** heads are large, to 4 in. wide; rays 1 to 1.5 in. long, six to eight (or 14), yellow; disk flowers many; achenes four-sided or flattened, slate colored; pappus an irregular crown of scales; May to August.

DISTRIBUTION: Mixed Conifer Belt to Subalpine Belt, at 3,500 to 10,600 ft on open (mostly volcanic) slopes south to Mono and Fresno Counties.

REMARKS: Mules ears grows in profuse carpets on many slopes, sometimes indicating areas that have been heavily grazed by sheep, cows, or horses. Often growing together and easily confused with mules ears is balsamroot (*Balsamorhiza sagittata*), which has smaller and more brightly yellow flowers as well as distinct arrowhead-shaped (sagittate) leaves. Another similarly flowered composite is California helianthella (*Helianthella californica* var. *nevadensis*), also called California sunflower. Helianthella has long, narrowly lanceolate three-veined leaves and grows in dry open areas below 8,000 ft.

Borages (Family Boraginaceae)

Flowers regular, in one-sided coiled spikes; calyx and corolla five-lobed; stamens alternating with corolla lobes; fruit of four nutlets.

FIDDLENECK   *Amsinckia menziesii* var. *intermedia*
Pl. 74

Stems 1 to 2 ft, branching, erect or bent downward; herbage pale yellowish green, hairy. **LEAVES** are 1 to 6 in. long, oblong, tapering. **FLOWERS** are in long curved spikes, yellow; peduncles short or none; calyx lobes slender; corolla .33 to .4 in. long, .08 to .25 in. broad at tip; nutlets ridged and granular; March to June.

DISTRIBUTION: Mostly in the Foothill Belt below 5,000 ft in grassy open spaces.

REMARKS: Fiddleneck may grow among other plants or grasses but also in nearly pure stands when its blossoms color whole hillsides.

VELVETY STICKSEED   *Hackelia velutina*
Pl. 75

Stems 1 to 2 ft, erect, hairs on lower half; herbage velvety. **LEAVES** are 1 to 3 in. long, oblong, tapering to tip, petioles short or absent. **FLOWERS** are .38 to .75 in. in diameter, in loose raceme, blue or pink; calyx lobes oblong, .25 in. long; corolla tube .14 to .2 in. long, much exceeding calyx, its lobes rounded; nutlets .25 in. long, evenly armed with prickles on upper side; June to August.

DISTRIBUTION: Mostly in Upper Montane Belt at 5,000 to 10,000 ft, from Tulare County to Nevada County on dry wooded slopes.

REMARKS: The similar smooth stickseed (*H. nervosa*) ranges from Fresno County north. It lacks hairs on the lower stem and has smaller .25 in. flowers.

MOUNTAIN BLUEBELLS   *Mertensia ciliata*
Pl. 76

Stems 2 to 5 ft, several, erect. **LEAVES** are 2 to 7 in. by .75 to 1.5 in., oblong or ovate, narrowed to broad petiole or without petiole on upper stem. **FLOWERS** are drooping, somewhat clustered; calyx lobes shorter than corolla, oblong to linear; corolla tubular, about .5 in. long, light blue with small, yellow-tipped crests in opening of tube; style extends beyond corolla; nutlets not barbed; May to August.

DISTRIBUTION: Mixed Conifer Belt to Subalpine Belt at 5,000 to 10,200 ft in moist open or shady places.

POPCORN FLOWER   *Plagiobothrys nothofulvus*
Pl. 77

Stems 1 to 2.5 ft, erect, one or several from base; herbage rough haired, with purple sap. **LEAVES** are 1 to 4 in. long, mostly in basal rosette, narrow, lance shaped. **FLOWERS** are in loose racemes, pedicels short; calyx .13 in. long, cleft to middle; corolla .17 to .33 in. in diameter, white, with crests at throat; nutlets with rectangular ridges; March to May.

DISTRIBUTION: Foothill Belt mostly below 2,500 ft in grassy fields and on hillsides; on both slopes.

Mustards (Family Brassicaceae)

Sepals and petals four; herbage with pungent taste; seeds in capsule (silique).

HOLBOELL'S ROCK CRESS   *Arabis holboellii*

Stems 1 to 2.5 ft, one or several, erect. **LEAVES** grow to 1.5 in. long at base of stem, lancelike, mostly entire; stem leaves clasping, densely hairy underneath. **FLOWERS** are downward hanging, white, pinkish, or purplish, petals .25 to .5 in. long; stamens six; capsules nearly straight in shape but drooping downward, 1.5 to 3 in. long; May to July.

DISTRIBUTION: Mixed Conifer Belt to Alpine Belt, 6,000 to 11,000 ft, and among pinyon pines and junipers on east side in dry stony places.

LEMMON'S DRABA   *Draba lemmonii* var. *lemmonii*

Stems 1 to 3.25 in., from a compact leafy cushion. **LEAVES** are .13 to .5 in. long, entire, thick, oblong, hairy, and densely clustered. **FLOWERS** are yellow,

.17 in. long, in short clusters; capsule ovate, .25 to .33 in., twisted; July to August.

DISTRIBUTION: Subalpine and Alpine Belts at 8,500 to 13,000 ft, in damp rocky places often in rock clefts; north to El Dorado County.

WESTERN WALLFLOWER   *Erysimum capitatum*

Pl. 78

Stems 1 to 2.5 ft, erect, usually unbranched. **LEAVES** are 1.5 to 5 in. by .13 to .5 in., narrow, rough and hairy, entire or toothed. **FLOWERS** are in terminal clusters; flower diameter .25 to .5 in., capsule 3 to 4 in. by .15 in., straight, four-sided; March to July.

DISTRIBUTION: Common to 12,000 ft on dry slopes.

REMARKS: Two forms of this species occur in the Sierra, one (subsp. *perenne*) has yellow flowers and constrictions in the capsule between each seed, while the other (subsp. *capitatum*) has orange flowers and lacks constrictions.

STREPTANTHUS or MOUNTAIN JEWELFLOWER
Streptanthus tortuosus

Pl. 79

Stems .5 to 3 ft, high, simple or many-branched. **LEAVES** .5 to 1.5 in. long, mostly oblong-ovate, clasping around stem. **FLOWERS** are pale yellow or purplish veined, .25 to .5 in. long, petals curling out of pinkish urn-shaped calyx; seeds in 3-in.-long thin capsule; May to August.

DISTRIBUTION: Foothill and Mixed Conifer Belts at 1,000 to 8,500 ft on dry rocky slopes.

REMARKS: Small bushy varieties with purplish or yellow sepals grow at 7,000 to 11,500 ft.

Bellflowers (Family Campanulaceae)

Calyx and corolla five-lobed; stamens five; juice milky.

CALIFORNIA HAREBELL   *Campanula prenanthoides*

Pl. 80

Stems 1.5 to 2 ft, slender, erect, angled, often branched. **LEAVES** are .5 to 1.5 in. long, oblong to lance shaped, edges toothed. **FLOWERS** are clustered on short pedicels, mostly in leaf axils; calyx lobes short, awl shaped; corolla .33 to .5 in. long, bright blue, bell shaped, lobes long, narrow, and tapered; style three-lobed, extending well beyond corolla; capsule hemispherical or top shaped; June to September.

DISTRIBUTION: Foothill and Mixed Conifer Belts on west slope, 800 to 6,000 ft in dry to moist wooded places.

PORTERELLA

Porterella carnosula

Pl. 81

Stems .75 to 12 in. **LEAVES** are .5 in. long, sessile, and narrowly ovate to triangular. **FLOWERS** are .25 to .5 in. wide, two upper petals narrow, three lower petals rounded, dazzling combination of blue purple, sharp white, and yellow center; June to August.

DISTRIBUTION: Vernal pools and wet meadows, 5,000 to 10,000 ft in northern Sierra.

Pinks (Family Caryophyllaceae)

Nodes of stem usually swollen; leaves opposite; sepals and petals five.

KING'S SANDWORT

Arenaria kingii **var.** *glabrescens*

Pl. 82

Stems 4 to 12 in., a delicate and inconspicuous plant. **LEAVES** are needlelike, in basal tuft. **FLOWERS** are small with five spreading petals, stamens 10 with red anthers; June to August.

DISTRIBUTION: Common on dry rocky slopes south to Tulare County, 6,000 to 11,000 ft.

CALIFORNIA INDIAN PINK

Silene californica

Pl. 83

Stems 6 to 12 in. (or to 3.5 ft among bushes), one or more, leafy. **LEAVES** are 1 to 3 in. long, narrow to broadly oval, tapering to tip. **FLOWERS** have a tubular calyx, five-cleft; corolla brilliant crimson, diameter to 1 in., petals bent outward, deeply four-cleft; stamens 10; styles three to four; March to August.

DISTRIBUTION: Foothill and Mixed Conifer Belts of west slope; to 5,000 ft in open woods of canyons.

REMARKS: Douglas's Catchfly (*S. douglasii*) is a common mountain plant of dry open areas from 5,000 to 9,000 ft. Unlike the showy Indian pink, this slender catchfly has small white petals that flare out in indistinct rays from a swollen and ribbed calyx.

Stonecrops (Family Crassulaceae)

Leaves succulent; sepals, petals, and pistils five; stamens 10.

SIERRA STONECROP

Sedum obtusatum

Pl. 84

A matlike succulent; stems 3 to 6 in., erect. **LEAVES** are to 1 in. by .25 in., thick, in basal rosettes of rounded bluish green leaves. **FLOWERS** are clustered, petals .25 to .38 in. long, yellow or white, joined at base into a tube; June to July.

DISTRIBUTION: Mixed Conifer Belt to Alpine Belt, Tulare County to Nevada County, at 5,000 to 13,000 ft on rocky slopes.

REMARKS: Pacific stonecrop (*S. spathulifolium*), living on shaded moss-covered rocks up to 7,500 ft, has petals separate to the base. Rosy sedum (*S. roseum* var. *integrifolium*) has a dense mat of leaves with deep maroon flowers in tight clusters; this stunning sedum is circumboreal throughout the Northern Hemisphere and occurs in the Sierra from 6,000 to 12,000 ft in damp rocky places.

Dodder (Family Cuscutaceae)

Twining, threadlike stems; leaves absent or vestigial scales; flowers with four to five lobes, stamens four to five, styles two.

CALIFORNIA DODDER *Cuscuta californica*
Pl. 85

Stems slender, twining, yellow to orange, fastened by suckers and parasitic on other plants. **LEAVES** are reduced to minute scales. **FLOWERS** are .06 to .13 in. long, in loose cymes, waxy-white, urn shaped; calyx colored like corolla, deeply five-cleft; corolla nearly globose, with five slender narrow lobes; May to August.

DISTRIBUTION: Foothill Belt to Upper Montane Belt, below 8,200 ft on many herbs and shrubs.

REMARKS: This apparently leafless plant lacks green coloring (chlorophyll). It germinates in the soil but later becomes completely parasitic on other plants, covering them in an orange or yellow mat of twining threads.

Heaths (Family Ericaceae)

Leaves basal or reduced to scales; sepals and petals five; stamens 10; style one.

PINEDROPS *Pterospora andromedea*
Pl. 86

Stems 1 to 4 ft, erect, stout, reddish, fleshy, sticky. **LEAVES** are reduced to reddish brown scales crowded at base of stem. **FLOWERS** are many in dense raceme, calyx reddish brown, deeply five-parted; corolla .25 in. long, urn shaped, yellowish, petals united, with five short bent lobes; June to August.

DISTRIBUTION: Mixed Conifer and Upper Montane Belts, 2,600 to 8,500 ft in humus of dry forests.

REMARKS: This plant lacks chlorophyll and is parasitic on living root fungi.

WHITE-VEINED WINTERGREEN
Pyrola picta
Stems 6 to 15 in. **LEAVES** are 1 to 2.25 in. long, basal, ovate or elliptic, evergreen, mottled or white veined. **FLOWERS** are in terminal raceme on erect reddish stalk, nodding, green white; corolla nearly .5 in. in diameter, petals separate, concave; June to August.

DISTRIBUTION: Mixed Conifer Belt to Subalpine Belt, 3,000 to 9,500 ft; growing in humus of dry, somewhat shaded forests, sometimes forming small colonies.

White-veined wintergreen

SNOW PLANT
Sarcodes sanguinea
Pl. 87

Stems 9 to 18 in. high and 1 in. or more thick, erect, stout, fleshy. **LEAVES** are reduced to reddish scales. **FLOWERS** are .5 to .75 in. long, crowded along stem in a raceme; corolla .25 to .33 in. long, red, fleshy, bell shaped, with five outwardly bent rounded lobes; May to July.

DISTRIBUTION: Mixed Conifer and Upper Montane Belts, 4,000 to 8,000 ft growing in forest humus, often at edges of melting snowbanks.

REMARKS: This unusual plant, with its bright red color against a carpet of pine needles, never fails to attract attention. It is protected against collection by state law. Snow plant is a saprophyte, deriving nutrients from decaying plant material in the soil.

Peas (Family Fabaceae)

Leaves usually compound; flowers irregular, butterfly-like; corolla of five petals (an upper banner, two wings at sides, and two below joined as a keel); stamens 10.

WHITNEY'S LOCOWEED   *Astragalus whitneyi*
Pl. 88

Stems 1 to 12 in., widely branched; herbage silvery, hairy. **LEAVES** are .5 to 4 in. long, pinnately compound, leaflets five to 21, linear-oblong, .25 to .75 in. long. **FLOWERS** are three to 16, creamy white or tinged with purple; pod to 2 in. long, inflated and papery, yellow green with burnt red splotches; May to September.

DISTRIBUTION: On dry stony places and sand flats south of Lake Tahoe, 6,800 to 12,000 ft.

REMARKS: The name locoweed refers to the effects of some poisonous species on livestock.

SIERRA NEVADA PEA   *Lathyrus nevadensis* var. *nevadensis*

Stems 4 to 20 in., sprawling, with twining tendrils to aid in climbing other plants. **LEAVES** are one-pinnate, four, six, or eight leaflets (in even combinations, unlike the odd number of leaflets in *Astralagus*). **FLOWERS** are large showy, bright purple pink (also white to blue purple); April to June.

DISTRIBUTION: Foothill Belt to Upper Montane Belt below 8,000 ft on dry slopes; south to Tuolumne County.

REMARKS: Perhaps 11 species of wild peas grow in the Sierra, a number that includes both native and introduced species, including the widespread and familiar sweet peas (*L. latifolius* and *L. odoratus*) that have escaped cultivation. All *Lathyrus* are separated from the similar vetches (*Vicia*) in having their leaflets rolled while in the bud as opposed to being folded in the bud as in the vetches.

MEADOW LOTUS
Lotus oblongifolius

Stems 7 to 10 in., multibranched and bushy in appearance. **LEAVES** are pinnately compound, three to 11 leaflets .5 to .75 in., oblong to elliptic. **FLOWERS** are two to six in small clusters, yellow banner petal with white keel and wings; pods straight, 1 to 1.5 in. by .08 in., slightly bent, tips short; May to September.

DISTRIBUTION: Foothill Belt to Upper Montane Belt below 8,500 ft in wet places.

Lupines (Genus *Lupinus*)

Annual or perennial; stems short and single or many branches and bushy. **LEAVES** are palmately compound, alternate, leaflets usually five to 17. **FLOWERS** are in terminal racemes, mostly blue or purple, a few yellow or white; calyx two-lipped; fruit a two-sided pod (legume), with row of two to 12 seeds. Many (60 to 80) species in California; a few Sierra species are mentioned here.

BREWER'S LUPINE   *L. breweri*
Pl. 89

To 8 in. high in silvery-haired, leafy mats. **FLOWERS** in dense clusters, to 2 in. long, with flowers .25 in. long, blue, banner with white center; June to August.

DISTRIBUTION: Mixed Conifer Belt to Subalpine Belt at 4,000 to 11,000 ft on dry stony slopes and meadow edges.

BROAD-LEAF LUPINE   *L. latifolius*
To 7 ft tall. **FLOWERS** are on long erect stalks, white to blue, hairs on keel margins; May to September.
DISTRIBUTION: Moist forest openings, 3,000 to 11,000 ft.

LARGE-LEAF LUPINE   *L. polyphyllus*
Stems 3 to 5 ft. **FLOWERS** are in spikelike cluster up to 16 in. long, dark blue, no hairs on keel margins; May to July.
DISTRIBUTION: Wet areas from 4,000 to 8,500 ft.

Clover (Genus *Trifolium*)
Stems erect or spreading. **LEAVES** are palmate, leaflets generally three. **FLOWERS** are in spherical heads, white, yellow, pink, red, or purple; calyx five-toothed, lobes usually equal; pods spherical to elongate, one- to three-seeded.
REMARKS: Of roughly 33 species in the Sierra some are introduced and others are native. Many are recognized by the presence or absence of an involucre, a group of leaflike bracts more or less united under the flower head.

LONG-STALKED CLOVER   *T. longipes*
Stems 3 to 10 in. involucre absent; leaflets three, narrow and long, pointed. **FLOWERS** are in a small .5 in. head at the end of a long, slender stalk, dull white and reddish purple; June to September.
DISTRIBUTION: Moist habitats to 9,000 ft.

CARPET CLOVER   *T. monanthum*
Stems many, 1 to 4 in., spreading, often forming mats; involucre vestigial; leaflets .06 to .5 in. long, ovate to lance shaped. **FLOWERS** are one to two (or four) in a loose cluster, .5 in. long, white (often pink-veined) with purple centers; June to August.
DISTRIBUTION: Mixed Conifer Belt to Subalpine Belt, 5,000 to 11,500 ft in wet places.

RED CLOVER   *T. pratense*
Pl. 90
Stems 4 to 12 in.; involucre absent; leaflets three, obovate, with pale white chevron mark on each leaflet. **FLOWERS** in large 1 in. head, bright reddish.
DISTRIBUTION: A valued animal-feed plant that has become naturalized in disturbed areas throughout the Sierra.

Gentians (Family Gentianaceae)

Leaves opposite; lobes of calyx and corolla four, stamens four.

EXPLORER'S GENTIAN *Gentiana calycosa*

Stem 6 to 24 in., several sprouting from a rootcrown. **LEAVES** are somewhat fleshy, opposite and clasping the stem, ovate. **FLOWERS** are up to 2 in. long, petals five, flaring slightly at ends, deep blue with pale whitish to greenish spots on inner surface, narrow threadlike fringes in nodes between each petal; July to September.

DISTRIBUTION: Wet meadows and rocky seeps from 4,000 to 10,500 ft.

REMARKS: Alpine Gentian (*G. newberryi*) has larger white (often blue-tinged) flowers with dark spots. It occurs in high mountain meadows or open areas above timberline from 7,000 to 12,000 ft, south to Tulare County.

HIKER'S GENTIAN *Gentianopsis simplex*

Pl. 91

Stems 4 to 14 in., several from base, leafy below, each ending with one flower. **LEAVES** are in three to six opposite pairs, lanceolate. **FLOWERS** are .5 to 2 in. long, corolla fused below but twisting and flaring separately higher, petals deep blue purple with ragged tips; July to September.

DISTRIBUTION: Mixed Conifer Belt to Subalpine Belt at 4,000 to 9,500 ft in wet meadows.

REMARKS: The similar Sierra gentian (*G. holopetala*) lacks the ragged tips or twists in its petals. It occurs in Plumas County and from Tuolumne County south, in wet meadows from 6,000 to 12,000 ft.

GREEN GENTIAN *Swertia radiata*

Pl. 92

Stems 2 to 6 ft, single stout stalk, biennial plant reaching its full height and flowering in its second year. **LEAVES** are whorled, oblong, fleshy, 4 to 10 in. long. **FLOWERS** are greenish white with purple dots, each petal with a pair of hairy, pink nectar glands, hundreds per plant borne in leaf axils; July to August.

DISTRIBUTION: On somewhat moist open slopes, 6,800 to 9,500 ft; occurs in Plumas County and El Dorado County south to Fresno County (south to Inyo County on east slope).

Geranium (Family Geraniaceae)

Sepals and petals five; stamens 10.

RICHARDSON'S GERANIUM
Geranium richardsonii

Pl. 93

Stems 1 to 3 ft. **LEAVES** are palmately five- to seven-lobed with many smaller lobes. **FLOWERS** with rounded petals, 1 in. long, rose pink to white, and purple-veined; July to August.

DISTRIBUTION: Mixed Conifer and Upper Montane Belts at 4,000 to 9,000 ft in damp woods and meadows, Nevada County south.

Waterleafs (Family Hydrophyllaceae)

Leaves opposite or alternate; calyx and corolla five-lobed; stamens five, alternate with corolla lobes.

VARIABLE-LEAVED NEMOPHILA
Nemophila heterophylla

Stems 4 to 16 in., weak and often tangled or sprawling on other plants. **LEAVES** are variable, five- to seven-lobed with each lobe rounded and well separated, entire or toothed. **FLOWERS** are .25 to .5 in. wide, white; March to July.

DISTRIBUTION: Foothills and lower Mixed Conifer Belt to 5,000 ft in shady areas of grasslands and slopes; on west slope north of Madera County.

TIMBERLINE PHACELIA
Phacelia hastata

Stems 2 to 8 in., often sprawling near ground, plant covered in stiff white hairs. **LEAVES** have sunken veins, mostly entire but

sometimes lobed or variously compound. **FLOWERS** are white, .25 in. wide, stamens protruding up to .5 in. beyond corolla giving a fuzzy look; July to September.

DISTRIBUTION: Gravelly and rocky sites, 7,000 to 13,000 ft.

REMARKS: There are 95 species of _Phacelia_ in California and many occur in the Sierra. A number of these species are common and widespread, ranging from the foothills to alpine peaks. They are noted for the fuzzy caterpillar appearance of their flowers that is caused by long exserted stamens.

St. John's Worts (Family Hypericaceae)

Leaves opposite, black-dotted; sepals and petals five.

ST. JOHN'S WORT   *Hypericum formosum* var. *scouleri*
Pl. 94

Stems 1 to 3 ft, erect, slender. **LEAVES** are .5 to 1.25 in. long, ovate or oblong, black-dotted on edges. **FLOWERS** are .5 to .75 in. in diameter, in branching clusters of three to 25 on each stem; sepals .13 in. long, ovate, black-dotted; petals .33 in. long, yellow; stamens many, in three groups; capsules .25 in. long, three-lobed; seeds brownish; June to August.

DISTRIBUTION: Mostly in Mixed Conifer Belt at 4,000 to 7,500 ft in wet meadows; occasional in chaparral.

REMARKS: The introduced Klamath weed (*H. perforatum*) has narrow sepals, the capsule is unlobed, and the seeds are shiny black. It also has many flowers, 25 to 100 per stem. It occurs in pastures and partially cleared areas below 6,500 ft. Poisonous to livestock, it has been eradicated over large areas by Klamath Weed Beetles (*Chrysolina quadrigemina*) that help to control the plant in its native Europe.

Irises (Family Iridaceae)

Leaves parallel veined, mostly basal; "petals" six, stamens three, ovary inferior. Flowers in this family are composed of six petal-like segments of the perianth (the calyx and corolla).

SIERRA IRIS   *Iris hartwegii*
Pl. 95

Stems 6 to 12 in., several, from creeping rootstock about .25 to .5 in. thick. **LEAVES** are many, .25 in. wide. **FLOWERS** are commonly in pairs on a pedicel .5 to 3.75 in. long, petals 1.5 to 2 in. long, yellow with lavender veins or pale lavender with deeper colored veins and yellow at the middle; May to July.

DISTRIBUTION: Mixed Conifer Belt, 2,500 to 6,000 ft in dry open forest.

REMARK: The western blue flag (*I. missouriensis*) with whitish or pale blue flowers and a 1 in. thick rootstock grows in moist meadows at high elevations, mainly on the east slope where it persists in grazed area.

BLUE-EYED GRASS   *Sisyrinchium bellum*
Pl. 96

Stems 6 to 18 in., distinctly flattened and two-edged, from fibrous roots. **LEAVES** are grasslike. **FLOWERS** are .67 in. long, petals blue, yellow at base, ending with a sharp tip in a notch; stamens united, their anthers alternating with the three stigmas; March to August.

DISTRIBUTION: Wet meadows and stream banks, 3,500 to 5,000 ft.

Mints (Family Lamiaceae)

Leaves opposite; stems square; aromatic; flowers irregular; calyx five-lobed; corolla tubular, two-lipped, often two lobes in upper lip and three in lower; stamens in tube of corolla, four (sometimes two stamens with anthers and two without); ovary four-lobed.

GIANT HYSSOP or HORSEMINT   *Agastache urticifolia*
Pl. 97

Stems 2.5 to 5 ft, erect, simple, widely spreading. **LEAVES** are 1.4 to 3 in. long, ovate, toothed, petioles .4 to 1 in. long. **FLOWERS** are crowded in a terminal spike to 7 in. long; calyx equally five-toothed, lobes tapering, pinkish; corolla .4 to .6 in. long, rose or violet, upper lip two-lobed, lower lip spreading; stamens four, extending beyond corolla; June to August.

DISTRIBUTION: Mixed Conifer and Upper Montane Belts at 1,000 to 10,000 ft in moist places.

REMARKS: This plant has a strong mint odor and the leaves make a potent tea.

MOUNTAIN PENNYROYAL or COYOTE MINT   *Monardella odoratis-*
Pl. 98   *sima* subsp. *pallida*

Stems 6 to 14 in., erect, several in dense cluster, green; perennial; herbage gray-green. **LEAVES** are .5 to 1.5 in. long, narrowly oblong, tapered to tip, petioles short or absent. **FLOWERS** in terminal heads .6 to 1 in. in diameter, surrounded by thin purplish bracts; calyx .25 to .33 in. long, tubular, with five short lobes, hairy; corolla .6 in. long, pale purple, tubular, extending well beyond calyx, upper lip erect, cleft for about half its length, lower lip three-parted; stamens four, all fertile, the longer pair extending beyond corolla; style two-cleft at tip; June to September.

DISTRIBUTION: Mixed Conifer Belt to Alpine Belt at 3,000 to 11,000 ft on dry slopes.

REMARKS: A few aromatic leaves from this plant make a fragrant tea that should be drunk in moderation and never during pregnency. Blossoms of pennyroyal are visited at night by hummingbird moths. Of other Sierra species, the western pennyroyal or mustang mint (*M. lanceolata*), an annual, has purple stems with few leaves and a hairless calyx. It grows mostly in the foothills, but occurs up to 9,000 ft.

SELF-HEAL   *Prunella vulgaris*
Pl. 99

Stems 4 to 12 in., erect. **LEAVES** are 1 to 3 in. long, oblong-ovate, petioles short. **FLOWERS** are in dense terminal heads; calyx two-lipped, purplish, stiffly haired; corolla .4 to .8 in. long, pinkish or lavender, upper lip forming hood, lower lip three-lobed, middle lobe slightly fringed; stamens four, in pairs beneath upper lip; May to September.

DISTRIBUTION: Foothill Belt to Upper Montane Belt; to 7,500 ft in moist semi-shaded meadows and forests; grows south to El Dorado County with additional occurrences in Fresno and Tulare Counties.

REMARKS: Two varieties of self-heal occur in the Sierra: one (var. *lanceolata*) is native, its stem leaves are three times longer than wide; the other (var. *vulgaris*) is introduced from Europe and has stem leaves that are two times longer than wide. Both have been used extensively for their various healing properties.

GRAY-LEAVED SKULLCAP
Scutellaria siphocampyloides

Stems 10 to 22 in., erect. **LEAVES** are oblong to lanceolate, 1 in. long. **FLOWERS** are .75 to 1 in. long, solitary or in pairs in upper leaf axils, bluish violet; calyx with two short lips, upper lip a projecting hood; corolla 1 in. long, upper lip beaklike; May to July.

DISTRIBUTION: Dry graveled or rocky sites, mostly in Foothill Belt, but up to 8,000 ft, primarily west slope.

Lilies (Family Liliaceae)

Leaves parallel veined; "petals" six; stamens six (or three without anthers). Flowers in this family are composed of six petal-like segments of the perianth (the calyx and corolla).

SIERRA ONION   *Allium campanulatum*
Pl. 100

Stems 4 to 12 in., stout; bulb to 1 in. long, on creeping rootstalk with coarse roots, bulb scales white or red-tinged. **LEAVES** are two, basal, grasslike, and 12 in. long. **FLOWERS** are in head, many, petals to .5 in. long, pink or rose purple, style one; July to September.

DISTRIBUTION: Foothill Belt to Subalpine Belt, at 2,000 to 9,000 ft on dry slopes in woods or open rocky areas.

REMARKS: Several species of wild onion grow in the Sierra. Many have a strong odor and their fibrous bulbs may be used to flavor hearty camp soup or stew.

Mariposa Lilies (Genus *Calochortus*)

Stems from a bulb. **LEAVES** are narrow, one or two at base, few on stem. **FLOWERS** have small, leaf-shaped sepals, green or colored; petals usually large, showy, and broadly wedge shaped, each with a large glandular pit (often dark) near base and few or many hairs; stamens six; about 14 species in Sierra Nevada.

WHITE GLOBE LILY   *C. albus*

Stems 12 to 36 in., branched; **FLOWERS** are several, white to pale rose, petals 1 to 1.75 in. long, folded over each other and forming a closed globe; April to June.

DISTRIBUTION: Foothill Belt, Butte County to Fresno County, up to 5,000 ft on shady hillsides, often in rocky soil.

LEICHTLIN'S MARIPOSA LILY   *C. leichtlinii*

Stems 8 to 24 in., simple; petals white with yellow hairs at base and dark maroon patch; June to August.

DISTRIBUTION: Open rocky sites on both slopes, 4,000 to 11,000 ft.

SIERRA STAR TULIP
C. minimus

Stems 1 to 4 in., one basal leaf 3 to 10 in. by .33 to .5 in.; one to three flowers, petals white, to .5 in. long, without hairs, anthers pale lilac; May to August.

DISTRIBUTION: Open woods on west slope from Placer County to Tulare County, 4,000 to 9,500 ft.

YELLOW STAR TULIP
C. monophyllus

Stems 3 to 8 in.; petals bright yellow, .5 to .75 in. long, hairy; April to May.

DISTRIBUTION: Foothill and lower Mixed Conifer Belts, south to Tuolumne County at 1,200 to 3,600 ft.

Yellow star tulip

CAMAS   *Camassia quamash*
Pl. 101

Stems 12 to 30 in., from an onionlike bulb. **LEAVES** are basal, grasslike, shorter than stem. **FLOWERS** are in raceme of five to 25, .75 to 1 in. long, blue (rarely white), style one, three-cleft at tip.

DISTRIBUTION: Upper Mixed Conifer and Upper Montane Belts, at 4,500 to 7,500 ft in wet meadows south to Tulare County.

REMARKS: The sweet and starchy bulbs of camas were much sought after by Native Americans throughout western North America. The similar and highly toxic death camas (*Zigadenus venenosus*) has whitish flowers and sometimes grows in the same sites as the edible camas, so extreme care is always needed when harvesting their bulbs.

SOAP PLANT
Chlorogalum pomeridianum

Stems 2 to 5 ft, nearly leafless. **LEAVES** are many, basal, 9 to 24 in. by .5 to 1.5 in., with keel, wavy edged. **FLOWERS** are few in long, spreading cluster, narrow petaled, .75 in. long, white, purplish-veined, style one, three-cleft at tip; bulb 3 to 4 in. long, diameter to 2 in., with dense coat of coarse brown fibers; May to August.

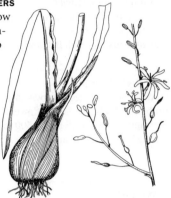

DISTRIBUTION: Foothill Belt to 5,000 ft on dry, open, and stony ground.

REMARKS: The delicate flowers open in the afternoon and close by morning. Scales of the bulbs form a soapy lather when mixed with water. Native Americans roasted the bulbs for food and used its fibers for brushes.

Brodiaea (Genera *Dichelostemma, Triteleia*)

Stems erect or long and twining. **LEAVES** are few, grasslike, dying early. **FLOWERS** are terminal, in open umbels on long pedicels or in dense head, sepals and petals united in tube at base, tips spread, blue, violet, pinkish, white, or yellow; stamens with anthers three or six.

BLUE DICKS
D. capitatum

Stems 6 to 15 in., erect. **FLOWERS** to .67 in. long, deep blue, four to 15 in dense compact head; March to May.

DISTRIBUTION: Grassy hillsides in Foothill Belt of west slope and on east side amid pinyon pine and juniper.

TWINING BRODIAEA
D. volubile

Stems to 3 ft high and erect or twining over bushes for 7 to 8 ft. **FLOWERS** are 18 to 30 in dense head, diameter to 6 in., rose red or pinkish, pedicels .5 to 1 in., flowers .5 to .67 in. long; April to July.

DISTRIBUTION: Foothill Belt at 500 to 2,500 ft on open brushy slopes.

WHITE BRODIAEA
T. hyacinthina

Pl. 102

Stems 24 in. **FLOWERS** to .75 in. wide, 10 to 40 in head, white segments with dark midvein and purple-tinged borders; May to July.

DISTRIBUTION: Widespread in wet meadows below 7,500 ft.

PRETTY FACE   *T. ixioides*
Pl. 103

Stems 6 to 18 in. **FLOWERS** are pale to golden yellow with dark vein on each segment, 16 to 40 in loose umbel, pedicels 1 to 4 in., flowers .5 to .75 in. long; May to July.

DISTRIBUTION: Foothill Belt and up to 10,000 ft on sandy soil.

ITHURIEL'S SPEAR   *T. laxa*

Stems 12 to 28 in., rigid. **FLOWERS** are violet purple, eight to 48 in loose open umbel, pedicels 2 to 3.5 in., flowers 1.25 to 1.75 in. long; April to June.

DISTRIBUTION: Foothill Belt at 500 to 4,600 ft in open grasslands; bulbs eaten raw by Native Americans.

FAWN LILY   *Erythronium purpurascens*

Stems 4 to 10 in., erect, from narrow bulb. **LEAVES** are two, basal, to 10 in. long, tapering to bottom, wavy margined. **FLOWERS** are one to five, 2 in. wide, petals bent back, white or cream, orange or bright yellow at base, turning purple after pollination; stigma three-lobed; flowering immediately after snowmelt.

DISTRIBUTION: Open woods and meadows in the Mixed Conifer Belt, 4,000 to 8,000 ft.

PURPLE FRITILLARY or SPOTTED   *Fritillaria*
MOUNTAIN BELLS   *atropurpurea*
Pl. 104

Stems 1 to 2 ft, erect, from a bulb. **LEAVES** are 3 to 5 in. long, in clusters of two to three along stem. **FLOWERS** are nodding, each to .5 in. long, mottled purplish brown and yellow; anthers yellow; April to June.

DISTRIBUTION: Forest openings and rocky slopes, 6,000 to 10,500 ft.

Lilies (Genus *Lilium*)

Stems 1.5 to 7 ft, erect, from a bulb. **LEAVES** are 3 to 5 in. long, narrow, scattered or in whorls. **FLOWERS** are large, showy, one or a few in raceme; stigma three-lobed.

LEOPARD LILY   *L. pardalinum*
Pl. 105

Stems 3 to 8 ft. **FLOWERS** 1 to 4 in. wide, orange with heavy purplish spotting on strongly recurved petals; May to July.

DISTRIBUTION: Mostly in large colonies along stream banks, 3,000 to 6,500 ft.

ALPINE LILY

L. parvum

Stems to 7 ft. **FLOWERS** are 1 to 1.25 in. long, orange yellow with purple spotting; July to September.

DISTRIBUTION: Mixed Conifer and Subalpine Belts, at 3,500 to 9,000 ft in boggy places or near streams.

WASHINGTON LILY
L. washingtonianum

Stems 4 to 6 ft. **FLOWERS** are 3 to 4 in. long with petals curling back, pure white, often purple-dotted, aging purplish, fragrant; July to August.

DISTRIBUTION: Mixed Conifer Belt at 3,000 to 7,500 ft in forest or thickets on dry slopes.

FALSE SOLOMON'S SEAL

Smilacina racemosa

Pl. 106

Stems 1 to 3 ft, from horizontal rootstock. **LEAVES** alternate, 3 to 5.5 in. long, broad, clasping stem at base; tip pointed, rough with short hairs. **FLOWERS** are in 2 to 4 in. panicles, small, white; stigma three-lobed; berry red with purple dots, one-seeded; March to June.

DISTRIBUTION: Shaded woods below 8,500 ft.

CORN LILY

Veratrum californicum var. *californicum*

Pl. 107

Stems 3 to 6 ft, stout, leafy, resembling cornstalk; rootstock short, thick, fibrous. **LEAVES** are 6 to 12 in. by 4 to 8 in. oval, tip pointed, sheathing stem at base, upper leaves narrower, shorter. **FLOWERS** are in 12 to 16 in. long panicle, woolly, flowers many, to .75 in. long, white, greenish at base, three styles; July to August.

DISTRIBUTION: Mixed Conifer Belt to Alpine Belt at 4,500 to 8,500 ft or higher; in wet meadows and along stream banks.

REMARKS: This plant resembles but is not related to the eastern skunk cabbage (*Symplocarpus*); it is also called false hellebore from its resemblance to *Helleborus* of Europe. This plant is highly poisonous if consumed in even small portions. Corn lilies grow rapidly as soon as the snows begin to melt, sometimes pushing up through the last snow and seeming to grow inches a day.

Loasa (Family Loasaceae)

Stinging hairs on leaves; calyx five-lobed; petals five; style one; ovary inferior.

BLAZING STAR
Mentzelia laevicaulis
Pl. 108

Stems 2 to 4 ft, rough hairs. **LEAVES** are .75 to 10 in. long, longest at base of stem, elliptic, margins ruffled and toothed. **FLOWERS** are up to 6 in. wide, petals lancelike and pointed, golden yellow, stamens many; June to October.

DISTRIBUTION: Widespread on dry rocky soil and roadsides on both slopes below 8,500 ft.

Mallows (Family Malvaceae)

Sepals and petals five; stamens united into a tube.

MALLOW
Sidalcea oregana subsp. *spicata*
Pl. 109

Stems 1 to 3 ft, lower parts with long bristles. **LEAVES** are lobed with ruffled margins on lower stem; upper leaves are deeply parted with many linear segments. **FLOWERS** are in a dense spike, rose pink, petals usually notched at apex; June to August.

DISTRIBUTION: Moist habitats to 8,500 ft.

REMARKS: Of eleven species in the Sierra, several have very limited ranges and are endangered. One common species is white-veined mallow (*S. glaucescens*), which lacks bristles and has bright lavender flowers that are heavily veined white on each petal. It occurs in dry forests and open areas from 3,000 to 11,000 ft.

Water Lily (Family Nymphaeaceae)

Leaves floating or erect; flowers large.

YELLOW POND-LILY
Nuphar luteum subsp. *polysepalum*
Pl. 110

Rootstock in water. **LEAVES** are 7 to 14 in. by 6 to 11 in., floating, heart shaped. **FLOWERS** have diameter of 3 to 5 in., calyx bright yellow or reddish-tinged, sepals petal-like, 9 to 12; petals 12 to 18, to .5 in., long, under many stamens with dark red anthers; fruit diameter to 1.5 in., ovate; April to September.

DISTRIBUTION: Mixed Conifer Belt and higher, from Mariposa and Mono Counties north at 3,500 to 7,500 ft in ponds and lakes.

Evening Primroses (Family Onagraceae)

Flowers usually regular; sepals and petals four; stamens eight, pollen cobwebby; ovary inferior.

DIAMOND CLARKIA
Clarkia rhomboidea

Pl. 111

Stems 1 to 3 ft, erect. **LEAVES** are .5 to 2 in. by .5 to .75 in. lanceolate to ovate, petioles short. **FLOWERS** are few in elongated spikes, rose purple; petals .25 to .5 in. long, with short broad lobe at base; stamens eight, those opposite petals short; stigma four-lobed; ovary four-celled; capsule 1 in. long, straight or slightly curved; May to August.

DISTRIBUTION: Foothill Belt to Upper Montane Belt below 8,000 ft on dry slopes.

REMARKS: Other species throughout the Sierra have flowers that are lavender, pink, purple, or white.

FIREWEED
Epilobium angustifolium subsp. *circumvagum*

Pl. 112

Stems 2 to 6 ft, erect. **LEAVES** are 4 to 6 in. long, narrow, lancelike. **FLOWERS** are in long racemes; calyx cleft nearly to ovary; corolla slightly irregular, lilac purple; petals .5 to .67 in. long, slightly notched at tips; stamens purple, filaments expanded at base, style longer than stamens; ovary four-celled; seeds with long tuft of hairs at tip; July to September.

DISTRIBUTION: Mixed Conifer Belt to Alpine Belt below 10,000 ft on moist ground, especially in fire-swept areas.

REMARKS: Other species occur from the foothills to 13,000 ft, and amidst pinyon pines and junipers on the east slope. In some species the petals are deeply lobed and white or pinkish.

CALIFORNIA FUCHSIA
Epilobium canum

Pl. 113

Stems 4 to 20 in., hairy. **LEAVES** are .75 to 1.75 in. by .5 in., ovate to elliptic. **FLOWERS** are 1 to 1.5 in. long, tubular; petals .3 to .6 in. long, two-cleft; stamens and style project beyond corolla; sepals and petals red; capsule linear, four-angled; seeds with tuft of hairs at one end; August to October.

DISTRIBUTION: Dry slopes and ridges below 10,000 ft.

REMARKS: Formerly known as *Zauschneria californica*.

GAYOPHYTUM
Gayophytum diffusum

Stems 6 to 24 in., widely branched. **LEAVES** are .5 to 2 in. long, linear or lance shaped. **FLOWERS** are in leafy racemes, widely spaced along branchlets; calyx lobes bent at tips; petals to .25 in. long, white turning pink with age, two small yellow dots at base; stamens eight; capsule four-valved, up to .25 in. long; seeds naked; June to August.

DISTRIBUTION: Mixed Conifer Belt to Subalpine Belt, 3,000 to 11,000 ft on dry slopes.

REMARKS: Other forms occur over the same range, and one species grows among pinyon pines and junipers on the east side.

EVENING PRIMROSE *Oenothera elata* subsp. *hirsutissima*

Stems 2 to 4 ft, stout, erect; herbage minutely hairy. **LEAVES** are 4 to 9 in. long, ovate to lance shaped. **FLOWERS** have calyx tube with lobes bent down; petals 1 to 2 in. long and equally broad, yellow aging to orange red; stamens eight; anthers attached near middle; stigma one, with four symmetrical lobes; ovary four-celled; seeds angled; June to September.

DISTRIBUTION: Mixed Conifer and Upper Montane Belts, 3,000 to 9,000 ft in moist places.

REMARKS: The evening primrose is a favorite browse for deer. It blooms in the early evening and is pollinated solely by night-flying hummingbird moths (Sphingidae).

Orchids (Family Orchidaceae)

Leaves parallel veined, sheathing stem or scalelike; flowers irregular; petals six, one (the "lip") unlike others; stamens one to two, united with pistil; ovary inferior.

SPOTTED CORALROOT *Corallorhiza maculata*

Pl. 114

Roots branching, coral-like; stem 8 to 13 in., erect. **LEAVES** are small, scalelike. **FLOWERS** are in a terminal cluster, 2 to 7 in. long, flowers about .25 in. long, lower petal (lip) finely toothed, white, purple-spotted; June to August.

DISTRIBUTION: Coniferous forest at 3,000 to 9,000 ft among pine needles and humus.

REMARKS: The rarer striped coralroot (*C. striata*) has larger flowers with purple stripes. These saprophytic orchids get their nutrients from decaying organic matter and thus have no green foliage of their own. The plants produce thousands of microscopic seeds but only those that establish an association with soil fungi are able to survive.

RATTLESNAKE PLANTAIN *Goodyera oblongifolia*

Pl. 115

Stems 7 to 14 in. **LEAVES** are in a basal cluster, dark green, midrib whitestriped and branching out into white veins, wavy margins. **FLOWERS** are small, white to greenish, in a raceme on a tall erect stalk; July to August.

DISTRIBUTION: Dry forest floor below 5,500 ft.

SIERRA REIN ORCHID   *Platanthera leucostachys*
Pl. 116

Stems 9 to 30 in., base thick, leafy, from a tuber. **LEAVES** are 4 to 9 in. by .5 to 1 in., lanceolate, sheathing stem. **FLOWERS** are white, .5 in. long, in dense spike 4 to 8 in. long; May to August.

DISTRIBUTION: From middle elevations to 11,000 ft in moist places.

Poppies (Family Papaveraceae)

Sepals two or three, dropping early; petals generally four (sometimes six or more); stamens many.

BLEEDING HEART   *Dicentra formosa*
Pl. 117

Stems 8 to 18 in. high. **LEAVES** are from creeping rootstock, compound, many-lobed, 3 to 9 in. long, petioles 4 to 12 in. long. **FLOWERS** are in a cluster at tip of stem, rose purple, to .75 in. long, heart shaped, petals joined to above middle, flared at ends; March to July.

DISTRIBUTION: On west slope in Mixed Conifer Belt below 7,000 ft in damp shaded places.

CALIFORNIA POPPY   *Eschscholzia californica*
Pl. 118

Stems 9 to 24 in., leafy, erect or spreading. **LEAVES** are 4 to 12 in. long including petioles, of many linear segments. **FLOWERS** are deep orange to pale yellow, diameter .5 to 2 in., petals fan shaped, usually four; sepals two, united as a cap that falls when the flower opens; February to September.

DISTRIBUTION: Central Valley into Mixed Conifer Belt, up to 6,500 ft on open or grassy sites.

REMARKS: California's state flower sometimes covers whole hillsides with its bright golden blossoms. The scientific name honors J. F. Eschscholtz, a Russian naturalist who visited California on Kotzebue's ship in 1824 and collected the first herbarium specimens of this flower.

Gilias (Family Polemoniaceae)

Leaves alternate or opposite; calyx and corolla five-lobed; stamens five, inserted on corolla, alternate with its lobes.

GRAND COLLOMIA   *Collomia grandiflora*

Stems 8 to 36 in., erect. **LEAVES** are 1 to 3 in. long, linear or lance shaped. **FLOWERS** are crowded in headlike clusters at ends of stems with leafy bracts below; corolla 1 in. long, trumpet shaped, pale salmon color, creamy yellow or white; tube three times length of calyx and lobes broadly oblong; April to July.

DISTRIBUTION: Foothill Belt to Upper Montane Belt below 8,000 ft on dry slopes.

SCARLET GILIA   *Ipomopsis aggregata*
Pl. 119

Stems 1 to 2.5 ft, erect, usually simple, minutely hairy. **LEAVES** are 1 to 2 in. long, mostly alternate, pinnately divided into narrow linear lobes .4 to .8 in. long. **FLOWERS** are in a long panicle; calyx .13 to .25 in. long, lobes lance shaped; corolla .75 to 1.25 in. long, tubular, spreading, throat open, lobes .33 to .5 in. long, tapering to sharp tips; reddish to pink or white, rarely yellow; June to August.

DISTRIBUTION: Mixed Conifer Belt to Subalpine Belt at 3,500 to 10,300 ft on open sandy flats and rocky ridges.

WHISKER BRUSH   *Linanthus ciliatus*
Pl. 120

Stems 1 to 12 in. **LEAVES** are opposite, densely hairy, deeply lobed into linear segments, spine tipped, in whorls. **FLOWERS** are fused into a tube at base, flaring out into a flat disk of five square-tipped petals, pink with corolla throat yellow and with dark purple dot; April to August.

DISTRIBUTION: Dry forest openings and slopes below 10,000 ft.

SPREADING PHLOX   *Phlox diffusa*
Pl. 121

Stems leafy, creeping, forming low dense mats. **LEAVES** are .25 to .5 in. long, linear, rigid. **FLOWERS** are white (turning pinkish purple after pollination), base tubular, outer parts of petals bent at right angles forming a flat disk; April to August.

DISTRIBUTION: Mixed Conifer Belt to Subalpine Belt, 4,000 to 12,000 ft on rocky ledges or sandy slopes.

REMARKS: Granite gilia (*Leptodactylon pungens*), or prickly phlox as it is sometimes called, is frequently confused with spreading phlox. The gilia is recognized by its spine-tipped leaves, and funnel-like flowers that twist in the bud.

SKY PILOT   *Polemonium eximium*
Pl. 122

Stems several, 2 to 9 in., simple, erect. **LEAVES** are in a dense basal tuft, 1 to 5 in. long, sticky and musky, pinnately compound; leaflets 0.4 to .2 in. long, greater than 12 per leaf, each deeply three- to five-lobed. **FLOWERS** are showy, clustered in a head; corolla .5 to .6 in. long, basal tube white, roundish lobes blue and about twice as long as the tube; July to August.

DISTRIBUTION: Alpine ridges and summits of the highest peaks from Yosemite National Park south, 10,000 to 13,000 ft.

PLANTS

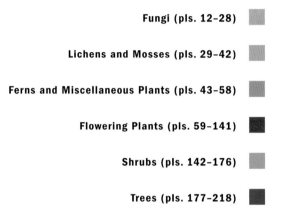

Plate 12. Coccora

Plate 13. Oyster mushroom

Plate 14. Giant lentinus

Plate 15. Honey mushrooms

Plate 16. Deer mushroom

Plate 17. Cobweb-gilled fungus

Plate 18. Sulfur tuft mushroom

Plate 19. King bolete

Plate 20. White-pouch fungus

Plate 21. Red-belted conk

Plate 22. Turkey tail

Plate 23. Sulfur shelf

Plate 24. Yellow coral mushroom

Plate 26. Witch's butter

Plate 25. Chanterelle

Plate 27. Black morel

Plate 28. Saddle fungus

Plate 29. Witch's hair

Plate 30. Tree-hair lichen

Plate 31. Cladonia

Plate 32. Oakmoss lichen

Plate 33. Wolf lichen

Plate 34. Flame firedot

Plate 35. Brown tile lichen

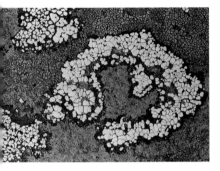

Plate 36. Yellow map lichen

Plate 37. Forked tube lichen

Plate 38. Cumberland rock-shield

Plate 39. Star moss

Plate 40. Dark rock moss

Plate 41. Peat moss

Plate 42. Common liverwort

Plate 43. Five-finger fern

Plate 44. California maiden-hair fern

Plate 45. Lady fern

Plate 46. Leathery grape fern

Plate 47. American parsley fern

Plate 48. Common horsetail

Plate 49. Bird's-foot fern

Plate 50. Goldback fern

Plate 51. Polypody

Plate 52. Western sword fern

Plate 53. Bracken fern

Plate 54. Giant chain fern

Plate 55. Broad-leaf cattail

Plate 56. Water plantain

Plate 57. Grass

Plate 58. Sedge

Plate 59. Cow parsnip

Plate 60. Ranger's buttons

Plate 61. Spreading dogbane

Plate 62. Purple milkweed

Plate 63. Yarrow

Plate 64. Heart-leaf arnica

Plate 65. Alpine aster

Plate 66. Anderson's thistle

Plate 67. Wandering daisy

Plate 68. Woolly sunflower

Plate 69. Bigelow's sneezeweed

Plate 70. White-flowered hawkweed

Plate 71. Common madia

Plate 72. Canada goldenrod

Plate 73. Mules ears

Plate 74. Fiddleneck

Plate 75. Velvety stickseed

Plate 76. Mountain bluebells

Plate 77. Popcorn flower

Plate 78. Western wallflower

Plate 79. Streptanthus

Plate 80. California harebell

Plate 81. Porterella

Plate 82. King's sandwort

Plate 83. California Indian pink

Plate 84. Sierra stonecrop

Plate 85. California dodder

Plate 86. Pinedrops

Plate 87. Snow plant

Plate 88. Whitney's locoweed

Plate 89. Brewer's lupine

Plate 90. Red clover

Plate 91. Hiker's gentian

Plate 92. Green gentian

Plate 93. Richardson's geranium

Plate 94. St. John's wort

Plate 96. Blue-eyed grass

Plate 95. Sierra iris

Plate 97. Giant hyssop

Plate 98. Mountain pennyroyal

Plate 99. Self-heal

Plate 100. Sierra onion

Plate 101. Camas

Plate 102. White brodiaea

Plate 103. Pretty face

Plate 104. Purple fritillary

Plate 105. Leopard lily

Plate 106. False Solomon's seal

Plate 108. Blazing star

Plate 107. Corn lily

Plate 109. Mallow

Plate 110. Yellow pond-lily

Plate 111. Diamond clarkia

Plate 112. Fireweed

Plate 113. California fuchsia

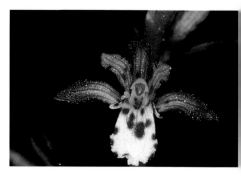

Plate 114. Spotted coralroot

Plate 115. Rattlesnake plantain

Plate 116. Sierra rein orchid

Plate 117. Bleeding heart

Plate 118. California poppy

Plate 119. Scarlet gilia

Plate 120. Whisker brush

Plate 121. Spreading phlox

Plate 122. Sky pilot

Plate 123. Nude buckwheat

Plate 124. Mountain sorrel

Plate 125. Pussypaws

Plate 126. Miner's lettuce

Plate 127. Sierra primrose

Plate 128. Monkshood

Plate 129. Western pasque flower

Plate 130. Red columbine

Plate 131. Marsh marigold

Plate 132. Tall larkspur

Plate 133. Wood strawberry

Plate 134. Sticky cinquefoil

Plate 135. Giant red Indian paintbrush

Plate 136. Tincture plant

Plate 138. Elephant's head

Plate 137. Common monkeyflower

Plate 139. Common mullein

Plate 140. Purple nightshade

Plate 141. Oak mistletoe

Plate 142. Poison oak

Plate 143. Rabbitbrush

Plate 144. Pinemat manzanita

Plate 145. Greenleaf manzanita

Plate 146. White heather

Plate 147. Alpine laurel

Plate 148. Western Labrador tea

Plate 150. Western azalea

Plate 149. Red mountain heather

Plate 151. Scotch broom

Plate 152. Bush chinquapin

Plate 153. Huckleberry oak

Plate 154. Wax currant

Plate 155. Alpine gooseberry

Plate 156. Sierra currant

Plate 157. Sierra gooseberry

Plate 158. Spanish bayonet

Plate 159. Wild mock orange

Plate 160. Virgin's bower

Plate 161. Snow brush

Plate 162. Tobacco brush

Plate 163. Holly-leaf redberry

Plate 164. Sierra coffeeberry

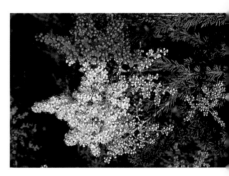

Plate 165. Chamise

Plate 166. Birch-leaf mountain mahogany

Plate 167. Toyon

Plate 168. Oceanspray

Plate 169. Bitter cherry

Plate 170. Bitterbrush

Plate 171. Interior rose

Plate 172. Mountain ash

Plate 173. Mountain spiraea

Plate 174. California button willow

Plate 175. Fremontia

Plate 176. California wild grape

Plate 177. Incense-cedar

Plate 178. McNab cypress

Plate 179. Piute cypress

Plate 180. Sierra juniper

Plate 181. White fir

Plate 182. Red fir

Plate 183. Whitebark pine

Plate 184. Knobcone pine

Plate 185. Foxtail pine

Plate 186. Lodgepole pine

Plate 187. Limber pine

Plate 188. Jeffrey pine

Plate 189. Sugar pine

Plate 190. Singleleaf pinyon pine

Plate 191. Western white pine

Plate 192. Ponderosa pine

Plate 193. Gray pine

Plate 194. Douglas-fir

Plate 195. Pacific yew

Plate 196. Mountain hemlock

Plate 197. California nutmeg

Plate 198. Giant sequoia

Plate 199. Mountain maple

Plate 200. Bigleaf maple

Plate 201. Mountain alder

Plate 202. Water birch

Plate 203. Mountain dogwood

Plate 204. Pacific madrone

Plate 205. Tan oak

Plate 206. Canyon live oak

Plate 207. Blue oak

Plate 208. California black oak

Plate 209. California buckeye

Plate 210. California bay laurel

Plate 211. Oregon ash

Plate 212. California ash

Plate 213. California sycamore

Plate 214. Fremont cottonwood

Plate 215. Quaking aspen

Plate 216. Black cottonwood

Plate 217. Lemmon's willow

Plate 218. Arctic willow

REMARKS: Showy polemonium (*P. pulcherrimum*) grows at 8,000 to 11,000 ft on rocky slopes in the central and northern Sierra and is recognized for having fewer numbers of larger unlobed leaflets on each leaf. Great polemonium (*P. occidentale*) stands 2 to 3 ft high and grows in wet meadows at 6,000 to 10,000 ft.

Buckwheats (Family Polygonaceae)

Calyx five- or six-parted; no corolla; stamens four to nine.

NUDE BUCKWHEAT
Eriogonum nudum

Pl. 123

Stems 1 to 3 ft high, erect, smooth, spreading into an open cluster. **LEAVES** are 1 to 2 in. long, arising from a woody taproot, oblong-oval, hairy below. **FLOWERS** are on slender pedicels, two to six in a small, ball-shaped head; calyx shiny, .08 to .13 in. long, usually white, sometimes rose or yellow, six-parted; stamens nine, styles three; June to October.

DISTRIBUTION: At all elevations in dry, usually rocky, places.

REMARKS: Of about 50 Sierra species, the sulfur flower (*E. umbellatum*) is most conspicuous. Its stems are 3 to 12 in. high, and the sulfur colored flowers are in dense heads. It blooms from June to August on dry slopes and ridges at 2,500 to 10,000 ft. Also common is Lobb's buckwheat (*E. lobbii*) with a dense cluster of round bluish basal leaves and long-stemmed balls of creamy flowers that lie prostrate on ground. It is found at mid- to high elevations on rocky ledges or sandy slopes.

MOUNTAIN SORREL
Oxyria digyna

Pl. 124

Stems 4 to 16 in., stout. **LEAVES** are fleshy, rounded, heart shaped, with varying degrees of red margins or tints, edible with sour lemony taste (rich in vitamin C). **FLOWERS** are in a panicle on erect stalk, green with red tints, lobes four, stamens six, styles two; July to September.

DISTRIBUTION: Open rocky ledges, 7,000 to 13,000 ft.

WESTERN BISTORT
Polygonum bistortoides

Stems 6 to 24 in., several, root woody. **LEAVES** are 3 to 5 in. long at base of stem, narrow; upper leaves smaller. **FLOWERS** are .17 to .33 in. long, white, in a dense cylindrical raceme, .75 to 1.5 in. long; calyx five-lobed; stamens eight; June to August.

DISTRIBUTION: Mixed Conifer Belt to Subalpine Belt, in wet meadows.

REMARKS: Davis' knotweed (*P. davisiae*) has bluish green leaves with two to five small, greenish white flowers in each leaf axil. This knotweed is abundant above 7,000 ft, especially on volcanic hillsides from Tuolumne County north, where it forms pink to red carpets of turning leaves in late summer.

Purslanes (Family Portulacaceae)

Leaves succulent; sepals two (to eight); petals open only in sunshine.

PUSSYPAWS *Calyptridium umbellatum*
Pl. 125

Stems 3 to 15 in., several. **LEAVES** are 1 to 2 in. long, spoon shaped, in a dense basal rosette. **FLOWERS** are in dense terminal heads; sepals two, papery; petals four, pink or white; stamens three; May to August.

DISTRIBUTION: Mixed Conifer Belt to Subalpine Belt at 2,500 to 12,000 ft, in sandy or gravelly soil.

REMARKS: Flower stalks contain red pigments that absorb the sun's heat and help this ground-hugging plant regulate its internal temperatures by lifting flower clusters off the ground during the day then lowering them back onto the ground by night.

MINER'S LETTUCE *Claytonia perfoliata*
Pl. 126

Stems 4 to 10 in. (or 16 in.), several, erect. **LEAVES** are united into a .5 to 2 in. diameter disk just below the flower cluster; other leaves .5 to 2 in. long, basal, narrow. **FLOWERS** are in a raceme, in twos and threes, or bundles; petals white to pinkish, .25 in. long, sepals two, petals five, stamens five; February to May.

DISTRIBUTION: Below 5,000 ft in shady moist places.

REMARKS: The basal leaves and stems are eaten as greens by many people.

TOAD LILY *Montia chamissoi*

Stems 1 to 12 in. **LEAVES** are slightly fleshy, in several opposite pairs along stem, oblanceolate. **FLOWERS** are small, petals five, white, anthers pink and laying against inner petal surfaces looking like pink spots; June to August.

DISTRIBUTION: Wet meadows, 4,000 to 11,000 ft; abundant and spreading by aboveground runners.

Primroses (Family Primulaceae)

Leaves basal; flowers regular, the parts in fours or fives; stamens on tube at base of corolla, opposite lobes.

SIERRA SHOOTING STAR
Dodecatheon jeffreyi

Stems 12 to 21 in., with an umbel of 5 to 15 nodding flowers. **LEAVES** are basal, 2 to 15 in. long, oblong to lance shaped, tapering basally to winged petioles. **FLOWERS** are .67 to 1 in. long with a short tube and widened throat; petals long, bent backward, pink crimson, yellow at base, edged with purple; stamens on throat of corolla; filaments united below; June to August.
DISTRIBUTION: Mixed Conifer Belt to Subalpine Belt, 2,300 to 10,000 ft in wet places.
REMARKS: Five other species of shooting stars range from the foothills to alpine fell-fields.

SIERRA PRIMROSE
Primula suffrutescens

Pl. 127
Stems 2 to 4 in. creeping, with leaves basal and an umbel of several flowers. **LEAVES** are .75 to 1.5 in. long, narrowly wedge shaped, toothed at tip. **FLOWERS** have a five-lobed calyx corolla .5 to .75 in. long, diameter to 1 in., tubular, with five notched lobes bent outward, red purple with yellow throat; July to August.
DISTRIBUTION: Subalpine and Alpine Belts, 8,000 to 13,500 ft, mostly around rocks and cliffs.
REMARKS: Only hikers in the High Sierra will see the deep-colored display of this attractive flower in late summer.

Buttercups (Family Ranunculaceae)

Leaves mostly palmately divided or lobed; flowers of varied forms.

MONKSHOOD
Aconitum columbianum

Pl. 128
Stems 1.5 to 5 ft, from thick roots. **LEAVES** are roundish, 2 to 3 in. wide, palmately five-lobed and subdivided. **FLOWERS** are in racemes, blue (rarely white or cream), irregular; sepals five, upper one .5 in. long, hooded; petals two, hammer shaped, hidden by hood; stamens many; pistils three to five; July to August.

DISTRIBUTION: Mainly in Mixed Conifer Belt at 4,000 to 8,000 ft in moist places, especially willow thickets.

REMARKS: Bumblebees are the pollinators of this highly poisonous plant.

WESTERN PASQUE FLOWER   *Anemone occidentalis*
Pl. 129

Stems 4 to 24 in., hairy. **LEAVES** are five-parted and further subdivided into narrow lobes. **FLOWERS** are regular, white or purplish; sepals five (six), petal-like, oval, 1 in. long; petals none; stamens many; achenes several, each with 1 in. feathery tail; June to August.

DISTRIBUTION: Mixed Conifer Belt to Subalpine Belt at 5,500 to 10,000 ft on rocky slopes, often in presence of snowbanks.

RED COLUMBINE   *Aquilegia formosa*
Pl. 130

Stems 1.5 to 3.5 ft, several, branching, smooth. **LEAVES** are at base of stem on long petioles, two to three times alternately compound (divided into three segments), leaflets .75 to 1.75 in. long, deeply lobed.

FLOWERS are regular, scarlet, center yellow; sepals five, flat; petals five, formed as hollow backward-pointing spurs; stamens many; pistils five; April to August.

DISTRIBUTION: Up to 8,000 ft in moist, shaded sites.

REMARKS: The alpine *A. pubescens* is smaller and minutely hairy, with yellow, white, or blue flowers; it occurs from Mariposa County to Tulare County at 9,000 to 12,000 ft in rocky places, blooming from June to August. The long-spurred flowers of red columbines are pollinated by hummingbirds, while *A. pubescens* is pollinated by sphinx moths.

MARSH MARIGOLD   *Caltha leptosepala* var. *biflora*
Pl. 131

Stems 4 to 12 in., from fibrous rootstock. **LEAVES** are roundish, 2 to 4 in. wide, basal, on long petioles. **FLOWERS** are regular, white (or bluish on back); sepals six to nine, petal-like, .5 in. long; petals none; stamens many; pistils five to 10+; May to July.

DISTRIBUTION: West slope at 4,500 to 10,500 ft in wet meadows or on marshy slopes.

TALL LARKSPUR   *Delphinium glaucum*
Pl. 132

Stems 3 to 6 ft, stout, leafy, from root cluster. **LEAVES** are 3 to 5 in. wide, smooth, 5 to 7 palmately lobed. **FLOWERS** are irregular, in a 6- to

18-in.-long raceme, blue or purplish, many (over 50); sepals .5 in. long, base of uppermost formed as a backward-pointing spur; petals four, the lower ones cleft to middle; stamens many; pistils three; July to September.

DISTRIBUTION: Mixed Conifer Belt to Subalpine Belt at 5,000 to 10,600 ft along streams or in wet meadows.

REMARKS: The smaller *D. nuttallianum* has fewer deep blue flowers (less than 12) in May through July; it is found in moist to dry forests or meadows at 5,000 to 10,000 ft. Twelve species of larkspurs occur in the Sierra.

WESTERN BUTTERCUP   *Ranunculus occidentalis*

Stems 4 to 24 in. **LEAVES** are deeply three-lobed, toothed. **FLOWERS** are bright, shiny yellow on thin ascending stalks, petals five (six); March to July.

DISTRIBUTION: Moist meadows, below 7,500 ft.

REMARKS: The water plantain buttercup (*R. alismifolius*) differs in having long, narrow leaves with smooth margins; it grows from 4,000 to 12,000 ft where its bright yellow flowers may carpet wet meadows.

FENDLER'S MEADOW-RUE   *Thalictrum fendleri*

Stems 2 to 6 ft. **LEAVES** are thin, divided into three to four sets of three leaflets. **FLOWERS** have male and female parts on separate plants, no petals, sepals four to five, greenish white and inconspicuous, male flowers tassel-like with 15 to 30, long, hanging stamens, female flowers consist of prominent swollen stigmas; May to August.

DISTRIBUTION: Moist habitats, 4,000 to 10,000 ft.

Roses (Family Rosaceae)

Sepals and petals five; stamens 10 to many; pistils one to many.

WOOD STRAWBERRY   *Fragaria vesca*

Pl. 133

Stems 4 to 5 in., often as runners, rooting at nodes. **LEAVES** are basal, each with three leaflets 1 to 1.25 in. long, roundly ovate, coarsely toothed, densely silky below. **FLOWERS** are loosely clustered, white, diameter .5 to 1 in.; calyx persistent, with five small bracts, alternate with petals; stamens about 20; pistils many; berry diameter .38 in., red; March to June.

DISTRIBUTION: Foothill and Mixed Conifer Belts below 7,000 ft in shaded damp places.

REMARKS: The mountain strawberry (*F. virginiana*), at 4,000 to 10,500 ft, blooms from May to July. Its central leaflet generally has fewer than 13 teeth on the margin, while the wood strawberry has 12 to 21 teeth. Cultivated strawberries have escaped in places; some may be from roots brought by early settlers. Cultivated or wild, strawberries in the Sierra have a delicious flavor.

STICKY CINQUEFOIL   *Potentilla glandulosa*
Pl. 134

Stems 6 in. to 4 ft, branching, erect, glandular; often reddish. **LEAVES** are mainly basal, 4 to 8 in. long, those at top smaller; pinnate, five to nine leaflets 1 to 3 in. long, roundish ovate, edges notched. **FLOWERS** are terminal, pale yellow, diameter .33 to .5 in.; stamens 20+; pistils 10 to 80, ripening to form dry achenes; May to August.

DISTRIBUTION: Widespread from foothills to 12,400 ft in many habitats.

REMARKS: Six subspecies of sticky cinquefoil occur in the Sierra, accounting for the species' broad elevational range. Graceful cinquefoil (*P. gracilis*) differs in having large palmate leaves with prominent teeth. It favors moist meadows and forest openings below 10,000 ft.

Saxifrages (Family Saxifragaceae)

Leaves mostly basal; sepals and petals five; ovary superior or inferior.

ALUMROOT   *Heuchera micrantha*

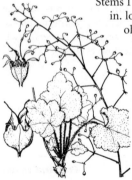

Stems 1 to 3 feet, hairy. **LEAVES** are mostly basal, 1 to 3.5 in. long, rounded and shallowly lobed, hairy, petioles up to 12 in. long. **FLOWERS** are in an open loose panicle, to .13 in. long, white or reddish; calyx bell shaped, greenish; stamens five; styles two; May to July.

DISTRIBUTION: Mixed Conifer and Upper Montane Belts at 2,500 to 7,000 ft on moist banks.

REMARKS: A smaller species (*H. rubescens*), 5 to 12 in. high with reddish calyx and longer flower clusters, inhabits dry rocky places mainly on the east slope at 6,000 to 12,000 ft, reaching alpine fell-fields.

BOG SAXIFRAGE   *Saxifraga oregana*

Stems 1 to 3 ft, bare. **LEAVES** are 2 to 7 in. long, oblong-oval, narrowed at base, mostly in cluster at base of stem. **FLOWERS** are in terminal clusters, white, petals .17 to .33 in. long; calyx five-cleft; stamens 10; styles two; May to August.

DISTRIBUTION: Mixed Conifer Belt to Subalpine Belt at 3,500 to 11,000 ft in wet meadows and boggy seeps.

REMARKS: Eight species of saxifrage occur in the Sierra, several of which are smaller alpine forms. The name saxifrage means "rock-breaker."

Figworts (Family Scrophulariaceae)

Leaves opposite or alternate; flowers tubular or saucer shaped; calyx five-cleft; corolla usually two-lipped, upper lip two-lobed or as a single hood or beak, lower lip three-lobed or of three sacs; stamens usually four fertile and one sterile.

GIANT RED INDIAN PAINTBRUSH *Castilleja miniata* subsp. *miniata*
Pl. 135

Stems 1 to 3 in. **LEAVES** are narrow, lanceolate with sharp tips, 1.25 to 2.33 in. long. **FLOWERS** are inconspicuous greenish tubes hidden among bright red hairy bracts; May to September.

DISTRIBUTION: Widespread in moist areas below 11,000 ft.

REMARKS: Approximately 21 species of paintbrush occur in the Sierra, but extensive variation and hybridization makes separation into species problematic in many cases. Some are parasitic on roots of other plants. Another common species is Applegate's Indian paintbrush (*C. applegatei*), which is distributed as widely as the giant red Indian paintbrush, but recognized by its distinctly wavy-edged leaves. Hummingbirds frequent patches of blooming paintbrush.

TINCTURE PLANT   *Collinsia tinctoria*
Pl. 136

Stems 6 to 24 in., erect, simple or branching; herbage sticky, staining brownish if rubbed. **LEAVES** are to 4 in. long, opposite, simple, ovate to lance shaped, petioles short or absent. **FLOWERS** are in successive whorls along stem; calyx .2 to .33 in. long, bell shaped, deeply five-cleft, the lobes linear or oblong; corolla .5 to .75 in. long with short tube, deeply two-lobed, upper lip two-cleft, lower three-cleft, middle lobe enclosing four stamens and style, creamy white (or pale lavender) with pale yellow throat and purple markings; capsule about .17 in. long; May to August.

DISTRIBUTION: Mostly in Mixed Conifer Belt of west slope at 2,000 to 7,500 ft in stony places or partially shaded grassy areas.

REMARKS: Below 3,000 ft grows a stunning purple version of the tincture plant known as Chinese houses (*C. heterophylla*), which has white upper petals sharply etched with red purple lines and spots. Blue-eyed Mary (*C. torreyi*), which grows in damp sandy places in the coniferous forest at 3,000 to 10,000 ft, is a small 2- to 4-in.-high plant with much smaller flowers.

COMMON MONKEYFLOWER   *Mimulus guttatus*
Pl. 137

Stems 1 to 30 in., erect or trailing. **LEAVES** are in pairs, ovate, coarsely toothed, upper pairs clasping stem. **FLOWERS** are .75 to 1.5 in. long, trumpet shaped, lower lip variously dotted with brownish red spots, throat hairy, in groups of five or more; May to August.

DISTRIBUTION: Common in many wet habitats below 8,000 ft.

REMARKS: There are 39 other species from the foothills up to 11,000 ft. In very wet meadows the diminutive primrose monkeyflower (*M. primuloides*) sparkles with moisture held by long silky hairs. This mat-forming species has small single flowers that are more regular in shape than those of the common monkeyflower. Lewis' monkeyflower (*M. lewisii*) has beautiful rose pink flowers that are 1.25 to 2 in. long. It is widespread in wet meadows from 4,000 to 10,000 ft.

ELEPHANT'S HEAD   *Pedicularis attollens*
Pl. 138

Stems 6 to 28 in., perennial, often in clusters. **LEAVES** are finely divided into 10 to 40 fernlike segments, leaves progressively smaller up stem. **FLOWERS** have a hooded and beaked upper lip, bearing an uncanny resemblance to an elephant's head, pink purple in dense terminal spike; June to August.

DISTRIBUTION: Mostly in coniferous forest above Mixed Conifer Belt at 5,000 to 12,000 ft in wet meadows.

REMARKS: Other species include the widespread pinewoods lousewort (*P. semibarbata*) with yellow, reddish-tipped flowers that arise from within a dense basal clump of leaves.

MOUNTAIN PRIDE   *Penstemon newberryi* var. *newberryi*

Stems many (shrublike), woody below, forming a creeping mat less than 1 ft high. **LEAVES** are to 1.5 in. long, opposite, ovate, finely toothed, petioles short. **FLOWERS** are several, near ends of stems; calyx .5 in. long, five-parted, lobes lance shaped; corolla 1.25 to 1.5 in. long, bright red, tubular, upper lip deeply two-lobed, lower three-lobed; stamens four, anthers densely woolly, fifth stamen short, sterile, bearded at tip; capsule with many angled seeds; June to August.

DISTRIBUTION: Rocky slopes and open forests, 5,000 to 11,000 ft.

REMARKS: Twenty-four other species of penstemon grow at all elevations in the Sierra. Meadow penstemon (*P. rydbergii* var. *oreocharis*) is very common in montane meadows from 5,000 to 9,000 ft, sometimes forming dazzling carpets of deep blue purple. It has dense whorls of flowers arranged along a 6 in. to 2 ft. tall stem. Another widely observed species is showy penstemon (*P. speciosus*), noted for its large, rather pot-bellied, flowers that come in shades of red, purple, and blue, as well as its thick blue-green leaves. It is widespread on open rocky slopes from 5,000 to 9,000 ft.

COMMON or WOOLLY MULLEIN   *Verbascum thapsus*
Pl. 139

Stems 3 to 6 ft, stout, erect, densely woolly. **LEAVES** mostly alternate, those at base in rosettes, 6 to 12 in. long, oblong-ovate, clasping stem. **FLOWERS** are in a dense spike 1 to 3 ft long and 1.25 in. thick; calyx .33 in. long; corolla .8 to

1 in. diameter, wheel shaped, with five nearly equal lobes, yellow; stamens five, all with anthers; June to September.

DISTRIBUTION: Waste places and along roads; an abundant and widespread introduced weed below 7,000 ft.

Nightshade (Family Solanaceae)

Calyx five-cleft; corolla five-lobed, tubular or saucer shaped; stamens five, inserted on corolla, alternate with its lobes.

PURPLE NIGHTSHADE   *Solanum xanti*
Pl. 140

Stems 1.5 to 3 ft, several, spreading; herbage minutely hairy, stem hairs sticky. **LEAVES** are .8 to 1.6 in. long, ovate. **FLOWERS** are six to 10 in an umbrella-like cyme; corolla .5 to .83 in. wide, saucer shaped, angularly lobed, blue; anthers grow together as an erect yellow cylinder; fruit is like a small green tomato with a persistent five-lobed calyx; February to August.

DISTRIBUTION: Dry places near chaparral or woods, to 9,000 ft.

Violets (Family Violaceae)

Flowers slightly irregular; sepals five; petals five, unequal; two upper, two lateral, one lower spurred at base; stamens five; stigma one.

WESTERN DOG VIOLET   *Viola adunca*

Stems leafy, to 8 in. long. **LEAVES** are .33 to 1 in. long, round-ovate to heart shaped, edges toothed. **FLOWERS** have .33- to .5-in.-long petals, violet turning purple, the side petals white-bearded; March to July.

DISTRIBUTION: Mixed Conifer Belt to Subalpine Belt, 3,300 to 8,500 ft on damp banks and in meadows.

REMARKS: The 15 species of violets in the Sierra are a familiar and welcome sight in many habitats throughout the entire region. Their colors range from purple to white to yellow depending on the species.

Mistletoes (Family Viscaceae)

Leaves opposite, male and female flowers on separate plants; regular; sepals three; no petals; stamens three; ovary inferior.

OAK MISTLETOE *Phoradendron villosum*
Pl. 141

Evergreen, bushlike, parasitic on trees; stems 1 to 3 ft long, hairy. **LEAVES** are many, thick, oval, .5 to 1.5 in. long. **FLOWERS** are small, greenish on a fleshy, jointed short spike; berry round, pulpy, pink.

DISTRIBUTION: Foothills to middle elevations, chiefly on black oak and canyon live oak.

REMARKS: Several other species have scalelike leaves, these include *P. juniperinum* on Sierra juniper and *P. libocedri* on incense-cedar. The related western dwarf mistletoe (*Arceuthobium campylopodum*), has scalelike yellowish or brownish leaves and flattened berries and is common on ponderosa and Jeffrey pines.

SHRUBS

A SHRUB IS A perennial plant with several woody stems branching from the base. Some woody species may be either trees or shrubs according to local conditions. The growth requirements of different species vary—wet to dry, cool to hot, or sunlit to shady—in the foothills, middle elevations, or sub-alpine areas.

California's most distinctive shrub association is the chaparral, a dense assemblage of plants low to medium in height, with multiple stiff branches, large, deep root systems, and leaves that are mostly small, hard, flat, and evergreen. Foothill chaparral includes bush poppy, chamise, toyon, poison oak, Sierra coffeeberry, holly-leaf redberry, fremontia, yerba santa, several species of ceanothus and manzanita, and others. It grows where soil moisture is limited, winters are cool, and summers are warm to hot and dry. Chaparral covers hundreds of square miles on interior hills and ridges that are typically deficient in humus. The growth, blossoming, and fruiting of chaparral species occurs chiefly in the short period that combines warmth with some topsoil moisture. Chaparral is subject to frequent fires, to which many of the species are specially adapted—some stumps sprout vigorously after a burn, and seeds of others germinate readily only after a fire.

Mountain chaparral grows in the conifer forest at higher elevations under different climatic conditions. Common members are huckleberry oak, bush chinquapin, bitter cherry, western serviceberry, and other kinds of ceanothus and manzanita.

A third shrub assemblage, with plants spaced more widely, is the Sagebrush Belt of the Great Basin and lower east slope of the Sierra Nevada. The major element is sagebrush in company with rabbitbrush, bitterbrush, and others adapted to scant moisture, cold winters, and hot, dry summers. Sagebrush "spills upward" into the high eastern Sierra and even onto the west slope. Each of these shrubby environments include distinctive species of herbaceous plants, insects, reptiles, birds, and mammals.

Sumac (Family Anacardiaceae)

Acrid or milky sap; ovary one, bearing three short styles.

POISON OAK   *Toxicodendron diversilobum*
Pl. 142

Height 2 to 8 ft; erect or spreading, sometimes vinelike climbing to 75 ft on tree trunks. **LEAVES** are alternate, compound, usually three-parted, leaflets 1 to 4 in. long, variable, roundish or ovate, lobed or toothed; deciduous. **FLOW-ERS** are in panicles appearing with leaves; flowers .13 in. long, greenish white, petals five, spreading; April to May. **FRUIT** grows to .25 in. diameter, berrylike, whitish or brown, stony seeded.

DISTRIBUTION: Common from borders of Central Valley streams through Foothill Belt to lower mountain slopes and valleys up to 5,000 ft.

REMARKS: Poison oak (not an oak but related to the eastern poison ivy) is a widespread California shrub. In fall its brilliant red foliage adds color to many slopes and roadsides, while its whitish fruits provide an important food source for a wide variety of birds and mammals. The plant's juice produces an irritating rash, sometimes severe, on the skin of many persons. Contact with the leaves, with clothing that has touched the foliage, or with smoke from burning plants serves to carry the oily substance. Washing thoroughly with soap or applying special skin preparations reduces the trouble.

Sunflowers (Family Asteraceae)

Blossoms in dense heads on enlarged receptacle surrounded by many bracts; individual flowers of two kinds: strap-shaped ray flowers and small tubular disk flowers.

SAGEBRUSH   *Artemesia tridentata*

Height 3 to 6+ ft; distinct trunk with gray shreddy bark; much branched; herbage aromatic, all grayish white or silvery, finely woolly. **LEAVES** are evergreen, narrowly wedge shaped, .75 to 1.75 in. long, usually three- (or four-) toothed at tip. **FLOWERS** are in many dense narrow panicles, 6 to 18 in. long; flowers narrow, to .08 in. long; no ray flowers; four to six disk flowers; late July to November. **FRUIT** is oblong achene, top disklike.

DISTRIBUTION: Along east slope south to Inyo County and on west slope from Mariposa County to Kern County at 1,500 to 10,600 ft on high flats and mountain slopes.

REMARKS: The gray-hued sagebrush is the most widespread and best-known shrub of the Great Basin, being the dominant plant over thousands of square miles. It shelters a distinctive fauna of insects, reptiles, birds, and mammals. This and other varieties or species of artemesia are spread among forests of the east slope, and some are also present in dry areas well to the west of Sierra summits.

RABBITBRUSH   *Chrysothamnus nauseosus*
Pl. 143
Height 1 to 10 ft; main stems fibrous barked; stems erect, much-branched, flexible, leafy, woolly, gray green to white, ill-smelling. **LEAVES** are evergreen, linear, .75 to 2.5 in. long by .17 in. wide, more or less woolly. **FLOWERS** are in terminal round-topped cymes, heads small; no ray flowers; five to six disk flowers, yellow; August to November. **FRUIT** is five-angled achene, smooth to hairy.

DISTRIBUTION: East slope and northern Sierra up to 12,000 ft on dry slopes and open woodlands.

REMARKS: Roadsides, flats, and slopes of the dry east slope and Great Basin support rabbitbrush (of several species and varieties) in abundance. The colorful, yellow blossom masses are seen from late summer until snow arrives.

SINGLE-HEAD GOLDENBUSH *Ericameria suffruticosa*

Height 6 to 16 in.; branches erect, clustered; covered with minute glandular hairs. **LEAVES** are evergreen, oblanceolate, .5 to 1.5 in. long, dark green, folded inward with wavy margins. **FLOWERS** have one to six haphazardly arranged ray flowers; disk flowers 20 to 40, yellow; July to October. **FRUIT** is five-angled achene, pappus white.

DISTRIBUTION: Open rocky slopes, 8,000 to 12,000 ft.

REMARKS: Eight species of *Ericameria* occur in the Sierra Nevada; all have heavily glandular flowers with a strong lemony odor.

Birch (Family Betulaceae)

Male flowers in catkins; female in groups of three.

CALIFORNIA HAZELNUT *Corylus cornuta* var. *california*

Height 5 to 12 ft; many spreading loose stems. **BARK** is smooth, finely haired when young. **LEAVES** are 1.25 to 3 in. by .75 to 2.5 in., roundish, tip rounded or bluntly pointed, thin, glandular-hairy, margin double toothed. **FLOWERS** include hanging, wormlike, male catkins; female flowers are in small, round, scaly clusters appearing before leaves; stigmas two, long, bright red; January to April. **FRUIT** is one to two hard nuts, each .5 in. long in a hairy tube.

DISTRIBUTION: Primarily on the west slope in the Mixed Conifer Belt at 2,500 to 6,000 ft; in cool, shaded canyons along streams.

REMARKS: The sweet nuts of this plant are favored by many birds and small mammals.

Sweet-Shrub (Family Calycanthaceae)

Leaves opposite, entire, no stipules; sepals and petals alike.

SPICEBUSH *Calycanthus occidentalis*

Height 4 to 12 ft, erect, bushy. **BARK** is smooth, brown. **LEAVES** are 2 to 6 in. by 1 to 2 in., narrowly ovate, tapered at end, one main vein, rough above, smooth below, aromatic when crushed. **FLOWERS** are bright brownish red, petals fleshy, diameter 1.5 to 2.5 in., solitary at ends of branches; stamens many; April to August. **FRUIT** is 1 in. long, urnlike.

DISTRIBUTION: Foothill Belt of west slope at 600 to 3,500 ft along streams or moist canyon slopes.

REMARKS: The distinctive flowers, fruits, and aroma have resulted in various common names including wine-flower, strawberry-bush, and sweet-scented shrub.

Honeysuckles (Family Caprifoliaceae)

Leaves opposite; corolla five-lobed.

DOUBLE-FLOWERED HONEYSUCKLE   *Lonicera conjugialis*

Height 2 to 6 ft. **LEAVES** are .75 to 3 in. long, opposite, elliptic to round. **FLOWERS** grow in pairs, dark red, two-lipped (upper lip four-lobed, lower lip bent downward), ovaries fused; June to July. **FRUIT** is paired and fused berries, bright red and semitranslucent.

DISTRIBUTION: Mixed Conifer Belt to Subalpine Belt at 4,000 to 10,500 ft; moist woods and stream banks.

CHAPARRAL HONEYSUCKLE   *Lonicera interrupta*

Height 1 to 2 ft, rigid woody trunk, branches vine-like, climbing on other shrubs or sprawling over ground for many feet; young branches often smooth purplish. **LEAVES** are evergreen, .75 to 1 in. long, opposite, elliptic to roundish, upper pairs fused around stem, green above, whitish below. **FLOWERS** grow in spikes 2 to 5 in. long; corolla .5 in. long, yellow, tubular at base, upper lip four-lobed, lower lip one-lobed; May to July. **FRUIT** is a globular berry, diameter .25 in., red.

DISTRIBUTION: Foothill and Mixed Conifer Belts at 1,500 to 4,000 ft on dry slopes.

REMARKS: Five species of *Lonicera* occur in the Sierra Nevada; all have flowers in pairs with a swollen base to one side of each flower.

BLUE ELDERBERRY   *Sambucus mexicana*

Height 4 to 10 ft as shrub, occasionally as tree 25 to 30 ft; branches slender, semihollow and filled with spongy pith, brownish. **LEAVES** are deciduous, pinnately compound, 5 to 8 in. long; leaflets five to nine, usually narrowly oblong, 1 to 6 in. by .5 to 2 in. edges finely toothed, smooth to sparsely hairy. **FLOWERS** grow in flat-topped, compound clusters, 2 to 8 in. wide; individual flowers are small, white or cream; calyx minute or absent, five-lobed; corolla saucerlike, five-lobed; stamens five; April to September. **FRUIT** is a berry, diameter .25 in., blue to black with whitish bloom.

DISTRIBUTION: Many plant communities up to 10,000 ft; commonly on streamside slopes.

REMARKS: Bushes of blue elderberry become covered with masses of large white flower clusters as warm weather arrives. Later they bear quantities of small bluish berries that are relished by many kinds of birds. With some labor they yield excellent material to make pies, jellies, or wine. Red elderberry (*S. racemosa*) has dome-shaped clusters of blossoms and bright red berries that are unpalatable or even toxic to humans; it occurs in Upper Montane and Subalpine Belts at 6,000 to 11,000 ft.

SNOWBERRY   *Symphoricarpos albus* var. *laevigatus*

Height 2 to 6 ft; erect or spreading, branches slender. **BARK** is thin, light

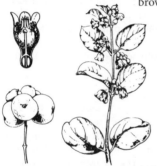

brown, later shreddy, gray or dark brown. **LEAVES** are deciduous, ovate to nearly round, .75 to 2 in. by .5 to 1.5 in., edge smooth or irregularly lobed, dull green, usually smooth. **FLOWERS** grow in short clusters, pink; calyx minute; corolla bell shaped, four- or five-lobed; stamens four to five, on corolla; May to June. **FRUIT** is a white globular berry, diameter .5 in.

DISTRIBUTION: Foothill Belt of west slope south to Tuolumne County; to 2,000 ft (occasionally to 4,000 ft) in shaded woods, on stream banks, or on north-facing slopes.

REMARKS: Other species of snowberry (*S. mollis, S. rotundifolius*) are low or sprawling shrubs with smaller leaves and whitish to pinkish flowers. They grow up to 10,000 ft, and on the east slope from Mono County to Lake Tahoe on drier sites (ridges and forest openings).

Dogwoods (Family Cornaceae)

Sepals four, minute; petals four; stamens four; ovary inferior. Flowers in dense umbel-like cluster sometimes surrounded by showy bracts.

AMERICAN DOGWOOD   *Cornus sericea*

Height 5 to 15 ft, branches smooth, red or purplish. **LEAVES** are deciduous, 2 to 4 in. long, ovate, rounded at base, tip pointed; four to seven pairs of distinct furrowed veins, lower surface with many two-branched hairs. **FLOWERS** grow in many round-topped clusters, diameter 1.5 to 2 in.; flowers small, petals .17 in. long, white, sometimes finely haired; May to July. **FRUIT** is spherical, flattened, diameter .25 in., white to blue.

DISTRIBUTION: Mainly in Mixed Conifer Belt of west slope at about 5,000 to 7,000 ft in moist places.

REMARKS: Streamsides and damp slopes at middle elevations often support small thickets of this reddish-stemmed dogwood (sometimes called red osier). The blackfruit dogwood (*C. sessilis*), with few yellowish flowers and larger oval and shiny fruits, occurs at 500 to 5,000 ft in the foothills from Calaveras County north, blooming in March and April.

Heaths (Family Ericaceae)

Petals joined and corolla bell or urn shaped (except *Ledum*).

Manzanitas (Genus *Arctostaphylos*)

Height generally 3 ft or more; branches crooked; many plants have dead woody stems with strips of red bark carrying nutrients up to still-living branches. **BARK** is red, smooth. **LEAVES** are evergreen, thickish, firm. **FLOWERS** grow in terminal clusters; calyx four- or five-parted, broad lobed; corolla urn shaped with four or five recurved lobes at small opening; stamens 10. **FRUIT** is usually a flattened sphere with nutlets enclosed in soft pulp.

REMARKS: Manzanita, with its irregular reddish branch system, is a common element of foothill chaparral and part of the mixed conifer forest; one ground-sprawling species grows at 6,000 to 10,000 ft. The many clusters of small, urn-shaped flowers are followed by large crops of reddish or brownish berries that are eaten by some birds and by foxes and bears; the seeds are relished by chipmunks. Of 57 species in California, about eight are in the Sierra. Hybrids sometimes occur where two species are present.

PINEMAT MANZANITA   *A. nevadensis*
Pl. 144

Height 6 to 18 in.; main stems on ground or rocks, rooting freely; bark smooth, reddish brown, peeling in thin pieces. **LEAVES** .75 to 1.5 in. by .25 to .75 in., elliptic, thick, leathery, patterned with dark veins, mostly shiny green above and below. **FLOWERS** are usually white, .25 in. long, in short racemes; May to July. **FRUIT** is globose, diameter .25 in., smooth, dark brown.

DISTRIBUTION: Upper Mixed Conifer and Upper Montane Belts at 6,000 to 10,000 ft from Tulare County north; often mixed with huckleberry oak in dense carpetlike mats on forest floor or sprawling over granite.

GREENLEAF MANZANITA
A. patula
Pl. 145

Height 3 to 7 ft; stems several, usually from swollen base; old bark smooth, reddish brown; branchlets with glistening golden gland-tipped hairs. **LEAVES** are 1 to 1.75 in. by .75 to 1.5 in. broadly ovate to roundish, smooth, bright shiny green. **FLOWERS** are pinkish, .25 in. long, in dense panicles; May to June. **FRUIT** is .25 to .5 in. in diameter, chestnut brown to blackish.

DISTRIBUTION: Mainly in Mixed Conifer Belt at 2,500 to 5,000 ft (north) or 5,000 to 9,000 ft (south); in open forest.

WHITELEAF MANZANITA
A. viscida
Height 4 to 12 ft; stems and branches crooked with smooth red bark, young branches slender, whitish, and sticky. **LEAVES** are ovate, 1 to 2 in. by .75 to 1.5 in., whitish, smooth on both surfaces. **FLOWERS** grow in open panicles or racemes with all parts sticky, rosy to white, .4 in. long; February to April. **FRUIT** is globular, diameter .25 in., light brown to deep red, often sticky surfaced.

DISTRIBUTION: Common in Foothill Belt south to Amador County; in chaparral and adjacent woodlands.

WHITE HEATHER
Cassiope mertensiana
Pl. 146

Stems to 12 in. high, erect, rigid. **LEAVES** are evergreen, .13 in. long, thick, boat shaped, narrow, in four rows pressed against stem. **FLOWERS** are drooping at top of erect flower stem, bell shaped, white to pink, .25 in. long, five-lobed; stamens 10 (or eight); July to August. **FRUIT** is a globular capsule.

DISTRIBUTION: Subalpine and Alpine Belts at 6,000 to 11,500 ft on rocky ridges and moist slopes.

REMARKS: Only mountain climbers in high country will find the cassiope, or white heather. Amid granite ledges, the perennial wiry stems and basal branches often form dense mats that are brightened by the small, bell-like flowers in late summer.

ALPINE LAUREL
Kalmia polifolia
Pl. 147

Height to 1.5 ft, spreading. **LEAVES** are evergreen, oblong, narrow, .25 to .75 in. long, edges rolled under, shiny green above, densely white haired below. **FLOWERS** are solitary in upper leaf axils; calyx deeply five-parted; corolla five-lobed, bowl shaped, diameter .5 to .75 in., bright pink to rose purple; stamens 10, short, in pouches on petals; June to August. **FRUIT** is a valved capsule.

DISTRIBUTION: West slope in Mixed Conifer Belt and above, from 5,000 to 12,000 ft; in wet places.

REMARKS: Borders of lakes or meadows and swampy places up to timberline are the home of the pale alpine laurel, a plant deadly for sheep and cattle. The stamens are held outward by the petals; when stamens or corolla are touched, the elastic filaments spring inward and pollen is shaken from the anthers.

WESTERN LABRADOR TEA   *Ledum glandulosum*
Pl. 148

Height 2 to 5 ft, erect, rather rigid. **LEAVES** are evergreen, crowded toward ends of branches, alternate, .75 to 2.5 in. by .5 to .75 in., oblong, edges often rolled under, dark green and smooth above, paler with gland-dotted felt below. **FLOWERS** are small, white, in crowded terminal clusters; flower diameter to .5 in.; sepals five; petals five, spreading; stamens 10, separate, longer than petals; June to August. **FRUIT** is a five-celled oval capsule, .17 in. long.

DISTRIBUTION: West slope to 10,000 ft; lake margins and damp places.

REMARKS: The leaves, elsewhere known as trapper's tea, give a pleasant odor when bruised. The plant is somewhat poisonous for livestock.

SIERRA LAUREL
Leucothoe davisiae

Height 2 to 5 ft, erect, branches mostly smooth; in small to extensive thickets. **LEAVES** are evergreen, alternate, .75 to 2.75 in. by .4 to .6 in., oblong or oval, thick, somewhat leathery, minutely toothed, shiny deep green above, duller and paler below. **FLOWERS** grow in erect racemes 2 to 4 in. long; flowers white, hanging; calyx star shaped; corolla bell shaped, .25 to .4 in. long, five-lobed; stamens 10; June to July. **FRUIT** is a spherical capsule, .25 in. long, smooth.

DISTRIBUTION: Sparse at 4,000 to 8,500 ft on moist ground; poisonous to livestock.

RED MOUNTAIN HEATHER   *Phyllodoce breweri*
Pl. 149

Stems 4 to 12 in. high, erect from branching base on ground. **LEAVES** are evergreen, alternate, crowded on stems, .25 to .5 in. long, needlelike because margins are tightly rolled under. **FLOWERS** grow in crowded terminal clusters; sepals five; corolla bell shaped, five-lobed, diameter to .5 in., rose purple, petals joined at base, tips spreading; stamens seven to 10 and style one, all protruding from corolla; June to August. **FRUIT** is a spherical capsule.

DISTRIBUTION: Subalpine and Alpine Belts at 6,500 to 12,000 ft from Tulare County north in swampy places.

REMARKS: Wet acid soils of the High Sierra are the home of our red heather, where it grows in irregular patches that may be small or large. Soon after the snow departs the small, upright, leaf-clothed stems bear clusters of little rose-purple flowers making carpets of bright color.

WESTERN AZALEA   *Rhododendron occidentale*
Pl. 150

Height 2 to 10 ft, loosely branched. **LEAVES** are deciduous, clustered at ends of twigs, elliptical, 1 to 4 in. by .5 to 1 in., thin, smooth or scatteringly haired. **FLOWERS** are clustered, large, showy; sepals five, small; petals five with ruffled edges, joined as bell-shaped corolla 1.25 to 1.75 in. long, white or pinkish, upper lobe with yellow splotch; stamens five, style one, all protruding well beyond corolla; May to July. **FRUIT** is a capsule, oblong, .38 to .75 in., hairy.

DISTRIBUTION: Mainly in Mixed Conifer Belt at 3,500 to 7,500 ft along streams and on moist slopes.

REMARKS: The handsome fragrant azalea is a showy shrub of late spring and early summer, found on damp sites in the forest. Often the blossoms lean out over a stream. The foliage is poisonous to livestock.

WESTERN BLUEBERRY   *Vaccinium uliginosum* subsp. *occidentale*

Height 1 to 2.5 ft; compact, stems smooth and stoutish, branchlets many, clustered, erect. **LEAVES** are deciduous, .38 to .75 in. by .13 to .38 in., elliptic to oval, tapered to base, light green and smooth above, whitened below. **FLOWERS** are solitary or two to four in cluster; calyx four- or five-lobed; corolla white, cylindric, four-lobed; June to July. **FRUIT** is an elliptic berry, .25 in. long, blue black with white bloom.

DISTRIBUTION: Mixed Conifer and Subalpine Belts at 5,000 to 10,000 ft in wet meadows or near streams.

REMARKS: Six species of *Vaccinium* occur in the Sierra Nevada providing an assortment of edible, and mostly tasty, berries. *Vaccinium* is the only member of the Heath family in California that has an inferior ovary.

Peas (Family Fabaceae)

Corolla irregular, butterfly-like: top petal (banner) shorter than two side (wing) petals, two lower (keel) petals longer; fruit a two-sided pod.

WESTERN REDBUD   *Cercis occidentalis*

Height 8 to 20 ft; many long stems clustered at base. **LEAVES** are alternate, simple, diameter 2 to 3.5 in., round, heart-shaped at base, smooth;

deciduous. **FLOWERS** grow in clusters appearing before leaves; calyx to .4 in. wide, bell shaped, five-lobed; petals five, red purple, .5 in. long, irregular; stamens 10; March to May. **FRUIT** is a pod 1.5 to 3 in. by .5 to .6 in., flat, maturing dull red.

DISTRIBUTION: Dry slopes and stream banks below 5,000 ft on west slope.

REMARKS: Redbud flowers appear in fluorescent magenta masses from late winter through spring, followed by leaves that are bronzy green and later glossy green. The clusters of reddish brown pods persist into the next winter. Root nodules contain nitrogen-fixing bacteria that contribute significant amounts of nitrogen to foothill ecosystems.

SCOTCH BROOM   *Cytisus scoparius*

Pl. 151

Height 3 to 10 ft; branches green, ribbed, broomlike. **LEAVES** are few, three-parted, leaflets to .17 in. long; evergreen. **FLOWERS** grow in terminal racemes from leaf axils; sepals five, forming two-lipped tube; corolla .75 in. long, bright yellow, butterfly like, petals five, broad; stamens 10; January to June. **FRUIT** is a pod 2 in. by .5 in., flat, hairy, black.

DISTRIBUTION: Naturalized in Foothill Belt.

REMARKS: Scotch broom is a fast-spreading weed in the Sierra foothills. The plant is a pest on forest and range lands as well as on roadsides and developed areas, where it often gains a foothold on disturbed soils and spreads quickly into adjacent habitats.

Oaks (Family Fagaceae)

Male flowers in catkins; female in groups of one to three; nut in scaly cup or spiny bur.

BUSH CHINQUAPIN   *Chrysolepis sempervirens*

Pl. 152

Height mostly under 5 ft, round topped, spreading. **BARK** is smooth, brown or

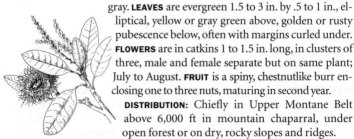

gray. **LEAVES** are evergreen 1.5 to 3 in. by .5 to 1 in., elliptical, yellow or gray green above, golden or rusty pubescence below, often with margins curled under. **FLOWERS** are in catkins 1 to 1.5 in. long, in clusters of three, male and female separate but on same plant; July to August. **FRUIT** is a spiny, chestnutlike burr enclosing one to three nuts, maturing in second year.

DISTRIBUTION: Chiefly in Upper Montane Belt above 6,000 ft in mountain chaparral, under open forest or on dry, rocky slopes and ridges.

REMARKS: Sprouts from burls following fires. Rodents and birds eat the sweet nuts.

SCRUB OAK   *Quercus berberidifolia*

Height 2 to 15 ft, branches rigid, tough. **LEAVES** are .75 to 1 in. long, stiff, shape various, oblong to elliptical, usually with spiny-tipped teeth, sometimes entire (lacking spines or lobes). **FRUIT** is an acorn .75 to 1.13 in. long, oval or cylindric, rounded or pointed, cup .5 in. by .75 in. or smaller, shallow or deep, scales are warty and set in spiral pattern.

DISTRIBUTION: Foothill Belt of west slope up to 5,000 ft, less common to north; often in chaparral and steep dry hillsides.

REMARKS: This small oak has the sturdy characteristics of its tree relatives expressed in shrub form so that it blends in with other members of the foothill chaparral. Sprouts from stumps after a fire and may grow so dense as to be virtually impenetrable and to exclude other plants.

HUCKLEBERRY OAK   *Quercus vaccinifolia*

Pl. 153

Height 2 to 4 ft, spreading or prostrate. **BARK** is smooth, grayish; branches slender, flexible, ending in broomlike tufts. **LEAVES** are .5 to 1.25 in. by .4 to

.6 in., elliptical and blunt tipped or narrower and pointed, sometimes spiny edged; gray green above, paler below. **FLOWERS** grow in catkins; May to July. **FRUIT** is an acorn .5 in. by .25 in., cup thin, shallow, with thin hairy scales; maturing in second fall.

DISTRIBUTION: Mainly in Upper Montane Belt but occurs from 3,000 to 10,000 ft; mostly on west slope south to Fresno County, but on east side of some passes and about Lake Tahoe; on dry ridges and rocky slopes.

REMARKS: The bushy huckleberry oak is the only oak of higher elevations, where it is part of a mountain chaparral community that includes greenleaf and pinemat manzanita, mountain whitethorn, and bush chinquapin. In some areas this oak plays an important role in stabilizing steep, erosion-prone slopes. Its little acorns are relished by chipmunks, squirrels, and other rodents.

Silk Tassel (Family Garryaceae)

Branchlets four-sided.

SILK TASSEL   *Garrya fremontii*

Height 4 to 10 ft, branches erect, usually yellowish green. **LEAVES** are evergreen, opposite, elliptical, tapered at ends, 1.25 to 2.5 in. long, usually thick and leathery, smooth and shiny above, grayish below. **FLOWERS** have male and female parts on separate plants, on hanging, tassel-like catkins with no petals and boat-shaped bracts; male catkins 3 to 8 in. long, in clusters of two to five, flowers yellowish, sepals four, stamens four; female catkins 1.5 to 2 in. long (to 3.5 in. with fruit), sepals two or absent; single pistil with two styles that extend beyond fused bracts; January to April. **FRUIT** is berrylike with two hard seeds, later dry on outside, diameter .25 in., buff to black.

DISTRIBUTION: Foothill and Mixed Conifer Belts at 2,000 to 7,000 ft on dry, rocky slopes.

REMARKS: Silk tassel is a tough-leaved member of the chaparral in the foothills or lower forest. The bark, leaves, and fruit contain a bitter alkaloid (garryine) sometimes used as a tonic, so that some related species are called "quinine bush." Four species in the Sierra Nevada differ mainly in the characteristics of hairs on their leaves.

Gooseberries (Family Grossulariaceae)

Sepals, petals, and stamens each in fives.

Currants and Gooseberries (Genus *Ribes*)

Height 1 to 6 ft, stems often sparingly branched, smooth or with prickles. **LEAVES** are alternate, palmately lobed. **FLOWERS** are red and white, in racemes or single, the parts in fives; petals inserted on throat of calyx, alternating with stamens; styles two. **FRUIT** is a berry, red or yellow.

DISTRIBUTION: Foothill Belt to Subalpine Belt at 3,000 to 12,000 ft in canyons or on mountain slopes.

REMARKS: Gooseberry stems bear spines, the flowers are one or few in a group, and the berries are spiny or smooth. Currants have unarmed stems, few or many flowers in a raceme, and smooth berries. The Sierra has eight species of gooseberries and five species of currants. At one time, forest employees destroyed many of the plants because they are intermediate hosts for white pine blister rust, a disease that affects five-needled pines such as sugar pine. At higher elevations, these plants sometimes produce heavy fruit crops in late summer that attract squirrels, birds, and people.

WAX CURRANT　　　　　　　　　　　　　　　　　*R. cereum*

Pl. 154

Height 3 to 8 ft; branches erect; no spines. **LEAVES** grow to 1.5 in., round, shallowly lobed, strong spicy odor. **FLOWERS** grow in clusters of three to seven; tubular shape; white to pink; June to July. **FRUIT** is bright red.

DISTRIBUTION: Dry open habitats from 5,000 to 13,000 ft.

ALPINE GOOSEBERRY
Pl. 155   *R. montigenum*

Height to 2 ft; low spreading form, sometimes prostrate at higher elevations, one to five spines at each branch node. **LEAVES** grow to 1 in. long, deeply lobed with serrated margins, hairy and sticky, glandular. **FLOWERS** are saucer shaped in clusters of three to seven; sepals .13 in. greenish white; petals less than .06 in. long, red; June to August. **FRUIT** orange red with glandular bristles; sweet and edible.

DISTRIBUTION: Subalpine and Alpine Belts, 7,000 to 14,000 ft, in forest openings or rocky slopes.

SIERRA CURRANT
Pl. 156   *R. nevadense*

Height 3 to 6 ft; erect to somewhat spreading; no spines. **LEAVES** grow to 3 in., thin, three- to five-lobed. **FLOWERS** grow in dense clusters of eight to 20; tubular with pinkish, erect sepals and scarcely visible white petals; April to July. **FRUIT** is dull blackish blue; edible.

DISTRIBUTION: Open forests 3,000 to 8,000 ft.

SIERRA GOOSEBERRY
Pl. 157   *R. roezlii*

Height 1 to 3 ft; long spreading branches, short rigid twigs; one to three spines per node. **LEAVES** grow to 1 in., three- to five-lobed with toothed margin. **FLOWERS** are single or few together, hanging; distinctive shape, red purple sepals curled back to reveal pinkish white petals arranged in erect tube; April to June. **FRUIT** is red and armed in stout prickles; edible.

DISTRIBUTION: Open forests 3,000 to 8,000 ft.

Waterleaf (Family Hydrophyllaceae)

Stamens five, inserted near base of corolla, alternating with corolla lobes.

YERBA SANTA   *Eriodictyon californicum*

Height 2 to 8 ft, erect, open, branchlets and leaves usually sticky. **LEAVES** are 2 to 4+ in. by .4 to 2 in., lance shaped, margins rolled under, edge toothed, leathery, brownish green, smooth, shiny and sticky above, lower surface with fine felt between veins. **FLOWERS** grow in terminal compound clusters; sepals five, nearly separate; corolla funnel-like, petals five, .38 to .63 in. long, lavender or pale blue (rarely whitish); stamens five, on corolla tube; May to July. **FRUIT** is a capsule, four-valved.

DISTRIBUTION: Foothill Belt up to 6,000 ft in dry open chaparral and on roadsides.

REMARKS: Leaves of yerba santa give a pleasant aromatic odor when crushed. They have been brewed into a syrupy remedy for colds and also dried and used as a miner's tobacco.

Lily (Family Liliaceae)

Leaves parallel veined.

SPANISH BAYONET   *Yucca whipplei*

Pl. 158

Plant with very dense rosette of leaves at base. **LEAVES** are gray green, 12 to 21 in. by .75 in., daggerlike, rigid, narrow, sharp tipped, margins toothed. **FLOWERS** grow in dense panicle 3 to 6 ft long on stalk 8 to 21 ft high; flowers 1 to 2 in. long, hanging, creamy white, fragrant; sepals and petals, three each, fleshy; stamens six; April to May. **FRUIT** is a capsule to 2 in. long, cylindrical.

DISTRIBUTION: Walker Pass and north to Kings River on foothills of west slope; east slope of southern Sierra.

REMARKS: Spikes of this yucca stand conspicuously in the drab southern brushlands. The waxy, fleshy flowers open at night and are pollinated by a small moth (*Pronuba*) that carries pollen from flower to flower; the moth's eggs are laid in the blossoms. After producing flowers and seeds the yucca dies. New plants grow from rooted basal shoots or seeds. Birds eat the fleshy fruit covering, and rodents take the seeds.

Poppy (Family Papaveraceae)

Sepals two, shed at flowering; stamens many; pistil one.

BUSH POPPY

Dendromecon rigida

Height 2 to 8 ft, stiff whitish stems, freely branched. **BARK** is shreddy, yellow gray to white. **LEAVES** are evergreen, 1 to 4 in. by .25 to 1 in., broadly lance-like, leathery, gray or yellow green. **FLOWERS** are solitary on 1 to 3 in. peduncles, showy, large golden yellow petals .75 to 1.25 in. long; April to July. **FRUIT** is a slender capsule, 2 to 4 in. long.

DISTRIBUTION: Foothill Belt of west slope below 6,000 ft, in chaparral or on dry ridges.

Mock Orange (Family Philadelphaceae)

Sepals and petals four to five each, fragrant; stamens many.

WILD MOCK ORANGE *Philadelphus lewisii*
Pl. 159
Height 4 to 10 ft, loosely branched. **BARK** is smooth, reddish on young shoots, gray on older stems. **LEAVES** 1.25 to 3.25 in. by .75 to 1.5 in., ovate, three- to five-veined from base. **FLOWERS** .75 to 1 in. diameter, white, in conspicuous racemes; stamens 20 to 40; May to July. **FRUIT** is a capsule, .4 in. long.
DISTRIBUTION: Sparse in Foothill and Mixed Conifer Belts of west slope at 800 to 4,500 ft south to Tulare County; on slopes, canyons, or forest openings.
REMARKS: Native Americans used the slender shoots to make shafts for arrows.

Buttercup (Family Ranunculaceae)

Leaves opposite, compound; achenes many, feathery.

VIRGIN'S BOWER *Clematis ligusticifolia*
Pl. 160
A woody vine climbing bushes or trees to 40 ft. **BARK** of old stems is stringy, gray. **LEAVES** are compound, leaflets five to seven, 1 to 3 in. long, rounded at base, tapered at tip, bluntly toothed; petioles long, twining around twigs like tendrils. **FLOWERS** are many, in panicles, long stalked, flowers .5 to .75 in. diameter, sepals four, greenish white; no petals; stamens 25 to 40, in clusters; March to August. **FRUIT** are in groups of achenes, each achene with a 1 to 2 in. feathery tail.
DISTRIBUTION: Foothill and Mixed Conifer Belts up to 4,000 ft; in moist canyons.
REMARKS: Climbing on shrubs and trees, this bushy vine has showy white flower masses in spring, followed by displays of the hairy fruits from May to August. Spanish Californians made an infusion of the herbage to treat cuts on horses.

Buckthorns (Family Rhamnaceae)

Flowers small; calyx tube lined with a flattish, central disk.

Ceanothus (Genus *Ceanothus*)

LEAVES are simple, petioled, opposite or alternate, deciduous or evergreen, often three-veined from base. **FLOWERS** are small, in clusters, showy, white or blue; sepals five, united at base to ovary; petals five, stalked, scoop shaped; stamens five, opposite petals. **FRUIT** is a three-lobed capsule.

REMARKS: From the foothills into subalpine areas there are many types of ceanothus; 14 of 43 species in California occur in the Sierra. Mostly they are shrubs but some form spreading ground mats. Some are common and widespread, often in chaparral; others are local or scarce. The group has no common name; "buck brush" and "deer brush" refer to frequent browsing on leaves and stems by deer. The bushes give shelter and nest sites for birds, and the seeds are eaten by rodents and birds. In spring and early summer the masses of white or blue flowers add much to local floral displays.

SNOW BRUSH or MOUNTAIN WHITETHORN   *C. cordulatus*
Pl. 161

Height 2 to 5 ft, diameter 3 to 9 ft, round topped, flattish (where depressed by snow); branchlets many, spiny, whitish. **LEAVES** are alternate, small, .25 to 1 in. by .25 to .5 in., ovate, light green above, whitish below. **FLOWERS** grow in clusters to 1.5 in. long, white, strongly scented; May to July.

DISTRIBUTION: Abundant in open forests at 3,000 to 9,500 ft on both slopes.

BUCK BRUSH   *C. cuneatus*

Height 3 to 8+ ft; bark gray; branches dense, rigid, diverging, irregular. **LEAVES** are opposite, wedge shaped, wider at tip, .25 to 1 in. by .25 in., one-veined. **FLOWERS** grow in small clusters, white (rarely blue), sweet odored; March to May.

DISTRIBUTION: Foothill Belt at 300 to 6,000 ft on dry slopes.

FRESNO MAT   *C. fresnensis*

Nearly prostrate, in mats 6 to 10 ft wide; few branches erect to 12 in.; twigs round. **LEAVES** grow to .5 in. long, opposite, elliptical, margin entire or finely toothed at end, leathery, dark green. **FLOWERS** grow in small umbels, blue; May to June.

DISTRIBUTION: Mixed Conifer Belt at 3,000 to 7,000 ft; Plumas County to Fresno County.

DEER BRUSH   *C. integerrimus*

Height 3 to 12 ft; bark green to yellow; branches loose, some drooping. **LEAVES** are deciduous, large, .75 to 2 in. by .4 to 1.5 in., thin, elliptic, light green. **FLOWERS** grow in long, cylindrical clusters, 2.5 to 6 in. by 1 to 4 in., white (occasionally blue), showy and fragrant; May to July.

DISTRIBUTION: Abundant in Foothill and Mixed Conifer Belts at 500 to 7,000 ft in many habitats on dry slopes and ridges.

MAHALA MAT   *C. prostratus*

Height 2 to 6 in. high, in prostrate mats 2 to 8 ft wide; branches many, often rooting at nodes; twigs angled. **LEAVES** are .25 to 1 in. by .1 to .6 in., opposite, wedge shaped, thick, firm, dark green, margin three- to nine-toothed. **FLOWERS** grow in clusters, small, blue (pinkish with age); April to May. **DISTRIBUTION:** Mixed Conifer Belt at 3,000 to 6,500 ft on forest floor, road edges, etc., south to Calaveras County.

TOBACCO BRUSH   *C. velutinus*
Pl. 162

Height 2 to 5+ ft, spreading, round topped; branchlets brownish. **LEAVES** are large, 1.5 to 2.5 in. by .75 to 1.25 in., rounded to elliptical, edge finely toothed, varnished dark green above, pale below, with strong cinnamon odor. **FLOWERS** grow in clusters 2 to 4 in. long, white; May to August. **DISTRIBUTION:** Mainly in Upper Montane Belt and edges of adjacent areas, but occurs from 3,500 to 10,000 ft on both slopes.

HOLLY-LEAF REDBERRY   *Rhamnus ilicifolia*
Pl. 163

Height 4 to 12 ft; stout shrub, or treelike; branchlets many, rigid, short; terminal bud covered by scales. **LEAVES** are .75 to 1.5 in. by .5 to 1 in., ovate to roundish, one-veined from base, margins spiny (like tiny holly leaves), smooth and dark green above; evergreen. **FLOWERS** are minute, greenish, rarely with petals one to six, growing from leaf axils; February to June. **FRUIT** grows to .33 in. long, oval, bright red.

DISTRIBUTION: Foothill Belt of west slope south to Tulare County; below 6,000 ft on dry slopes.

REMARKS: Hoary Coffeeberry (*R. tomentella*) is also widespread on dry slopes but is recognized by its larger (1 to 3 in. long), white- or silvery-haired leaves that lack spiny margins.

SIERRA COFFEEBERRY   *Rhamnus rubra*
Pl. 164

Height 2 to 6 ft; erect; branchlets slender, deep reddish or bright gray; terminal bud not covered by scales. **LEAVES** are .5 to 1.5 in., narrowly oblong, minutely toothed, tip usually pointed, gray or green; semideciduous. **FLOWERS** grow in short umbels in leaf axils, petals small, inconspicuous, greenish; flower parts in fives; May to August. **FRUIT** is a globular berry, diameter .25 in., green, becoming reddish then black, with two seeds.

DISTRIBUTION: Common on both slopes, mainly in Mixed Conifer Belt, at 3,000 to 7,000 ft.

REMARKS: Coffeeberry has puckery-tasting bark with purgative qualities like its relative cascara (*R. purshiana*), which occurs from El Dorado County north and has 2- to 8-in.-long leaves.

Roses (Family Rosaceae)

Stamens 10 to many, inserted with petals on calyx or on edge of disk lining calyx tube; leaves alternate.

CHAMISE
Adenostoma fasciculatum

Pl. 165

Height 2 to 12 ft; diffusely branched, stems straight. Bark is shreddy, reddish or grayish brown. **LEAVES** are tiny and needlelike, in evergreen bundles clothing stems. **FLOWERS** are a terminal panicle, dense, 1.5 to 4 in. long; flowers minute; sepals five, united around receptacle; petals five, white; stamens 10 to 15; pistil one; February to July. **FRUIT** is an achene in hardened receptacle.

DISTRIBUTION: Foothill Belt of west slope, 500 to 5,000 ft, in chaparral.

REMARKS: Often in nearly pure stands, this "greasewood" is in some areas a common chaparral plant from the lower foothills up to the Mixed Conifer Belt. The thickets sometimes are almost impenetrable for humans or pack animals but afford favorable shelter for many small native creatures. After a fire these plants sprout abundantly from stumps.

WESTERN SERVICEBERRY
Amelanchier alnifolia

Height 3 to 25 ft; erect. **BARK** is gray, but younger twigs are reddish brown. **LEAVES** are deciduous, bluish green, .75 to 1.75 in. by .5 to 1 in., oval or roundish, one-veined from base, margin entire at base but toothed on outer half. **FLOWERS** are in racemes 1 to 2 in. long; sepals five, joined at base, free ends persisting on fruit; petals five, slender, .5 to .75 in. long, white, falling early; stamens many; pistil one; May to June. **FRUIT** is berrylike, .25 in. diameter, spherical, purplish, pulpy, edible.

DISTRIBUTION: Foothill to Upper Montane Belt at 2,500 to 9,000 ft in many habitats from dry rocky slopes to moist shaded forests.

REMARKS: Serviceberry often grows in large thickets that become white with blossoms. The leaves vary in shape, toothing of margins, and amount of woolly covering. Native Americans and early settlers ate the berries, which are sweetish but not very tasty.

BIRCH-LEAF MOUNTAIN MAHOGANY
Cercocarpus betuloides

Pl. 166

Height 5 to 12 ft as shrub or 25 ft as tree; branches spreading; branchlets short, spurlike, leaves clustered near tip. **BARK** is smooth gray or brown. **LEAVES** are evergreen .5 to 1 in. by .4 to 1 in., elliptic, tapered toward base, finely toothed toward tip, above dark, below pale to whitish, woolly. **FLOWERS** are two or three in cluster; calyx base a slender tube, outer ends spread, five-toothed, whitish, .25 in. wide; no petals; stamens 15+; pistil one; March to April. **FRUIT** is a hard achene with feathery twisted plume 2.5 to 3 in. long in reddish calyx tube.

DISTRIBUTION: West slope mostly below 8,000 ft; mostly in chaparral; very rare on east slope.

REMARKS: Birch-leaf mountain mahogany is a common browse plant of deer and livestock. The alternate name mountain ironwood refers to its beautiful, hard wood. Dense stands appear gray when the bushes are clothed with the feathery-plumed achenes. The curl-leaf mountain mahogany (*C. ledifolius*) on the east slope has slender untoothed leaves with curled edges and a prominent midrib. It grows as a shrub or a tree with a spreading crown, contorted branches, and sometimes a large rough-barked trunk.

KITKITDIZZE   *Chamaebatia foliolosa*

Height 12 to 24 in.; low, much-branched. **BARK** is smooth, gray brown; foliage is evergreen, heavily resin scented. **LEAVES** are sticky and hairy, pinnately divided three or more times creating a fernlike appearance. **FLOWERS** grow to 1.5 in. wide in loose clusters; sepals five, slender; petals five, broad, white; stamens many, in rows; May to July. **FRUIT** is an achene in a persistent calyx.

DISTRIBUTION: Common on west slope, Kern County to Sierra County, in Mixed Conifer Belt and lower edge of Upper Montane Belt; often in extensive uniform carpets under pine forest.

REMARKS: Old-timers walking through dense, fernlike fields of this sticky plant called it mountain misery or tarweed. On warm days the resinous leaves and stems are fragrant. The name, kitkitdizze, is that given to it by the Miwok Indians, who steeped the leaves in hot water and drank the infusion as a cure for various diseases.

TOYON   *Heteromeles arbutifolia*
Pl. 167

Height 5 to 15 ft; erect, bushy, young branches woolly. **LEAVES** are evergreen, 2 to 4 in. by .75 to 1.5 in., elliptical, narrowed at ends, leathery, toothed, shiny dark green above, paler below. **FLOWERS** grow in dense terminal panicle 2 to 3 in. high; sepals five, joined at base, persistent; petals five, distinct, spreading, white; stamens 10, in pairs opposite sepals; pistils two to three; June to July. **FRUIT** grows to .33 in. long, ovoid, berrylike, bright red.

DISTRIBUTION: Mainly in Foothill Belt of west slope up to 3,500 ft on rocky slopes or in canyon bottoms.

REMARKS: From November to January the clusters of bright red "Christmas berries" contrast with the dark green foliage to make toyon a most handsome shrub. It is planted commonly in home gardens and city parks. The berries are highly sought after by robins, waxwings, and other birds as food in winter.

OCEANSPRAY
Holodiscus discolor

Pl. 168

Height 3 to 18 ft; erect or spreading, intricately branched, stems hairy. **BARK** is brown to ashy, shreddy on older shoots. **LEAVES** grow to 3 in. long, simple, deciduous, ovate, ends coarsely toothed. **FLOWERS** many in oblong panicle 4 to 10 in. long, creamy white to pinkish; petals five, rounded; pistils five, distinct; June to August. **FRUIT** is a pod, one-seeded, to .13 in. long.

DISTRIBUTION: Forest edges and mountain chaparral up to 6,000 ft.

REMARKS: Oceanspray plants may be short or tall, with few or many flowers, depending on soil conditions and elevation. The similar cliffspray (*H. microphyllus*) grows on rocky outcrops at 6,000 to 13,000 ft and is recognized by its smaller leaves (under .75 in.) and flower clusters that are less than 3 in. long. The characteristics of these two species blend in some areas as the result of hybridization, but they are always notable for the fragrant smell of their crushed leaves.

BITTER CHERRY
Prunus emarginata

Pl. 169

Height 4 to 12 ft (rarely, a tree to 20+ ft); branches slender, very long. **BARK** is gray or reddish. **LEAVES** are deciduous, .75 to 2 in. by .4 to 1 in., elliptic to obovate, rounded at tip, edge finely toothed, one or two small glands near base, smooth and dark green above. **FLOWERS** are 3 to 10 in flat-topped cluster; flower .5 in. wide; sepals five, united at base; petals five, white, roundish; stamens 15 to 30; pistil one; April to July. **FRUIT** is .33 in. long, bright red, with stony pit, pulp very bitter.

DISTRIBUTION: Upper Mixed Conifer and Upper Montane Belts at 4,000 to 8,500 ft; in open forests and montane chaparral, often in large dense thickets.

REMARKS: In summer many stream banks, moist slopes, and roadsides at middle elevations have an almondlike fragrance from this cherry. Later the little fruits, too bitter for humans, are eaten by several kinds of birds. Five species of *Prunus* occur in the Sierra. Western chokecherry (*P. virginiana* var. *demissa*) is a showy shrub with many white flowers in 5-in.-long cylindrical racemes. Sierra plum (*P. subcordata*) has stiff, thorny branches; rounded leaves; and one to seven flowers in an umbel-like cluster.

BITTERBRUSH
Purshia tridentata

Pl. 170

Height 1.5 to 6 ft, diffusely branched. **BARK** is brown or gray, young twigs woolly, glandular. **LEAVES** are mostly deciduous, in bundles, .25 to .5 in. long, wedge shaped, tip three-lobed, margins with fine glands, strongly rolled under, woolly green above, white below. **FLOWERS** .67 in. wide, usually single; calyx tube with resin granules; petals five, to .33 in. long, spoon shaped, creamy yellow; stamens 18 to 30; pistil one; April to July. **FRUIT** is a hairy, featherlike achene joined to persistent style.

DISTRIBUTION: Common on east slope at 4,000 to 7,000 ft on arid flats and slopes (some high on west slope).

REMARKS: Bitterbrush or antelope brush is a silvery-barked shrub bright with small yellow flowers when blooming. On the dry eastern side of the Sierra this shrub—rich in carbohydrates, proteins, and fats—is useful as browse for deer and livestock in a region dominated by unpalatable sagebrush. Dried flower parts contain germination inhibitors to prevent seedlings from establishing around the parent plants. Rodents that collect bitterbrush seeds strip off these flower parts and plant the seeds in small caches then return in spring to eat the young seedlings.

INTERIOR ROSE   *Rosa woodsii* var. *ultramontana*

Pl. 171

Height 2 to 10 ft; erect, stout, diffusely branched; thicket-forming stems gray to red brown with slender, straight prickles, young shoots bristly. **LEAVES** are pinnate, of five to seven leaflets .5 to 1.5 in. long, oval, toothed. **FLOWERS** grow in clusters of one to five, rose to light pink; sepals with long, slender tips, persisting on fruit; petals five, stamens and pistils many; receptacle globular, ripening into hard fruit; May to June. **FRUIT** is a red, rounded, and hardened floral tube, enclosing several achenes.

DISTRIBUTION: Common on east slope up to 10,000 ft; on moist slopes or stream banks.

REMARKS: Wild roses of about six species occur scatteringly or in thickets in many damp situations, such as open meadows or along shaded watercourses. The flowers are abundant and fragrant. The small, hard fruits (commonly known as rosehips) are food for some birds and mammals, and they are a natural source of vitamin C.

BLACKCAP RASPBERRY   *Rubus leucodermis*

Height 3 to 6 ft; stems and petioles with recurved spines; stems have white waxy bloom. **LEAVES** are of three to seven ovate leaflets, double-toothed margin; green, slightly hairy above, white, woolly below. **FLOWERS** are few, at ends of short branches from previous year, in clusters, diameter .5 in., white; calyx five-parted; sepals .25 in., hairy; petals five, shorter; April to July. **FRUIT** is a purple to blackish berry, .5 in. in diameter.

DISTRIBUTION: Foothill and Mixed Conifer Belts at 2,500 to 7,000 ft in canyon bottoms or on moist slopes.

REMARKS: Wild raspberry thickets are local in occurrence. The tasty berries often are eaten by birds as soon as they are ripe.

THIMBLEBERRY   *Rubus parviflorus*

Height 3 to 6 ft, erect, stems not spiny. **BARK** is gray, peeling in long strips. **LEAVES** 2 to 7 in. long and wide, simple, deciduous, five-lobed, irregularly toothed; sparingly haired above, soft, woolly below; petioles 1 to 2 in. **FLOWERS** grow in a terminal cluster of four to seven, diameter 1 to 2 in.; petals five, white, .75 in. long; numerous yellow pistils and stamens; April to August. **FRUIT** is a red berry .5 to .75 in. wide.

DISTRIBUTION: Mixed Conifer to Upper Montane Belt at 3,000 to 8,000 ft along streams in moist shade.

REMARKS: The large, thin-pulped berries are edible and often eaten by birds. Thimbleberry grows as a smaller plant at higher elevations because taller stems break under heavy snows.

CALIFORNIA BLACKBERRY   *Rubus ursinus*

Usually trailing or climbing, some stems to 20 ft long; stems slender and round with straight slender spines. **LEAVES** are evergreen, 3 to 6 in. long, lobed or pinnately divided into three or five leaflets to 3 in. long, oblong to triangular, doubly toothed, midribs and veins prickly. **FLOWERS** are .75 to 1.25 in. broad, usually in clusters; petals five, white; January to May. **FRUIT** is a black, sweet berry to .5 in. long.

DISTRIBUTION: From Central Valley into Mixed Conifer Belt along streams and on moist ground.

REMARKS: A century and more of settlement in the foothills of the Sierra has resulted in abandoned cultivated berry vines as well as those of native blackberries. Fencerows and hedges sometimes are overrun by thickets that afford both food and spiny "briar patch" protection for various birds and mammals. The introduced Himalayan blackberry (*R. discolor*) is now common and widespread in moist or disturbed areas below 5,000 ft. This invasive weed is recognized by its stout, ribbed stems and curving wide-based spines.

MOUNTAIN ASH   *Sorbus californica*

Pl. 172

Height 2 to 9 ft; erect, many-branched. **BARK** is smooth, dull red. **LEAVES** are deciduous, pinnate with seven to nine leaflets, each 1 to 1.5 in. by .5 to 1 in., elliptic, finely toothed. **FLOWERS** in flat-topped clusters, diameter 2 to 3 in., flower diameter .5 in., white; sepals five; petals five; stamens about 20; styles two to five; June to August. **FRUIT** grows to .33 in. diameter, berrylike, scarlet, pulp bitter.

DISTRIBUTION: Mixed Conifer to Subalpine Belt at 5,000 to 11,000 ft, along streams and on moist slopes or flats.

REMARKS: The mountain ash is a showy component of mountain streamsides. In late summer or fall the large clusters of brilliant red berries contrast strikingly with the greenery of other plants.

MOUNTAIN SPIRAEA
Pl. 173   *Spiraea densiflora*

Height to 3 ft; stems slender, in dense clumps. **BARK** is gray or reddish. **LEAVES** are .5 to 1.5 in. by .25 to .75 in., ovate to elliptic, outer part unequally toothed. **FLOWERS** are at top of stem in flat-topped cluster, diameter .5 to 1.5 in., pink or rose; flower diameter .13 in., calyx five-lobed; sepals erect; petals five, rounded; July to August. **FRUIT** is a five-chambered pod, several seeded.

DISTRIBUTION: From Mixed Conifer to Subalpine Belt at 5,000 to 10,000 ft in rocky moist soil, forest edges and moist meadows.

Madder (Family Rubiaceae)

Leaves opposite; blossom heads spherical; corolla four-cleft.

CALIFORNIA BUTTON WILLOW
Pl. 174   *Cephalanthus occidentalis* var. *californicus*

Height 3 to 12+ ft; young branches commonly in threes, smooth and green, yellow, or reddish. **BARK** when older is gray or brown and furrowed. **LEAVES** are deciduous, simple, opposite, or in whorls of three (to five), 3 to 8 in. by .75 to 1.5 in., ovate or elliptic, often wavy edged, glossy pale green. **FLOWERS** in spherical heads, diameter .5 to 1.5 in., each of many small flowers; sepals four, forming 13-in. green tube; corolla white, funnel shaped, 1.25 in. long; stamens four; July to September. **FRUIT** is hard, wedge shaped, two to four nutlets, .25 in. long.

DISTRIBUTION: Central Valley and into the Foothill Belt up to 3,300 ft; along flowing streams.

Figwort (Family Scrophulariaceae)

Calyx five-cleft; stamens four, inserted on two-lipped corolla.

BUSH MONKEYFLOWER   *Mimulus aurantiacus*

Height 9 in. to four ft; erect or spreading, branchlets often sticky and downy haired. **LEAVES** are evergreen, opposite, 1 to 3 in. by .19 to .6 in. wide, narrowly oval or linear, edge rolled under, yellowish to dark green and sticky above, paler and woolly below. **FLOWERS** are many, yellow, cream, or salmon colored; calyx tubular, five-angled, .75 to 1.25 in. long; corolla 1.5 in. or longer, lower part funnel shaped, outer portion spread as two upper and three lower lobes; stamens four, inserted on corolla; April to August. **FRUIT** is a capsule .5 to .75 in. long.

DISTRIBUTION: Common, mainly in Foothill Belt, on dry rocky slopes.

REMARKS: These plants are often found along roadside cuts, providing colorful displays for passersby. Many regional forms have at times been split into distinct species.

Cacao (Family Sterculiaceae)

Stamens five, united into a tube at base.

FREMONTIA
Fremontodendron californicum

Pl. 175

Height 6 to 15 ft, a loosely branched shrub (or small tree to 30 ft); branchlets long, flexible, tough, with many short, hairy spurs on leaves or flowers. **LEAVES** are evergreen, ovate, entire or three-lobed, .25 to 1.5 in. long, thick, rough dark green above, with dense gray or whitish felt below. **FLOWERS** are single, showy; calyx lemon yellow, diameter 1.5 to 2 in., of five rounded petal-like sepals united at base; no petals; style one, slender; May to June. **FRUIT** is a capsule, ovoid, densely hairy, .75 to 1.13 in. long, persistent.

DISTRIBUTION: Foothill Belt of west slope, at 1,500 to 5,300 ft, abundant south of Mariposa County; in chaparral and woodlands, and on rocky slopes.

REMARKS: Fremontia, also called flannelbush because of its hairy covering, is a showy shrub with many conspicuous large, yellow blossoms. It has been brought into cultivation for gardens.

Grape (Family Vitaceae)

Woody vines climbing by tendrils.

CALIFORNIA WILD GRAPE
Vitis californica

Pl. 176

Stems 5 to 50 ft long, climbing by tendrils. **LEAVES** are 1.5 to 5 in. wide, alternate, roundish to shallowly three-lobed, base heart shaped, edge toothed, surfaces woolly; tendrils opposite leaves, branched, twisted. **FLOWERS** are five-parted, many, small, in branched clusters, greenish, fragrant; May to July. **FRUIT** is a juicy berry, diameter .25 to .5 in., purplish, covered with white bloom.

DISTRIBUTION: Central Valley and Foothill Belt to 3,000 ft; on trees near streams.

REMARKS: Wild grape climbs most often on oaks and cottonwoods. Sometimes its foliage blankets and kills the tree by exclusion of sunlight. The sweet-smelling blossoms attract many bees. The berries are edible but have large seeds.

TREES

A TREE IS A perennial plant usually with a single woody trunk. Most mature trees are 15 ft or higher, although the Utah juniper varies from a 20-ft tree to a 2-ft many-stemmed shrub, depending on local conditions. Unlike the eastern states with their broadleaved deciduous forests, the Sierra is covered largely by evergreen conifers; 23 of 47 tree species in this handbook are conifers, compared with 25 of 239 species occurring in the southeastern United States.

Trees are the dominant plants over most of the Sierra. They make their own habitat by adding organic matter to the soil and by creating shade and moisture conditions that favor particular associations of plants and animals. One of the most fascinating associations is between the roots of trees and underground mycorrhizal fungi. In exchange for photosynthetic byproducts—mainly sugars and amino acids—tapped from the tree roots, fungi provide water and minerals to the trees. In addition, mycorrhizal fungi form an underground web of fungal threads that facilitate the transfer of food, minerals, and defense compounds between trees. The health of an entire stand can thus depend on this remarkable symbiosis.

Only native trees are included in this handbook. Ornamental trees have been planted around Sierra settlements, but only one, the "Tree of Heaven" (*Ailanthus altissima*), introduced by Chinese settlers in the Mother Lode, has become naturalized. The tree is deciduous, often shrublike, with light green compound leaves having a disagreeable odor.

A fairly reliable estimate of the age of a tree can be obtained by counting growth rings in wood near its base—on the stump of a felled tree or by extracting a small cylinder from a living tree. Huge ponderosa or sugar pines may be 500 to 600 years old, and giant sequoias 900 to 2,100 years old. Only bristlecone pines (*Pinus longaeva*) on ranges east of Owens Valley are older. The largest (oldest) trees are mostly in national or state parks. Throughout this section, height and diameter measurements that are given in parentheses represent record sizes above the normal range indicated.

A *forest* is a dense stand of trees, with or without shrubs below. In some forests the crowns make an overlapping canopy that largely excludes sunlight from the ground underneath. Many Sierra forests are more open than those of humid regions, although some stands of red fir or lodgepole pine are closed and dark underneath. By contrast, the lower flanks of the Sierra support more open woodlands—trees in moderate numbers interspersed with shrubs and grass as in the oak-pine woodland of the western foothills and the pinyon or juniper woodlands on the east side. An ancient, mature forest may persist for millennia unless destroyed by fire, disease, or human activities.

There has been a major lumber industry in Sierra conifer forests since the 1850s. The trees used are mostly ponderosa and Jeffrey pines, Douglas-fir, incense-cedar, some white fir, and giant sequoia. Young lodgepole pine trunks serve for walls in some mountain cabins. Oak is cut mainly for firewood.

Conifers

Conifers (cone-bearing trees) have both leaves that are either needle shaped or scalelike and naked seeds borne in cones. These trees are evergreen

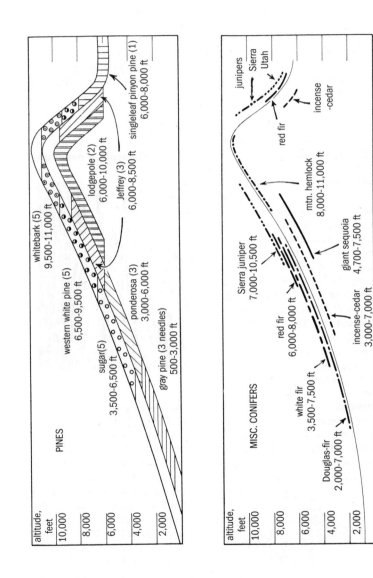

altitude, feet

PINES

whitebark (5)
9,500–11,000 ft

western white pine (5)
6,500–9,500 ft

sugar (5)
3,500–6,500 ft

lodgepole (2)
6,000–10,000 ft

Jeffrey (3)
6,000–8,500 ft

singleleaf pinyon pine (1)
6,000–8,000 ft

ponderosa (3)
3,000–6,000 ft

gray pine (3 needles)
500–3,000 ft

altitude, feet

MISC. CONIFERS

junipers
Sierra
Utah

red fir

incense-cedar

mtn. hemlock
8,000–11,000 ft

Sierra juniper
7,000–10,500 ft

red fir
6,000–8,000 ft

giant sequoia
4,700–7,500 ft

white fir
3,500–7,500 ft

incense-cedar
3,000–7,000 ft

Douglas-fir
2,000–7,000 ft

Figure 9. Distribution of coniferous trees across the Sierra Nevada by altitude.

(keeping their needles year-round), allowing them to photosynthesize during colder, winter months when broadleaved trees have dropped their leaves. In this group both male and female reproductive features are found on each tree (monoecious). Most conifers can be identified easily by their needles and their cones and by their growth form. Bark texture and pattern are also characteristic of each Sierra tree. Pine trees are often conspicuous and reliable guides to the plant belts (fig. 9). In many parts of the world, pines are variable and difficult to identify but in the Sierra the species are easily recognized; when learned they will aid in understanding other aspects of local natural history.

Cypresses (Family Cupressaceae)

INCENSE-CEDAR
Pl. 177

Calocedrus decurrens

Height 50 to 150 ft, diameter 2 to 7 ft; trunk tapered from broad base. **BARK** is cinnamon brown; irregular scaly flakes on young trees and branches, becoming thick and furrowed on older trees. **NEEDLES** are small and flat, scalelike, pointed, adhering to branchlets in alternate pairs. **CONES** are .75 to 1 in. long, of two broad, flat, seed-bearing scales.

DISTRIBUTION: Throughout Mixed Conifer Belt at 2,000 to 7,000 ft; common on west slope, occurs on east slope north of Mono County; found in a variety of dry and moist sites.

REMARKS: The flattened, fanlike sprays of foliage, tapered trunk, and fragrant wood are features of the incense-cedar. It rarely grows in pure stands but mingles with other conifers of the Mixed Conifer Belt. Young trees are clothed with branches from their pointed tops to their bases, whereas older ones have open, irregular crowns with branches only on the upper third of their trunks (they also have heavy, shreddy bark and buttressed bases). It has been suggested that this species is becoming more dominant because it wasn't a favored timber tree in the past and fire suppression has allowed its prolific seedlings to survive. In winter, small birds search for insects under flakes of cedar bark. The wood is durable and best known for its use in pencils.

McNAB CYPRESS   *Cupressus macnabiana*

Pl. 178

Height 10 to 30 (55) ft, diameter 1 to 2 (3) ft; juniperlike in appearance but with unique cones, trunk often bears oozing nodules and streaks of pitch. **BARK** is dark brown with reddish tinge, thin, laced with fine seams and ridges. **NEEDLES** grow in slightly flattened juniperlike sprays, blue to gray green, pungent; in opposite pairs with prominent gland dot on back of each needle; older stems sometimes bristly with dried, retained needles. **CONES** are .5 to 1 in. in diameter, generally rounded, thick and woody, with six to eight scales having hornlike projections.

DISTRIBUTION: In few scattered groves on west slope from Yuba County to Amador County, 1,000 to 2,800 ft; on dry slopes in chaparral and foothill woodland areas.

REMARKS: This poorly known and little-studied species grows best on soils shunned by other woody plants. The spotty distribution of such soils, derived from serpentine, gabbro, or greenstone, accounts for the widely disjunct pockets of McNab cypress. Growing as both multi-branched shrubs and single-trunked trees, this species typically forms dense, uniform stands wherever it does occur. Older trees often carry large numbers of old, weathered cones that release their seeds after a hot fire.

Piute cypress (*C. nevadensis*) occurs in only a dozen or so groves in the Greenhorn and Piute Mountains of the southern Sierra at elevations of 4,000 to 6,000 ft. Its cones are up to 1.5 in. in diameter and lack any hornlike projections (pl. 179). Some authorities (including *The Jepson Manual*) consider this to be a subspecies of the Arizona cypress (*C. arizonica*), as it may rightly be.

SIERRA JUNIPER   *Juniperus occidentalis*

Pl. 180

Height 15 to 35 (even 85) ft, diameter 1 to 5 (14) ft. **BARK** grows to .67 in. thick, shreddy, dull red. **NEEDLES** grow to .13 in. long, in threes, gray green, scalelike, overlapping, closely pressed on branchlets, with gland dot on back of each needle; pungent ginlike smell when rubbed or crushed. **CONES** are rounded and berrylike, to .33 in. diameter, blue black with whitish waxy surface.

DISTRIBUTION: Upper Montane and Subalpine Belts on both slopes at 7,000 to 10,500 ft; mainly on granite ridges.

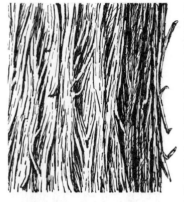

REMARKS: Sheltered Sierra junipers on granite flats have rounded dome-like crowns, a good clothing of branches, and a short conical trunk often 4 to 5 ft in diameter. More often, however, the tree is found on rocky summits exposed to fierce winter storms, where it becomes spectacularly deformed. Long, heavy roots cling to the granite, the trunk is short and often deformed, scored by lightning and bleached by wintry blasts, and the foliage masses are broken and irregular. Such junipers attract photographers because of the irregular form and weathered, exposed wood patterns. For several Sierra birds such as American Robins and Townsend's Solitaires, the abundant crops of berrylike cones are welcome food in fall and early winter. Juniper seeds do not readily germinate unless they have first passed through the digestive tract of birds or other animals.

The Sierra juniper is more properly a geographic race (var. *australis*) of the widespread western juniper that has found a unique home on Sierra Nevada slopes and rocky faces. Another juniper in the Sierra is the Utah juniper (*J. osteosperma*), which occupies low slopes on the east side between Mono and Plumas Counties. This is a small tree (typically under 25 ft tall with a diameter under 12 in.) whose scalelike needles are arranged in opposite pairs and lack the gland dots that are evident on Sierra juniper needles. Utah juniper cones are reddish brown (bronzy) and coated with the same kind of waxy frosting as those of their close relative.

Pines (Family Pinaceae)

WHITE FIR
Abies concolor

Pl. 181

Height 60 to 200 ft, diameter 4 ft; crown is narrowly cylindrical or spirelike. **BARK** on young trees is smooth, whitish; and on old trees is 2 to 4 in. thick, broken into rounded vertical ridges, gray or drab brown; branches in whorls around trunk, branchlets extending laterally as flat sprays. **NEEDLES** are .5 to 2.5 in., flat, often grooved on upper surface and keeled on lower; twisted at base. **CONES** are nearly cylindric, 2 to 5 in. by 1 to 1.75 in., erect on upper branches; cone scales fan shaped, wider than long; bracts half the length of scales.

DISTRIBUTION: Mixed Conifer and Upper Montane Belts along the length of the Sierra; widespread and on both slopes in northern Sierra but in narrow, fragmented belt on the west slope in southern Sierra; 2,500 to 7,500 ft in north and 5,000 to 8,000 ft in south; favors moist and shaded sites.

REMARKS: The white fir is common in the main timber portion of the Sierra, usually on better soil with more moisture than is needed by ponderosa pine. At lower elevations it mixes readily with pon-

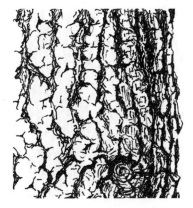

derosa and sugar pines, incense-cedar, and Douglas-fir, often becoming dominant in sites where wildfires have been suppressed. At higher elevations it forms extensive forests with red fir, the Sierra Nevada's other "true fir." These two firs are rather similar in appearance but separated by their needles and bark color. White firs have flattened needles that can't be easily rolled while red firs have four-sided needles that will roll if rubbed between two fingertips. A small piece of bark broken from the trunk of an older tree will reveal a pale tan color in white fir or wine red in red fir. Both firs have barrel-shaped cones

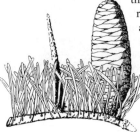

that stand upright on high branches, where they remain until mature; then the scales and seeds are shed piecemeal, leaving the central axis still attached to the branch. Green cones may be dislodged and can fall in storms, and many are cut by tree squirrels, but it is unusual to find them lying intact on the ground. Cones cut by Chickarees are stored for winter food. In refrigeration, under winter snow, the seeds will keep until used.

RED FIR   *Abies magnifica*
Pl. 182

Height 60 to 200 ft, diameter 2 to 4+ ft; mature crown short, narrow, round topped. **BARK** on young trees and at tops of old ones is smooth and whitish; on old trees it is deeply furrowed with dark red ridges, 2 to 3 in. thick; branches (except topmost) downcurved, then upcurved at ends; foliage dense, dark blue green. **NEEDLES** are .75 to 1.5 in., four-sided, whitish in first year, curved at base and bent outward all around branchlet. **CONES** are oval, 4 to 8 in. by 2.5 to 3.5 in., brown, scales with upturned edges.

DISTRIBUTION: Upper main forest belt, mostly on west slope at 5,000 to 7,000 ft (north) and 6,000 to 9,000 ft (south); on moist slopes or around wet meadows, also on rocky ridges or plateaus.

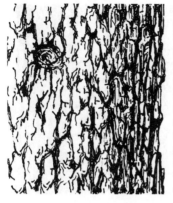

REMARKS: In the upper Sierra this fir is a stately element—stout, straight trunks soaring as high as 230 ft and to a girth of 10 ft. On many north-facing slopes red firs form a dark forest with scant ground cover. Shafts of sunlight between the densely foliaged crowns make a sharp contrast with the big, somber, dark red fluted columns of the mature trees. At higher elevations, red firs are particularly striking because chartreuse wolf lichens (*Letharia vulpina* and *L. columbiana*) coat their trunks down to the level of winter's average snowpack, 5 ft or more above the ground. Where winter storms are severe, red firs suffer many casualties because their wood is easily broken. The crowns of some are snapped off, others break at midlength, and many are felled completely. Because of the scarcity of other food-producing plants, a red fir forest is inhabited mainly by birds that find forage on the big conifers—woodpeckers, nuthatches, and creepers on the trunk; chickadees, kinglets, and warblers in the dense needle foliage; and various seed-eaters harvesting from the maturing cone crops in fall. Cavities in damaged firs provide nest retreats not only for many of these birds but for Chickarees, chipmunks, and other mammals—even martens on occasion.

WHITEBARK PINE   *Pinus albicaulis*

Pl. 183

Of varied form, from tree of 40 ft, to dwarfs of 6 ft with two or more trunks, to shrubby mats. **BARK** is thin, whitish, smooth or in scaly plates on trunk. **NEEDLES** grow in fives, 1 to 2 in. long, rigid, blunt tipped, clustered at ends of flexible branches, persisting four to eight years. **CONES** are 1 to 3 in. long, dark purple when young, turning brown by end of second year; scales thick and pointed at tip, not opening to reveal seeds like cones on other pines; cones torn apart on trees by birds and squirrels, rarely found intact on ground; pollen cones crimson.

DISTRIBUTION: Subalpine Belt, mainly on rocky summits at 7,500 to 9,500 ft (north) and 9,500 to 12,000 ft (south); Lake Tahoe to Mt. Whitney.

REMARKS: The sturdy whitebark pine lives near timberline, where it is buffeted by winter storms and summer winds. It grows slowly; a 5-in. branchlet may be 12 to 17 years old. Occasional trees in protected sites are upright, with unusually stout trunk, but most individuals are of distorted shape. Some have prostrate trunks 12 to 18 in. in diameter and broad mats of densely placed twigs and needles over which a person may scramble. This shrubby or prostrate growth form is known as *krummholz* (a German word meaning elfin timber or crooked wood), a trait shared by other tree species that reach timberline. White-tailed Jackrabbits often find shelter under these

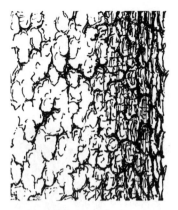

mats, as indicated by accumulations of their droppings. Cones bear wingless seeds that Clark's Nutcrackers and squirrels eat, the nutcrackers collecting huge numbers (each bird gathering as many as 98,000 seeds in eight days of harvesting), which they carry off and bury to eat later in the year.

KNOBCONE PINE   *Pinus attenuata*
Pl. 184

Height 20 to 30 (80) ft, diameter 6 to 12 in. or more; slender, often multi-trunked, trees bristling with sessile cones. **BARK** is thin, smooth, pale brown on branches and young trees; thick, dark brown, and irregularly fissured on older trunks. **NEEDLES** grow in threes, 3 to 5 in. long, slender, pale yellow green. **CONES** are narrowly pointed and curved, 3 to 6 in. long; yellow brown when young, but weathering to gray brown; in tight persistent clusters on trunk, often becoming buried within growing wood; scales thick on outer side of cone and armed with small, curved thorns.

DISTRIBUTION: Small groups on rocky, chaparral hillsides at 2,500 to 4,000 ft; on west slope in two main clusters: one in Mariposa County, the other from Nevada County to El Dorado County.

REMARKS: Named for its curious, knobby cones this tree is a bit of an enigma in the Sierra, rarely encountered because of its odd distribution and familiar to few naturalists. The thick prickly cones have the strange habit of remaining adhered to the trunk and major branches for a tree's entire life. Even if they become engulfed within rings of growing wood, the seeds within the cones remain viable. Instead of falling to the ground on an annual basis, these seeds are protected until a hot fire melts the resin that holds the scales together. Apparently, this species tolerates serpentinite soils where it doesn't have to compete with dense chaparral shrubs.

FOXTAIL PINE   *Pinus balfouriana*
Pl. 185

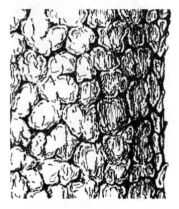

Height 20 to 45 ft, diameter to 6 ft at base; a stout-based tree with bright reddish bark. **BARK** is reddish brown, checked into square plates; branches short and irregular giving the tree a ragged appearance.

NEEDLES grow in fives, .75 to 1 in., bright green above, whitish beneath, persisting 10 to 15 years. **CONES** are 2.5 to 5 in. by 1.75 to 2 in., egg-shaped; deep purple; scale tips thickened on upper surface only and bearing very short bristles.

DISTRIBUTION: Found almost entirely within Sequoia and Kings Canyon National Parks; on granite outcrops at 9,000 to 11,300 ft; separate population in the Klamath Mountains of northwestern California.

REMARKS: To find this hardy alpine tree one must climb to high elevations in either of its separate and limited areas of occurrence. In the Sierra it grows in scattered stands, usually apart from other plants, on bare, rocky, elevated slopes or cirques. There it is exposed to extremes of daily and seasonal temperature, intense sunlight, severe winds and snowstorms, and long summer droughts. The trunk is strongly tapered (stout at the base and quickly narrowing to the tip) and in older trees the dead tips (possibly killed by lightning) project through the dense green crown foliage as bleached spires. These trees look ancient and are estimated to live as long as 1,500 years, though no one has found a tree this old. The common name derives from the way in which the short, curved stiff needles densely clothe the terminal 10 to 20 in. of a branch, nearly parallel to the stem and all around it—like a foxtail.

LODGEPOLE PINE   *Pinus contorta* subsp. *murrayana*
Pl. 186

Height 50 to 80 (125) ft, diameter 6 to 30 in. or more; straight-trunked tree with narrow crown. **BARK** is thin (to .25 in.), smooth, flaking off in thin scales, pale reddish to gray. **NEEDLES** grow in twos, 1 to 2.75 in. long, densely clothing branchlets, persisting two to three years. **CONES** are 1 to 1.75 in.

long, nearly globular when open, pale brown; growing against branches with no apparent stalk; scales thin with sharp points.

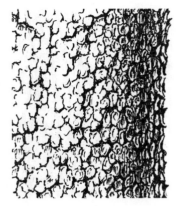

DISTRIBUTION: Throughout higher Sierra from upper edge of Mixed Conifer Belt nearly to timberline at 5,000 to 7,000 ft (north), 6,000 to 10,000 ft (center), and 7,000 to 11,000 ft (south); in meadows, on moist slopes and broad ridges, often the only tree in boggy situations or "frost pockets" where cold air sits; occasionally down to 4,000 ft, as in Yosemite Valley.

REMARKS: This pine ranges from Baja California north to Alaska and east to South Dakota. In the northern part of its range it often occurs in dense pure stands of slender polelike trunks, but in California its form is varied. Some

trees here are symmetrical and tall, and others have short trunks with heavy branches. In regions of heavy snow some young lodgepoles are bent and held down throughout the winter, whereby their trunks develop a permanent bend (pistol butt or snow knee) near the base, but unlike other conifers reaching timberline they don't grow in twisted windswept shapes or shrubby mats. The cones ripen and open at the end of summer but some remain closed, even for several years. This reserve seed stock helps to regenerate a stand destroyed by fire. In such circumstances young trees may shoot up in profusion, shading one another so that lower branches are soon lost and an immature pole forest results. Ghostly forests of bleached standing dead trees result from stands killed by Lodgepole Needle Miners (*Coleotechnites milleri*) or Western Pine Beetles (*Dendroctonus brevicomis*). Lodgepole cones, green or ripe, are cut by Chickarees to obtain the seeds. Chipmunks, crossbills, nutcrackers, and others also levy on the ripe seed crop. This tree is mistakenly called tamarac(k) pine (resulting in many "Tamarack" place names in the Sierra Nevada), but the true tamarack (*Larix*) does not grow in California. The wood is very pitchy.

LIMBER PINE
Pinus flexilis

Pl. 187

Height 15 to 60 ft, diameter to 3 or 4 ft; in tree form or dense shrubby mats at high elevations. **BARK** on trunk grows to 2 in. thick in dark brown, deeply furrowed, rectangular plates with thin scales; branches tough, flexible light gray or silvery. **NEEDLES** grow in fives, 1 to 2.25 in., dark yellow green, in dense brushlike tufts on ends of branches. **CONES** are 3.5 to 6 in., oval, bright green (never purple like whitebark pine) ripening to pale brown; scales only somewhat thickened, rounded at tip; scales opening to reveal seeds; open, weathered cones found on ground; pollen cones are bright yellow.

DISTRIBUTION: Scattered on east slope from Mono Pass to Monache Peak at 9,300 to 10,000 ft; and on west slope on the South Fork of Kings River at 10,500 to 12,000 ft; usually on dry, rocky, shallow soils.

REMARKS: Few people see the limber pine in the Sierra because of its small and rather inaccessible range. Its growth habits are unlike those of most pines. On young trees the branches are in separate whorls extending horizontally, then dipping toward the ground. Older trees have branches 16 to 18 ft long, those at the top angling gracefully downward. The branch system seems to develop at the expense of the trunk, which remains stunted. Old trees grow very slowly and may reach 2,000 years in age. In common with whitebark pine, which it closely resembles, its seeds are collected and dispersed by nutcrackers.

JEFFREY PINE
Pl. 188

Pinus jeffreyi

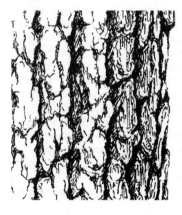

Height 60 to 170 ft, diameter to 4 (or 7) ft. **BARK** on young or old trees is reddish brown, divided into rough plates by deep, rather closely spaced furrows. **NEEDLES** grow in threes, 5 to 10 in. long, dull, grayish blue-green (with white bloom). **CONES** are heavy and beehive shaped, 4.75 to 8 in. by 4 to 5.5 in., purple, then russet brown, each scale with inturned prickle.

DISTRIBUTION: In Upper Montane Belt on west slope at 5,200 to 8,000 ft (north), 5,800 to 8,500 ft (center), and 6,000 to 9,000 ft (south); and on east slope often in pure stands, ranging downward into the Sagebrush Belt.

REMARKS: The Jeffrey pine very closely resembles the ponderosa pine but is a distinct species chemically, ecologically, and physiologically. Compared with the latter, its bark is darker and more narrowly furrowed, with a vanilla odor. The needles average thicker in diameter and duller in color; when crushed they often have a distinctive odor, like that in a firm winter apple. The cones are larger and heavier with smooth exterior; the prickle on each scale turns inward, not outward as on ponderosa pine cones. If a cone is held in the hand, remember the old adage "Prickly Ponderosa, Gentle Jeffrey" to tell which cone you are holding. Primarily a tree of the east slope, Jeffrey pine also occurs in a belt on the west slope immediately above ponderosa pine, sometimes mingled with that tree. From the latitude of Lake Tahoe northward the two species occur together in many places, especially in the eastern part of the Sierra. In these zones the two species frequently hybridize. At its lower limits in the southern Sierra, Jeffrey pine grows on meadow margins in company with lodgepole pine, but at higher levels it is often on rather barren rocky sites. In  pure stands, such as around Mammoth Lakes, it forms a somewhat open forest where the trunks are conspicuous. As is true with many larger conifer species, once a Jeffrey reaches maturity its pyramid-shaped crown begins to flatten out and the tree stops growing taller while still adding girth.

SUGAR PINE   *Pinus lambertiana*

Pl. 189

Height 100 to 210 ft, diameter 3 to 7 ft; at maturity a tall, straight-trunked tree with relatively few long, horizontal branches forming a wide, flat crown. **BARK** is 2 to 4 in. thick, vertically ridged with a surface of loose purple or cinnamon scales. **NEEDLES** grow in fives, 2 to 3.5 in. long, rigid, sharp pointed. **CONES** hang from stalks at ends of higher branches, 13 to 18 in. long and 4 to 6 in. in diameter when open, scales thin.

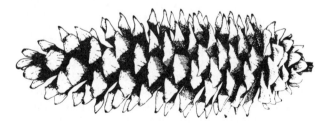

DISTRIBUTION: Mainly in Mixed Conifer Belt on west slope at 3,500 to 6,500 ft (north) and 4,500 to 9,000 ft (south).

REMARKS: A big mature sugar pine on a mountain crest, with long cones hanging at the ends of its spreading branches, conveys the feeling of a beneficent patron. This magnificent tree (the world's largest pine) is a striking element in the main forest belt, although other conifers usually outnumber it. The cones ripen and shed their seed in their second summer of growth but commonly remain in place until the following winter or spring. Because of their size and

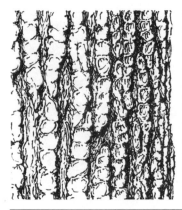

bright tawny coloring, these cones are much sought out for decorative use. The soft wood has high commercial value and the tree is extremely susceptible to white pine blister rust *(Cronartium ribicola)*; in consequence sugar pines, especially the giants of old, have become scarce in many forests. Wounds in the wood of a living tree result in a fluid exudation that hardens into white nodules. Native Americans and early settlers learned to chew this gum, which is sweet with a pine sugar.

SINGLELEAF PINYON PINE   *Pinus monophylla*
Pl. 190

Height 8 to 25 (45) ft, diameter 12 to 15 in.; trunk often divided near ground into several spreading stems. **BARK** on young trees is smooth, dull gray; and on old trees grows to 1 in. thick, rough and furrowed, with thin scales, dark brown. **NEEDLES** are single (rarely double), 1.25 to 2 in. long, stiff, curved, sharp pointed, and circular in cross section, grayish, persisting five years. **CONES** are nearly spherical, 1 to 2.25 in. by 2.5 to 3.5 in.; scales four-sided, thick and blunt.

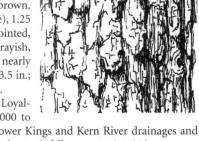

DISTRIBUTION: East slope from Loyalton, Sierra County south; at 6,000 to 8,000 ft; also on west slope in lower Kings and Kern River drainages and Walker Pass; on dry rocky slopes where rainfall averages 10 to 20 in. per year.
REMARKS: As gray pines characterize low slopes of the west side, so does this species on the east side. Young pinyon pines are covered by needles from base to tip, forming a conical exterior that cloaks the branches and bark. Older trees become irregular with more exposed framework. These pines occupy dry, exposed slopes below the Jeffrey pines of the east side, sometimes accompanying Sierra junipers. More often they are in the upper part of the Sagebrush Belt along with Utah juniper, mountain mahogany, and bitterbrush. Native Americans gather pinyon nuts for food, and these nutritious seeds are a staple diet for many birds and mammals. Surprisingly, this tree was not even present in the region until about 10,000 years ago but was apparently introduced and spread rapidly by Clark's Nutcrackers carrying seeds to new sites. This is the only one of the world's roughly 110 pines with single needles.

WESTERN WHITE PINE

Pinus monticola

Pl. 191

Height 50 to 125 ft, diameter to 6 ft; branches are regularly spaced creating a tiered pagoda-like effect, with upper branches curving upward at the end. **BARK** is smooth and gray in young trees, or checked into small, square, dark-purple-tinged or reddish plates in older trees. **NEEDLES** grow in fives, slender, 1 to 3.75 in., bluish green with whitish tinge, persisting one to three years. **CONES** grow on long stalks in clusters of one to seven at ends of high branches; 6 to 8 in. long, slender and tapered; blackish purple when young, later tawny; diameter 3 to 3.5 in. when open, scales thin.

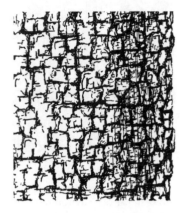

DISTRIBUTION: Upper Montane and Subalpine Belts south to southern Tulare County; above 5,500 ft in the north, and from 8,000 to 11,000 ft in the south.

REMARKS: Sometimes called the silver or mountain pine, this species is scattered throughout the upper part of the main timber belt and higher but is nowhere abundant except in small patches. It grows widely spaced and open to the sun, being quite intolerant of deep shade. Because this tree has a low level of genetic variability it has proven highly susceptible to white pine blister rust. This fungal pathogen, introduced to North America in a shipment of pine seedlings from France, has spread far and wide, leaving dead white pines in its wake.

PONDEROSA PINE

Pinus ponderosa

Pl. 192

Height 60 to 225 ft, diameter to 8 ft; a tall straight-trunked tree. **BARK** of older trees is 2 to 4 in. thick, yellowish (or reddish) tan, divided by shallow furrows into large scaly-surfaced plates 1 to 4 ft tall by 3 to 18 in. wide; bark of younger trees is narrowly furrowed, red brown to blackish; branches are short, usually upturned at ends, forming spirelike or flat-topped crown; branchlets orange, darkening with age. **NEEDLES** grow in threes, 5 to 10 in. long, glossy, yellowish green, in tufts on ends of branchlets, persisting about three years. **CONES** are near ends of branches, 2 to 5 in. by 2.75 to 3.5 in., reddish brown, each scale tip with out-turned prickle; seeds shed in second year, cone later falling, leaving some scales on tree.

DISTRIBUTION: On west slope at 1,500 to 5,000 ft (north), 3,000 to 6,000 ft (center), and 5,000 to 7,000 ft (south), scattered individuals and patches

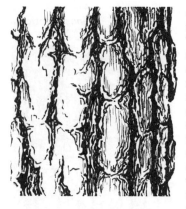

occur at both lower and higher elevations; also on east slope from Lake Tahoe northward.

REMARKS: This tree has another common name, yellow pine, which refers to the pale color of bark on mature trees, unlike that of any other local conifer. This pine is the commonest and most widely distributed of western conifers, and it defines the main forest on the western flank of the Sierra Nevada. Its vertical range seemingly depends on two different factors—at least 25 in. of annual precipitation at the lower limit, and prolonged winter freezing at the upper. Between these limits it grows in various environments—fertile moist slopes and plateaus, rocky ridges, and rather arid sites. Common forest associates are the black oak, incense-cedar, sugar pine, and white fir. The largest ponderosa pines are usually along ridges where the traveler may walk over needle-carpeted ground with little underbrush among the great trunks of this impressive tree. Frequent fires are required to maintain this openness (mature trees being protected by their thick bark) and to clear ground where seedlings establish themselves. The wood is fine and straight grained, usually with abundant resin, and supplies much of the lumber produced in California.

GRAY PINE or FOOTHILL PINE
Pl. 193

Pinus sabiniana

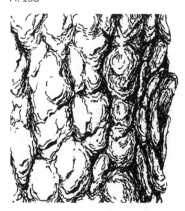

Height 40 to 90 ft, diameter 1 to 4 ft; trunk often slanting and frequently divided at 10 to 15 ft above the ground into several slender upright branches, forming an open broomlike top. **BARK** on older trees grows to 2 in. thick, gray brown, vertically furrowed. **NEEDLES** grow in threes, 7 to 12 in. long, sparse, gray green to blue. **CONES** are heavy and armored with stout, curved 1-in. hooks; 6 to 10 in. by 5 to 7 in., nearly globular.

DISTRIBUTION: Along western foothills at about 500 to 3,000 ft and on south end of Sierra at 2,500 to 5,000 ft; absent from Kings River to South Fork of the Tule River.

REMARKS: The foothill-loving gray pine bears little resemblance to its stately relatives in the deep green forests above. It is grayish green, with several upper "trunks" and an airy canopy. The foliage is so open that it affords scant shelter in the heat of summer. The wood is coarse grained and pitchy and warps badly. Small wonder that early settlers, who gave the name "Digger" to local Native American tribes as a term of contempt, applied it also to this tree. The abundant seed crops (pine nuts) were relished by the Native Americans, who also ate the soft central core of green cones in early summer. The large nuts, rich in proteins and fats, are staple food for gray squirrels, woodpeckers, jays, and various foothill birds. To the traveler of today the gray pine is a picturesque element of the landscape because of its varied, and sometimes otherworldly, growth pattern. Along with Jeffrey pine, this species contains explosive resins that earn these two the name "gasoline trees."

DOUGLAS-FIR   *Pseudotsuga menziesii*
Pl. 194

Height 70 to 110 ft or more, diameter up to 6 ft or more; a magnificent straight-trunked tree that in some parts of its range can grow over 300 ft high and 14 ft in diameter. **BARK** on young trees is thin, smooth, ashy brown; on old trees it is thick, soft, dark brown, with broad ridges and deep furrows; lower branches drooping (and shed early if heavily shaded), upper branches flat or upturned at ends. **NEEDLES** are .5 to 1.5 in., narrow, blunt at tip, upper surface with center groove, ridged below, yellow to blue green with two pale lines along underside. **CONES** mature in first fall 1.75 to 3 in. by 1.25 to 1.75 in. when open, red brown; scales broad, thin, with a protruding three-pointed bract.

DISTRIBUTION: Mixed Conifer Belt of west slope south to San Joaquin River; at 2,000 to 7,000 ft; mainly on shaded slopes and canyons.

REMARKS: Unsure how to classify this conifer, early botanists called it Oregon pine for a time then classified it briefly as a true fir or as a hemlock;

John Muir even called it Douglas spruce. When related trees were discovered in China and Japan the new genus *Pseudotsuga*, meaning "false hemlock," was created. Unlike true firs (*Abies*), which have little, rounded, subterminal buds, Douglas-fir has long, pointed, shiny brown buds at the tips of smaller twigs. In lower sections of the Sierra Nevada's main forest belt Douglas-fir grows mainly on moist, fertile, shaded slopes alone or mixed with ponderosa and sugar pines, incense-cedar, white fir, and black oak. In the Pacific Northwest it is prized for logs yielding large, long, and straight-grained timber. The seeds of this tree are a staple item in the diet of many forest mammals and some birds.

MOUNTAIN HEMLOCK
Tsuga mertensiana

Pl. 196

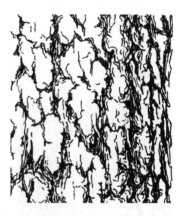

Height 15 to 150 ft, diameter 6 to 30 in. or more; a narrow-crowned tree with drooping top and branch tips, may grow in shrubby mats above roughly 10,000 ft. **BARK** is red brown, 1 to 1.5 in. thick, in broad, flat ridges, deeply furrowed. **NEEDLES** grow to 1 in. long, narrow, blunt pointed, flattish above, ridged below, slightly curved, growing from all sides of branchlet and pointing in all directions (often forming starlike clusters), deep green with bluish cast. **CONES** are 1.5 to 3 in. by .5 to .75 in., narrowed at both ends; purple when young, later red brown; often abundant on a tree; scales thin, rounded at tip.

DISTRIBUTION: Upper edge of forest at 6,000 to 11,600 ft.

REMARKS: This graceful tree lives at high elevations where snow lingers well into summer. It forms small, open groves, commonly in sheltered north- or east-facing canyons. When winter snowfall is heavy, the tips of saplings are bent over to touch the ground, but they recover when summer returns. Lower branches may take root where they make contact with the ground, resulting in the formation of dense thickets. In protected sites at lower elevations this hemlock becomes a large forest tree, either as pure stands or mixed with western white pine, lodgepole pine, or red fir. Wherever present, its tapered form and nodding top add pleasantly to many a rocky vista.

Yews (Family Taxaceae)

PACIFIC YEW

Taxus brevifolia

Pl. 195

Height 25 to 50 (75) ft, diameter 1 to 2 (4) ft; grows in both small tree and large shrub forms. **BARK** is thin, peeling off in papery curls, red brown. **NEEDLES** are .5 to 1 in. long, deep green, straight, pointed, with raised midribs, in flat two-ranked sprays on branchlets. **FRUIT** is berry-like (looking much like a huckleberry), scarlet.

DISTRIBUTION: Rare and scattered on west slope at 2,500 to 4,000 ft; south to Calaveras County in moist, well-shaded sites.

REMARKS: Only chance or persistent

searching will reveal the occasional tree of this species in the Sierra or elsewhere in California. It is more common in the Pacific Northwest. The powerful anticancer drug taxol can be extracted from the bark of this slow-growing tree. Birds and perhaps mammals disperse seeds after eating the attractive red fruit (technically an aril, a single seed partially surrounded by fleshy pulp).

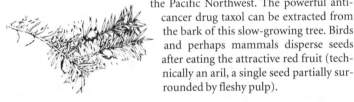

CALIFORNIA NUTMEG
Torreya californica

Pl. 197

Height to 50 ft, diameter 6 to 36 in. **BARK** grows to .63 in. thick, pale brown, finely checked with scaly ridges. **NEEDLES** are 1.25 to 2.5 in., narrow, rigid, bristle tipped, glossy green above, yellowish green below with two white grooves, arranged in flat two-ranked spray; base of needle extends along stem. **FRUIT** is olivelike, 1 to 1.75 in. long, yellow

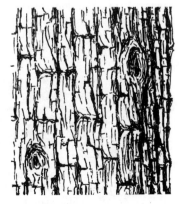

green streaked with purple, exterior wrinkled, pulp thin and resinous.

DISTRIBUTION: Uncommon on west slope near upper edge of Foothill Belt south to Tulare County; 2,000 to 4,500 ft in moist canyons.

REMARKS: California nutmeg is a handsome tree with dark green foliage that sometimes grows in shrubby form. The fruit resembles the true nutmeg (of the Molucca Islands) but has no value for flavoring. The needles, branchlets, or green bark, when crushed, emit a sharp odor, so this tree has had at times the nickname stinking cedar.

Bald Cypress (Family Taxodiaceae)

GIANT SEQUOIA
Pl. 198

Sequoiadendron giganteum

Height 150 to 275 (310) ft, diameter 5 to 20 (27) ft; young trees have a conical crown with branches to the ground, old trees are massive with long open trunks that taper little while the crown is a short, irregular dome. **BARK** is 4 to 24 in. thick, in broad rounded ridges and deep furrows; soft, spongy, and composed of fine fibers; cinnamon brown. **NEEDLES** are awl shaped to .5 in. long, blue green, lying flat on slender drooping branchlets. **CONES** are egg shaped and green when young, 1.75 to 2.75 in. long, of 34 to

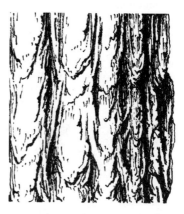

40 thick diamond-shaped scales, maturing to reddish brown in second fall.

DISTRIBUTION: Mixed Conifer Belt on west slope; 4,600 to 7,000 ft from Placer County to Tulare County; favors drainage bottoms and edges of meadows near springs or seeps.

REMARKS: Greatest of all Sierra plants is the giant sequoia, which lives in 75 isolated groves in a narrow belt on the west slope. All but eight of these groves occur in southern Fresno and Tulare Counties. The greatest known age of a giant sequoia is 3,200 years, and the famous General Sherman Tree (275 ft high by 27.5 ft diameter) is estimated to be 2,500 years old. In aged mature trees the base is broadly buttressed, while the trunk is a huge clear column with a slight taper that is free of branches for 100 to 150 ft. The fibrous nonresinous bark is highly resistant to fire. Freshly cut wood is pink, aging to dark red, fairly strong, and highly resistant to decay. The small cones are produced in abundance, each having 200 to 300 seeds, and stay on the tree for decades holding onto their seeds. Seeds are released when hot fires dry the cones or when Chickarees cut the cones to eat the green scales (discarding the tiny seeds). Fires are essential for clearing debris and allowing seedlings to reach bare soil. Even though controlled fires are being introduced in some areas, young trees are still scarce, prompting worry that older trees will not be replaced. The giant sequoia is a living fossil having had far wider distribution in past geologic time.

Broadleaf Trees

Broadleaf trees are deciduous (with the exception of live oaks, madrone, California laurel, and tan oak), losing their leaves in fall and replacing them in spring. Because the Sierra Nevada endures a summerlong dry season and broadleaf trees lose substantial amounts of water through their large, fleshy leaves, many deciduous trees are limited to growing on moist soils or near water. Blue oaks of the arid foothills are one notable exception in that they have developed special features (waxy coating on their leaves and reduced leaf size, among other characteristics) allowing them to survive summer drought. Many species in this group have separate male and female trees (dioecious), with individual plants producing either pollen or fruit.

Maples (Family Aceraceae)

MOUNTAIN MAPLE
Acer glabrum

Pl. 199
Height 5 to 15+ ft, diameter 2 to 3 in., shrub or tree, branches slender, upright. **BARK** is smooth, grayish on older surfaces, generally reddish brown on young twigs. **LEAVES** grow 1 to 3 in. broad, palmately three-lobed (middle lobe being longest), margin unequally serrated; shiny green above, pale green below, veins yellowish, leaf stems red. **FLOWERS** grow in small clusters of about 10, yellowish green; samaras in clusters, smooth, wings to 1 in. long.

DISTRIBUTION: Mixed Conifer and Upper Montane Belts on both slopes at 3,000 to 9,000 ft along stream margins or on hillsides.

REMARKS: Mountain maple (or Rocky Mountain maple) grows in thickets on stream borders or damp hillsides, sometimes in company with shrubs. In shaded niches, the maples hold their leaves on a horizontal plane to maximize exposure to sunlight. Red blotches are commonly present on the leaves, being galls caused by eriophyid mites. Squirrels and chipmunks favor this maple's seeds. A variety that grows on the east slope (var. *diffusum*) and eastward across the Great Basin is characterized by its gray twigs.

BIGLEAF MAPLE   *Acer macrophyllum*
Pl. 200

Height 30 to 80+ ft, diameter 1 to 4+ ft; broad open crown. **BARK** on younger trees is green and smooth, brownish gray with narrow interwoven ridges or checked in small squarish plates on older trees. **LEAVES** are 4 to 10 in. broad, roundish in outline, in five broad palmate divisions, dark shiny green above, paler below. **FLOWERS** are small, in drooping clusters, yellow, fragrant; fruit a bristly samara, wings 1 to 1.5 in. long.

DISTRIBUTION: On west slope from upper Foothill Belt through Mixed Conifer Belt at 2,000 to 4,500 ft (north), to 5,600 ft (central), higher in south; south to Kaweah region but most numerous from Nevada County north; along stream borders.

REMARKS: This is the large maple of the west. The trees are scattered in shaded canyons, in company with other stream-margin species, and often have tall straight trunks. In these moist environments the bark and branches can become moss covered and the tree may send out "canopy roots" that grow from branches to absorb moisture and nutrients in the moss. The wood is hard, close grained, and reddish brown; the sap contains sugar. Winged maple seeds, called samaras, spiral as they fall and can be carried a fair distance in a strong wind. Large seed crops provide nutritious food for Chickarees and finches or other birds.

Birches (Family Betulaceae)

WHITE ALDER
Alnus rhombifolia

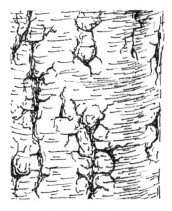

Height 30 to 115 ft, diameter to 24 in.
BARK is smooth, thin, whitish or grayish brown with dark upside-down "V" marks where branches start; becoming reddish brown and scaly at base of trunk in older trees.
LEAVES are 2 to 4 in. long, oblong, tapered to base, tip rounded, wavy bordered, light yellowish green; midrib and major veins not indented above.
FLOWERS grow in catkins; 4.5 to 5.5 in. long, slender and hanging on male trees; on female trees short, erect, ripening into brown woody cone .5 to .75 in. long.

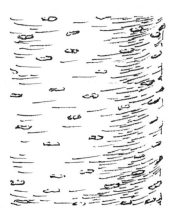

DISTRIBUTION: From Central Valley up into Mixed Conifer Belt on west slope to 2,500 ft (north) and 6,000 to 8,000 ft (south); along rivers and smaller streams.
REMARKS: More tolerant of shade than cottonwoods, the white alder lines many canyon bottoms and gorges having permanent water. The tall trunks and open crowns are attractive, as are the small upright cones. White alder leaves drop while still green in the fall and don't assume the colors of some other deciduous trees.

MOUNTAIN ALDER
Alnus tenuifolia

Pl. 201

Height 8 to 30 ft; in shrub or tree form, trunk often bent. **BARK** is smooth, thin, dark gray-brown; on larger trunks lightly seamed, scaly, red-tinged; young twigs red. **LEAVES** are 1 to 3 in. long, roundish, edge double toothed, dark green; major veins indented above. **FLOWERS** grow in catkins to 3 in. on male trees, maturing as cones to .63 in. long on female trees.
DISTRIBUTION: From Tulare County north at 5,000 to 8,000 ft on wet slopes.
REMARKS: Mountain alder grows in dense pure thickets with leaning,

sometimes almost horizontal, stems on mucky slopes, lake borders, and gulches saturated with water. Seedlings abound in shady or open sites, but older trees need top light. This species, as with all alders, is able to absorb atmospheric nitrogen due to Actinomycetes fungi that live in special nodules on the alder's roots. This nitrogen is then incorporated into the plant's tissues and added to the ecosystem as the alder's leaves and stems fall and decompose. Mountain alder thickets are often nearly impenetrable but offer good harbor for small animals and birds. Some authorities (including *The Jepson Manual*) call this species *Alnus incana* subsp. *tenuifolia*.

WATER BIRCH   *Betula occidentalis*
Pl. 202

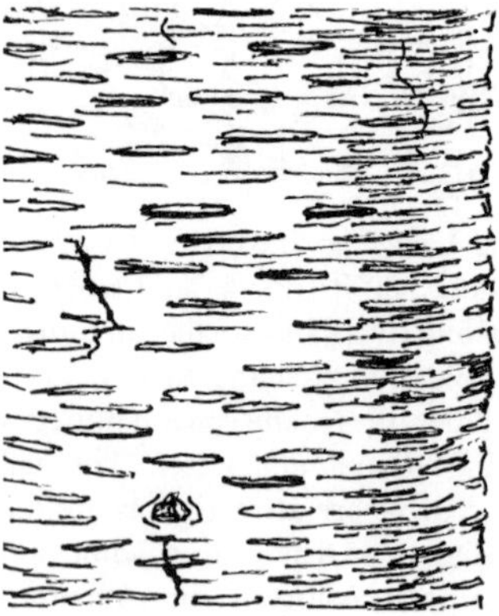

Height 10 to 25 ft, diameter 6 in. **BARK** is smooth, red brown, twigs have a warty texture due to numerous resin glands. **LEAVES** are 1 to 2 in. long, round ovate, sharply toothed (serrate). **FLOWERS** grow in catkins; 2 to 2.5 in. long on male trees, on female trees 1.5 in. long when fruiting.

DISTRIBUTION: Found on east slope along streams running into Owens Valley, mostly Inyo County and southern Mono County.

REMARKS: The birch grows as either a slender tree or tall shrub. In both forms, buds at the bases of the trunks sprout prolifically resulting in dense clumps of 100 or more stems. These streamside thickets provide important shaded habitat for trout and other fish as well as nesting habitat for birds. Water birch leaves turn a brilliant gold color in the fall.

Dogwood (Family Cornaceae)

MOUNTAIN DOGWOOD or PACIFIC DOGWOOD   *Cornus nuttallii*
Pl. 203

Height 10 to 30 (60+) ft, diameter usually less than 10 in. but rarely up to 2 ft. **BARK** is thin, smooth, ashy brown or reddish with small thin scales on old trees, young twigs are green. **LEAVES** are 3 to 5 in., narrow or oval, tip pointed, minutely haired, veins conspicuous, pale green. **FLOWERS** are small, greenish yellow, in buttonlike cluster surrounded by four to six showy petal-like, broad, white bracts 1.5 in. or longer; fruit scarlet, of 25 to 40 drupes in tight cluster.

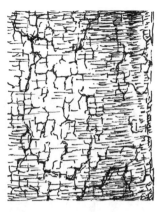

DISTRIBUTION: Mixed Conifer Belt on west slope at 2,500 to 5,100 ft or higher; in shaded forest understories.

REMARKS: May or June brings out the showy white "blossoms" of this dogwood, highly visible in dense green woods of the lower coniferous forest. What at first glance looks like a single white flower is in fact a tight ball of inconspicuous flowers surrounded by a ring of petal-like bracts that create the appearance of a single large flower. Later in the summer these flowers mature into clusters of bright red fruit that are highly sought by Band-tailed Pigeons and other birds. With fall the leaves turn pink to rosy red, making bright color patches among the dark greens of pines and firs.

Heath (Family Ericaceae)

PACIFIC MADRONE *Arbutus menziesii*
Pl. 204

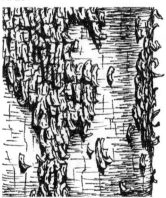

Height 20 to 80+ ft, diameter 2 to 3 ft; often multitrunked and widely branched. **BARK** is thin, smooth, red or tan and peeling on twigs and branches, scaly and reddish brown on old trunks. **LEAVES** are evergreen, 3 to 6 in. long, narrowly elliptical, above shiny dark green, below whitish. **FLOWERS** grow in large drooping clusters, white, corolla .25 in. long, urn shaped; fruit berrylike and in clusters, diameter to .5 in., red or orange.

DISTRIBUTION: Mixed Conifer Belt of west slope south to Tuolumne County in forest on various soils.

REMARKS: Against the somber coniferous forest the madrone stands in contrast. As summer growth begins the bark peels off in thin layers, leaving a pale green satiny surface that ages to terra cotta or light red. The dense blossom clusters are followed by clumps of reddish berrylike fruits in fall. Many birds, including American Robins and Cedar Waxwings, gather in large numbers to feast on these fruits through winter.

Oaks (Family Fagaceae)

TAN OAK *Lithocarpus densiflorus*
Pl. 205

Height 50 to 100 ft, diameter 1 to 3 ft; tree or shrub. **BARK** is smooth on

young trees, later in squarish plates, gray brown; young twigs woolly. **LEAVES** are 2.5 to 4.5 in. by 1 to 1.75 in., evergreen, oblong, veins strong and ending in teeth at margin, smooth, shiny above, woolly, red brown below. **FLOWERS** grow in catkins, erect, 2 to 4 in. long. **ACORN** is short, thick, 1 to 1.5 in. long, cap "hairy," maturing in second fall.

DISTRIBUTION: Sparse on west slope, Butte County to Mariposa County at 2,000 to 5,000 ft; mostly in Mixed Conifer Belt.

REMARKS: This tree is an odd intermediate between oaks and chestnuts and is the only North American representative of a genus that has 100 species in Asia. Tan oak (also known as tanbark oak or simply tanbark) is more common in the northern Coast Ranges than in the Sierra. Here it occurs scatteringly in dense forests. A shrubby form (var. *echinoides*), 2 to 10 ft high, with

thick small leaves (1 to 2 in. long) and small acorns is found from Placer County to Mariposa County. Acorns of tan oaks were an important food for Native Americans. White settlers later developed an industry around using extracts from the bark to tan leather hides, cutting so many trees that turn-of-the-century botanists worried the species could go extinct.

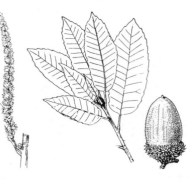

CANYON LIVE OAK *Quercus chrysolepis*
Pl. 206

Height 20 to 50+ ft, diameter 1 to 5 ft, crown rounded, spreading. **BARK** is rather smooth, whitish. **LEAVES** are 1 to 2 in. long, evergreen, thick and leathery, tip pointed, margin entire or toothed (even on same branch);

green above, yellow with fine fuzz or powder below. **ACORN** is 1 to 1.25 by .75 to 1 in. ovate to cylindric, tip usually pointed, cup thick, rounded, felted with yellow fuzz, suggesting a yellow turban.

DISTRIBUTION: Locally common from upper part of Foothill Belt through Mixed Conifer Belt of west slope at 1,500 to 5,000 ft (north), 3,000 to 8,000 ft (south); on valley walls and floors and on ridges.

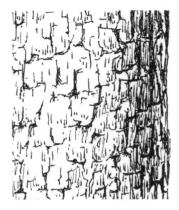

REMARKS: Canyon live oaks densely clothe many sunlit canyon walls on the west slope, sometimes growing as clones. The wood is dense and straight grained and seasons well, hence it was used by early settlers and mountain packers, who gave it many names, including golden-cup, canyon, white, and maul oak. Acorns and leaf insects of these trees are food for many birds and mammals; Band-tailed Pigeons can swallow the acorns whole! More than 50 kinds of gall-forming insects utilize this oak.

BLUE OAK

Pl. 207

Quercus douglasii

Height 20 to 60 ft, diameter 1 to 2 ft; a small to medium-sized oak. **BARK** is whitish, in small thin scales on trunk and small branches. **LEAVES** are variable in size and outline, 1 to 3 in. by .5 to 3 in., oblong, shallowly lobed, entire or with few teeth, bluish green above, paler below. **ACORN** .75 to 1.5 in. by .5 to .75 in., oval or tapering; cup small, .33 to .5 in. long.

DISTRIBUTION: Common in west slope Foothill Belt up to 3,000 ft; on dry grassy or rocky slopes.

REMARKS: When heading east into the mountains one meets scattered blue oaks well before other plants of

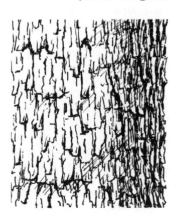

the Foothill Belt. As one continues, they become common, in pure stands or among gray pines and live oaks, always recognizable by their distinctive bluish-tinged leaves. The blue oak affords perches and nesting places for the Nuttall's Woodpecker, Western Kingbird, Ash-throated Flycatcher, Western Scrub-Jay, Oak Titmouse, and associated birds. The distinctive bluish cast on this oak's leaves is from a waxy coating that, along with the leaves' small size, helps reduce moisture loss.

A stunted form of Oregon oak (*Q. garryana* var. *breweri*) is found in scattered stands among dry foothill chaparral on the west slope. These "Brewer's oaks" superficially resemble small blue oaks except that their leaves are more deeply lobed and lack the bluish tones of blue oaks.

CALIFORNIA BLACK OAK
Quercus kelloggii

Pl. 208

Height 30 to 80 ft, diameter 1 to 4.5 ft; crown broad, rounded. **BARK** is smooth and gray on young trees, becoming dark and narrowly fissured on older trees. **LEAVES** are 4 to 10 in. by 2.5 to 6 in., deeply and irregularly lobed; each lobe ending in one to three (or more) coarse teeth; above lustrous green, below paler. **ACORN** is 1 to 1.5 in. by .75 in., deep in large thin-scaled cup, maturing in second season.

DISTRIBUTION: Common on west slope in Mixed Conifer Belt at 3,000 to 7,500 ft; on slopes and in valleys on good to rocky soil; on east slope in the far northern Sierra, and at scattered sites in the southern Sierra.

REMARKS: Black oak is a prominent member of the Mixed Conifer Belt along the western flank of the Sierra, scattered among conifers on slopes and forming pure stands at lower fire-prone elevations. In spring its reddish leaf buds produce pale green leaves that contrast with the dark greens of the conifers. In fall the ground becomes carpeted with their crisp golden

brown leaves while leaves on the trees may assume yellow or red colors. Tree squirrels and some owls nest in rotted cavities of the trunks and limbs; woodpeckers, jays, gray squirrels, and deer relish the acorns; and the summer foliage is host to many birds for foraging and nesting.

VALLEY OAK
Quercus lobata

Height 40 to 125+ ft, diameter 2 to 9 ft; round topped, often broader than high. **BARK** is thick, with cubelike checks; main branches huge, branchlets cordlike, drooping. **LEAVES** are 3 to 4 in. by 2 to 3 in., with three to five pairs of broad rounded lobes, green above, paler below, yellow-veined. **ACORN** is long, conical, 1.5 to 2.25 in. by .5 to .75 in., maturing reddish brown, cup warty.

DISTRIBUTION: Central Valley and broad level foothill valleys of west

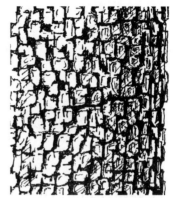

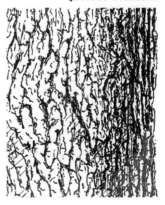

slope to 2,000 ft (north) or 4,000 ft (south); on loamy well-watered soil.

REMARKS: Most majestic of California oaks is the valley oak that grows on broad, fertile lowlands. The crown is wide and rounded, the trunk huge, and the long drooping branchlets sometimes reach the ground. In summer the leaf crown provides welcome shade from the sun's heat, and in fall jays, woodpeckers, and other birds harvest its acorns—as Grizzly Bears did formerly. Agriculture, grazing, and development of river floodplains favored by this species have greatly reduced its populations.

INTERIOR LIVE OAK
Quercus wislizenii

Height 30 to 75 ft, diameter 1 to 3 ft; dense rounded crown, often broader than tall. **BARK** is smooth and gray on young trees, becoming dark and fissured on older trees. **LEAVES** are 1 to 2.5 in. long, evergreen, thick and leathery, tip tapered or rounded, margin entire or toothed (a single leaf may be both entire and toothed), smooth green appearance. **ACORN** is 1.25 to 1.63 in. long, slender, tapered, deeply set in cup with thin brown scales.

DISTRIBUTION: Common on west slope from border of Central Valley through

Foothill Belt at 2,000 to 5,000 ft; on slopes or in stream bottoms, good or poor soils.

REMARKS: At all seasons the rounded evergreen or "live" oak is easily recognized. The dense, dark foliage gives protected roosting places for many birds. Insects on the leaves are sought by vireos, some warblers, titmice, and their associates. Evergreen oaks that keep their leaves benefit from being able to photosynthesize year-round but suffer tissue damage wherever snow or frost is severe, thus limiting them to slightly lower elevations than black oaks and other deciduous oaks.

Buckeye (Family Hippocastanaceae)

CALIFORNIA BUCKEYE
Aesculus californica

Pl. 209

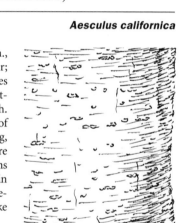

Height 10 to 45 ft, diameter 8 to 20 in., or several stems 3 to 6 in. diameter; usually a small tree but sometimes shrublike, crown open, spreading, flattish. **BARK** is smooth, gray to whitish. **LEAVES** are palmate on 4 to 5 in. stem, of five to seven lobes, each 3 to 5 in. long, pointed, margin toothed. **FLOWERS** are in erect clusters 4 to 6 in. long, blossoms many, white, petals .5 in. long; fruit in pear-shaped pod, seeds 1 to 2 in. diameter with smooth reddish-brown skin like a chestnut.

DISTRIBUTION: Foothill Belt of west slope up to 5,000 ft; on hillsides or stream borders.

REMARKS: The buckeye, or horse chestnut, puts forth a showy display of white flower clusters in May or June, then sheds its drying shriveled leaves in late summer to leave the pearlike seed pods hanging from the tips of bare branches. No other local deciduous tree has the same habit of closing shop during the heat of summer.

Laurel (Family Lauraceae)

CALIFORNIA BAY LAUREL
Umbellularia californica

Pl. 210

Height 40 to 60 ft, diameter 1 to 2 ft; evergreen tree or shrub, crown dense, of erect slender branches. **BARK** is thin, scaly, dark brown. **LEAVES** are 3.5 to 5 in.

by .67 to 1.25 in., evergreen, oblong, short petioled; emit sharp pungent odor when bruised. **FLOWERS** are four to 10 in group; sepals .33 in. long, cream-colored; fruit (drupe) rounded to 1 in. long, ovate, greenish, ripening to dark purple.

DISTRIBUTION: In upper Foothill and Mixed Conifer Belts of west slope at 1,200 to 4,000 ft (north), 2,500 to 6,500 ft (center), and higher (south), south to Tule River basin; in moist canyons.

REMARKS: In the northern Coast Ranges this tree is common and often

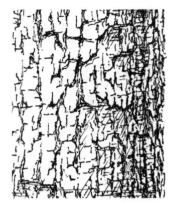

large (up to 130 ft). In the Sierra the trees are smaller, sometimes growing as shrubs in drier areas. The wood (called pepperwood because of its odor) is heavy, hard, and strong. At times this tree is known as California bay, California laurel, or bay laurel; under the name Oregon myrtle it is favored by woodworkers and made into trays and bowls. Fruits resemble those of the avocado, a plant to which laurel is closely related.

Olives (Family Oleaceae)

OREGON ASH
PI. 211
Fraxinus latifolia

Height up to 80 ft, diameter to 3 ft. **BARK** gray brown, becoming fissured with age. **LEAVES** are 6 to 12 in. long, pinnately compound with five to seven sessile leaflets. **FLOWERS** appear before leaves, in small clusters, petals absent; fruit paddle shaped with single wing extending from tip (like half of a

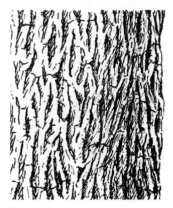

Young bark

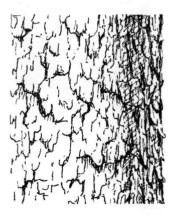

Old bark

maple fruit), in hanging clusters on female trees only.

DISTRIBUTION: Foothill Belt of west slope up to 3,000 ft; in vicinity of streams.

REMARKS: Three species of ash occur in the Sierra Nevada with Oregon ash being the tallest. South of the Kern River it is gradually replaced by velvet ash (*F. velutina*), an extremely similar species that is believed to hybridize extensively with Oregon ash in the southern Sierra. A smaller shrubby (rarely tree like) species, also occurring in the Foothill Belt of the west slope, is California ash (*F. dipetala;* pl. 212). This small ash seldom exceeds 10 ft in height and is recognized in having two white petals per flower and four-sided twigs (Oregon and velvet ash have cylindrical twigs).

Sycamore (Family Platanaceae)

CALIFORNIA SYCAMORE or WESTERN SYCAMORE
Pl. 213

Platanus racemosa

Height 40 to 90 ft, diameter 1 to 3 ft; branches long, irregular, crown open. **BARK** is smooth; sheds thin reddish-brown surface sheets yearly, exposing green, yellow, or white areas beneath, giving mottled appearance. **LEAVES** are 4 to 12+ in., broader than long, in three to five palmate lobes, light yellowish green. **FLOWERS** are in ball-like clusters scattered on slender axis (male and female separate); balls fall apart in winter, releasing seedlike nutlets.

DISTRIBUTION: Central Valley and Foothill Belt up to about 2,500 ft; along stream bottoms.

REMARKS: Solitary sycamores growing along lowland rivers or creeks are broad and open framed, but those living in deep canyons are taller and narrower in form. Not widely distributed in the Sierra Nevada, they occur in numbers only along some low-elevation stream courses. Goldfinches feed on the seed heads in fall or winter as the tree's leaves turn yellow.

Willows (Family Salicaceae)

FREMONT COTTONWOOD
Populus fremontii subsp. *fremontii*
Pl. 214

Height 40 to 90 ft, diameter 1 to 3 ft. **BARK** is whitish in young trees, becoming dark brown, 1 to 5 in. thick, roughly fissured. **LEAVES** are 2 to 4 in. wide, triangular with broad base and tapered tip; margins coarsely scalloped; yellow green; flattened stalks nearly as long as leaves. **FLOWERS** grow in caterpillar-like catkins; dense and 2 to 4 in. long in male trees, more loosely arranged in female; seeds with many long white hairs, turning catkins into soft cottony masses.

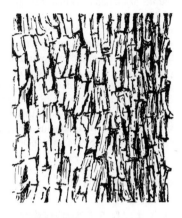

DISTRIBUTION. On west side from Central Valley into Foothill Belt, up to 2,500 ft; on east slope along lower reaches of Truckee, Carson, and Walker Rivers; on moist soil along stream courses.

REMARKS: This is a common cottonwood in the lowlands west of the Sierra. Along with willows it helps to make up the streamside or riparian growths so richly populated by birds in nesting time. Raccoons, Wood Ducks, and other hole-inhabiting animals use rotted cavities in the trunks. Clusters of mistletoe on cottonwoods produce berries attractive in winter to robins, waxwings, and bluebirds. Cuttings of cottonwood branches readily root when stuck into moist soil. Both cottonwood and willow leaves turn yellow in the fall.

QUAKING ASPEN
Populus tremuloides
Pl. 215

Height 10 to 60 ft, diameter to 10 in. or more. **BARK** is smooth, chalk white to

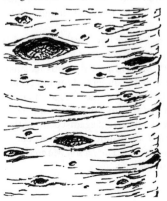

olive green, easily damaged and forming dark brown scars. **LEAVES** are .75 to 2 in. long, round ovate, tip sharp, margin toothed or entire. **FLOWERS** grow in catkins, 1.5 to 2.5 in. long on male trees, 2 to 4 in. on female trees; seeds minute, brownish, white-haired.

DISTRIBUTION: Throughout Sierra on both slopes at 5,000 to 8,000 ft (north), 6,000 to 10,000 ft (south); most numerous on east slope between Lake Tahoe and Mono Lake; in swampy meadows or gravelly slopes and bases of lava jumbles.

REMARKS: At higher elevations aspen is the most conspicuous deciduous tree, especially in fall when its foliage turns golden yellow or red, adding bright color to many slopes. Often it occurs in groves with straight vertical trunks branched only near the crown, but where exposed to severe storms and heavy snows the trunks may be distorted, some nearly prostrate. The leaves, having flattened petioles, quiver in any breeze, making a pleasant rustling sound. Under a thin white outer layer that sloughs off easily, aspen bark is greenish and photosynthetically active. While aspens produce copious numbers of seeds, they reproduce largely by cloning, sending out many long adventitious roots that develop primordia that turn upward to become duplicates of the parent tree. Members of a clone all have a similar appearance and turn colors in the fall at the same time, readily separating them from their neighboring clone clusters. Beavers introduced at higher elevations in the Sierra favor aspen bark for food.

BLACK COTTONWOOD   *Populus trichocarpa*
Pl. 216

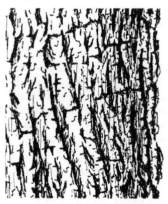

Height 40 to 125 ft, diameter 2 to 4 ft. **BARK** is smooth, yellowish white, becoming ashy gray with age and developing rough fissures. **LEAVES** are 4 to 8 in. long, ovate, heart shaped at base, tapered at tip, finely toothed, dark green above, rusty brown and later whitish below; stalk is one-third to one-half the length of leaf, rounded below, channeled above. **FLOWERS** grow in catkins; to 5 in. long in male trees, female catkins shorter and mature into grapelike clusters that split open in summer to release cottony seeds.

DISTRIBUTION: Sparingly distributed throughout the Sierra Nevada, mostly 3,000 to 10,000 ft; mainly along stream banks or moist bottom lands.

REMARKS: River canyons in the lower forest belt are lined by this tree, which has dark tapered leaves. Along such canyons it may ascend to 10,000 ft in a few places. It is intolerant of shade but by rapid growth sends its small crown up into full light, where it competes with conifers. Many insects live on the foliage and twigs in summer, and the tree provides forage and nesting places for various species of birds in that season. Sticky, aromatic resin covers young buds and new leaves, acting as a deterrent against plant-eating insects. Bees collect this resin (which acts as an disinfectant against bacteria) for their hives. Some authorities (including *The Jepson Manual*) call this species *Populus balsamifera* subsp. *trichocarpa*.

WILLOWS

Genus *Salix*

Pls. 217, 218

Trees or shrubs of rapid growth and light wood. **BARK** is bitter flavored; young shoots smooth, yellow or red, trunk bark of older trees fissured and dark. **LEAVES** are simple, narrow, short petioled. **FLOWERS** grow in catkins, usually erect, appearing before or with leaves.

REMARKS: The slender pointed leaves, flowering catkins or pussy willows, and close adherence to water—stream banks, lake borders, wet meadows, and seepage slopes— make willows as a group easy to recognize. Over 20 species occur in the Sierra (some being trees and others shrubs), but precise identification usually requires blossoms, seed capsules, and a botanical key. Willow trees 6 to 50 ft high, such as red and black willows (*S. laevigata* and *S. gooddingii*), border waters below 5,000 ft. These are a major element of the lowland riparian habitat, and they accompany the larger streams where margined by soil up into the Mixed Conifer Belt. In the lower elevations they, and associated wetland plants, often form dense thickets, sometimes all but impenetrable by humans. Here from late April into June are the largest nesting bird populations. (One census at Snelling in late May, 6 to 9 a.m., totaled 41 species and 425+ birds.) Other animals also abound in these places. At 5,000 to 10,000 ft in swampy meadows the Lemmon's willow (*S. lemmonii*) grows in dense clumps that are the summer domain of White-crowned Sparrows, Lincoln's Sparrows, blackbirds, some flycatchers and warblers, and other small birds. The arctic willow (*S. arctica*) is the dwarf of this group. Its erect branches, 2 to 4 in. high, rise from creeping stems that make carpetlike growths bordering alpine streams at 8,500 to 12,000 ft.

MISCELLANEOUS ANIMALS

MANY PEOPLE THINK of insects as the smallest animals, but there is an immense variety of even smaller animals in the Sierra landscape and its waters. Some are frequently encountered, others must be searched for, and the tiniest of them are found only with a microscope. Representative common forms are included here.

Among the animals discussed in this section are members of Arthropoda, a phylum shared with insects, the most numerous group of animals on earth. Insects are discussed separately in the next section; the arthropods covered in this section include crustaceans, spiders and their allies, centipedes, and millipedes. All arthropods have movable appendages (legs and feet, mouthparts; e.g., grasshopper), a body subdivided into many segments (whether few or many, alike or differing), and a body wall that is firm or rigid. The Sierra forms included here range in size from microscopic proportions to 6 in. or longer.

Much remains to be learned about the smallest animals of the Sierra Nevada—the species present, their distribution and habits, and their ecology.

Simple Animals

PLANKTON

Freshwaters contain varying numbers of microscopic floating plants (e.g., algae, diatoms) and animals (protozoans, rotifers, etc.). Collectively these are called plankton. In sunlight the algae and diatoms, both containing chlorophyll, multiply and become the plant food that is eaten by many aquatic insect larvae, water snails, freshwater clams, and other small creatures. Plankton are thus the start of the aquatic food chain that leads up to the fishes. Plankton abound in quiet lowland waters but are scarce in swift mountain streams and scant or absent in alpine lakes. In consequence, fishes and other aquatic animals are numerous in lakes and streams at lower elevations but fewer in waters of the High Sierra.

FRESHWATER SPONGES   Genera *Spongilla, Ephydatia*
Pl. 219

In tufts of irregular or flat masses growing on stones, sticks, or plants; firm textured, surface bristly, with many large and small pores; color green, yellow, or brown.

DISTRIBUTION: Near quiet lake and stream margins, especially in alkaline waters, up to 6,500 ft; on objects in water.

FRESHWATER HYDRAS   Genus *Hydra*
Length 1 in. or less; body green or brown, a slender cylinder, flexible, highly contractile, with six to 10 delicate tentacles around

mouth at upper free end of body; side of body sometimes with one or more buds (the starts of new hydra).

DISTRIBUTION: On vegetation or debris in quiet cooler waters.

FRESHWATER JELLYFISH
Craspedacusta sowerbyi

Transparent, gelatinous, shape of inverted bowl, diameter to .8 in.; margin with many slender, delicate tentacles in three rows; young stage smaller, only eight tentacles.

DISTRIBUTION: Occasionally in lakes.

REMARKS: If one carefully searches, or tows a small-meshed net, in permanent lowland lakes during the warmer months he or she may find this only freshwater relative of the marine jellyfishes. Its small alternate stage is somewhat like hydra but with a branched tubular body and no tentacles.

PLANARIANS
Genera *Dendrocoelopsis, Dugesia, Phagocata*

Length .67 to 1 in.; thin, slender, soft; front end bluntly triangular with two black eyespots; body tapered, flexible, contractile, often brown, black, orange, or any combination of these colors; mouth midway on undersurface with a tubular proboscis extended to capture food.

DISTRIBUTION: On leaves and plant debris, or under stones, in cool, quiet waters or swift streams. One species, *Phagocata tahoena,* is endemic to Lake Tahoe and surrounding springs.

REMARKS: Planarians avoid strong light, hiding by day under objects in the water. After dark they come out to feed on small live or dead animals. Often they can be attracted to small pieces of meat placed on the bottom.

FRESHWATER BRYOZOANS
Pectinatella magnifica,
Plumatella repens

Mature form is an oval or rounded gelatinous mass, watery to firm, diameter to 4 in. or more; surface with many small starlike colonies; each colony includes several microscopic individuals (zooids) with short retractile tentacles, firm body enclosure, and complete digestive tract.

DISTRIBUTION: Occasionally in reservoirs and lakes on both east and west slopes.

REMARKS: *Pectinatella magnifica* has jellylike colonies that can be found on submerged rocks or wood. *Plumatella repens* produces branching, twiglike colonies on the same substrates. Late in the season bryozoans produce small dark-colored bodies (*statoblasts;* diameter to .03 in.) that overwinter after the colony dies. When the water again becomes warm, each begins to produce a colony of the form described above.

HORSEHAIR WORMS
Genera *Gordius, Paragordius*

Length .5 to 12 in., diameter to .1 in.; body thin, cylindrical, firm, opaque; front end blunt; color yellow, gray, brown, or black.

DISTRIBUTION: In shallow ponds, puddles, stream borders, or water troughs at lower elevations.

REMARKS: The long, slim adults wriggle slowly in quiet water where the females deposit eggs. From these, the microscopic larva hatch and soon attach to leaves at the water's edge that may be exposed when water levels recede. If such vegetation is eaten by crickets, grasshoppers, or some kinds of beetles, the larva burrows into soft parts of the insect's body to grow, becoming adult in a few weeks. The worms emerge when their hosts return to water. People formerly believed that these worms, seen in water, were horsehairs that had come to life.

EARTHWORMS
Class Oligochaeta

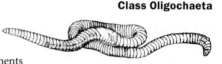

Length to 6 in. (or more); body soft, cylindrical, blunt at both ends, divided into many similar ringlike segments separated by slight grooves; able to extend, contract, and twist in any direction.

DISTRIBUTION: In damp soils up to middle elevations.

REMARKS: It is uncertain if there were any native earthworms in the Sierra prior to the arrival of Europeans. Others doubtless have been introduced with potted plants brought into the mountains and by anglers who have released worms from elsewhere into meadows with the hope of establishing convenient supplies for fish bait. Earthworms feed on decaying plant materials that they draw into their burrows in the soil. They respond to changes in temperature and soil moisture, living near the surface when the ground is damp and moderately warm, but burrowing deeper in the drought of summer or chill of winter.

Mollusks (Phylum Mollusca)

About 50 species of snails, slugs, clams, and mussels live in the Sierra. Most of them measure .13 to .75 in., and fully half are rare. The majority are land snails that eat decomposing leafy vegetation on the ground at night or on damp days; they remain hidden during summer dryness or winter cold. Each lays a number of small, gelatinous eggs, usually in a crevice or under a stone or log. Of the aquatic forms, the water snails feed on microscopic algae (green or brown scum on rocks or twigs), while the clams and mussels feed on plankton.

On snail shells, a whorl is one complete coil, while a spire is the central point or tip on the upper side.

SIDEBAND SNAILS   Genus *Monadenia*

Diameter to 1 in., height to .5 in., whorls
5.5 to six; shell and spire low; opening
U-shaped, edge rolled outward and
whitish; surface slightly shiny with
faint diagonal lines; pale cinnamon
brown, outer whorl with two buffy
bands enclosing one dark band.
DISTRIBUTION: West slope of central
Sierra at 3,500 to 5,000 ft.

SHOULDERBAND SNAILS   Genus *Helminthoglypta*

Diameter .75 to 1.25 in., height .4 to .75 in., whorls five to 5.5; shell height
moderate, spire low; opening U-shaped, upper edge thin, lower edge rolled
outward and pinkish; surface faintly roughened with fine diagonal lines;
color olive buff with one narrow brownish band.
DISTRIBUTION: Central and southern Sierra (few in north), Mariposa
County to Kern County, from lower foothills up to 7,000 ft under boulders,
fallen wood, or other shelter; usually near moisture (16 species).

CHAPARRAL SNAILS   Genus *Trilobopsis*

Diameter .25 to .33 in., height to .2 in., whorls five; shell low, thin; opening
relatively large, with three "teeth," edge thin, flared, its inner end extends
over cavity (*umbilicus*) in center of shell below; surface matte or finely
hairy; color pale yellowish brown, no band.
DISTRIBUTION: From Mariposa County north in Foothill Belt and up to
Mariposa Big Trees (four species).

HESPERIAN SNAILS   Genus *Vespericola*

Diameter to .6 in., height to .4 in., whorls 5.25 to six; shell slightly higher
than *Trilobopsis;* opening moderate, with one or no "teeth," edge flared, its
inner end partly over umbilicus; color pale yellowish brown.
DISTRIBUTION: Foothill Belt from El Dorado County north (two species).

QUICK GLOSS   *Zonitoides arboreus*

Diameter .17 in., height .1 in., whorls 4.5; shell low, thin, translucent, glossy,
color olive buff; opening nearly circular, edge thin, not rolled.
DISTRIBUTION: Common above 2,000 ft on west slope in rotting logs; also
widespread over North America, especially in cultivated areas.

WESTERN GLASS-SNAIL — *Vitrina pellucida*

Diameter .2 in., height .08 in., whorls three, the last composing most of the shell, which is delicate, shiny, transparent, and faintly greenish; opening large, circular, edge not rolled.

DISTRIBUTION: Common from Tulare County north at 6,000 ft or higher among aspens.

PACIFIC BANANA SLUG — *Ariolimax columbianus*

Pl. 220

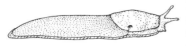

Length to 6 in.; body soft, flexible, and contractile, slimy surfaced, olive green to brown, sometimes brown spotted; a saddlelike mantle on forepart; "head" with two pairs of soft retractile tentacles; "foot" occupying most of undersurface, edges with alternating dark and light vertical lines; shell internal.

DISTRIBUTION: Mostly in foothills to 5,000 ft south to Tuolumne County on damp, leafy ground. The smaller, grayish *Deroceras laeve* occurs in wet meadows above 5,000 ft.

FOREST DISC — *Discus whitneyi*

Diameter .25 in., height .13 in., whorls 3.5 to 4.5; all visible on both upper and lower surfaces of shell; shell thin, outer whorl circular in section, surface with fine diagonal ribbing, light brown; opening large, thin edged.

DISTRIBUTION: Above 5,000 ft on west slope.

AMBER SNAILS — Genus *Succineidae*

Diameter .2 in., height .25 to .33 in.; shell high, thin, translucent, pale brown; opening oval, higher than wide.

DISTRIBUTION: Throughout Sierra above 4,000 to 5,000 ft, usually near water.

EAR SNAIL — *Lymnaea auricularia*

Diameter to .75 in., height to 2 in.; shell high, with tall, pointed spire on top, outer surface with faint curving striations, thin, translucent, and yellowish (when cleaned); opening on right side, higher than wide, edge rolled only at lower left part.

DISTRIBUTION: Common in slower streams, lakes, and ponds at all elevations.

REMARKS: In life the exterior usually has a greenish brown covering (*periostracum*) that protects the limy shell from being dissolved by any acids present in the water. This and other freshwater snails have lungs and come to the surface to breathe at intervals.

TADPOLE PHYSELLA
Physella gyrina

Diameter .25 in., height .5 in.; shell vertically oval in outline, spire low; shell thin, shiny, transparent (when cleaned), faintly brownish; opening on left side, higher than wide, edge slightly rolled out at bottom.

DISTRIBUTION: Common in waters at low elevation. Many species are in this genus, including introduced species.

KEEL SHELL
Helisoma newberryi

Diameter .5 in., height .4 in., whorls three; shell somewhat angular with slight keel around outer whorl, surface ribs fine, irregularly curved, color yellowish brown; opening on right side, irregular, somewhat ear shaped, flared on lower part, edge thin.

DISTRIBUTION: In mountain streams and lakes south to Lake Tahoe; under stones.

UBIQUITOUS PEACLAM
Pisidium casertanum

 Length to .25 in.; shell oval, swollen at middle; brown, green, buff, or light blue.

DISTRIBUTION: In quiet streams, springs, and ponds up to 8,600 ft.

PHILIPPINE CLAMS
Genus *Corbicula*

Length to .25 in.; shell oval to round, swollen at middle; brown or yellow, with heavy growth lines. Nonnative invasive species introduced to San Francisco Bay and spreading throughout North America.

DISTRIBUTION: In quiet streams, springs, and ponds up to 4,000 ft.

WESTERN PEARLSHELL
Margaritifera falcata

Length to 3.5 in.; shell thick, elliptical, somewhat angular, ridged with concentric growth lines and with horny brown or blackish covering (*periostracum*); interior of shell pearly, in life often pale blue or orange.

DISTRIBUTION: Streams and rivers up to middle elevations, on bottom in sand or mud.

REMARKS: This species and other mussels (*Anodonta californica* and *Gonidea angulata* are also found in the Sierra) burrow and crawl slowly on stream bottoms, leaving narrow grooves in the surface mud. Their eggs are fertilized and begin developing in a pouch within the female parent; then millions of the microscopic young (*glochidia*) are discharged into the water. For growth to continue, each must attach to the gills or skin of a fish and live as a parasite for several weeks, ultimately escaping as a minute clam. These "larval" stages sometimes heavily infest trout in hatcheries, resulting in the loss of many of the fish. Flesh of this clam is tough and rather unpalatable but is eaten by some persons. Shells of Midwestern relatives (*Unio*) of this mollusk are cut to make the "pearl" buttons used on clothing.

Crustaceans (Subphylum Crustacea)

All have two pairs of antennae (insects have one pair), and varying numbers of paired appendages for locomotion, feeding, and respiration. Sowbugs live in moist places on land, but other crustaceans are aquatic. The smaller kinds feed on microscopic material (plankton) and in turn are eaten by small fishes and insect larvae.

FAIRY SHRIMP   **Genus *Branchinecta***

Length about 1 in.; thorax of 11 segments, each with a pair of leafy appendages bearing gills; abdomen of nine segments; translucent, greenish or reddish; swims upside down.

DISTRIBUTION: High Sierra at 7,000 to 12,800 ft in small pools, often of snowmelt.

REMARKS: These delicate creatures swim inverted, often near the surface, by wavelike action of their slender appendages. The related *Eubranchipus,* of wide occurrence in springtime pools, has additional paired appendages between the antennae. *Streptocephalus sealli* may be found from 6,000 to 12,000 ft in wet meadows and pools without fish and may be vivid blue, green, yellow, or transparent. The San Francisco Brine Shrimp (*Artemia franciscana*), .4 in. long, with eight abdominal segments, lives in salty ponds around the Owens Valley. The Mono Lake Brine Shrimp (*A. monica*) is endemic to Mono Lake.

WATER FLEA   ***Daphnia pulex***

Length .1 in.; head free, one (fused) eye, second antenna long, two-branched and bristly, used for swimming; body thin, in folded oval shell (seemingly of two parts) with one spine at rear; transparent.

DISTRIBUTION: Common in ponds and lakes.

REMARKS: Many other species of water fleas are in the genera *Simocephalus, Moina,* and *Alonella.*

OSTRACODS or SEED SHRIMP   Genus *Ostracodes*

Length .04 in.; body thin, completely enclosed in two-part smooth, oval-hinged shell; antennae finely hairy, project from shell, used for swimming; seven pairs of appendages; whitish or greenish.

DISTRIBUTION: Throughout Sierra in ponds and lakes.

COPEPODS   Genus *Copepodes*

Length to .08 in.; body is egg shaped, shell large at front; abdomen of five segments, tapered, with hairlike projections at end, in female with two external oval egg cases; nine trunk segments, last four without appendages.

DISTRIBUTION: Common in ponds and lakes.

SOWBUGS   Genus *Porcellio*

Length to .5 in.; oval, convex above, shell of separate segments extended as plates at sides; appendages beneath on most segments; gray or brown.

DISTRIBUTION: On land in moist places under logs or stones.

REMARKS: Sowbugs are scavengers on humus. The related pill bugs (isopods) roll up when disturbed.

AMPHIPODS or SCUDS   Genera *Hyalella, Gammarus*

Length to .5 in.; body thin, humped, segments separate (thorax six, abdomen seven), appendages slender; brown.

DISTRIBUTION: In or near water, in springs, or under wet stones or logs.

CRAYFISH   *Pacifastacus leniusculus*

Pl. 221

Length to 6 in.; a firm, rounded shell over top and sides of head and thorax; abdomen of six separate, jointed segments; first pair of legs large, with stout pincers for grasping prey; four pairs of walking legs; reddish brown.

DISTRIBUTION: In quiet stream pools or lakes (down to 30 ft in Lake Tahoe); hides in vegetation or under stones, but is conspicuous on white, sandy bottoms. Introduced from the Columbia River into the Sacramento and San Joaquin Rivers; now spread into the Sierra Nevada.

Spiders and Their Relatives (Class Arachnida)

No antennae; one pair of chelicerae (mouthparts), one pair of pedipalps, and four pairs of walking legs; mostly terrestrial. All are predators with the exception of some mites and harvestmen.

Spiders (order Aranae) differ from other arachnids in having a narrow waist (*pedicel*) that clearly separates the cephalothorax from the abdomen. They are also unique among arachnids in producing silk with abdominal appendages (*spinnerets*), in injecting venom with their chelicerae, and in having male pedipalps modified for sperm transfer.

Spiders can be divided into two suborders, Mygalomorphae and Araneomorphae. Represented here by trap door spiders (family Antrodiaetidae) and tarantulas (genus *Aphonopelma*), mygalomorphs are considered the more primitive group, having two pairs of book lungs and chelicerae that move along a vertical (i.e., longitudinal) axis. Araneomorphs have one pair of book lungs and chelicerae that move along a horizontal (i.e., transverse) axis. This latter group can be further divided into those with two claws, those with three claws, and those with a *cribellum*—a flat, platelike, silk-spinning organ just in front of the spinnerets. Species that have lost their third claw have also abandoned the use of snare webs; most have become wandering hunters, although some—such as crab spiders (genus *Misumena*)—are sedentary.

Harvestmen (order Opiolones, pl. 222) are sometimes referred to as daddy longlegs, an ambiguous term (also used for some spiders and crane flies) that should best be avoided. Harvestmen superficially resemble spiders, because of their long legs, but have the abdomen broadly joined to the cephalothorax, lack the ability to produce silk, and are not venomous. Although not dangerous to humans, they do produce pungently aromatic chemicals that may challenge our olfactory sense. Genera in this order are sometimes divided into short- and long-legged forms; lacking official common names, the following names are intended only to be useful labels.

SCORPIONS   **Order Scorpiones**

Length to 3 in.; flattened; head region with small chelicerae, pedipalps with stout pincers (*chelae*); thorax with four pairs of legs and one pair of comblike ventral appendages (*pectines*); abdomen narrowed posteriorly into jointed flexible tail with sharp poisonous stinger at tip; color yellow or brown.

DISTRIBUTION: *Paruroctonus* can be found throughout the Sierra, others are at lower to middle elevations; most abundant at rock outcrops, also under logs or stones.

REMARKS: Scorpions (genera *Paruroctonus, Serradigitus,* and *Uroctonus*) hide by day and come out at night to feed on insects and small, ground-dwelling animals. Prey is caught by the pincers, killed by the stinger, and torn apart with the chelicerae to eat. In Sierra species the sting is less painful than a bee sting and not dangerous to humans. Young are born alive and ride on the female's back until their first molt. Scorpions are unusual because all species fluoresce under ultraviolet light.

TRAP DOOR SPIDERS   Family Antrodiaetidae
Length of body about .75 in. These spiders live in burrows and make a variety of entrances, with trap doors, curtains, and even turrets. At night they come to the burrow entrance and wait for insect prey to approach. They are among the most primitive of spiders as they have vestigial segmentation on the abdomen.
DISTRIBUTION: Throughout the Sierra.

TARANTULAS   Genus *Aphonopelma*
Pl. 223
Length of body about 1.5 in., leg spread 3 to 4 in.; hairy, brownish; tarsal claws two.
DISTRIBUTION: Low to middle elevations in the Sierra.
REMARKS: Tarantulas are mostly ground dwellers, active at night. They do not bite unless provoked; the bite is painful but not dangerous.

TRIANGLE SPIDERS   Genus *Hyptiotes*
Length .2 in. A cribellate spider. The triangle spider is so called because it constructs a triangular web. Two sides are attached to a branch and the spider holds the third, remaining motionless until the arrival of an insect, at which point it shakes the web to ensnare the prey.
DISTRIBUTION: Found throughout the Sierra, on foliage and in hidden recesses.

BLACK WIDOW SPIDER   *Latrodectus hesperus*
Pl. 224
Length to .6 in.; female globose, shiny black, usually with a red hourglass mark on the underside of the abdomen, rarely with a red spot on back; male smaller, narrower, with white lines on sides; young orange and white; tarsal claws three, legs without spines; web irregular, tough, sticky, retreat funnel shaped.
DISTRIBUTION: Common at lower elevations under rocks, in hollow logs, in old outbuildings, or under houses.
REMARKS: The bite is much feared and rightly so because the venom is a nerve poison, producing severe symptoms in humans and even causing death if left untreated (in about five percent of untreated cases). Fortunately the spider is not aggressive, usually trying to escape rather than attack a person. If accidentally disturbed it can bite only through soft skin. Treatment must be by a physician.

After mating the female sometimes kills and eats the male. Her eggs are laid in creamy yellow or tan egg cases about .5 in. in diameter, suspended in the web.

ORB-WEAVERS   Family Araneidae
Length to 1 in. These spiders construct orb webs, which are flat, vertical, and with radii converging at the center. The spiders come in a variety of forms and colors—though all possess three claws—and may rest in the center of the web or in an adjacent retreat. Males, once mature, leave their webs and spend the rest of their lives searching for females.
DISTRIBUTION: Found throughout the Sierra, generally on foliage, trees, or grass.

WOLF SPIDERS   Family Lycosidae
Pl. 225
Length to 1 in.; brown with various mottled patterns; female carries a spherical egg case attached to her spinnerets and later the young on top of her abdomen; although possessing three claws, wolf spiders do not spin webs but are wandering hunters.
DISTRIBUTION: Found throughout the Sierra, on ground, especially at marshy areas, or under stones.

CRAB SPIDERS   Genus *Misumena*
Length .4 in. With their two claws, these brightly colored spiders resemble crabs in general appearance. They sit and wait in flowers for prey to arrive. Related genera live on the ground and are brown in color.
DISTRIBUTION: Found throughout the Sierra.

JUMPING SPIDERS   Genus *Salticidae*
Length to .5 in. These two-clawed diurnal spiders can be distinguished by their huge front eyes and the square shape of the cephalothorax.
DISTRIBUTION: Found throughout the Sierra.
REMARKS: Jumping spiders hunt in daylight by slowly stalking their prey until a short distance away then making sudden, quick jumps to capture the prey; they have no web for snaring prey but rather a closely woven retreat made for night or hibernation. There are many species in the Sierra, some on the ground, others only on foliage.

SNAIL-EATING HARVESTMEN   Genus *Taracus*
Length .2 in. A short-legged form. These strange harvestmen have chelicerae longer than their bodies, probably used to reach into snail shells.

DISTRIBUTION: This genus of western endemics occurs throughout the Sierra. They are moisture loving and are most commonly found in and under decomposing logs.

SCULPTURED HARVESTMEN — Genus *Ortholasma*
Length .25 in. A short-legged form. These harvestmen have small, normal chelicerae and a very flat body ornamented with lacy projections.
DISTRIBUTION: This genus occurs throughout the Sierra. They can tolerate more xeric conditions and are found under a variety of ground litter.

LONG-LEGGED HARVESTMEN — Genus *Leiobunum*
Length .25 in. A long-legged form. These harvestmen have very round bodies and extremely long legs. They often aggregate in caves and cavelike habitats and bob rhythmically when disturbed. Although generally predators, they will readily feed on a wide variety of foods.
DISTRIBUTION: This genus occurs throughout the Sierra.

ROBUST HARVESTMEN — Genus *Protolophus*
Length .33 in. A long-legged form. These harvestmen have larger bodies and shorter legs than *Leiobunum*. Males have fat pedipalps, which are slender and branched in females and juveniles. They do not aggregate.
DISTRIBUTION: This genus occurs throughout the Sierra. They hide during the day and wander about in search of food at night.

PSEUDOSCORPIONS — Order Chelonethi
Length to .2 in. They have pedipalps which resemble those of scorpions, but they are much smaller and lack a tail; brown.
DISTRIBUTION: Found throughout the Sierra, under rocks, in leaf litter, in decomposing logs, and on or under loose bark of dead trees.

SUN SPIDERS, SOLPUGIDS, WINDSCORPIONS — Order Solifugae
Length to 1 in.; hairy; cephalon with large, swollen, pointed chelicerae; pedipalps leglike, giving appearance of five pairs of legs; no waist; abdomen of 10 segments, unmodified.
DISTRIBUTION: At low elevations on ground in open sandy places.

RED-SPIDER MITES — Genus *Tetranychus*
Almost microscopic; oval, compact, eight legs; mouthparts minute, piercing; red or yellow, sometimes with black spots.

DISTRIBUTION: On leaves of many broadleaved trees and shrubs, causing pale spotting.

REMARKS: Different species of mites feed on nearly all kinds of Sierra plants. Some produce gall-like swellings on leaves of willows. Still others feed on birds and mammals, producing scabs and itching. Another group lives in streams and ponds; their larvae appear as small red sacs attached to dragonflies and other insects. There are no chiggers in the Sierra that bite humans.

TICKS Genus *Dermacentor*

 Length .25 in.; body oval, flat, with shield behind head on back; chelicerae and pedipalps formed into small beak; legs eight in adults, six in young; brown or gray.

DISTRIBUTION: Widespread at low and middle elevations in the Sierra.

REMARKS: Female ticks suck blood of deer and other large mammals, swelling to .75 in. long, then dropping to the ground, where each lays thousands of eggs. The larvae hatch and climb bushes to the tips of branches, waiting to attach to a host mammal walking by. Larvae, nymphs, and adults feed on different hosts, usually of increasing size. In the northern Sierra and beyond (to Montana) ticks of this genus may transmit the spotted fever disease to humans. Other ticks (e.g., *Ornithodorus*) lack the shield. They are common on squirrels, chipmunks, and other rodents and may leave their nests under mountain cabins to bite people. They transmit relapsing fever and hence should be avoided—by not permitting rodents to nest in or around residences. The Deer Tick (*Ixodes pacificus*) is small, reddish brown with a black spot at the anterior end; this species is a vector of Lyme disease. There is no immediate sensation when a tick bites. After walking through woods or chaparral where host animals are common, people should search their skin and clothing and remove any ticks present. When removing a tick, take care that the mouthparts are not broken off and left in the skin to cause a secondary infection.

Centipedes and Millipedes
(Classes Chilopoda, Diplopoda)

Head with one pair each of antennae and jaws; trunk slender, of few or many like segments, each with one or two pairs of legs.

CENTIPEDES Genus *Scolopendra*

Pl. 226

Length to 4 in.; slender, flat; segments 21, each with one pair of legs; first pair of body appendages four-jointed, hooklike, with poison ducts; pale reddish brown.

DISTRIBUTION: Common under loose bark and on ground beneath stones and other items.

REMARKS: Different species of centipedes have various numbers of segments and legs; some are small and almost white. None in the Sierra is dangerous to humans—as are some large tropical species. Centipedes prey on insects and other small animals.

MILLIPEDES   Families Spirobolidae, Polydesmidae, Platydesmidae
Pl. 227

Length to 4 in.; cylindrical; body wall hard; segments about 100, each with two pairs of legs.

DISTRIBUTION: In moist places on ground or in rotten logs.

REMARKS: These "thousand-legged worms" glide smoothly along with wavelike movements of the many legs. When disturbed they coil up and may secrete an offensive odor from stink glands. They eat dead plants and roots, as well as animal materials.

INSECTS

OF LAND ANIMALS—both vertebrate and invertebrate—insects are by far the commonest, with beetles alone accounting for one out of every four named species in the world. One million of the world's insects have been described, but it is estimated that the total number of insect species is closer to 10 to 15 million. The abundance and dominance of insects in terrestrial ecosystems is due in part to their ability to fly, the specialized role of each stage of their life cycles, and the diversity of body forms they have evolved. More than 30,000 kinds of insects probably inhabit the Sierra, and new species are being found yearly.

Both adult and larval insects live in or on every type of soil, plant, and water, where they play a central and critical role in all aspects of the economy of nature (pls. 228–232). Bees and other flower-visiting insects are essential for pollinating flowers of many wild and cultivated plants, providing an essential service for some human food crops. Termites and some beetles reduce fallen trees to humus by their feeding and by the bacteria and molds they spread. Ants serve as predators, harvesters, and scavengers. Many beetle and fly larvae help decompose and consume carrion and dung. Every kind of insect is preyed upon by one or more of the other species of insect. Insects are also eaten by spiders, scorpions, and vertebrates ranging from fishes to mammals. Some species damage forests and crop plants, and some carry diseases to plants, animals, and humans.

Characteristics

Insects are small relative to vertebrates, with three pairs of legs and typically with two pairs of wings and one pair of sensory *antennae* (fig. 10). The body covering is usually hard, but, even when it is soft, it does not grow so it must be shed or molted at intervals during growth stages to allow for an increase in size. The body consists of a series of segments grouped in three major parts—a movable head, a rigid thorax, and a flexible abdomen. The end of the abdomen often has a pair of short appendages (*cerci*), and in females it has an egg-laying apparatus (*ovipositor*). The legs and antennae are segmented to permit movement. Each leg is of several parts: hip or shoulder segment (*coxa*), thigh (*femur*), tibia, and foot (*tarsus*); the last is of one to five segments (or none), usually with two claws. Eyes are of two kinds—simple (*ocelli,* with single lenses) and compound (masses of hundreds of individual eyes) that see by "mosaic" vision. Nearly all adult insects have two compound eyes, and some have two or three simple eyes as well. Respiration occurs by many microscopic tubes (*tracheae*) that carry air from openings (*spiracles*) in the body wall to the blood system (the blood being yellow or greenish) that reaches all interior parts. Insects possess an acute sense of smell by means of chemoreceptors located on antennae, mouthparts, ovipositors, and other parts of the body. Aided also by their mobility, insects can thus locate food sources or mates at great distances. Insects are cold-blooded (lacking temperature regulation) and must adjust their daily and yearly cycles to avoid extremes of heat and cold.

Most insects, such as grasshoppers, have chewing mouthparts. These comprise a flaplike upper lip (*labium*), a pair of strong upper jaws

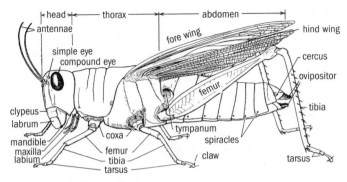

Figure 10. Insect structure: the grasshopper.

(*mandibles*), a pair of lower jaws (*maxillae*) usually with sensory feelers (*palps*), and a fused lower lip (*labium*) with central plates and lateral lobes and palps. In the center is a fleshy tongue (*hypopharynx*). From this general type the true bugs have evolved tubelike sucking mouthparts, with the mandibles and maxillae being modified as slender, piercing stylets. Moths and butterflies have a coiled tube (*proboscis*) for sucking plant nectar. Two-winged flies have mouthparts adapted for sucking (mosquitoes) or soft lapping (house flies). Bees combine mandibles for chewing with a labium and palps for sucking nectar from flowers.

Life Cycles

Among primitive insects, such as bristletails, the egg at hatching yields a small individual similar in form to an adult. At each of several molts the animal increases in size, finally becoming a sexually mature adult. This group undergoes no metamorphosis or transformation in form during growth. Next, with grasshoppers, true bugs, many aquatic insects, and related forms, the young, called *nymphs*, at hatching resemble adults but lack wings. At successive molts, wing pads on the middle (meso-) and hind (meta-) thorax increase in size. At the last molt the nymph becomes an adult with membranous wings. This type of growth is called incomplete metamorphosis (fig. 11).

Finally, in the lacewings, moths and butterflies, beetles, flies, and wasps, the young hatch as wormlike *larvae* (caterpillars, grubs, or wrigglers) with six true legs on the thoracic segments (in some groups the abdominal segments are also supported by pairs of *prolegs* that are lost in the adult stage). This is the stage of feeding and molting in order to grow, with the young being totally unlike the adult in form and habits. Wing pads develop internally. The full-grown larva transforms through a final molt into a *pupa* (the *chrysalis* of butterflies), which often is formed within a silken cocoon. Within the pupa, larval structures are broken down and those of the adult develop from primordial tissue. From this stage the adult emerges and its wings unfold—a complete metamorphosis. This

NO METAMORPHOSIS
Bristletail

INCOMPLETE METAMORPHOSIS
Grasshopper

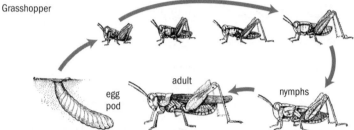

COMPLETE METAMORPHOSIS
Alfalfa Butterfly

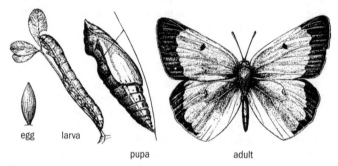

Figure 11. Insect life histories.

"resting" pause (*diapause*), often occurring between the pupa and the adult life stages but possible at egg or larva stages, is one of the key evolutionary achievements of insects. It has given insects great versatility in exploiting different habitats because they can wait out unfavorable seasons (winter cold or summer drought) and synchronize their life cycles to match optimal conditions.

Collecting

Insects are ideal subjects for nature study because they are easy to find and collect (with a net or the hands) and easy to observe alive or to preserve. Due to the great number of insects, this hobby may be pursued with no harmful effects to insect populations and with great benefit to the collector. Specimens may be killed in a bottle containing plaster of Paris or wadded paper saturated with the volatile fluid, ethyl acetate. Hard-shelled adults dry quickly and require no skinning or preservative. They may be laid on cotton under glass or mounted by inserting a fine pin through the thorax (for beetles, through the right wing cover). Butterflies should be spread while soft so that the hind margins of the front wings form a line at right angles to the body and the hind wings are brought up to extend slightly under the front wings. Styrofoam or balsa wood is useful for a spreading board if a wide trough is cut to hold the thick body. Then the wings can be held in place with strips of paper pinned to the substrate. The specimen will dry in a few days and remain in the spread position. It may then be pinned in a box with corrugated cardboard or a cork bottom. If the specimen is to have scientific value, exact information on the place and date of capture and the name of collector is written on a small label put on the pin under the insect. A permit is required to collect insects in national or state parks, but elsewhere in the Sierra there are no restrictions.

In this handbook a number of common dragonflies and butterflies are highlighted (as with the plants and vertebrates) because they are popular and familiar organisms to study. Other insects are discussed mostly at the level of families and orders, with mention of examples found in the Sierra.

Taxonomy mostly follows Borror et al. (1989).

Springtails (Order Collembola)
Pl. 233

Length to .25 in.; no wings; chewing mouthparts (retracted in head); antennae four- to eight-jointed; abdomen of six segments, usually with a springing organ below. Young resemble adults. In logs, wet leaf mold, or soil; some on snow; eat decaying plants. *Entomobrya,* common on ground; *Podwa aquatica,* may blacken surface of ponds.

Silverfish (Order Thysanura)
Pl. 234

Length .5 to 1.75 in.; no wings; chewing mouthparts (sometimes retracted into mouth); antennae long; body flattened and slender with gray scales; abdomen of 10 to 11 segments with short appendages below and three slender "tails" at end. Young resemble adults. On ground, eat decayed plants.

REMARKS: Bristletails (Archeognatha) are very similar but now split off into their own order. They are distinguished by their more cylindrical bodies with the thorax somewhat arched; *Pedetontus californicus* is found in foothills, and *Mesomachilis* occurs under fallen needles or loose bark in the forest of the Mixed Conifer Belt.

Mayflies (Order Ephemeroptera)

Length to 1.75 in.; body soft, delicate; wings four, membranous, hind pair often reduced, all held vertically at rest; chewing mouthparts poorly

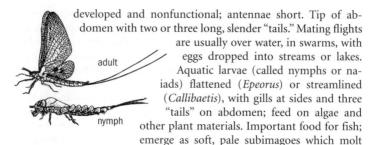

developed and nonfunctional; antennae short. Tip of abdomen with two or three long, slender "tails." Mating flights are usually over water, in swarms, with eggs dropped into streams or lakes. Aquatic larvae (called nymphs or naiads) flattened (*Epeorus*) or streamlined (*Callibaetis*), with gills at sides and three "tails" on abdomen; feed on algae and other plant materials. Important food for fish; emerge as soft, pale subimagoes which molt after a few hours into sexually mature adults. Adults live ephemeral lives of only a few hours or days.

Dragonflies and Damselflies (Order Odonata)

Length to 4 in., wing span to 5 in.; wings four, membranous, with strong veins and many cross veins; chewing mouthparts; eyes very large; antennae short, bristlelike; abdomen long, slender; brown or black with red, green, or blue and yellow patterns. Mating flights in tandem, male holding head or thorax of female by tip of his abdomen; female obtains sperm by touching end of her abdomen to receptacle on second abdominal segment of male. Eggs dropped onto water or inserted on or in stems of aquatic plants. Larvae (nymphs or naiads) in ponds or streams, stout, with short wing pads, lower jaws on long, hinged part (labium) to catch aquatic insects, small fish, and tadpoles. Adults prey on flying insects.

Dragonflies (suborder Anisoptera) are large, strong fliers; hind wings wider at base than fore wings; all wings held horizontally at rest. Legs crowded together and moved forward onto thorax, not used for walking but adapted for perching. In flight, legs held as sort of basket to scoop up insects. Dragonfly larvae breathe by gills within the rectum where oxygenated water circulates, often ejected forcibly, producing jet-propelled forward movement. They live underwater from a couple months to three years before transforming into short-lived adults (four to six weeks in some species).

Damselflies (suborder Zygoptera) are smaller than dragonflies; weak fliers; wings held vertically over back or loosely spread at rest. Larvae with three external leaflike gills at tip of abdomen, living underwater four to 12 months with a flight season lasting only a few weeks.

COMMON GREEN DARNER   *Anax junius*
Pl. 235

Length 3 in.; males have solid green thorax with blue abdomen; most females are brown and green but some are colored like males. Found about fields and waterways throughout the Sierra Nevada. From April to November, males may be seen sporadically patrolling their territories over fields and waterways. This large dragonfly is one of few North American species to migrate south in winter. Green Darners have separate populations that are either resident or migratory, with the migratory populations heading south to begin a second annual generation. In late summer large numbers may swarm in mountain meadows prior to migrating.

BLUE-EYED DARNER   *Aeshna multicolor*
Pl. 236

Length 3 in.; bright blue eyes and face; thorax and abdomen appear bluish in flight but are actually a mosaic of blue, black, and copper. Found around ponds, lakes, slow streams, or fields up to 8,000 ft. These large and powerful dragonflies are often seen feeding over fields during the day, though they may retreat to the shade of nearby trees at midday. Males also patrol large areas of water in an irregular pattern, wandering slowly about emergent vegetation. Seven species of *Aeshna* occur in the Sierra Nevada with field identification being difficult without good views of the thoracic stripes and appendages at the tip of the abdomen.

GRAPPLETAIL   *Octogomphus specularis*
Pl. 237

Length 2 in.; face yellow to pale green; eyes black; thorax black with large yellow, gray, or green patches; abdomen mostly black, with grapplelike appendages at the tip (male only). Occurs along fast-moving streams from foothills up to Mixed Conifer Belt. These attractive dragonflies are active from April until August, and males are commonly seen perching on stones amid riffles.

PACIFIC SPIKETAIL   *Cordulegaster dorsalis*
Pl. 238

Length 3.5 in.; pale face with blue eyes; thorax dark with wide yellow stripes; abdomen dark with large yellow dorsal spots on each segment. A big, striking, powerful dragonfly that frequently is seen patrolling long stretches along small wooded streams or roadsides up to 6,000 ft. Males fly at smooth, steady speeds a foot or two above streams. When laying eggs, females hover over shallow water and dip their abdomens vertically into the muddy bottom with a rapid motion, like that of a sewing machine.

TWELVE-SPOTTED SKIMMER   *Libellula pulchella*
Pl. 239

Length 2 in.; each wing has three large dark spots with white spots in between; abdomen whitish with blue tinge in males and brownish in females, with yellow stripe down each side; females lack white spots on wings. Eight species of *Libellula* occur in the Sierra Nevada, most being widespread along ponds, lakes, and rivers. From April until October, these dragonflies are commonly seen hovering over the surface of still waters. Other skimmers common in the Sierra Nevada include the Eight-spotted Skimmer (*L. forensis*), which has two dark spots on each wing (lacks dark wing tips of *L. pulchella*) and is common on the east side; the Four-spotted Skimmer (*L. quadrimaculata*), which is olive-colored and has a tiny black spot mid-length on each wing; the Widow Skimmer (*L. luctuosa*), which has a whitish, blue-tinged body and dark wing bases bordered by white at midwing, found at lower elevations on the west side; and the Flame Skimmer (*L. saturata*), which has a bright red orange body and reddish wing bases.

VARIEGATED MEADOWHAWK   *Sympetrum corruptum*
Pl. 240

Length 2 in.; variably colored with mosaic of reds and olives, looking reddish (adult males) or orangish tan (females and immature males) from a distance. Best field mark is a row of white spots along side of abdomen. Ten species of *Sympetrum* occur in the Sierra Nevada with *S. corruptum* the most common and widespread. In late summer and fall five to six species at a time may be found around wet mountain meadows and boggy lakes. All of these dragonflies are variously red and have a characteristic manner of holding their wings angled forward while at rest. Variegated Meadowhawks are found near still waters and slow streams up to 10,000 ft and also in clearings and along roadsides.

AMERICAN RUBYSPOT   *Hetaerina americana*
Pl. 241

Length 1.5 in.; male is dark bodied (bronzy) with brilliant ruby red patch at wing base; female is less colorful with pale eyes and orangish wing bases. Male rubyspots are a startling splash of color as they flit along small, shaded foothill streams. These damselflies range up into the Mixed Conifer Belt.

CALIFORNIA SPREADWING   *Archilestes californica*
Pl. 242

Length 1.75 to 2.38 in.; males have dark bodies with pale gray abdomen tips and blue eyes; females are brownish. The spreadwings are recognized for perching with wings held loosely open but not flat like dragonflies. California Spreadwings occur along foothill streams on the west slope, where they hang from the sunny leaves of willows and alders and make short flights to capture prey. This fall species is not seen in large numbers until September to October.

VIVID DANCER   *Argia vivida*
Pl. 243

Length 1.25 in.; males are a vivid blue and black, with thin black thorax stripes pinched at midlength; females either resemble males or are tan or pale gray where males are blue. Mostly found along streams or seeps at a wide range of elevations but frequently travels long distances from water. Several species of dancers, which hold their wings closed vertically above their abdomens, occur in the Sierra Nevada. Dancers are unique among damselflies in preferring to perch on logs, stones, or open ground rather than on vegetation.

NORTHERN BLUET   *Enallagma cyathigerum*
Pl. 244
Length 1.25 in.; colored much like the Vivid Dancer but thorax stripes wider and not pinched, and eyes are black instead of dark blue. The Northern Bluet is one of five common and widespread species of bluets in the Sierra Nevada. Unlike dancers, these damselflies hold their wings alongside their abdomens when at rest. Bluets are closely associated with aquatic habitats, where they fly low over still water surfaces and perch on floating debris or emergent vegetation.

Grasshoppers, Katydids, and Crickets (Order Orthoptera)

Length to 2.5 in.; wings usually present, fore wings tough, colored like body, hind wings membranous, large, folded fanlike at rest; chewing mouthparts; antennae many-segmented; hind legs large for jumping (except certain wingless forms). Some adults sing (stridulate) by rubbing together comblike edges of legs or wings. Young are like adults but with short wing pads. Eat green plants; a few predaceous.

GRASSHOPPERS   Family Acrididae
Length to 1.5 in.; antennae short; tarsi three-segmented. Plant feeders, sometimes destructive to vegetation, on meadows or rocky slopes; egg pods laid in ground. *Cratypedes neglectus,* wings yellow marked, in mountains; flies with clicking noise made by hind wings snapping in flight.

LONG-HORNED GRASSHOPPERS or KATYDIDS   Family Tettigoniidae
Pl. 245
Length to 2.5 in.; antennae very long; tarsi four-segmented; ovipositor on abdomen long, bladelike. Live in green foliage that they resemble. Males sing day or night. Eggs laid in rows on leaves or twigs. *Microcentrum rhombifolium,* the Broad-winged Katydid, with broad rhomboid fore wings, occurs up to middle elevations.

JERUSALEM CRICKETS   Family Stenopelmatidae
Pl. 246
Length to 1.25 in.; robust, wingless, head large; antennae long; tarsi four-segmented; abdomen cross-barred. On ground, feeds on roots and tubers,

eggs laid singly in ground. *Stenopelmatus fuscus* is commonly encountered in garden soils, where its fearsome appearance and bite may leave a lasting impression.

CRICKETS   **Family Gryllidae**

Length to 1.5 in.; antennae long; tarsi three-segmented; abdomen with two long tails, also long ovipositor in female; male chirps. Field Cricket (*Gryllus assimilis*): stout bodied, brown to black, under stones, eggs laid in ground; Snowy Tree Cricket (*Oecanthus fultoni*) has delicate pale green body, young white, on foliage where eggs are laid.

WALKINGSTICKS, TIMEMAS   **Superfamily Phasmatodea**
Pl. 247
Length to 1 in.; form of short stout "walking stick"; no wings; legs short, tarsi three- or five-segmented. Usually green or pink, resembling foliage that they eat. *Timema californica* ranges through the foothills to middle elevations, present in late winter and early spring.

ROCKCRAWLERS or GRYLLOBLATTAS
Family Grylloblattidae
Length to 1 in.; slender; no wings; legs short, tarsi five-segmented; two tail-like appendages. Live deep in crevices under snow or glaciers and in ground above 7,000 ft; nocturnal and active on snow surfaces mostly during winter months. *Grylloblatta bifratrilecta* occurs at Sonora Pass, and other species are known at elevations to 12,000 ft.

Termites (Order Isoptera)
Pl. 248
Length .25 to 1 in.; chewing mouthparts; antennae short, nine-plus segmented; young or workers and soldiers (with big heads and jaws) wingless, blind, soft bodied, whitish—sometimes called "white ants"; sexual forms male and female (queen) flat bodied, wings four, long, equal, filmy, shed after mating flight (usually after a rain). A social, colonial insect that lives in tunnels in soil or wood, feeds on wood (cellulose) and fungi digested by bacteria and protozoans in termite gut. *Reticulitermes,* small, in wood and soil; *Zootermopsis,* large, in pine logs up to 9,000 ft.

Stoneflies (Order Plecoptera)

Length to 1.5 in.; chewing mouthparts often reduced; antennae long, slender; wings four, membranous, hind wings larger, pleated over back at rest;

body pale green to brown; pronotum flat and rectangular. Eggs dropped on water or glued to rocks. Nymphs long and slender (*Alloperla*) or stout, with two "tails"; crawl out on streamside rocks or plants for molting to adult form, leaving dried skins. Nymphs eat plant tissues or aquatic insects. Important as fish food and as bait for anglers. Adults appear in any month. *Taenionema pacifica* ranges up to 7,000 ft. *Capnia lacustra* are wingless as adults; nymphs to depths of 100 to 400 ft in Lake Tahoe.

Psocids (Order Psocoptera)

Length to .25 in.; either winged or wingless and pale, or convex, winged, and pigmented; wings four, clear, held rooflike over body at rest; swollen area toward front of head between antennae; antennae slender. Young (barklice) and adults on bark or foliage of coniferous and other trees; booklice (*Liposcelis decolor*) in houses.

Chewing and Sucking Lice (Order Phthiraptera)

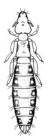

Length to .25 in.; Chewing lice have broad head, flat body, wingless, and chewing mouthparts; feed on feathers of birds (e.g., Duck Louse, *Anaticola crassicornis*) or rarely on hair of some mammals. Sucking lice have narrow head, retractable piercing-sucking mouthparts; suck blood of deer, ground squirrels (*Linognathoides laeviusculus*), rabbits, and other mammals. The tarsi of sucking lice are one-segmented and equipped with a single large claw for hooking onto hairs of a host.

Chewing Louse   Sucking Louse

True Bugs (Order Heteroptera)

Wings four (rarely absent), front pair leathery at forward end (*base*), membranous at distal half, tips overlap at rest, leaving an enlarged triangular area (*scutellum*) between bases; mouthparts form slender sucking tube attached forward on head; scent glands produce pungent odor. Young (nymphs) similar to adults but with wing pads.

Boxelder Bug

STINK BUGS   **Family Pentatomidae**

Length to .75 in.; five-sided outline; with simple eyes; beak four-segmented; antennae five-segmented; usually with triangular scutellum. Produce strong, characteristic odor when disturbed. Feed on many plants; Harlequin Cabbage Bug (*Murgantia histrionica*) on plants of cabbage family; a few (*Podisus*) prey on caterpillars.

LEAF-FOOTED BUGS   Family Coreidae

Resemble members of Lygaeidae but many parallel veins in wing membrane. Feed on squashes (*Anasa*).

SEED BUGS   Family Lygaeidae
Pl. 249

Length to .75 in.; with simple eyes; beak four-segmented; wing membrane with only five parallel veins. Often eat seeds on the ground. Small false chinch bugs (*Nysius*) on composites and other plants; cone bugs (*Gastrodes*) eat seeds of gray pine; milkweed bugs (*Oncopeltus, Lygaeus kalmii*) on milkweed.

BOXELDER BUGS   Family Rhopalidae

Similar to Coreidae except that they lack scent gland openings between the second and third pair of legs. Feed on box elder (*Leptocoris rubrolineatus*), legumes, and other plants.

FLAT BUGS   Family Aradidae

Length to .5 in.; oval, very flat, brown; no simple eyes; beak four-segmented, with long tube (setae) that uncoils to suck juices from fungi. Live under bark or in termite galleries (*Mezira*), on wood-rot and other fungi (*Aradus debilis*).

LACE BUGS   Family Tingidae
Pl. 250

Length to .25 in.; wings enlarged into lacy shield that hides flat body, wings whitish or clear, many-celled; no simple eyes; beak four-segmented. *Corythucha* feeds on undersurface of leaves of ash, alder, lupine, producing white areas and black fecal spots; cast skins of young often adhere to leaves; eggs inserted into leaf tissue.

ASSASSIN BUGS   Family Reduviidae

Length to 1 in.; with large, beady protruding eyes; beak three-segmented, touching groove between front legs. *Apiomerus* preys on bees in flowers. Kissing Bug or Bloodsucking Conenose (*Triatoma protracta*) is .75 to 1 in. long dark brown, sucks blood of wood rats (*Neotoma*), may attack humans when these rats nest in foothill houses. Kissing Bug bites are painful and may cause serious illness in persons who have become sensitized by repeated attacks. Similar-looking ambush bugs (*Phymatidae*) have slightly clubbed antennae and enlarged front femora to grab bees coming to flowers.

DAMSEL BUGS   **Family Nabidae**
Pl. 251

Length to .33 in.; slender, gray; beak long, four-segmented; with simple eyes. *Nabis americoferus,* agile, on plants or ground, preys on insects.

SWALLOW BUGS and BED BUGS   **Family Cimicidae**
Length to .25 in.; oval, body flat, light brown; no simple eyes; beak three-segmented, serving to pierce skin of mammals or birds and suck blood; wing pads short in adults. *Oeciacus vicarius,* in swallow nests; *Cimex lectularius,* in beds of humans (very rare species in California).

MINUTE PIRATE BUGS   **Family Anthocoridae**
Pl. 252

Length to .13 in.; oval; brown or black and white; with simple eyes; beak three-segmented; fore wings like plant bugs (Miridae). On flowers (*Orius tristicolor*), foliage of trees, and bark of conifers; prey on mites and minute insects. Both the pinkish nymphs and adults can inflict pinprick bites, especially on sweaty skin.

PLANT BUGS
Family Miridae

Length to .5 in.; oval or slender; no simple eyes; beak four-segmented, used to suck plant juices; fore wings with small area bent down on outer edge. One or more species on many kinds of Sierra plants, often in great numbers: *Lygus hesperus,* on lupines; *Platylygus,* stout, tawny, on pines; *Orthotylus,* slender, green, on willows; *Dacerla,* ant mimic, on pines and lupines. *Deraeocoris* preys on aphids.

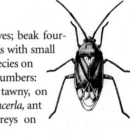

WATERSTRIDERS   **Family Gerridae**
Pl. 253

Length to 1 in.; body narrow; legs long, tarsi with claws attached above tip (avoiding breaking surface film on which strider walks); some have wings reduced or absent. *Gerris remigis,* on ponds and stream pools at all elevations; eggs laid on floating objects.

WATER BOATMEN   **Family Corixidae**
Length to .5 in.; oval; black or brown; swim underwater with *backside up,* using fringed oarlike hind legs. Lack gills and obtain air by rising to surface of water and capturing air bubble held as a silvery film on abdomen. Eat minute plants and animals gathered with forelegs.

Sigara, small, to .25 in.; *Hesperocorixa* to .5 in. In ponds and stream pools at all elevations.

BACKSWIMMERS
Family Notonectidae

Length to .5 in.; body narrow, convex above, concave below; swim *upside down* with long oarlike hind legs. Obtain air by touching tip of abdomen to water surface. Prey on other insects and may bite people. *Buenoa,* slender, to .33 in. long; *Notonecta unifasciata,* stout, to .5 in. long.

GIANT WATER BUGS
Family Belostomatidae
Pl. 254

Length to 3 in.; body long, oval, flat above; two short straplike posterior tubes under wings used to obtain air at surface of water; beak short, stout. Prey on young fish and insects by gripping them in its stout front legs; will bite humans severely if handled. *Lethocerus americanus,* length 2 to 3 in., attracted to lights at night, lays eggs on plant stalks at water surface; *Abedus,* length to 1.5 in., and *Belostoma,* length to .75 in., glue eggs on back of male, who carries them until hatching.

WATERSCORPIONS
Family Nepidae
Pl. 255

Length to 2 in.; slender, sticklike; front legs long, grasping, abdomen with two long breathing tubes. *Ranatra fusca,* usually hidden among sticks and plants in shallow water; predaceous.

TOAD BUGS
Family Gelastocoridae
Pl. 256

Length to .5 in.; rough surfaced; oval, eyes big; color matches shores of sandy or muddy ponds and streams; named for the froglike appearance of its head and eyes. *Gelastocoris oculatus* preys on small insects.

Cicadas, Hoppers, Aphids, and Others (Order Homoptera)

Those in suborder Auchenorryncha have antennae short, bristlelike; tarsi three-jointed; full winged. Mouthparts form slender sucking tube, attached below at back of head. Young (nymphs) usually like adults but with wing pads.

Spittlebugs

Those in suborder Sternorryncha have antennae usually well developed; tarsi one- or two-jointed; females usually slow moving or fixed.

CICADAS
Family Cicadidae
Pl. 257

Length to 1.5 in.; stout bodied; three simple eyes. Males sing or click to attract females, sometimes excruciatingly loudly, producing sound by a tymbal chamber and membrane. Eggs inserted in plant tissue. Nymphs molelike, forelegs huge, burrow in ground and feed on roots for one to 17 years. Singing cicadas (*Okanagana*) vibrate platelike membranes at base of abdomen; smaller, narrower black woodland cicadas (*Platypedia*) make clicking noise with wings. All wary, some ventriloquists.

TREEHOPPERS   Family *Membracidae*
Pl. 258
Length to .5 in. Like leafhoppers but prothorax projecting as spine or hump. In meadows and on oak trees (*Platycotis vittata*).

FROGHOPPERS or SPITTLEBUGS   Family Cercopidae
Length to .5 in. Like leafhoppers but plant-sucking nymphs surrounded by a white froth or "spittle." *Aphrophora permutata,* on conifers, chaparral, various shrubs, and other plants.

LEAFHOPPERS   Family Cicadellidae
Length to .33 in.; slender; two simple eyes; appearance similar to froghoppers but hind tibiae with rows of spines. Eggs inserted in plants. Nymphs resemble adults, feed on vegetation, will jump readily. Many species in mountain meadows and on willow or alder; *Empoasca abrupta,* in foothills. Planthoppers (*Fulgoroidea*) resemble leafhoppers but head projects forward.

JUMPING PLANTLICE or PSYLLIDS   Family Psyllidae
Length to .25 in.; pale-colored; antennae nine- or ten-segmented; legs enlarged for jumping; tarsi two-segmented. Common on alders along stream margins; also on willows and chapparal plants. The Potato Psyllid (*Paratrioza cockerelli*) breeds on plants of the nightshade family.

WHITEFLIES   Family Aleyrodidae
Length to .13 in.; body and wings covered with white powder; tarsi two-segmented; adults mothlike in appearance, nymphs scalelike, attached to manzanita and other plants. *Dialeurodes citri* is a valley and foothill species.

PLANTLICE or APHIDS   Family Aphididae
Length to .25 in; legs not developed for jumping; antennae three- to seven-segmented; tarsi two-segmented; some with four wings, many wingless (or successive winged and wingless generations, often on alternate host plants). Some produce waxy covering, and many secrete honeydew. Most Sierra

plants are fed upon by one or more aphids; aphids on manzanita produce a reddish rolled gall on the edges of leaves. The Green Bug (*Schizaphis graminum*) lives on wild and introduced grasses.

SCALE INSECTS and MEALYBUGS **Superfamily Coccoidea**

Length to .25 in.; tarsi one-segmented; males very small, lack mouthparts and do not feed, with one pair of wings and a pair of white "tails"; females wingless, stationary (scales) or slow moving (mealybugs); body covered with powdery or scaly wax; mouthparts threadlike, often longer than body, inserted through tough, woody bark to suck juices of pines, oaks, and other plants. On bark and needles of pines (*Matsucoccus*), on roots and foliage of many Sierra plants (mealybugs), and on bark of aspen and other deciduous trees (San José Scale, *Quadraspidiotus perniciosus*).

Thrips (Order Thysanoptera)

Length to .33 in.; body slender, wings four, narrow, fringed with long hairs; mouthparts for rasping and sucking; tarsi end in protrusible "bladder"; antennae six- to nine-segmented. Young with external wing pads. Young and adults suck fluids of flowers and leaves, producing pale spots. A few large black species prey on mites under bark of conifers and other trees.

Dobsonflies and Alderflies (Order Megaloptera)

Length to 2 in.; like Neuroptera, except hind wings broader at base than fore wings. Aquatic larvae (hellgrammites) long, with two slender, tapering gills on each abdominal segment; predaceous. Dobsonfly larvae (*Corydalus, Protochauloides*) among stones in shallow water at sides of streams; no central filament at tip of abdomen. Alderfly larvae (*Sialis*) have a terminal filament and live at the bottom of deep pools in streams and lakes. Both serve as trout food and fish bait.

Lacewings and Ant Lions (Order Neuroptera)

Antennae long; chewing mouthparts; wings four, both fore and hind wings similar in size and shape, net veined, transparent, held rooflike over body at rest; tarsi five-segmented. Larvae stout, spiny, three pairs of legs, jaws long and grooved to suck juices of other insects used as prey. Pupae in cocoons on plants or in ground.

GREEN LACEWINGS **Family Chrysopidae**

Pl. 259

Length to .75 in. *Chrysopa*, delicate, pale or bright green, eyes golden, wings lacy, green; on vegetation; each minute egg on end of threadlike filament; larvae bristly, feed on aphids, etc.

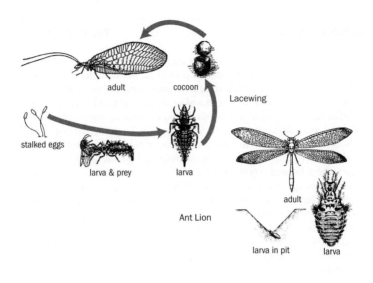

adult

cocoon

Lacewing

stalked eggs

larva & prey

larva

adult

Ant Lion

larva in pit

larva

ANT LIONS   Family Myrmeleontidae

Pl. 260

Length to 2 in. *Myrmeleon,* slender, with short, knobbed antennae; larvae or "doodlebugs" short, stout, live in small conical pit in sand or dust into which ants and other prey fall and are captured before they can escape.

Snakeflies (Order Raphidioptera)

Pl. 261

Like lacewings but fore part of thorax and head are long, cylindrical; female with long taillike ovipositor. Larvae slender, run both backward and forward; predaceous on small insects. *Agulla,* on oaks and many conifers.

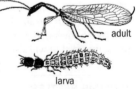

adult

larva

Beetles (Order Coleoptera)

Antennae usually 11-segmented; mouthparts for chewing; fore wings thick, leathery, meet along midline; hind wings folded under fore wings at rest. Larva worm- or grublike, usually with three pairs of legs; pupa usually free, not in cocoons. Over a quarter million species of the world's beetles have been described so far—more than twice as many as any other group of organisms. Beetles are extremely diverse in form, behavior, and habitat.

GROUND BEETLES
Pl. 262

Family Carabidae

Length to 1 in.; mostly blackish, long legged, head narrower than thorax; trochanters shaped like little footballs. Common at all elevations, under stones and at edge of water; nocturnal; larvae active, long, flattish above, with two cerci at end of body; prey on other insects and snails. Pupate in chamber in ground. *Scaphinotus,* large (to 1 in.), wing covers broadly rounded, preys on snails; up to Subalpine Belt. *Bembidion,* length to .17 in., black, at edge of ponds and streams. *Calosoma,* length to 1.5 in., stout, blue or black, on ground and hardwood trees in riparian areas, preys on caterpillars. Tiger beetles (Cicindelinae, pl. 263) are a distinctive group within the Carabidae that are brightly colored with a head as wide as the thorax; run and fly rapidly; in open, sandy places; larvae live in deep holes, move up and down by use of hooks on fifth abdominal segment, head of the first thoracic segment is modified into a roughened shield to plug the hole like a trapdoor; prey on insects on ground surface. *Cicindela longilabris* is metallic green and common in open areas around wet meadows; *C. plutonica* is metallic blue to black, rare around snowmelt ponds above treeline. *Omus californicus* all black, flightless, nocturnal.

PREDACEOUS DIVING BEETLES

Family Dytiscidae

Length to 1.5 in.; oval, smooth, shiny; long threadlike antennae; hind legs flat, fringed with hairs, move simultaneously like oars for swimming; air taken at surface by tip of abdomen and stored under wing covers when diving. Eggs laid on water plants; larvae (water tigers) long, slender, with two long cerci, prey on many insects. Pupate in small earthen chambers at edge of water. Many species at all elevations. *Dytiscus marginicollis* is black with metallic green cast; length to 1.5 in.; up to 6,000 ft.

larva

adult

D. dauricus similar except female with deep, close set grooves in elytra (wing covers); 6,000 to 12,000 ft. Larval *Dytiscus* prey on a variety of aquatic insects, but will also take salamanders, frogs, and small fish.

WHIRLIGIG BEETLES

Family Gyrinidae

Length to .5 in.; oval, lustrous, eyes divided horizontally, upper pair for surface vision, lower for sight underwater. Larvae long, slender, with two gills on each abdominal segment, two pairs on ninth segment. Pupate in mud chambers on plants above water. Whirl and gyrate in "schools" on surfaces of ponds and streams; predaceous.

divided eye

adult

WATER SCAVENGERS

Family Hydrophilidae

Length to 1 in.; with hind legs adapted for swimming (legs moved alternately unlike Dytiscidae); antennae short and clubbed. Eggs laid in cases;

larvae slender, some with lateral gills; cerci segmented; pupation in ground chamber on shore. Some nonaquatic species live in dung. *Tropisternus lateralis,* length to .5 in., metallic green to black with buff margins; temporary pools up to 7,000 ft.

ROVE BEETLES   Family Staphylinidae
Length to .75 in.; wing covers short, exposing six to seven abdominal segments. Scavengers in dung or predators. Larvae resemble those of ground beetles (Carabidae).

CARRION BEETLES   Family Silphidae
Length to 1.5 in.; body broad, flat above (*Oxelytrum*) or stout with short wing covers (*Nicrophorus*). Eggs laid in carrion, fungi, or decaying plants where larvae feed. Larvae broad, black, with lateral plates. *Nicrophorus* buries small animals as food for larvae.

SCARAB BEETLES   Family Scarabaeidae
Pl. 264
Length to 1.5 in.; body broad, deep, convex; legs spiny; antennal plates flattened, usually touching. Larvae stout, crescent-shaped white grubs, commonly feed on roots in soil; some live in dung. The 10-lined June Beetle (*Polyphylla decemlineata*) lives on roots and is attracted to lights in early summer. Other common scarabs are the metallic green pine chafers (*Dichelonyx*), small brown dung beetles (*Aphodius*), and large brown rain beetles (*Pleocoma*) that emerge during first heavy rains of fall when males fly to wingless females remaining in emergence holes. A bluish Sierra species (*Boreocanthon simplex*), like the sacred scarabs of Egypt, rolls dung into a ball on which it lays an egg before burying it to provide food for larvae. Males of the introduced Dung Beetle (*Onthophagus taurus*) have curved bull-like horns on each side of their head; to 7,000 ft.

WATER PENNIES   Family Psephenidae
Pl. 265
Length to .25 in.; oval, brownish, covered with fine hairs; abdomen of six segments below; legs with large claws. Adults terrestrial but crawl underwater to lay eggs. Larvae to .75 in. long, oval, flat, with gills on second to sixth abdominal segments, cling to rocks in swift-flowing streams. *Eubrianax* extends up to Upper Montane Belt.

RIFFLE BEETLES   Family Elmidae
Length to .1 in.; brown or black, covered with fine hairs; abdomen of five segments below; claws large. Larvae cylindrical, with six legs. Adults live in fast-flowing, well-aerated water, using oxygen from air trapped in film

against the body; cannot swim but crawl over the stream bottom or cling to roots of plants in water. *Optioservus,* black with red spots.

METALLIC WOOD BORERS   Family Buprestidae
Pl. 266

Length to 1.5 in.; spine on undersurface of thorax fits into groove; hind angles of thorax not spinelike. Larvae ("flat-headed" borers), legless, with prothorax (not head) large and flat; bore in wood of living or dead trees, making tunnels that are flat (shape of prothorax), not round like those of "round-headed" cerambycid larvae.

REMARKS: The most conspicuous of many Sierra species is the Golden Buprestid (*Buprestis aurulenta*); it is iridescent coppery green with gold margins. Eggs are laid on fire scars or the exposed pitchy wood of conifers. Larvae bore into heartwood, reducing the value of the tree for lumber. Pupation and transformation to adults takes place in tunnels during summer and early fall. Adults hibernate there, emerging the following summer. There are records of adults emerging from timbers in houses 25 or more years after the logs were milled. Other common buprestids are the large mottled brown *Chalcophora* on conifers; the small, smooth *Melanophila,* which are attracted by smoke and oviposit on conifers after a forest fire; and the black and white or yellowish *Acmaeodera* on chaparral plants. Adults of the last type frequent flowers.

CLICK BEETLES   Family Elateridae
Pl. 267

Length to 1.5 in.; spine on prosternum fits a groove in the metasternum; the latter has a catch so that the body can be arched when upside down and then suddenly bent forward, causing a click as the beetle is catapulted into the air. Hind angles of prothorax project, spinelike. Larvae (wireworms) long, slender and cylindrical, with three pairs of short legs. Feed on roots of plants in ground and pupate there. The eyed elater (*Alaus*) is dark gray with two large eyespots on the pronotum.

LIGHTNING BUGS   Family Lampyridae
Pl. 268

Length to .5 in.; head covered by large thorax, abdomen seven-segmented. Larvae slender, with six legs, prey on earthworms, snails, and insects in the ground. The Pink Glowworm (*Microphotus angustus*) of the Foothill Belt has winged males with grayish brown prothorax and wing covers. Females lack wings, resemble larvae, and glow with pale light in late summer and fall nights.

HIDE BEETLES   Family Dermestidae
Pl. 269

Length to .5 in.; oval, covered with hairs or scales; abdomen of five visible segments below, body grooved so that legs and antennae can be pulled in when beetle is alarmed. The small black or pale marked adults of *Anthrenus* are common on flowers. Larvae six-legged, covered with long hairs. Larvae and adults of the Hide Beetle (*Dermestes marmoratus*) frequent bird nests and animal carcasses, feeding on dried skin and feathers.

BARK-GNAWING BEETLES   Family Trogossitidae
Length to .5 in.; oval and brownish, or long and metallic green or blue; tarsi slender. Larvae narrow, white with black head and a two-spined plate at the end of the body. *Temnocheila chloridia* preys effectively on bark-gnawing beetles in Sierra conifers.

CHECKERED BEETLES   Family Cleridae
Pl. 270

Length to .75 in.; body slender, hairy; five or six ventral abdominal segments; brightly colored. Larvae cylindrical, hairy, prey on bee larvae, grasshopper eggs, and larvae of wood-boring beetles. A yellow and black species, *Trichodes ornatus* frequents flowers and has a life history similar to Meloidae. Some brown species of *Enoclerus* are important natural enemies of bark-gnawing beetles.

FLAT BARK BEETLES   Family Cucujidae
Length to .5 in.; flat, red with black antennae, eyes, tibiae, and tarsi; front coxal cavities open behind; hind tarsi of male may be four-segmented. Larvae flat, pale brown, with two short spines at hind end. *Cucujus clavipes* preys on wood-boring beetles under bark. Smaller brownish species occur in seeds and fruits.

LADYBIRD BEETLES   Family Coccinellidae
Pl. 271

Length to .33 in.; body round, convex, usually brightly colored and spotted. Eggs laid on plants. Larvae soft, spiny, pupate in last larval skin. Larvae and adults prey on aphids and scale insects. *Hippodamia convergens* breeds during spring in lowlands, and swarms of adults fly to heights of several thousand feet; some are carried by prevailing westerly winds into the Sierra. These black-spotted orange beetles hibernate by the many thousands in dense clusters at middle elevations under logs and needles covered with snow. In spring a reverse flight takes them back to feeding grounds. Collecting these beetles in the Sierra for release to prey on crop pests is useless because when winter ends they make a westward migratory flight before feeding.

DARKLING BEETLES   Family Tenebrionidae
Pl. 272

Length to 1.5 in.; black or brown, front coxal cavities closed behind; nocturnal. Larvae (false wireworms) long but thoracic legs short; labrum distinct.

Nyctoporis carinata, rough surfaced, under loose bark. Large black *Eleodes* leaves trails in sand or dust, its pointed rear end being raised when alarmed to emit pungent quinines as a defense mechanism against rodents and other potential predators.

BLISTER BEETLES   Family Meloidae

Length to .75 in.; front part of thorax narrow, necklike; claws toothed or cleft; soft bodied, black, some marked with yellow or red. Adults feed on rabbitbrush (*Chrysothamnus*) and other plants, laying thousands of eggs. The minute, first-stage larva wanders in search of a host—grasshopper egg pods in *Epicauta* and some related genera, and bee nests in others. At first, the larva of *Meloe* attaches to a bee (*Anthophora*) visiting a flower and rides to the bee's nest. There it molts to a grublike larva with reduced legs but well-developed mouthparts and feeds on bee larvae and stored pollen. After two more molts the legs disappear and a prepupa stage ensues, followed by pupation and emergence as an adult. Such a life history is known as hypermetamorphosis.

LONG-HORNED BEETLES   Family Cerambycidae

Pl. 273

Length to 2.33 in.; antennae long, bases usually partly surrounded by eyes. Larvae are grublike, cylindrical, and legless—the "round-headed" borers in dead or dying trunks and branches of forest trees. Adults of gray or brownish species live on bark, those of brightly colored yellow and black species (*Leptura*) live on flowers. The adults of some species make a squeaking noise when picked up. The brown *Prionus* with three lateral spines on the prothorax and *Ergates* with many thoracic spines are the largest Sierra species; larvae of *Prionus* bore into roots of oaks, those of *Ergates* bore into dead pine trees. Another pine sawyer (*Monochamus*) has antennae much longer than the body. Cerambycidae is a very diverse group with 150 to 200 species in the Sierra.

LEAF BEETLES   Family Chrysomelidae

Pl. 274

Length to .5 in.; antennae shorter than body, bases not at all surrounded by eyes. Larvae grublike, with six legs, feed on leaves or roots, or mine leaf tissue. The Cottonwood Leaf Beetle (*Chrysomela scripta*), .33 in. long, is yellowish with variable black markings above. Larvae eat all the leaf tissue except the network of veins, then pupate on the leaves. The Milkweed Beetle (*Chrysochus cobaltinus*) is .5 in. long, stout, and brilliant blue. The Klamath Weed Beetle (*Chrysolina quadrigemina*) is .25 in. long and bronze to metallic blue or green. Introduced from Europe as a biological control agent, this beetle has eliminated the poisonous Klamath weed from many places in the foothills and in the lower Mixed Conifer Belt.

WEEVILS   Family Curculionidae

Length to .5 in.; beak distinct, usually longer than broad; antennae elbowed. Larvae burrow into seeds, fruits, stems, or roots, and often pupate in a cocoon. The acorn weevil (*Curculio*) drills a hole in an acorn shell then lays eggs within; when acorns begin to drop from trees, larvae mature and enter the ground to overwinter. The pine reproduction weevil (*Cylindrocopturus*) is small; attacks growing tips of young pines, especially new plantings in burned areas. This is the most species-rich family of all insects, with more than 1,000 species in California of which probably half are in the Sierra.

BARK BEETLES   Family Scolytidae

Length to .33 in.; short, cylindrical; antennae clubbed; adults and larvae feed under bark, "engraving" branched channels. Bark beetles are a subfamily within the Curculionidae but are treated separately here because they play such an important role in western forests. The Western Pine Beetle (*Dendroctonus brevicomis*) is the most destructive insect on ponderosa pine. Adults emerge in spring and summer, ovipositing in weak or even apparently vigorous trees and excavating winding egg galleries between the bark and sapwood. Small, white larvae feed on the inner bark and then pupate in the outer bark, with two to four generations a year. New attacks are indicated by resin tubes at the entrance holes and by reddish foliage. Parasites and predators normally maintain a balance and prevent epidemic infestations. Every Sierra conifer is attacked by one or more species of bark beetles, and bark beetles kill more forest trees than all other natural agents combined (including fires).

Scorpionflies (Order Mecoptera)

Length to .5 in.; body slender, with four narrow wings or wing vestiges; head extended as a beak; chewing mouthparts; end of abdomen upturned. Larvae caterpillar-like, six legs on thorax and eight on abdomen. On soil and moss in damp places; predaceous. A small, black form (*Boreus*) emerges and mates on the surface of snow in February.

Caddisflies (Order Trichoptera)

Length to 1 in.; body and wings mothlike, but covered by hairs, not scales; wings four, roofed over body at rest; chewing mouthparts; antennae slender, many-segmented. Adults fly over streams at dusk and drop eggs on water or crawl into water and glue eggs to stones (*Phryganea*). Larvae grub-like, in silken cases camouflaged with sticks or pine needles (*Limnephilus*) or sand grains (*Lepidostoma*), or free in nets (*Hydropsyche*) in swift-flowing waters to catch floating plant or animal food; larvae are "caddis worms," a main source of trout food, often used as bait.

Moths and Butterflies (Order Lepidoptera)

This group includes moths and their showy relatives, the butterflies (discussed separately later). Adult mouthparts of all but the most primitive moths are joined into a long, spiraled tube (proboscis) that is uncoiled to suck nectar from flowers, tree sap, and other liquids; wings four, covered with microscopic overlapping scales; compound eyes typically large relative to head size; antennae many-segmented. Larvae (caterpillars) with three pairs of thoracic legs and two to five pairs of stumpy abdominal prolegs; glands on labium used to spin silk for many purposes: construction of shelters, guide trails, portable cases, and cocoons protecting the pupae within.

Moths

Moths are distinguished from butterflies by their plumelike or threadlike antennae, which are not swollen at their tips, and by the fact that they are mostly nocturnal. A few species are pests of timber, agricultural crops, or cultivated plants. Moths are placed into about 120 families, of which roughly 45 occur in the Sierra Nevada. Vastly more diverse in species and life history habits than butterflies, but usually less conspicuous. It is impossible in a guide of this size to adequately represent moth diversity (there are probably 400 species of Gelechiidae moths alone in the Sierra), and the species included here were chosen because they are often encountered or are otherwise conspicuous. Other species were chosen for their unique life history habits, even if these traits may not be representative of other species in the family.

FAIRY MOTHS   **Family Adelidae**
Wing span to .75 in.; hind tibiae bristled; wings fringed with elongated scales. Ovipositor modified to pierce plant tissue during egg laying. Larvae feed on stems, seeds, or fruit. *Adela trigrapha* males are black with three white bars across fore wings, and female fore wings are bright metallic blue with yellowish stripes; hind wings purplish; head with bright orange scales; antennae of females are longer than wings, and that of males are three times as long as wings. Day flying. Larvae feed at first on flowers of *Linanthus androsaceus;* later instars are in a portable case feeding on fallen leaves on the ground.

LEAFMINERS   **Family Gracillariidae**
Wing span to .63 in.; hind tibiae smooth scaled. Typically with long fringes on wings. Many species found on forest trees and shrubs. Larvae "mine" leaves by feeding within leaf, forming serpentine trails or blotchy patterns;

LOWER ANIMALS

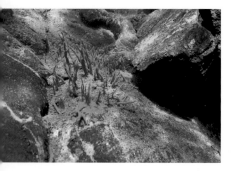

Plate 219. Freshwater sponges

Plate 220. Pacific Banana Slug

Plate 221. Crayfish

Plate 222. Harvestman with red mites

Plate 223. Tarantula

Plate 224. Black Widow Spider

Plate 225. Wolf Spider carrying eggs

Plate 226. Centipede

Plate 227. Millipede

Plate 228. Nest of mound-building ants

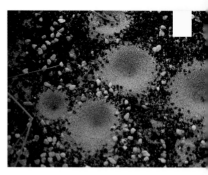

Plate 229. Ant lion larva pits

Plate 230. Galls

Plate 231. Galls on an oak branch

Plate 232. Pipevine Swallowtail larva feeding on vegetation

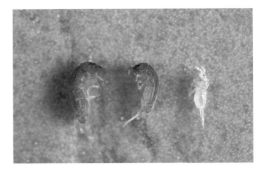

Plate 233. Springtails

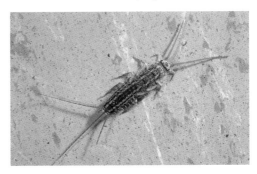

Plate 234. Silverfish

Plate 235. Common Green Darner

Plate 236. Blue-eyed Darner

Plate 237. Grappletail

Plate 238. Pacific Spiketail

Plate 239. Twelve-spotted Skimmer

Plate 240. Variegated Meadowhawk

Plate 241. American Rubyspot

Plate 242. California Spreadwing

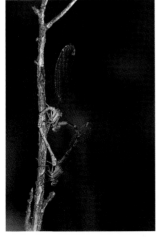

Plate 243. Vivid Dancer

Plate 244. Northern Bluet

Plate 245. Long-horned grasshopper

Plate 247. Walkingstick

Plate 246. Jerusalem Cricket

Plate 248. Termite

Plate 249. Seed bug

Plate 250. Lace bug

Plate 251. Damsel bug

Plate 252. Minute pirate bug

Plate 253. Waterstrider

Plate 254. Giant water bug with captured fish

Plate 255. Waterscorpion

Plate 256. Toad bug

Plate 257. Cicada

Plate 258. Treehopper

Plate 259. Green lacewing

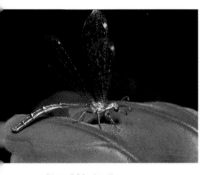

Plate 260. Ant lion

Plate 261. Snakefly

Plate 262. Ground beetle

Plate 263. Tiger beetle

Plate 264. Scarab beetle

Plate 265. Water penny

Plate 266. Metallic wood borer

Plate 267. Click beetle

Plate 268. Pink glowworm (female)

Plate 269. Hide beetle

Plate 270. Checkered beetle

Plate 271. Ladybird beetle

Plate 272. Darkling beetle

Plate 274. Leaf beetle

Plate 273. Long-horned beetle

Plate 275. Carpenter moth

Plate 276. Geometer moth

Plate 277. Giant silk moth

Plate 278. Sphinx moth

Plate 279. Tiger moth

Plate 280. Clodius Parnassian

Plate 281. Pipevine Swallowtail

Plate 282. Indra Swallowtail

Plate 283. Western Tiger Swallowtail

Plate 284. Pale Swallowtail

Plate 286. Checkered White

Plate 285. Pine White

Plate 287. Large Marble

Plate 288. Pacific Orangetip

Plate 289. Lustrous Copper

Plate 290. Golden Hairstreak

Plate 291. Great Purple Hairstreak

Plate 292. Nelson's Hairstreak

Plate 293. Gray Hairstreak

Plate 294. Spring Azure

Plate 295. Silvery Blue

Plate 296. Acmon Blue

Plate 297. Mormon Metalmark

Plate 298. Northern Checkerspot

Plate 299. Variable Checkerspot

Plate 300. Mylitta Crescent

Plate 301. Satyr Comma

Plate 302. California Tortoiseshell

Plate 303. Mourning Cloak

Plate 304. Red Admiral

Plate 305. Painted Lady

Plate 306. West Coast Lady

Plate 307. Common Buckeye

Plate 308. Lorquin's Admiral

Plate 309. California Sister

Plate 310. Common Ringlet

Plate 311. Monarch

Plate 312. Silver-spotted Skipper

Plate 314. Common Checkered-Skipper

Plate 313. Propertius Duskywing

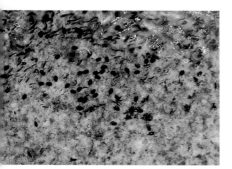

Plate 315. Moth fly larvae

Plate 316. Black fly larvae

Plate 317. Bee fly

Plate 318. Fruit fly

Plate 319. House fly

Plate 320. Ichneumon wasp

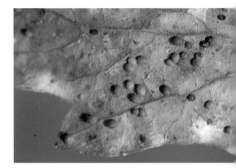

Plate 321. Gall wasp

Plate 322. Velvet ant

Plate 323. Yellowjacket

Plate 324. Thread-waisted wasp
hanging from ceiling nest

Plate 325. Digger bee

Plate 326. Honey Bee

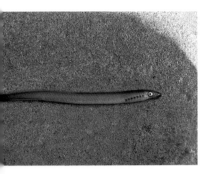

Plate 327. Pacific Lamprey

Plate 328. Tui Chub

Plate 329. Lahontan Redside

Plate 330. California Roach

Plate 331. Hardhead

Plate 332. Speckled Dace

Plate 333. Sacramento Sucker

Plate 334. White Catfish

Plate 335. Mountain Whitefish

Plate 336. Chinook Salmon

Plate 337. Kokanee

Plate 338. Rainbow Trout

Plate 339. California Golden Trout

Plate 340. Lahontan Cutthroat Trout

Plate 341. Brown Trout

Plate 342. Brook Trout

Plate 343. Threespine Stickleback

Plate 344. Prickly Sculpin

Plate 345. Green Sunfish

Plate 346. Bluegill

Plate 347. Largemouth Bass

Plate 348. Smallmouth Bass

Plate 349. Spotted Bass

Plate 350. California Tiger Salamander

Plate 351. Long-toed Salamander

Plate 352. California Newt

Plate 353. Yellow-eyed Ensatina

Plate 354. California Slender Salamander

Plate 355. Mount Lyell Salamander

Plate 356. Western Spadefoot

Plate 357. Western Toad

Plate 358. Yosemite Toad

Plate 359. Pacific Treefrog

Plate 360. Red-legged Frog

Plate 361. Mountain Yellow-legged Frog

Plate 362. Bullfrog

Plate 363. Western Pond Turtle

Plate 364. Western Fence Lizard

Plate 365. Coast Horned Lizard

Plate 366. Western Skink

Plate 367. Northern Alligator Lizard

Plate 368. Rubber Boa

Plate 369. Ring-necked Snake

Plate 370. Racer

Plate 371. Striped Racer

Plate 372. Gopher Snake

Plate 373. Common Kingsnake

Plate 374. Long-nosed Snake

Plate 375. Night Snake

Plate 376. Western Rattlesnake

the patterns are often indicative of which moth species or genus is involved. Live Oak Leafminer (*Cameraria agrifoliella*) has fore wings orange, white-barred, fringed at tip; hind wings narrow, broadly margined with fine hairs. Larvae flat, tapered behind, pale greenish; as larvae grow, their leaf galleries widen into broad blotches with greenish leaf cuticle covering; pupate in leaf blotch.

GELECHIID MOTHS — Family Gelechiidae

Wing span to .75 in.; hind tibiae hairy; wings usually narrow and pointed at tip. This and other families in the Gelechioidea have a great many species, diverse in habits; larvae are leaf miners, folders (tiers), stem gall makers, or feed on fruit and seeds. Lodgepole Needleminer (*Coleotechnites milleri*) has white, black-speckled wings. Eggs laid at needle bases, hatch in two weeks; young larvae mine into needles and spend first winter there; usually two more needles mined in following summer; grown larvae .33 in. head dark, body yellow to orange, a red line along back; pupate in last needle mined, in June. In Yosemite National Park adults fly in July and August of odd-numbered years. Occasionally destructive outbreak levels occur—perhaps when trees are weakened by drought, overcrowded due to fire suppression, or other factors—resulting in large "ghost forests" of lodgepole pine. Currently treated as a natural phenomenon that may actually help maintain meadows and open spaces.

PYRALID MOTHS — Superfamily Pyraloidea

Pyralidae and related families. Wing span to 1.75 in.; slender, hind wings fanlike and folded under fore wing at rest; palpi on head form a "snout." Larvae quite varied in feeding habits: leaf feeders, borers, scavengers, and fungus feeders. Weedfield Sable (*Pyrausta subequalis*): length to .67 in.; wings folded along body at rest; brownish fore wing, orange hind wing. Larvae probably feed on plantain (*Plantago*). Very common in weedy urban and rural areas, one of the most common moth species in California. Metal Mark (*Petrophila confusalis*): wing span .5 to .75 in., grayish red with white and brown marks and a row of black spots on hind wings. This light-bodied delicate moth swims or crawls underwater in streams or ponds to lay eggs on stones. The larvae, with many gill filaments on sides, spin webs on rocks and feed on algae. There are three generations per year, at up to 6,000 ft in the Sierra.

PLUME MOTHS — Family Pterophoridae

Wing span to 1 in.; all wings cleft, the hind ones deeply to form three lobes or "plumes." At rest, wings held at right angles to body. *Amblyptilia pica*: mottled brown, three dark spots near tip of fore wing; larvae feed on and make webs in flowers and leaves of paintbrush (*Castilleja*) and other herbs.

CLEAR-WINGED MOTHS   Family Sesiidae

Wing span to 1.5 in.; mimic wasps in form and flight habits; wings mostly scaleless, transparent; abdomen banded black, yellow, red; fly in daytime. Locust Clear-wing (*Paranthrene robiniae*): yellow and black, appears to mimic yellowjackets; larvae bore into locust, willow, and poplar trees.

CARPENTER MOTHS   Family Cossidae
Pl. 275

Wing span to 2.75 in.; body stout, tapered behind; hind wings small. Goat Moth (*Prionoxystus robiniae*): mottled gray above, with hind wings partly reddish orange in males, no orange in females. Larvae bore into wood of oaks and cottonwoods at lower elevations; life cycle two to three years.

LEAFROLLER MOTHS   Family Tortricidae

Wing span to 1.25 in.; fore wings abruptly widened at base and squared at wing tips so that resting moths are rectangular or bell shaped. Larvae of many species are leaf rollers or borers. Includes the notorious Codling Moth (*Cydia pomonella*), whose larvae bore into apples. Pine Tortrix (*Choristoneura lambertiana*) has fore wings speckled rust to orange with a reticulated pattern of black lines. Eggs laid in July or August, young larvae (budworms) hibernate in cocoons and resume feeding in spring, binding needles, new buds, and staminate cones with webs in which they pupate. Sierra populations feed mainly on Jeffrey pine.

GEOMETER MOTHS   Family Geometridae
Pl. 276

Wing span to 2.25 in.; in a few winter-active species females are wingless. Caterpillars lack the first three pairs of abdominal legs and loop or inch along as they move. Adults with broad wings, often angulate along margins, held out flat against surface at rest. Oak Winter Highflier (*Hydriomena nubilofasciata*) is highly variable—mottled black and white, greenish gray, or rust; to 1.25 in. Emerges during warm late winter days at midelevation and lays eggs on oaks; larvae emerge as leaves appear and occasionally partially defoliate black oaks. Darwin's Green (*Nemoria darwiniata*) is 1 to 1.25 in.; dull green moth, larvae lumpy and mottled and very cryptic on bark or flower buds, feeding on many trees and shrubs including oak and ceanothus. Pine Looper (*Sabulodes edwardsata*) has wings fawn-colored, fore wings broad, crossed by irregular brown band.

GIANT SILK MOTHS   Family Saturniidae
Pl. 277

Wing span to 5 in.; antennae of male feathery; wings usually with eyespots. Adults do not feed and live only a few days. Among the largest moths worldwide, often brightly colored and prized by collectors. Ceanothus Silk Moth (*Hyalophora euryalus*) is common in chaparral and forest communities. Larvae to 3 in., green with yellow and blue wartlike tubercles, spin oval cocoons on host (especially ceanothus, bitter cherry, manzanitas, and Douglas-fir); reddish adults with long eye spots often seen at outdoor lights in spring. Polyphemus Moth (*Antheraea polyphemus*) is tan to reddish brown; wing spots translucent, ringed with yellow, those on hind wings also with blue and black. Larvae to 3 in. long, on deciduous trees (particularly black oak) and shrubs, pupate in brownish oval cocoons to 2 in. long. Sheep Moth (*Hemileuca eglanterina*) has wing span to 3 in., purplish orange with black markings, flies in the daytime; larvae with stinging spines, feed on many chaparral plants; life cycle two years. Similar species *H. nuttalli* (white fore wing, yellow hind wing) and *H. hera* (white with black markings) can be common in late summer in the sagebrush communities on the eastern slopes.

TENT CATERPILLARS   Family Lasiocampidae

Wing span to 3.75 in.; proboscis reduced. *Malacosoma californicam* male rusty red, female tan, fore wings with two oblique pale lines. Larvae spin tentlike community webs among branches and leaves of ceanothus, bitterbrush, and other shrubs in spring; overwintering eggs cemented in rings around twigs; common at high elevations, mainly on east side. Other species occur on west side up to 4,000 ft.

SPHINX MOTHS or HUMMINGBIRD MOTHS   Family Sphingidae

Pl. 278

Wing span to 5 in.; wings narrow, often fly at dusk, wings beat rapidly, hover like hummingbirds at flowers when feeding with long proboscis. Larvae, typified by the unwelcome tomato hornworm, usually with "horn" (spine) at hind end, otherwise smooth, often with diagonal stripes on segments. Pupae naked, brown, in ground. White-lined Sphinx (*Hyles lineata*) is brown with reddish bars, fore wings with broad pale stripe from base to tip, veins white, hind wings with broad pinkish area. Adults may fly in daytime. Larvae green or black, in several color phases; on many plants, especially *Clarkia,* fireweed, and evening primroses. Can reach outbreak levels in neighboring Great Basin and desert regions. Bumble Bee Moth (*Hemaris diffinis*) has wing span to 2 in.; body greenish, wings clear with red brown borders. In flight resembles a bumble bee. Larvae green granulated with white; feed mostly on snowberry (*Symphoricarpus*).

TUSSOCK MOTHS   Family Lymantriidae

Wing span of male to 1 in.; female wingless. Tussock Moth (*Orgyia vetusta*): brownish gray, fore wings mottled, female stout, wingless. Larvae gray with red, blue, and yellow spots, hair tufts black and white, on oak, poplar, willow, and other trees. One brood per year.

NOCTUID MOTHS   Family Noctuidae

Wing span to 3 in. (6 in. in one species); mostly brown or variegated; rest by day against concealing backgrounds, such as bark of trees, and fly at night. Larvae naked, feed on foliage or fruits; cutworms live in ground, where they feed on roots or cut stems of young plants; armyworms "march" in search of food plants at night. Pupae in soil. Semi-looper (*Syngrapha celsa*) has fore wings variegated, gray with black and white; larvae with anterior prolegs reduced, hence walk by "looping"; feed on white fir and other conifers. Noctuids are the commonest moths in the Sierra. Many species are attracted to lights on calm, warm nights.

TIGER MOTHS   Family *Arctiidae*
Pl. 279

Wing span to 2.5 in.; wings usually contrastingly marked. Caterpillars are brown and black "woolly bears" that roll up into a ball when disturbed; often seen in fall in open spaces, seeking places to hibernate. Ornate Tiger Moth (*Grammia ornata*) is yellow, black, and reddish; adults common at lights in spring. *Lophocampa maculata* has fore wings yellow tan with wavy brown splotches, hind wings pale buff colored. Larvae with long black and white hairs and a wide band of yellow hairs at middle; on willow and other deciduous trees.

Butterflies
(Superfamilies Papilionoidea, Hesperioidea)

Butterflies are best thought of as a related group of fancy moths within the Lepidoptera. They are day-flying (diurnal) and have clubbed antennae.

The butterflies of the Sierra Nevada fall within five main families: parnassians and swallowtails; whites, sulphurs, and orangetips; hairstreaks, coppers, and blues; brushfoots; and skippers.

Parnassians and swallowtails (Papilionidae) have wing spans of 2.5 to 4 in.; well-developed front legs, and a short spur on the middle of the tibia; hind wings often have long or short "tails." These butterflies are yellow with black borders; stripes and veins are primarily black, though some have small blue or reddish spots on hind wings. Larvae have a forked organ (*osmeteria*) at the front that projects when disturbed and gives off a pungent odor. Pupae are rough surfaced, attached at the tip, and held upright by a threadlike silk girdle. Eight species exist in the Sierra.

Whites, sulphurs, and orangetips (Pieridae) have wing spans to 2.25 in. and are usually white or orange yellow marked with black, though sometimes they are red. Front legs are fully developed; tarsal claws are forked. Eggs are long and tapered; larvae are slender, without spines; pupae are supported by a fine thread. About 20 species occur in the Sierra.

Hairstreaks, coppers, and blues (Lycaenidae) are blue, brown, or coppery; the eyes are notched near the antennae, and the width of the face between the eyes is less than the length. Eggs are sea urchin shaped; larvae are slug shaped with small heads, some secreting a fluid attractive to ants that in turn defend the larvae from predators and parasites. Pupae are short and rounded, attached to the substrate by a filament. At least 52 species have been recorded in the Sierra.

Brushfoots (Nymphalidae) are distinguished by much-reduced front legs, hence their other common name, Four-footed Butterflies. Pupae are suspended at the tip of the abdomen with no girdle of thread. The Monarch has unscaled antennae; its larva is hairless, with four fleshy filaments; the pupa is smooth and cylindrical. In the ringlets, satyrs, and arctics, veins on the fore wings are swollen at the base, and the wings have "eyespots"; the larvae are smooth, thickest at the middle, and have a double tail. Fritillaries and the rest of the butterflies in this family lack the above-mentioned characteristics. Their larvae have spines and tubercles, and the pupae are rough surfaced. About 45 to 50 species occur in the Sierra; some authorities divide this large group into several families.

Skippers (Hesperiidae) have wing spans to 2 in.; wide heads, and antennae that are usually curved at their tips. Flight is often so rapid that wing movements are blurred. Hind wings (also fore wings in some groups) spread horizontally or at a 45-degree angle when at rest. Larvae lack spines or prominent hairs, have large heads and constricted necks, and usually stay in a nest made of rolled or tied leaves of the host plant. About 30 species occur in the Sierra.

CLODIUS PARNASSIAN   *Parnassius clodius*
Pl. 280

Wing span to 2.5 in.; white with dark bars on fore wings, and two small red spots (three in female) ringed with black on hind wings; antennae black; no tails. During mating, the male plugs the female's copulatory opening with a large pinkish white structure (sphragis); the female can thus mate only once. The largely crepuscular larvae are covered with fine black down, each segment with orange or yellow raised tubercles (seems to mimic poisonous millipedes), found on bleeding heart (*Dicentra formosa*) in Mixed Conifer Belt to Subalpine Belt; pupation in ground debris. The Sierra Nevada Parnassian (*P. behrii*) has two small yellow to orange spots on its hind wing; feeds on stonecrops (*Sedum*) above treeline from Carson Pass south.

PIPEVINE SWALLOWTAIL   *Battus philenor*
Pl. 281

Wing span to 4.75 in.; black with greenish blue iridescence, large orange spots below on hind wing. Larvae feed on Dutchman's pipevine (*Aristolochia californica*). Abundant in Foothill Belt on west slope, also on east slope in southern Sierra.

INDRA SWALLOWTAIL *Papilio indra*
Pl. 282

Wing span to 2.5 in.; inner half of each wing all black; tails about .13 in. Larvae feed on native plants of carrot family (Apiaceae). Upper Montane Belt to Alpine Belt, occasionally lower on serpentine outcrops.

WESTERN TIGER SWALLOWTAIL *Papilio rutulus*
Pl. 283

Wing span to 3.5 in.; tails .4 in. or more; inner parts of wings yellow with oblique black bars. Larvae on sycamore, cottonwood, and willow, from Foothill Belt to Upper Montane Belt; often on aspens at higher elevations and on east side (as at Monitor Pass). The larger Two-tailed Swallowtail (*P. multicaudata*) frequents canyons on both slopes, Foothill and Mixed Conifer Belts. The Anise Swallowtail (*P. zelicaon*) has reduced yellow patches on its wings and extensive black markings. Its larvae feed on plants of the carrot family from the Foothill Belt to the Alpine Belt. Adults assemble on rocky summits for mating, producing local aggregations.

PALE SWALLOWTAIL *Papilio eurymedon*
Pl. 284

Wing span to 3.5 in.; like Western Tiger Swallowtail but background color whitish, not yellow. Larvae on *Ceanothus* and *Rhamnus* in Foothill and Mixed Conifer Belts; adults seek hilltops and roam higher in Sierra.

PINE WHITE *Neophasia menapia*
Pl. 285

Wing span to 1.75 in.; white, fore wings with black at tips and line along front margin curving in beyond middle; hind wings with black (male) or orange (female) veins below. Weak fluttery flight high among treetops from July to September. Larvae dark green, with white stripe on each side and one on back, two short tails; on ponderosa, Jeffrey, and lodgepole pines.

CHECKERED WHITE, WESTERN WHITES *Pontia protodice,*
Pl. 286 *P. occidentalis*

Wing span to 2 in.; white, wings with black spots or streaks; hind wings below with blackish brown veins. These two very similar species occur at lower and higher elevations, respectively, with overlap at 5,000 to 7,000 ft. *P. occidentalis* flies to over 12,000 ft and aggregates on rocky summits for mating. Larvae on mustard and other plants of that family. Spring White (*P. sisymbrii*) has veins of hind wings below outlined in gray or pale brown; Mixed Conifer Belt to Alpine Belt, in unforested (rocky or arid) habitats. The Cabbage White (*Pieris rapae*), uncommon in the Sierra, is white with fore wings dark tipped, a small black spot above on each fore wing (two spots on females) and hind wings below unmarked. Larvae often on cabbage, but also feed on other plants of the mustard family; in Foothill and Mixed Conifer Belts, always near civilization. This species was naturalized from Europe in the 1800s.

LARGE MARBLE   *Euchloe ausonides*
Pl. 287

Wing span to 1.5 in.; white, fore wings with small white-flecked black bar at midwing, tips black and white; hind wings below marbled with green and yellow. Larvae on plants of mustard family, mostly in grassy areas on east slope and in Upper Montane and Subalpine Belts. The smaller California Marble (*E. hyantis*) lacks white flecks in black midwing bar and light spots within marbling are pearly. It occurs only in rocky unforested habitats in foothill canyons and Mixed Conifer Belt to near treeline. These two similar-looking butterflies have very different larvae: *ausonides* is striped lengthwise with violet gray and yellow; *hyantis* is brilliant green with a white line on each side. Adults of both species appear only briefly during springtime (which at higher elevations comes in July).

PACIFIC ORANGETIP or SARA ORANGETIP   *Anthocharis sara*
Pl. 288

Wing span to 1.5 in.; white above, tips of fore wings reddish orange and edged with black; much greenish marbling below especially on hind wings. Feeds on plants of the mustard family; in Foothill and Mixed Conifer Belts. Stella Orangetip (*A. stella*) is very similar but the ground color is either pale (male) or rich (female) yellow, not white. Upper Montane and Subalpine Belts from Bucks Lake, Plumas County south.

SIERRA SULPHUR or BEHR'S SULPHUR   *Colias behrii*

Wing span to 1.5 in.; color greenish with dark wing margins, fore wings with ill-defined dark spot near middle, hind wings with whitish spot. Larvae on dwarf bilberry (*Vaccinium caespitosum*). Confined to Subalpine Belt from Tuolumne County to Tulare County; best seen at Tuolumne Meadows from late July to early September.

LUSTROUS COPPER   *Lycaena cupreus*
Pl. 289

Wing span to 1.25 in.; coppery orange above with brown spots and wing margins; coppery below on fore wings and brownish gray on hind wings with brown spots. In Mixed Conifer Belt to Subalpine Belt at increasingly higher elevations southward. Larvae on docks (*Rumex*). The American Copper (*L. phlaeas alpestris*) is similar but with more brown above; it occurs in the Alpine Belt of the central and southern Sierra on alpine sorrel (*Oxyria digyna*). Several other coppers are found in the Sierra.

GOLDEN HAIRSTREAK   *Habrodais grunus*
Pl. 290

Wing span to 1.25 in.; dark brown above, yellowish brown below, faint spots and lines near margins; hind wing with a short tail. One brood; larvae on oaks, especially canyon live oak. Long flight season (June to October). Adults estivate in hot, dry weather and can be found sitting quietly, often in large numbers, inside bramble tangles, among dead leaves, or in other cool, damp places. Often flies at dawn, late afternoon, and dusk. Foothill and Mixed Conifer Belts.

GREAT PURPLE HAIRSTREAK   *Atlides halesus*
Pl. 291

Wing span to 1.5 in.; hind wings with two slender tails; iridescent blue, broad wing margins, and black veins above; black, ends of hind wings with white and blue spots below; tip of abdomen orange. Several broods; larvae green with short, velvety orange hairs; feed on mistletoe of broadleaf trees. Pupae brown, mottled black with short orange hairs. Foothill and Mixed Conifer Belts, common in riparian areas.

BEHR'S HAIRSTREAK   *Satyrium behrii*

Wing span to 1 in.; orange with dark brown wing margins above, gray below; with black spots; no tails. Larvae on bitterbrush (*Purshia*) among east slope Jeffrey pines. The Sooty Hairstreak (*S. fuliginosum*) is very dark slate gray. It is found in subalpine steppe, especially on volcanic mudflows such as those at Carson, Ebbetts, Sonora, and Monitor Passes.

NELSON'S HAIRSTREAK   *Callophrys nelsoni*
Pl. 292

Wing span to 1 in.; above coppery brown, below dark spotted near the short tails, a broken white line near margin of each wing. Larvae feed on incense-cedar (*Calocedrus decurrens*) in Mixed Conifer Belt. Juniper Hairstreak (*C. gryneus*) occurs on juniper on the east slope. The two are very similar but *gryneus* is green below.

WESTERN PINE ELFIN   *Callophrys eryphon*

Wing span to 1 in.; dark brown above, paler and mottled with angular dark lines edged by white below, giving checkered appearance; no tails. Larvae on pines in Mixed Conifer Belt to Subalpine Belt. Brown Elfin

(*C. augustinus*) is similar but less complexly marked, feeds on many diverse hosts from the Foothill Belt to near treeline.

GRAY HAIRSTREAK   *Strymon melinus*
Pl. 293
Wing span to 1.25 in.; dark slate gray above; corner of hind wing with one red spot and several blue and black spots; light gray with black and red marks near margin of hind wing below; each wing with white-edged black line; hind wing with slender tail. Widespread species on mallow, legumes, and other plants in Foothill and Mixed Conifer Belts, often straying higher. There are numerous other hairstreaks in the Sierra that can be difficult to tell apart. They often swarm on the flowers of California buckeye (*Aesculus californica*) in the foothills in early summer.

WESTERN TAILED-BLUE   *Everes amyntula*
Wing span to 1.5 in.; blue, wing edges dark above; a little orange on hind wing margins; gray with small black spots and a touch of orange below; tails hairlike, distinct. Larvae on legumes, especially *Astralagus,* upper Foothill Belt to Alpine Belt. Blues are a very difficult group for beginners to identify because the species are so similar.

SPRING AZURE   *Celastrina ladon*
Pl. 294
Wing span to 1.5 in; blue (male) or blue with black tip on fore wing (female) above; pale gray to whitish with faint, fine dark spots below; no orange. Larvae on various shrubs and trees: dogwood, ceanothus, buckeye, and possibly others. Found as high as the Upper Montane Belt. Two broods at lower elevations. At higher elevations usually the first nonhibernating butterfly to emerge in spring.

SQUARE-SPOTTED BLUE   *Euphilotes battoides*
Wing span to 1 in.; blue (male) above, sparsely black-spotted, pale bluish with squarish black spots and blackish stripe near wing margin below; brown (female) above with orange stripes at rear of hind wing, below like male. On buckwheat (*Eriogonum*) from Mixed Conifer Belt to Subalpine Belt. There are several other very similar species in this genus.

SILVERY BLUE   *Glaucopsyche lygdamus*
Pl. 295
Wing span to 1.25 in.; blue (male) or mostly brown (female) above; brownish gray, many rounded black spots sharply ringed with white below; no orange. Foothill Belt to Alpine Belt, larvae feeding on legumes.

SIERRA NEVADA BLUE — *Agriades podarce*

Wing span to 1 in.; blue (male) above with gray or silver cast, darker toward wing margins; brown (female) above, brownish gray with dark spots circled with whitish, no orange below. Upper Montane and Subalpine Belts in meadows. Larvae on shooting stars (*Dodecatheon*). This butterfly belongs to a species complex that reaches the shores of the Arctic Ocean and Eurasia. The very similar, recently discovered, *A. cassiope* feeds on white heather near treeline.

ACMON BLUE — *Icaricia acmon*
Pl. 296

Wing span to 1 in.; pale sky blue (male) or mostly brown (female) above, wing edges darker; hind wing with submarginal stripe of orange; gray with black spots below, hind wing orange near margin. Larvae on buckwheat and legumes, especially *Lotus*. Foothill Belt to Subalpine Belt.

MORMON METALMARK — *Apodemia mormo*
Pl. 297

Wing span to 1.25 in.; brown with black and white spots; fore wings with orange ground color on basal half; hind wings with orange at middle and narrowly white on outer margins. Larvae short, broad, dark violet, four rows of black and white spots with clumps of bristles. Pupae short, plump, corrugated, with wavy hairs, brown with two orange spots. On buckwheats in Mixed Conifer and Upper Montane Belts; extremely colonial and often flying late in the season (September to October) so easily overlooked. This is the only Sierra representative of the mainly tropical family Riodinidae. Metalmarks differ from the Lycaenidae in holding their wings open while perched and lacking silk attachments in the pupae.

GREAT BASIN FRITILLARY — *Speyeria egleis*

Wing span to 2.25 in.; orange above, veins and spots black; tan below with black and silver spots. On violets in Upper Montane and Subalpine Belts. Other similar species differ in size, background color, and precise pattern of black and silver spots; these species segregate by habitat but are otherwise difficult to tell apart. The brilliant orange Nokomis Fritillary (*S. nokomis*) is one of our most spectacular species (though females are yellow and brown); found in wet meadows on the east slope south of Lake Tahoe.

NORTHERN CHECKERSPOT — *Chlosyne palla*
Pl. 298

Wing span to 1.75 in.; like Variable Checkerspot but smaller and paler. Where the two species overlap, female Northern Checkerspots are blackish and apparently mimic the other species. On various members of the sunflower family (Asteraceae) in Mixed Conifer and Upper Montane Belts. Hoffmann's Checkerspot (*C. hoffmanni*), with wing bases mainly black, also occurs in high elevation forests.

VARIABLE CHECKERSPOT   *Euphydryas chalcedona*
Pl. 299

Wing span to 2.5 in.; dark brown to black with pale orange spots above; brick red with black veins and large white spots below. High elevation adults (subsp. *sierra*) are mostly red above. Larvae black with white stripe along back and broken stripe on each side; with numerous short spines. Pupae gray, spotted with orange and black. On monkeyflowers, figworts, and other flowers from Foothill Belt to Subalpine Belt. Other species common in Sierra.

MYLITTA CRESCENT   *Phyciodes mylitta*
Pl. 300

Wing span to 1.5 in.; orange above with rows of black bars and dots paralleling wing margins (female darker than male); irregularly checkered below with brown, tan, and whitish. On thistle (*Cirsium*) at all elevations. This species has probably become much more abundant and widespread due to the introduction of weedy host plants. California Crescent (*P. orseis herlani*) is slightly larger but similar in pattern; rare and local, mostly around the Tahoe Basin.

SATYR COMMA   *Polygonia satyrus*
Pl. 301

Wing span to 2 in.; eyes hairy, wing margins irregularly concave, hind wing with tail; orange brown with large black spots above and below; yellow tan (male) or brown (female) below. Larvae with seven rows of long bristles on large black head, body black, a greenish stripe along back and a V-shaped black mark on each segment. Pupae brown, angular. On nettle (*Urtica*) in Foothill and Mixed Conifer Belts. The similar Hoary Comma (*P. gracilis zephyrus*) is gray underneath; common in Mixed Conifer Belt to Subalpine Belt. Green Comma (*P. faunus*) males are heavily green-mottled beneath (females dull gray); uncommon in Mixed Conifer and Upper Montane Belts.

CALIFORNIA TORTOISESHELL   *Nymphalis californica*
Pl. 302

Wing span to 2.25 in.; eyes hairy; wing margins irregular; hind wing with short tail; dark brown above, centers of wings orange; this color reaching front margin of fore wings; mottled below, gray brown, with irregular, broad pale band on outer half of each wing. Larvae velvety black with broken yellow line along back; each segment with five branching spines supported on blue tubercles and small white dots between spines. Pupae ashy gray, two black projections on head; two spines near wing cases. Larvae may cause mass defoliation of foothill ceanothus species during spring, also of *Ceanothus velutinus* at higher elevations later in summer.

REMARKS: Adults hatch in late June, fly through summer, overwinter, then continue flying until April or May of the following year. Thousands sometimes gather to estivate in late summer above treeline, where astounded hikers report encountering them either alive or scattered dead across snowfields. In some years this species increases enormously and disperses by the millions, reaching such numbers that they can obstruct traffic on roads. Sometimes the flights continue for days. During an outbreak, ceanothus is defoliated over a wide area and the pupae, suspended from twigs, make a rustling sound when disturbed. The smaller Milbert's Tortoiseshell (*N. milberti*) also migrates but is seldom abundant; larvae found on nettles (*Urtica*) but adults often seen at coyote mint (*Monardella*) flowers at high elevations.

MOURNING CLOAK   *Nymphalis antiopa*
Pl. 303

Wing span to 3.5 in.; eyes hairy; wing margin somewhat irregular; dark brown to black above, sides of wings broadly margined with yellow paralleled by row of bluish spots; dusky, yellow-margined below. Overwinters as adult. Larvae black with rows of orange spots along back, feed on willow and cottonwood up through Upper Montane Belt.

RED ADMIRAL   *Vanessa atalanta*
Pl. 304

Wing span to 2.5 in.; eyes hairy; hind wings lack a tail; dark brown above; fore wing with oblique orange bar across middle and white dots near tip; hind wing with broad orange band along rear margin; mottled below, with oblique red stripe and white spots as above. On nettle, up through Mixed Conifer Belt. This species is migratory and can turn up almost anywhere.

PAINTED LADY   *Vanessa cardui*
Pl. 305

Wing span to 2.5 in.; blotched orange, tan, and black; fore wing above with white bar beyond middle of front margin and white spots near tip; ashy brown below blotched with darker color, fore wing partly orange or pink and black, hind wing with three or four eyespots near edge. Larvae lilac colored with scattered black spots and lines of yellow, black, and white; spines on seven rows of tubercles; feed on thistles, mallows, and other plants up through Upper Montane Belt. Pupae brown with rows of short spines. This is a rather irregular migrant from Mexico and desert regions; in April 2001, millions moved up the east slope for a week, tying up traffic in Reno. Other great migrations have occurred on the west slope. Migrants sometimes fly right over continuous snowfields.

WEST COAST LADY   *Vanessa annabella*
Pl. 306

Wing span to 2 in.; resembles Painted Lady but fore wing with red bar beyond middle of front margin above. On mallow and nettle, up through Upper Montane Belt. Not migratory but extremely common and widespread.

COMMON BUCKEYE   *Junonia coenia*
Pl. 307

Wing span to 2.25 in.; eyes hairless; pale brown above, fore wing with large eyespot, a second smaller spot on hind wing; fore wing above with dull white around eyespot reaching to front margin and two reddish bars on inner half; ashy, mottled below, markings of fore wings as above. Multiple broods per year. Larvae on plantain, monkeyflower, and various other plants, mostly in Foothill Belt but occasionally up through Upper Montane Belt. Intolerant of cold and cannot persist late in the season at high elevation or on the colder east slope.

LORQUIN'S ADMIRAL   *Limenitis lorquini*
Pl. 308

Wing span to 2.75 in.; enlarged end of antenna longer and more slender than in other butterflies; black above with broad white stripe across middle of both wings, fore wings orange-tipped; more brown below, with white stripe, also a pale stripe near edge of wings. Larvae olive brown, mottled, with white band on each side; head two-lobed; two rough horns on third segment, and pairs of tubercles behind. Pupae olive green to purple, mottled with white, a large lobe at base of abdomen. Larvae on willow, cottonwood, and other trees up through Upper Montane Belt. Thought to be a mimic of the California Sister.

CALIFORNIA SISTER   *Adelpha bredowii*
Pl. 309

Wing span to 3 in.; resembles Lorquin's Admiral; brownish black above, fore wing with large orange spot near tip; variegated brown, blue, and whitish below, with blue stripes on inner half and near margin of wings. Larvae on oaks in Foothill and Mixed Conifer Belts. A distasteful butterfly to birds.

COMMON RINGLET   *Coenonympha tullia california*
Pl. 310

Wing span to 1.25 in.; pale yellowish brown above; darker with irregular pale bars below; hind wings with many eyespots. Spring form nearly white;

summer form more yellow. On grasses in Foothill Belt. East slope populations (subsp. *ampelos*) are usually buff colored; the two subspecies intergrade in the Feather and Pit River drainages.

GREAT BASIN WOOD-NYMPH   *Cercyonis sthenele*

Wing span to 1.5 in.; light brown above, mottled gray below, each fore wing with two bold black eyespots ringed with yellow and white at center. On grasses in Foothill and Mixed Conifer Belts; locally abundant around Sierra Valley, Sierra County on east slope.

RIDINGS' SATYR   *Neominois ridingsii*

Wing span to 2 in.; grayish brown, wings with transverse white bars near edges, fore wing with two white-centered black eyespots. On grasses at high elevations. Apparently quite rare in most areas; flies only in even-numbered years in many locations.

CHRYXUS ARCTIC   *Oeneis chryxus*

Wing span to 2 in.; ashy with some paler areas above and below; fore wing with one to three small eyespots, hind wing with one spot at back and mottled below. Populations between Carson and Tioga Passes have a distinctive butterscotch color. On grasses in Alpine and upper Subalpine Belts. This is the most characteristic alpine butterfly of the Sierra, but flying in most areas only in odd-numbered years and taking two years to complete its life cycle.

MONARCH   *Danaus plexippus*
Pl. 311

Wing span to 4.5 in.; orange with veins and wing margins black, two rows of white spots. Larvae banded with black, white, and yellow. Pupae green, gold-spotted. Larvae on milkweed. Foothill and Mixed Conifer Belts, occasional adults higher in the mountains. Monarchs migrate to coastal and southern California for winter, then mate and disperse northward again the following spring.

SILVER-SPOTTED SKIPPER   *Epargyreus clarus*
Pl. 312

Wing span to 1.75 in.; dark brown, fore wings above with orange spot, hind wings below with large irregular silvery white spot. Caterpillars on legumes such as *Amorpha californica* and *Lotus crassifolius*; construct leafy daytime shelter, emerging at night to feed. Pupae brownish, on ground; one brood a year. Foothill Belt, commonest around Gold Country towns where the larvae are found on introduced Black Locust (*Robinia pseudoacacia*).

NEVADA CLOUDYWING   *Thorybes mexicanus nevada*

Wing span to 1.75 in.; dark brown, fore wings above with oblique rows of small pale spots, mottled gray below. From Upper Montane Belt to Alpine Belt. On meadow and meadow edges, but mating on rocky summits. Larval hosts are native clovers on wet soils. Active in first half of season only. The larger Northern Cloudywing (*T. pylades*) occurs in foothill canyons into the Mixed Conifer Belt.

PROPERTIUS DUSKYWING   *Erynnis propertius*
Pl. 313

Wing span to 1.5 in.; dark mottled brown, fore wings with small white spots. Larvae feed on oaks, ranging upward through Upper Montane Belt. Several smaller, similar species that are very difficult to identify occur in a variety of habitats from moist woods to chaparral to serpentine barrens.

COMMON CHECKERED-SKIPPER   *Pyrgus communis*
Pl. 314

Wing span to 1 in.; color highly variable but mainly dark brown with many white spots above, much paler below. Larvae feed on mallows at all elevations except the Alpine Belt. Two-banded Checkered-Skipper (*P. ruralis*): smaller and darker; found at edges of mountain meadows in spring from Upper Montane Belt to Alpine Belt. Larvae on *Horkelia* (Rosaceae).

JUBA SKIPPER   *Hesperia juba*

Wing span 1.5 in; orange above with black markings and two orange spots near tips of fore wings; pale orange below, two white spots near tips of fore wings and V-shaped white band on hind wings. Widespread above 5,000 ft on both slopes. Two flights: late spring and September to October. Larvae on bunchgrasses. The rare Sierra Skipper (*H. miriamae*) is found in Alpine Belt from Alpine County to Tulare County; color paler orange, wings with bluish sheen. Two other uncommon species, *H. lindseyi* and *columbia*, are confined to serpentine, gabbro, and limestone soils in the western foothills and the Inyo-Kern area.

WOODLAND SKIPPER   *Ochlodes sylvanoides*

Wing span to 1.5 in.; like *Hesperia* but lacks white markings on the underside of the hind wings and the two spots near tips of fore wings. All elevations below alpine zone, flying July to October. The Rural Skipper (*O. agricola*) is similar but smaller, found in western foothills up to Mixed Conifer Belt, May to early July only, mainly in rocky canyons.

SANDHILL TECUMSEH SKIPPER   *Polites sabuleti tecumseh*
Wing span to 1 in.; like Woodland Skipper but smaller, darker, and with hind wings speckled and barred below. Around meadows and high barren slopes mainly in the Upper Montane and Subalpine Belts.

True Flies (Order Diptera)

Two fore wings transparent, few veins; hind wings modified into a pair of small clublike *halteres* that help provide equilibrium during flight; mouthparts piercing-sucking or sponging, often forming a proboscis. Larvae lack segmented thoracic legs.

CRANE FLIES   Family Tipulidae

Length to 1.5 in.; wing span to 3 in. Resemble enlarged mosquitoes; two slender wings, legs long, fragile; a V-shaped groove on middle of thorax above. Larvae (leather worms) wormlike, head partly within thorax, two mandibles; live in moist soil of meadows or at edges of ponds or streams, some on bottom of swift streams. A wingless spiderlike snow gnat (*Chionea*), .2 in. long, occurs at high elevations.

MOTH FLIES   Family Psychodidae
Pl. 315
Length to .2 in.; densely hairy wings held rooflike over body, thus resembling small moths. Larvae breed in muck and swampy places in meadows or sewage drains (*Psychoda*). Others (*Maruina*) have eight suckers on lower surface and cling to rocks in splash areas of mountain streams; pupae are small black disks.

MOSQUITOES, PHANTOM MIDGES, DIXID MIDGES   Superfamily Culicoidea
Length to .5 in.; slender, delicate, 10 veins or their branches reach wing margins. Adults swarm for mating; larvae (wigglers) with distinct head; aquatic.
REMARKS: This group includes three families. (1) Phantom midges (Chaoboridae) with scaly-edged wings and plumelike antennae. They are nonbiting and attracted by lights at night. Larvae are predaceous and almost transparent, living in bottom mud of lakes and streams by day and rising to surface waters at night. (2) Dixid midges (Dixidae), without plumelike antennae or scaly wings, are nonbiting and inconspicuous. Their larvae are common at water's edge, having a U-shaped posture when resting or moving. (3) Mosquitoes (Culicidae), with scaly wings, a biting proboscis in

females and plumelike antennae in males. Related families of gnats, black flies, and mountain midges are treated separately below.

The more common mosquitoes in the Sierra Nevada are of three genera: (1) *Anopheles* has eggs that float individually, and larvae that rest parallel to the surface of water. Adult females have palpi about as long as proboscis, and they stand in a tilted position with head down when biting. *A. freeborni* occurs in the Central Valley and foothills; its larvae breed in sunlit pools containing algae or grasses and sedges. This was the carrier of malaria in early times and is still a hazard if persons with malarial parasites in their blood visit the region and infect local mosquitoes. (2) *Culex* has black eggs laid vertically in rafts that float on water. Larvae have a long breathing tube at end of body and hang downward from the surface. Pupae are stout "tumblers," with two short breathing "trumpets." Adults stand with the body nearly horizontal when biting. *C. tarsalis* breeds in sunlit pools up to 7,200 ft. It is the most efficient carrier of encephalitis in California. (3) *Aedes* lays eggs on moist surfaces, where they remain dry for several months, hatching when they are wetted by rains or snowmelt. Larvae have a short breathing tube and hang downward from the water surface. Females stand horizontally to bite. *A. sierrensis* breeds in tree holes, ranging in elevation from 3,500 to over 10,000 ft and emerge from April through July. The commonest breeding places are woodland or meadow pools resulting from snowmelt. In the Sierra, where there are many breeding places, mosquitoes are mainly avoided by screening tents and houses and using repellents.

MOUNTAIN MIDGES

Family Deuterophlebiidae

Length to .5 in.; long legged with broad fanlike wings; antennae of male much longer than body. Larvae have seven pairs of fingerlike lateral lobes, each with concentric small hooks to cling on surface of smooth rocks in mountain streams and waterfalls; pupae attach to

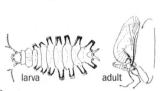

larva   adult

rocks. Adults emerge and fly briefly in early morning.

MIDGES

Family Chironomidae

Length to .5 in.; mosquitolike, but mouthparts reduced; wings scaleless, usually six veins or branches reaching margin; males have characteristic feathery antennae. Larvae (called bloodworms because they contain hemoglobin that makes them red) with distinct head, mostly in mud bottom of lakes. They are important fish food organisms. Adults gather in loudly humming swarms near lakes and streams throughout the Sierra. Other small mosquitolike insects include gnats that make galls on sagebrush, pines, and other plants (Cecidomyiidae) and those that breed in fungi (Mycetophilidae).

BLACK FLIES   Family Simuliidae
Pl. 316

Length to .25 in.; short, chunky, wings broad, legs short and thick, first tarsal segment dilated; antennae short and bare; mouthparts short, in female adapted for piercing. Larvae attach by anal end to rocks in running water and catch drifting food in mouth brushes. Pupae live within silken cocoons with breathing filaments; adults emerge from turbulent waters in protective air bubbles.

REMARKS: Simuliid larvae probably occur in every Sierra stream, but the adults are seldom seen because they usually bite wild mammals and birds. In the far north they are serious pests of livestock and humans, and in the tropics they transmit several human diseases.

SOLDIER FLIES   Family Stratiomyidae

Length to .75 in.; brightly colored, often metallic, somewhat flattened above, and lacking bristles; basal part of antennae held together with tips spread to form a "Y"; tarsi with three nearly equal pads beneath claws. Larvae tapered at both ends, surface hardened by limy secretion, often bristly; with mouth hooks; often aquatic, in mud, but some in decaying vegetation, rotting fruit, or under bark; feed mostly on algae and other microorganisms, but some species are carnivorous; pupate in last larval skin. Spotted Soldier Fly (*Stratiomys maculosa*) on streamside vegetation, especially flowers, where it resembles wasps in color.

HORSE FLIES, DEER FLIES   Family Tabanidae

Length to 1 in.; broad, flattish, some (*Tabanus*) gray to brown, others (*Chrysops*) marked with yellow and with patterned wings; antennae with third segment ringed; tibiae spurred; tarsal claws, with three equal pads; male feeds on nectar and pollen; mouthparts of female daggerlike, bite painful to humans but do not transmit disease. Eggs laid on plants over water. Larvae in muck near water; body cylindrical, tapered at both ends, with girdle of false feet on each segment; carnivorous; pupate in moist soil.

SNIPE FLIES   Family Rhagionidae

Length to .75 in.; gray or brown, some with yellow bands; body without bristles; third antennal segment not divided into rings; tarsi with three nearly equal pads beneath claws; tibiae with small spines at tips. Larvae of aquatic forms (*Atherix*) to 1 in. long, spiny at sides, two tapering gills behind, and eight pairs of stumpy prolegs; prey on other insects in streams. Adults lay eggs on branches over streams and die there, forming large clusters of dead flies. Adults of *Symphoromyia* are common biting pests on humans visiting the mountains. Wormlion (*Vermileo*) lays eggs in sand. Larvae tapered, with small heads, but hind ends thick with four small lobes; burrow in sandy soil, making craters like Ant Lion larvae; pupate in last larval skin in sand. Adults in Yosemite emerge in June. Feed on small ants and other insects that fall into pits; hundreds of pits often under mountain cabins, also at edge of granite boulders where there is a little protection from rain and snow. Adult does not bite.

ROBBER FLIES   Family Asilidae

Length to 1.75 in.; body long, narrow or tapering, with bristles and hairs, including hairy "beard" on face; top of head hollowed out between eyes; third segment of antennae not ringed; tarsi with only two pads under claws; proboscis well developed, adapted for piercing and sucking fluids in other insects. Eggs usually laid in soil; larvae feed on larvae of other insects. Adults swift in flight, capture other insects on the wing.

BEE FLIES   Family Bombyliidae

Pl. 317

Length to .75 in.; stout, usually densely hairy, often with patterned wings; third segment of antennae not ringed; tarsi with two pads under claws; long proboscis for drinking nectar from deep flowers. Eggs often laid near entrance to ground nests of wild bees; larvae feed on pollen and honey stores and on young bees; pupate in sealed cells of bees; others parasitic on cutworms, tiger beetles, sawflies, and grasshopper eggs. Adults on flowers or hovering in air.

HOVER FLIES, FLOWER FLIES   Family Syrphidae

Length to .75 in.; often brightly colored with yellow stripes, no bristles; third segment of antennae not ringed; tarsi with two pads under claws; on flowers and hovering. Eggs of hover flies in mud or decaying organic matter; larvae aquatic, "rat tailed" with anal breathing tube much longer than body; adults resemble bees or wasps and hover stationary in midair. Eggs of flower flies laid on plants; larvae stout or tapering to front end; prey on aphids and other insects.

FRUIT FLIES   Family Tephritidae

Pl. 318

Length to .5 in.; stocky with dark-patterned wings; tapered abdomen in females; males often observed walking about and flicking out their wings as courtship behavior; second antennal segment not cleft above. Larvae of *Euphranta canadensis* develop in fruit of gooseberries; others "mine" leaves of various plants; many, like *Aciurina maculata*, feed in flower heads of composites, where galls may be formed.

SHORE FLIES, BRINE FLIES Family Ephydridae

Length to .2 in.; brownish gray, mouth wide, face strongly arched; second antennal segment not cleft above and bristle on third segment usually plumelike only on upper side. Eggs of the brine flies, *Ephydra,* are laid in brackish or salty water. Larvae have eight pairs of stubby false legs and a long breathing tube behind; feed on algae. The brown pupae (in last larval skin) retain breathing tube; they may be attached underwater but often float on surface.

REMARKS: Millions of brine flies live near the shores of Mono Lake. In earlier years the Paiute Indians collected and dried larvae and pupae in the fall. The skins were removed by rubbing and winnowing in scoop-shaped baskets. The resulting kernel, called koo-chah-bee, was described by William H. Brewer in 1863 as "oily, very nutritious, and not unpleasant to the taste." Brine flies were also used to salt acorn meal cakes by west slope Native Americans.

SMALL FRUIT FLIES or VINEGAR FLIES Family Drosophilidae

Length to .2 in.; yellowish brown, second antennal segment lacks cleft above, bristle plumelike on both sides; wings clear. Life cycle of *Drosophila melanogaster* is 11 days at 77 degrees F. Oblong eggs have two appendages; pale larvae are .25 in. long; pupae shorter, with two hornlike breathing tubes. Larvae occur in decayed vegetable matter and in fermenting fruits and seepage from trees; in the Sierra they are not easy to find on wild food sources, but geneticists collect adults, using fermenting bananas as bait.

HOUSE FLIES, STABLE FLIES Family Muscidae

Pl. 319

Length to .5 in.; black, second antennal segment cleft above, antennal bristle plumelike or with dense hairs, mouthparts well developed. The House Fly (*Musca domestica*) breeds in animal excrement and other refuse. The white eggs soon hatch, and the pale tapered maggots develop rapidly; oval- to barrel-shaped and reddish brown pupae. Complete life cycle may take only eight or nine days in summer; overwinter as adults in sheltered places. Mouthparts of adult are of the sponging or lapping type, so bacteria are readily spread from breeding places to the food of humans. The stable fly (*Stomoxys*) has biting mouthparts.

LOUSE FLIES Family Hippoboscidae

Length to .5 in.; brownish to black, body flat, legs widely separated at bases; has wings but these are shed after the fly finds a host; sucks blood from various warm-blooded hosts. Deer louse flies (*Lipoptena*) are common in the Sierra and commonly alight mistakenly on humans, especially on sweaty skin; bird louse flies (*Olfersia*) occur on towhees, jays, juncos, and other birds. Related families (Streblidae, Nycteribiidae) are found only on bats.

BLOW FLIES   Family Calliphoridae

Length to .5 in.; resemble house flies but often metallic blue or green. The blue bottle (*Calliphora*) and green bottle flies (*Lucilia*) lay eggs on decaying flesh or on open wounds of animals, and larvae can feed on living tissue. They pupate on or in soil. Meat left exposed is commonly "blown," or covered with eggs of these flies.

TACHINID FLIES   Family Tachinidae

Length to .5 in.; stout, usually bristly, second antennal segment cleft above, antennal bristle bare or only slightly hairy, mouthparts usually well developed. Probably over 150 species in Sierra that parasitize other insects. Eggs are laid on the host insect or scattered over its food plant to be eaten by caterpillars or other hosts. The fly larva feeds on the internal organs of the host, usually not killing it until the host larva is ready to pupate. Adults are sometimes observed laying eggs but more commonly are seen resting on flowers.

BOT FLIES   Family Oestridae

Length to .5 in.; stout, second antennal segment with a cleft above, mouthparts reduced or vestigial. Eggs or young larvae are laid on skin or in nostrils of mammals. Larvae bore through flesh to the skin and form pouches (tumors) with breathing holes; when grown they emerge and drop to the ground to pupate. In the Sierra the Deer Bot Fly (*Cephenemyia pratti*) is common, and species of *Cuterebra* attack rabbits, wood rats, and mice.

Fleas (Order Siphonaptera)

Length to .25 in.; body compressed; no wings; mouthparts piercing-sucking; antennae short, in grooves; eyes simple or absent; hind legs adapted for leaping. Eggs laid in habitat of host; larvae cylindrical, legless, to .25 in. long, mandibles for feeding on organic debris; three larval stages. Pupae in cocoons. Life cycle from egg to adult usually about a month. Adults are intermittent ectoparasites, sucking blood of birds and

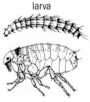

larva

mammals. Two common species in the Sierra are the Ground Squirrel Flea (*Oropsylla montanus*) to 6,000 ft elevation and the Chipmunk Flea (*Eumolpianus eumolpi*) at high elevations. Both bite humans and both are involved in transmission of plague from wild rodents. The Cat Flea (*Ctenocephalides felis*) is carried to the Sierra by humans and their domesticated animals.

Ants, Bees, and Wasps (Order Hymenoptera)

Wings four (or absent), membranous, few veins, interlocked in flight; mouthparts chewing or chewing-lapping; female with ovipositor for sawing, piercing, or stinging; pupae often in cocoons. Some species social, in colonies, others parasitic on insects; a few chew plant tissue or make galls on plants.

SAWFLIES   **Superfamily Tenthredinoidea**

Length to .33 in.; body robust; front tibia with one apical spur; ovipositor of female sawlike, concealed; males unknown in most species and females can lay eggs without mating. Larvae resemble caterpillar or slug. The pine sawfly (*Neodiprion*) is black or brown, male with feathery antennae. Eggs laid in slits cut in needles; greenish larvae scatter over foliage, feeding on needles until September, then drop to the ground and pupate in cocoons. New adults emerge the following spring. Other species feed on willow, cherry, and currant, also on ferns (which are used by very few Lepidoptera caterpillars).

HORNTAILS   **Family Siricidae**

Length to 1.5 in. plus .5 in. ovipositor in female; body straight sided; front tibia with one spur at end; female with long ovipositor and sheaths. Larvae long, cylindrical, grublike, legs reduced, bore into wood of trees and shrubs. The Western Horntail (*Sirex areolatus*) is dark metallic blue with brownish wings. Female drills into and oviposits an inch or more into freshly felled or injured conifers to lay eggs. Larvae make round holes in heartwood and sapwood; after one or two years pupal cells are formed near the surface of wood and adults cut emergence holes.

ICHNEUMON WASPS   **Family Ichneumonidae**

Pl. 320

Length to 1.5 in.; antennae not elbowed; trochanters (segment between coxa and femur) two-segmented; front wings with pigmented spot; abdomen long, slender, several segments distinct on upper surface; ovipositor to 3 in. long. Larvae are parasites of caterpillars and other insects and pupate in host. The largest Sierra ichneumonid is *Megarhyssa,* which loops its long ovipositor and bores through bark to lay eggs in tunnels of horntail wasps. Braconid wasps are like ichneumonids but usually smaller and pupate outside host.

CHALCID WASPS   **Superfamily Chalcidoidea**

Length to .13 in.; body metallic, antennae elbowed; trochanters two-segmented; hind femur swollen; ovipositor of female issues from below abdomen forward of tip. Seed chalcidoids (*Megastig-mus*) attack most Sierra conifers, drilling through young, green cones to lay eggs in seeds. Larvae reduce seeds to mere shells. Adults emerge in the second or third year. Other chalcids are parasites either on caterpillars and other larvae or on other parasites.

GALL WASPS Family Cynipidae

Pl. 321

Length to .25 in.; body compressed; antennae not elbowed; trochanters two-segmented; front wings without pigmented spot at outer third of front margin. Eggs laid in plant tissues, mainly on oaks; others parasitic on other wasps or flies. Cynipids alternate between a bisexual generation and a generation with only females. Some galls are woody and fleshy or thin skinned, spotted, and spherical; the latter type is produced on huckleberry oak by *Loxaulus maculipennis*. The California Oak Gall Wasp (*Andricus californicus*) produces the large "oak apples" 2 to 4 in. in diameter on valley and foothill oaks. Many small larvae inhabit a single gall. On valley and foothill oaks, seedlike galls .08 in. in diameter are produced by *Neuroterus saltatorius*. Fully grown "seeds" drop to the ground, and thousands are sometimes seen "jumping" as the larvae jerk back and forth in their tiny capsules, which presumably enables them to settle into cracks and other protected spots.

CUCKOO WASPS Family Chrysididae

 Length to .5 in.; metallic green, bluish, or golden; antennae elbowed; trochanters one-segmented; abdomen with only three segments visible above, flat below, curled under body for protection. Eggs are laid in provisioned cells in nests of solitary wasps and bees; larvae eat host's food and larvae, then pupate in a cocoon within the host cell.

ANTS Family Formicidae

Length to .75 in.; black or paler, sometimes reddish; trochanters one-segmented; waist at front of abdomen has one or two knoblike segments. Social, in colonies, with sexual females (queens), males, and wingless workers; queen removes her wings after mating flight and starts colony by laying eggs and caring for first young. Later she is fed and the brood is tended by workers. **REMARKS:** Most ants are scavengers and therefore useful in cleaning up organic material in fields or forests. A few are predaceous or eat seeds, and some colonize aphids and "milk" the honeydew. In the Sierra, Myrmicinae ants have been recorded up to 8,600 ft; these have a two-segmented pedicel, no simple eyes, a well-developed sting, and naked pupae. The other common group, Formicinae, has a one-segmented waist, simple eyes, and the pupae in cocoons. Instead of a structure to inject formic acid, the stinger is reduced; the ants gain protection by squirting a spray as much as 2 in. from the tip of abdomen. The Brown Ants (*Formica fusca*) nest in the ground, some forming crater nests in sandy soil. Red ants (*Formica*) make large mound nests of pine needles in open forests. The Amazon Ant (*Polyergus breviceps*), with narrow pointed mandibles, nests under logs and stones; it raids colonies of the Brown Ant, stealing pupae which are then raised and used as slaves. Carpenter ants (*Camponotus*) are the largest Sierra ants, the body of a wingless queen reaching .6 in. These ants tunnel in stumps, logs, and even milled lumber. They do not eat the wood but are general scavengers; also they tend aphids and the caterpillars of Lycaenid butterflies.

VELVET ANTS   Family Mutillidae
Pl. 322

Length to .5 in.; body black, densely covered with long hairs, usually reddish or orange in Sierra species; trochanters one-segmented; male winged, female wingless with a powerful sting; Mutillids have a thin, unknobbed "waist" or petiole. In the foothills often seen running about on sandy soil. Eggs are laid in burrows of solitary bees and wasps and the larvae feed on young of their hosts.

SPIDER WASPS   Family Pompilidae

Length to 1.6 in.; body dark blue or black, wings sometimes red or orange; legs long; trochanters one-segmented. Adults seen at flowers or on ground, running erratically and constantly flicking wings. Females sting spiders, paralyzing but not killing them. Then the spider is buried with an egg that soon hatches, the larvae feeding on the fresh spider. Tarantula hawks (*Pepsis*) are common throughout the Sierra except at highest elevations. The battle between a large *Pepsis* and an even larger tarantula is usually won when the wasp stings the spider in a part of the nervous system near the head.

YELLOWJACKETS, PAPER WASPS   Family Vespidae
Pl. 323

Length to .75 in.; yellow and black; trochanters one-segmented; wings folded lengthwise; sting potent, painful. Young females overwinter and each starts a colony that lasts one season. Nests are made of paper (chewed wood) with combs of cells to house eggs and larvae, which are reared on fragments of insects, meat, sweets. Many small females perform work of the social colony. Males are produced late in summer from unfertilized eggs. *Polistes* and *Mischocyttarus* (abdominal petiole long, narrow) make a flat, uncovered nest attached by a short stem, the cells opening downward; colonies number up to 200. *Vespula* (petiole short, abdomen appears broad at base) makes nests below ground or above ground (typical). *Dolichovespula* broadly fastens nests to tree limbs. Nests are large, with hundreds or thousands of cells and workers; those on trees are sometimes larger than a football. The cells are protected by a paper covering. In the Sierra, *Polistes fuscatus* occurs up to 8,000 ft and the vespulas are common everywhere, particularly late in the season as their colony sizes build up.

REMARKS: The common Yellowjacket (*Vespula pensylvanica*) is a ground nester. In some years it is excessively abundant—one per square yard in places. The cause of such outbreaks is not known. In these times the wasps are annoying to vacationers and picnickers. Yellowjackets do not pursue people; they merely seek bits of food from a table or lunch box. They sting only when molested. Protection is afforded by screening homes and, when plagued by wasps outdoors, by being calm and avoiding direct contact. Stings can be treated with an ice pack and then a paste of water and bicarbonate of soda. If stung many times, or if the reaction is severe, it is best to see a doctor.

THREAD-WAISTED WASPS, MUD DAUBER WASPS   **Family**
Pl. 324   **Sphecidae**

Length to 1 in.; waist long, slender; wings not folded lengthwise; trochanters one-segmented. Nests provisioned with caterpillars, grasshoppers, and spiders that have been stung, remaining alive but unable to move; each genus of wasp using specific kinds of prey. *Ammophila*, black with reddish legs and base of abdomen, buries caterpillars of moths in the ground with an egg, covers the hole, and taps the soil in place with a small pebble. The yellow-and-black Mud Dauber (*Sceliphron caementarium*) builds mud cells to 1.5 in. in length side by side under rocks or in eaves and rafters of houses. The cells are provisioned with spiders on which the white, grublike larvae feed.

MINING BEES   **Family Andrenidae**

Length to .5 in.; body clothed with branching hairs (as in all bees); trochanters one-segmented; tongue short, hind tarsi with pollen baskets. Places pollen and eggs in cells in tunnels dug in ground. Important pollinators of Sierra plants.

LEAFCUTTING BEES   **Family Megachilidae**

Length to .5 in.; abdomen with a dense mat of hairs for collecting pollen. Nests of *Megachile* are in hollow stems or in holes in wood, lined with disks cut from leaves of roses and other plants. Several cells are placed end-to-end, separated by disks and provisioned with a nectar-pollen paste. The 1-in. circular holes cut in leaves of wild rose are the work of these bees. Other species nest in the ground or externally in cells formed of resin and pebbles.

DIGGER BEES, CARPENTER BEES — Family Anthophoridae
Pl. 325

Length to .75 in.; stout, black or bluish, mandibles powerful, used to tunnel in solid wood of buildings, bridges, and other structures, or make deep burrows in ground. The Mountain Carpenter Bee (*Xylocopa tabaniformis*) makes burrows 5 to 12 in. long, provisioned with a honey-pollen mixture packed into a cell in which an egg is laid. The larvae feed for about a month, pupate two weeks later, and emerge after another two weeks. Since many bees may tunnel close together, timbers are sometimes weakened.

BUMBLE BEES — Subfamily Bombinae

Length .8 in.; densely hairy, black with yellow or reddish markings; tongue long for gathering nectar from clover and other plants. Bumble bees are a subfamily within the Apidae (honey bees forming another subfamily, Apinae, within the same family) but are treated separately here because they are such a familiar insect. An overwintering young queen starts a new colony (lasts one season) in an old rodent burrow; she lays eggs and collects pollen and nectar to feed the brood. After the first generation, small female workers take over the labor in the field and colony. Late in the season the colony is large with much brood and much stored food in honeypots. Then males and future queens are produced. After mating, the males and workers gradually die and the queens seek protected places under loose bark or other sites to hibernate. Bumble bees are dominant in northern latitudes including the Arctic; they occur from the Central Valley to the alpine fell-fields. They are important pollinators of many flowering plants.

HONEY BEES — Subfamily Apinae
Pl. 326

Length of queen to .8 in., worker to about .5 in.; golden brown to dark brown; eyes hairy, female workers with pollen baskets on hind legs; queens with relatively short wings; drones (males) broad, eyes large. The Honey Bee (*Apis mellifera*) native to the Old World has been imported and spread everywhere. In the Sierra, colonies often are not domesticated. Honey Bees seen visiting flowers at all elevations derive mostly from foothill colonies or others moved to high meadows by beekeepers during the short period when flowers are producing the most nectar. If wild colonies become established in trees they cannot survive Sierra winters. Because of their abundance and widespread nectar collecting, Honey Bees may deplete nectar sources before native bees and other pollinators gain access, with detrimental effects on populations of native species.

FISHES

THE CREST OF THE Sierra divides the waters and fish fauna in two. To the east are those that form the Lahontan drainage: the Susan, Truckee, Carson, and Walker Rivers and some lesser streams; while a few drain into Mono Lake, or Owens Valley (which forms part of the Death Valley drainage). The other waters flow westward, mostly into the Sacramento–San Joaquin River system. Since the 1850s there have been drastic changes to all river systems. Various species of warmwater fishes have been introduced into lowland streams and trout have been added to colder waters. For the most part, waters above 6,000 ft in elevation were fishless until trout were introduced into them. Most west-slope streams have been dammed, so that migrant fishes can no longer ascend them; and most reservoirs and lakes have been stocked with nonnative fishes that compete with native fishes for food and habitat. As a consequence, of the 40 species native to the Sierra Nevada, six are now formally listed as Threatened and Endangered, 12 are Species of Special Concern, and four others are in serious decline. By contrast, the 30 species of introduced fish are generally abundant and widespread.

Fish are streamlined, muscular animals that have a mostly simple body shape (fig. 12). Living in a world of water that is eight hundred times denser than air, they are able to remain effortlessly suspended and control their forward movement with powerful sweeps of their *caudal* fins. Paired *pectoral* fins assist in steering, while paired *pelvic* fins act as stabilizers to help keep the fish upright. Pectoral fins that are longer and pointed allow for precise control in fast hunting fish, while shorter, more rounded pectorals are usually found in sluggish feeders and bottom fish. *Dorsal* and *anal* fins assist in providing stability, and some species have spiny portions of the dorsal fins that serve as spiky armor to discourage potential predators. *Adipose* fins

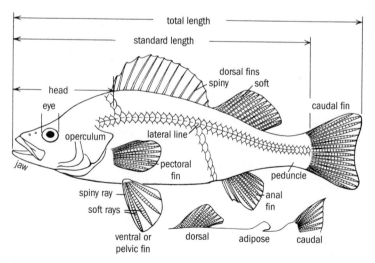

Figure 12. Structure of a fish.

are a special feature found on trout, salmon, catfish, and a few other groups. The *lateral line* is a sensory feature sometimes visible as a line of scales along the body. Unique to fishes, this series of pores serves as a highly sensitive turbulence and pressure change detector that allows fishes to "see" in the dark and monitor their surroundings. Most fishes have bony lips around the jaw, but some of the fish-eating (piscivorous) fishes have large sharp teeth in their throats called *pharyngeal teeth*. Because water contains a lower amount of oxygen than air, fishes must constantly pump water across their gills by gulping with their mouths and opening and closing their gills covers (*operculum*). Many (and perhaps all) fishes produce sounds (including courtship songs) but they lack ears because the density of their flesh equals about that of water and absorbs sound waves without distortion.

Taxonomy follows Moyle (2002).

Lamprey (Family Petromyzontidae)

PACIFIC LAMPREY   *Lampetra tridentata*
Pl. 327

Length to 24 in., diameter to 1.5 in.; body soft, cylindrical, compressed behind; skin smooth, slimy; mouth a circular funnel with horny teeth; top of head with one nostril; two small lateral eyes; gill openings seven pairs, separate; fins on back and tail soft (no paired fins); plain brownish or bluish gray.

DISTRIBUTION: Streams of west slope, occasionally up to 3,500 ft; once abundant but now restricted to reaches of streams below major dams.

REMARKS: The unusual lamprey (not a true fish) has no jaws, paired fins, or scales. To feed, it attaches to a fish by the sucking mouth, rasps a hole with the horny teeth, and sucks out blood and flesh. Mature lampreys ascend freshwater streams and make nests by moving rocks in the pebbly bottom; each female laying perhaps 200,000 eggs. The young hatch as small slender larvae (*ammocoetes*) without eyes or teeth. Each makes a U-shaped hole in sand or mud where it lives five to seven years, drawing in water for respiration and filter feeding. Gradually it becomes adult in form, migrates to saltwater to feed and grow, and finally returns to a stream during the summer months to spawn and die.

Minnows (Family Cyprinidae)

TUI CHUB   *Siphateles bicolor*
Pl. 328

Length to 13 in.; head large, conical, flat on sides; eyes large; lateral line curved downward; scales large; dorsal fin over pelvic fins; tail sharp forked; olive green above, at times brassy or silvery, white to yellow white below.

DISTRIBUTION: Waters of east slope, introduced into some west-slope streams and lakes.

REMARKS: Lakes and quiet parts of large streams are the habitat of the long-lived Tui Chub, which often gather in large schools and are usually associated with abundant aquatic vegetation. Their food includes plankton, some plant materials, and insects. The adhesive eggs are spawned in spring and spread over underwater vegetation. Young can form huge schools in shallow waters. Tui Chub in lakes are a major prey item of trout, Osprey, pelicans, grebes, and other predators.

LAHONTAN REDSIDE   *Richardsonius egregius*
Pl. 329

Length 3.5 in.; body compact, mouth large, terminal; base of pelvic fins ahead of dorsal; lateral line nearly straight; tail bluntly forked; back and upper sides green with a blood red. streak along upper side of body in breeding male (rosy in female) and another dusky streak on side; whitish crescent on cheek and belly.

DISTRIBUTION: Common in streams and lakes of Lahontan system on east slope, as well as in the Mokelumne River on the west slope.

REMARKS: This species has successfully colonized a number of reservoirs. Spawning involves very large aggregations of individuals gathering in shallow, gravel-bottomed areas. Schools commonly observed around piers in Lake Tahoe.

HITCH   *Lavinia exilicauda*

Length to 12 in.; body deep, compressed, tapering at ends; peduncle slender; head and mouth small, upper lip on level with lower part of pupil; eye large, well forward; dorsal fin small, pectoral short, anal long and high; caudal well forked; dark above, sides silvery; scales dark spotted.

DISTRIBUTION: Lowland streams, sloughs, and lakes up into Foothill Belt.

REMARKS: This native minnow is increasingly scarce in Sierra streams, where it fights a losing battle with a combination of altered habitats and introduced species. It was once a favored food item of Native Americans. The young fish feed on plankton and small insects near shore, while adults feed in open water. Spawning occurs during early spring rains, in small creeks or gravelly lake shallows.

CALIFORNIA ROACH   *Lavinia symmetricus*
Pl. 330

Length to 5 in.; head slender, snout slightly convex, mouth small, slightly oblique, low in head; eye large; lateral line downcurved at front; dorsal fin well behind pelvic fins; dusky above, sides pale, silvery below, scales black-dotted; may have dark stripe from snout to tail; base of pectoral fins orange; cheek silvery.

DISTRIBUTION: Tributary streams of Central Valley into Foothill Belt, where it survives in warm water and low oxygen levels that many other fish cannot tolerate.

REMARKS: The roach lives in small, clear creeks, feeding on insects, crustaceans, and algae. In spring it spawns several hundred adhesive eggs in shallow water over rocks or large gravel, often gathering in large excited aggregations of fish. Several isolated and genetically distinct populations of this species are poorly described.

HARDHEAD   *Mylopharodon conocephalus*

Pl. 331

Length to 36 in.; body long, compressed; head broad and short; mouth small, toothless; throat (pharyngeal) teeth large, blunt; scales small, loosely overlapped; lower lobe of caudal fin longer than upper, bronze green above, paler below.

DISTRIBUTION: Scattered populations in deep clear streams on west slope below 4,000 ft. California Species of Special Concern.

REMARKS: The Hardhead is second in size only to the pikeminnow. Like that species it has been recorded from Alturas to Bakersfield in many west-slope streams, although dams have now resulted in populations becoming fragmented, or declining and disappearing altogether. It feeds on insects and plant materials and spawns in spring.

SACRAMENTO PIKEMINNOW   *Ptychocheilus grandis*

Length 24 to 48 in.; head and body long, slender; mouth large, extending to front of eye, toothless; throat (pharyngeal) teeth large and sharp; scales small; lateral line nearly straight; front of dorsal fin behind that of pelvic fins; lobes of caudal fin equal; olive or brownish green above, silvery below, scales dark margined; fins red or orange in spring; young with black caudal spot.

DISTRIBUTION: Common in rivers and larger streams of west slope well into Mixed Conifer Belt.

REMARKS: This second largest of American minnows is common in the Sierra, where it has adapted to living in river systems altered by humans. When young it eats aquatic insects, later it preys on small frogs and other fishes. Although frequently killed by disappointed trout anglers, there is no evidence its predation has a negative effect on salmon or trout populations in the Sierra.

SPECKLED DACE   *Rhinichthys osculus*

Pl. 332

Length 2 to 3 in.; slender, snout pointed; upper lip joined to skin of snout; tail stout, forked; above brownish or yellowish green, with dark blotch on operculum, some with imperfect stripe on side; fins red tinted in spawning season.

DISTRIBUTION: Only fish widely native to both sides of the Sierra; abundant and widespread in streams and lakes of Lahontan drainage but in danger of disappearing from Owens Valley region; found on west slope mainly north of Cosumnes River.

REMARKS: The Speckled Dace is a small minnow, seminocturnal and secretive in habits, but common on riffles in small streams and among the shelter of rocks and gravel along lakeshores. It seldom lives over sand or in quiet waters. Nearly always seen in small groups. The food is of small insects and algae. In spring the few large eggs are deposited among rocks in riffles.

Suckers (Family Catostomidae)

SUCKERS
Pl. 333

Genus _Catostomus_

Length to 24 in.; body slender, somewhat cylindrical; eye high on tapered head; mouth below tip of snout, toothless; lips thick and covered with papillae, lower lip with broad free margin and divided into two lobes; scales small (in some species), crowded at front; pelvic fins under dorsal; anal fin short, high; tail forked; body dark above, pale below, breeding male with reddish side band.

DISTRIBUTION: Common in streams on both slopes, some to above 6,000 ft.

REMARKS: Suckers graze over rocks and other objects in stream bottoms, often in schools, using their thick soft lips to gather algae and other edible materials. Small trout may follow suckers around, consuming insects disturbed by their feeding. Suckers deposit nonadhesive eggs in small depressions in gravels of riffles. Three species are found in the Sierra: Sacramento Sucker (_C. occidentalis_) is widespread and abundant on the west side; Tahoe Sucker (_C. tahoensis_) is abundant in the Lahontan drainage; and Mountain Sucker (_C. platyrhynchus_) is in the same range as the Tahoe Sucker but rarer and not surviving in reservoirs (California Species of Special Concern). They all have a similar appearance but differ in the structure of their lips and the number of rows of fleshy papillae on the upper lips.

Bullhead Catfishes (Family Ictaluridae)

BROWN BULLHEAD

Ameiurus nebulosus

Length 12 to 18 in.; weight 1 to 2 (7) lb.; upper jaw usually longer than lower; four pairs of "feelers" on snout, those on top much shorter; tail fin squarish, not forked; skin scaleless, leathery; dorsal and paired fins each with stout spine; dorsal nearer snout than adipose; anal fin with rays longest at front; yellowish brown, with dark mottling.

DISTRIBUTION: Introduced in 1874, now in lakes and streams on both sides of the Sierra.

REMARKS: This common bullhead is another successful transplant from eastern waters. The species is best adapted to large bodies of water at lower elevations and individuals living at higher elevations in the Sierra are stunted. Long "feelers" on the snout are used to detect prey items. Females evacuate nest sites by carrying materials away in their mouths, and both sexes take turns aerating the incubating eggs by fanning their tails back and forth.

WHITE CATFISH   *Ameiurus catus*
Pl. 334

Length to 24 in.; usually smaller; body slender in young, heavier and head broader with age; mouth small with four pairs of "feelers" (barbels on snout), those on top shortest; tail fin forked, upper lobe longer; an adipose fin; skin scaleless, leathery; dorsal and pectoral fins each preceded by stout spine; dorsal fin midway between snout and adipose fin; base of anal fin shorter than head; front anal rays shortest; bluish olive above, silvery white below.

DISTRIBUTION: Introduced in 1874, now common in rivers of Central Valley and foothill reservoirs.

REMARKS: Several catfishes of eastern states were introduced into California many years ago and all have become common. Peeled of its tough skin, catfish is a favored food.

Salmon and Trout (Family Salmonidae)

MOUNTAIN WHITEFISH   *Prosopium williamsoni*
Pl. 335

Length to 16 in.; slender; body nearly cylindrical in cross section; mouth small, weak (toothless), ventral, reaching only to front of large eye; tail deeply forked; adipose fin present; scales large; back bluish, sides silvery, adipose and caudal fins steel blue.

DISTRIBUTION: Lake Tahoe, Donner Lake, and the Truckee, Carson, and Walker Rivers.

REMARKS: This native whitefish, related to the trouts, spawns in October to December, ascending tributaries of Lake Tahoe and various rivers. Males then have small tubercles on head and on scales near the tail. Like trout, they feed mainly on aquatic insects. They readily take wet flies and bait and are considered very tasty when cooked.

CHINOOK SALMON   *Oncorhynchus tshawytscha*
Pl. 336

Length 24 to 60 in., weight 16 to 18+ lb.; body robust, compressed, deepest near middle; head conic, mouth wide, teeth moderate (jaws of breeding male curved, teeth large at front); an adipose fin; peduncle slender; dusky above, sides with olive or bluish tinge, silvery below; back, dorsal fin, and tail with round black spots; breeding fish tinged with red.

DISTRIBUTION: Streams of Central Valley and foothills on west slope; migratory. State and Federal Endangered (winter and spring runs).

REMARKS: Originally this Pacific Coast salmon ascended major west-slope streams to spawn by the millions in tributaries well above the Foothill Belt. Dams built on most streams now exclude them, and spawning is mainly in the Sacramento River and the lower reaches of its tributaries. The salmon make nests in bottom gravel to receive the eggs, in the manner of Rainbow Trout. When four to 12 months old the young migrate to the ocean to live and grow for two to five years. After maturing they cease feeding, return to freshwater streams, spawn, and die. There are four distinct runs: winter, spring, fall, and late fall. All runs are declining. The Kokanee (*O. nerka*, pl. 337) was introduced during the 1940s into Lake Tahoe, Donner Lake, and other lakes and reservoirs; still being actively planted.

RAINBOW TROUT *Oncorhynchus mykiss*
Pl. 338

Length to 45 in., weight 20+ lb.; variable in color but back often bluish gray, belly silvery white; side stripe reddish to violet; black spots minute to .13 in. on upper half of head and body; lower side of head often reddish (no "cutthroat" red stripes on lower jaw, no brown or red spots, no wavy bars); dark parr marks on sides usually disappear early in life.

DISTRIBUTION: Originally the rainbow was *the* trout of all cool streams west of the Sierra crest. For well over a century it has been transplanted or reared and planted in many suitable California waters, and most caught by anglers are domesticated trout from hatcheries. Also it has been established in most eastern states, Europe, New Zealand, and many other parts of the world.

REMARKS: Wild rainbows spawn during the winter and spring (December to June, or later at higher elevations) in small, clear, cool, and swift streams. A pair will meet over clean gravel where the flow keeps the site well aerated and clear of silt. The female uses her tail to flip little rocks aside and form a nest, or redd. The two move over the redd, the female expels some ripe eggs, and the male ejects white milt containing sperm. She promptly moves gravel over the eggs, which meanwhile are fertilized by the sperm and absorb water until they are spherical. At 40 degrees F, the eggs hatch in about 80 days, but sooner in warmer water. Each young, or fry, at hatching has a yolk sac hanging on its lower surface—a food supply while it lives amid the gravel. When the yolk is consumed, the little trout, or fingerling, emerges to start feeding on minute insects in the stream. Growth depends on water temperature and food supply. In a cold brook after one year the fish may be only 3.5 in. long and after two years only 5 in., whereas a 2-in. fingerling planted in a rich, warm lake may reach 14 in. in a year.

Ocean-going rainbows known as Steelhead live in streams tributary to the Sacramento River and migrate into the ocean when a year or two old, remain in saltwater for one to two years, and then return to spawn in their parent streams. When freshly returned they are gray above and silvery on the belly with less of the red or violet seen on resident rainbows, but these colors are highly variable. Steelhead formerly spawned on the same west-slope rivers as Chinook Salmon but now are largely absent from Sierra Nevada and are listed as Threatened in the Central Valley.

CALIFORNIA GOLDEN TROUT *Oncorhynchus mykiss aguabonita*
Pl. 339

Length to 28 in.; olive back, sides golden yellow; belly, cheeks, and operculum bright red as are the pectoral, pelvic, and anal fins; side stripe rosy; parr marks on sides persist in streams (up to one year in lakes); dark spots few on back, more on dorsal and caudal fins; dorsal and anal fins white-tipped, sometimes edged with black.

DISTRIBUTION: Originally in few high streams of Kern River drainage; transplanted to many waters from Placer County to Tulare and Inyo Counties. Most transplanted populations probably hybrids with coastal races of Rainbow Trout.

REMARKS: This beautiful form of Rainbow Trout developed in the high southern Sierra, several streams having slightly unlike races (including the Little Kern Golden Trout, *O. m. whitei;* and Kern River Rainbow Trout, *O. m. gilberti).* In those remote waters golden trout abounded and were easily caught. All types are now threatened in their native range by introduced Brown Trout and livestock, but recovery efforts are under way.

LAHONTAN CUTTHROAT TROUT *Oncorhynchus clarki henshawi*
Pl. 340

Length to 3 ft, weight to 30 lb.; usually dark yellow olive from back to belly, with broad pinkish side stripe; body and fins with few or many scattered black spots; two red "cut-throat" stripes on membrane of lower jaw; minute (basibranchial) teeth on base of tongue.

DISTRIBUTION: Once the only trout found on east slope, in lakes and streams of the Lahontan drainage, but now rare and mostly replaced by nonnative trout. Federal Threatened.

REMARKS: Cutthroat trout once abounded in Lake Tahoe and other eastside waters. In early days it was caught commercially to supply mining camps. Overfishing, competition from nonnative trout, and exotic diseases reduced the population drastically. Another distinct form is the Paiute Cutthroat Trout (*O. c. seleneris*), once native to Fish Valley, Alpine County, where it has been largely replaced by nonnative trout. Populations of this Federal Threatened fish now persist at other sites where they have been introduced.

BROWN TROUT *Salmo trutta*
Pl. 341

Length to 2 ft; back dark or olive brown, sides golden or greenish brown, belly white or yellow (no bright side band or wavy marks); head, body, and dorsal fins with large, distinct dark spots, some orange-edged; lower sides with red or orange spots, pale bordered.

DISTRIBUTION: In many Sierra waters; prefers deep pools along streams but can tolerate warm water in summer; smaller fish are found in riffles and runs.

REMARKS: Five species of trout inhabit Sierra lakes and streams. They differ from salmon in having 12 or fewer rays in the anal fin, but a good visual guide in the field is that the anal fin is higher than long in trout and longer than high in salmon (high meaning distance from tip to base). True trouts

(*Salmo* and *Oncorhynchus*) have darkish spots on a lighter background, fewer than 190 scales in the lateral line, and a row of teeth in the center of the roof of the mouth. Chars (*Salvelinus*) have light spots on darker background and smaller scales (190+).

The Brown Trout, planted in California waters since 1893, is now widely established. This is the only trout with both black and red spots. It is wary, often escaping hooks and enemies to become old, deep bodied, heavy, and cannibalistic; extremely territorial, it readily ousts native trout from favored haunts. Skilled anglers enjoy attempts to catch this elusive species. It spawns in fall. Growing young have dark parr marks (vertical bands on sides) and pale-ringed dark spots.

BROOK TROUT   *Salvelinus fontinalis*

Pl. 342

Length to 2 ft, weight 9+ lb.; tail scarcely forked; scales very small; back and sides dark olive green with light wavy lines on dorsal fin and back; sides with red or light gray spots, some red spots with blue borders; front edge of pelvic and anal fins usually white.

DISTRIBUTION: Widely planted throughout California since 1871 but established mainly in mountain lakes and meadow streams at 5,000 to 9,000 ft.

REMARKS: Brook Trout does best in high lakes, where it spawns from September to December in the gravels of springs emerging from the lake bottoms or in tributary creeks. It is the fish primarily responsible for eliminating native Mountain Yellow-legged Frogs and other amphibians from most lakes into which it has been introduced.

LAKE TROUT   *Salvelinus namaycush*

Length to 3+ ft, weight 15 lb.; tail deeply forked; no bright color; body gray, pale to blackish, with large pale spots except on belly; dorsal and caudal fins with dark, wavy lines.

DISTRIBUTION: Introduced in lakes of Truckee River drainage: Tahoe, Donner, Fallen Leaf, Stony Ridge, and others, where it had a role in eliminating native Lahontan Cutthroat Trout.

REMARKS: Introduced in 1889 from Michigan, this trout lives deep in lakes and is caught usually on large heavily weighted spinners. It becomes large and feeds on other fish. Unlike other trout, which make gravel nests, this species sheds its eggs loosely over rocks or shelves in lake bottoms.

Livebearer (Family Poeciliidae)

WESTERN MOSQUITOFISH   *Gambusia affinis*

Length of female 1.5 to 2 in. and of male .5 to 1 in.; male smaller and scarcer than female; head flat, body relatively deep, especially in female; dorsal fin far back in female, its base behind that of anal fin in both sexes; male with spinelike mating organ (as long as head) projecting from back of anal fin; light olive, scales dark edged; a triangular bar below eye.

DISTRIBUTION: Introduced in 1922 from southeastern United States and now common in clear sluggish streams and ponds.

REMARKS: This diminutive fish swims near the surface, feeding on small insects and crustaceans. It has been widely planted in California to aid in control of mosquitoes but its success has been mixed. The eggs are fertilized internally and the young develop there. They are about .4 in. long when hatched, in broods of eight to 11; a female may produce several broods in a season.

Stickleback (Family Gasterosteidae)

THREESPINE STICKLEBACK   *Gasterosteus aculeatus*
Pl. 343
Length to 4 in.; body spindle shaped, caudal peduncle very slender; mouth small, lower jaw projecting; eye large; scaleless but sides often with row of vertical plates (five to 25), smaller toward tail; two large and one small spines on back ahead of dorsal fin; small erectile spines at anal fin, and one large spine low on each side at midbody; greenish olive above, silvery below; spring breeding colors: male throat and belly scarlet, fins greenish, eyes blue; female throat and belly pinkish.

DISTRIBUTION: Lower foothill and Central Valley streams; introduced in waters of east slope.

REMARKS: Sticklebacks occur in fresh or brackish waters throughout the Northern Hemisphere. They eat insects and plankton and become prey of trout and Largemouth Bass. The male builds a nest of twigs held together by a secretion from his kidney. Several females may spawn in one nest, which then is guarded by the male until hatching.

Sculpins (Family Cottidae)

SCULPINS   Genus *Cottus*
Pl. 344
Length 3 to 5 in.; mouth large; eyes small, on top of broadly rounded head; body slender, scaleless, with patches of prickles; pectoral fins relatively large, dorsal fin double, pectoral close behind operculum; grayish olive with darker mottling.

DISTRIBUTION: West-slope streams and well into Mixed Conifer Belt (Riffle Sculpin, *C. gulosus*); in west-slope reservoirs and lower elevation rivers (Prickly Sculpin, *C. asper*); or on east slope in Truckee River and other streams of Lahontan system (Paiute Sculpin, *C. beldingi*).

REMARKS: These small fishes, often called muddlers or bullheads, live among loose rocks in stream riffles, keeping position by use of their large pectoral fins. Their coloration matches bottom materials, providing effective camouflage. They feed largely on aquatic insects and are often important prey of trout.

Sunfishes (Family Centrarchidae)

SUNFISHES   Genus *Lepomis*
Pls. 345, 346

Length to 8 in.; body short, high, thin, back elevated; mouth small, terminal; form of body and height of spines varies with age and condition; color brilliant, yellow or greenish, sexes alike.

DISTRIBUTION: In many waters of both slopes.

REMARKS: Several species of small deep-bodied sunfishes have been brought from eastern states to California and become common, especially in lowland waters. These include the Green Sunfish (*L. cyanellus*), Bluegill (*L. macrochirus*), and Redear Sunfish (*L. microlophus*). They serve as food for larger alien fishes (mainly bass) and are caught by many anglers.

LARGEMOUTH BASS   *Micropterus salmoides*
Pl. 347

Length to 37 in., weight to 23 lb.; mouth reaching beyond eye in adult; cheek scales in 10 to 11 rows; above dark green, lower sides greenish silvery, belly white; three dark oblique stripes on cheek and operculum; some dark spots above and below lateral line; young with blackish line along entire side; caudal fin pale at base, then blackish, white-tipped.

DISTRIBUTION: Introduced in 1891, now abundant and widespread in ponds, reservoirs, and degraded streams of the west slope; recently expanding to Lake Tahoe.

SMALLMOUTH BASS   *Micropterus dolomieu*
Pl. 348

Length to 28 in.; weight to 14 lb.; body long ovate, deeper with age; mouth large but ending before eye; cheek scales minute, about 15 to 18 rows; scales on trunk moderately small; edges of spiny dorsal fin notched; dark bronzy green above, dark spots on sides in young, three bronzy cheek bands radiating from eye, a small dusky spot at end of operculum; white below; dorsal fin bronze-spotted, edge dusky; caudal fin yellow at base, then black, white-tipped.

DISTRIBUTION: Introduced and now abundant and widespread in west-slope streams at least into foothills.

REMARKS: The two basses are rated among the gamiest of fishes in lakes and reservoirs. They rise either to fly or minnow bait and by their rushes and leaps test the angler's skill. The Smallmouth favors cleaner and cooler waters, while the Largemouth does well in shallow warm places. In large waters having both gravel and mud bottoms the two may occur together, along with Spotted Bass (*M. punctulatus,* pl. 349) and Redeye Bass (*M. coosae*). Where bass are abundant, native fishes tend to disappear.

AMPHIBIANS

SALAMANDERS, NEWTS, toads, and frogs have moist glandular skins and are cold-blooded (they don't generate warmth and their body temperature mirrors that in the environment around them). The Sierra species are small and must live in damp or wet places, avoiding both the dry heat of summer and the freezing of winter. They hibernate (not technically hibernation, but brumation) in winter (except at lower elevations), and in arid landscapes remain hidden below ground in midsummer. In consequence they are limited in occurrence and activity. Lungless land salamanders (from *Ensatina* to *Hydromantes* in this section of this guide) lay their eggs in moist chambers under rocks or logs or in burrows. All the other amphibians spawn in water. The true frogs (*Rana*) live in or close to water, where they may be found in the daytime. Toads and Pacific Chorus Frogs leave the water after egg-laying and hide in damp retreats by day.

Half of the amphibians in the Sierra Nevada are at risk of extinction due to a variety of causes. Species once so abundant that early naturalists had to tread carefully to avoid crushing them are now teetering on the edge of extinction. Bullfrogs and various nonnative fishes introduced into warm waters and trout introduced into mountain lakes have had a huge impact on a number of species, while air pollution (including herbicides and pesticides) is suspected of causing further declines. But in some cases the reasons for plummeting numbers are simply unknown.

Taxonomy used here follows Stebbins (2003).

Mole Salamanders (Family Ambystomatidae)

CALIFORNIA TIGER SALAMANDER   *Ambystoma californiense*
Pl. 350

Length 6 to 9 in.; stocky salamander with broad, rounded snout; small eyes; black above with irregular lemon yellow or whitish spots; belly grayish.

DISTRIBUTION: Foothill Belt on west slope; grasslands and open oak woodlands below 1,500 ft; occurs in widely scattered colonies from Sacramento County to Tulare County. Candidate for Federal listing.

REMARKS: Rarely seen on the surface except in the winter breeding season, tiger salamanders spend much of their time living underground. In California they live in ground squirrel and pocket gopher burrows. During winter rains, they move to fish-free ponds to mate. Females lay their eggs singly and hatchlings appear by mid-February, metamorphosing into small salamanders before ponds dry in the summer heat. Habitat loss due to agriculture, development, and introduction of exotic species such as Western Mosquitofish and Bullfrogs have rendered this species vulnerable to local extinctions.

LONG-TOED SALAMANDER   *Ambystoma macrodactylum*
Pl. 351

Length 4 to 6.25 in.; upper surface dark brown or black with yellow or greenish yellow spots that may run together along middle of back; undersurface sooty or brown; sides and belly with minute white spots; side of body with 12 to 13 grooves.

DISTRIBUTION: Mixed Conifer and Upper Montane Belts to 10,000 ft from northern Tuolumne County north to Alaska; in vicinity of ponds or lakes.

REMARKS: Named for the long fourth toes on their hind feet, Long-toed Salamanders move to ponds and lakes to mate soon after ice melts in spring. The female lays 85 to 400 eggs, each in a soft gelatinous covering about .63 in. in diameter that makes eggs in clumps look widely spaced. Eggs are deposited singly or in clumps of five to 100 on the bottom or attached to plants along the margin. After a couple of weeks the larvae hatch. They are olive or brownish gray, with three pairs of gills. They feed and grow to about 3 in. long, then lose the gills and transform into small adults; at high altitudes this change is usually in the second year. In summer, adults hide by day under rocks and in or under decaying logs.

Newt (Family Salamandridae)

CALIFORNIA NEWT   *Taricha torosa*
Pl. 352

Length 5 to 7.75 in.; upper surface and sides uniform reddish brown; undersurface uniformly yellow to orange, no spotting; skin thick and warty.

DISTRIBUTION: Foothill and Mixed Conifer Belts of west slope to about 6,500 ft; spawns in quiet streams, ponds, or reservoirs.

REMARKS: This common amphibian emerges from underground shelters toward the end of winter. Adults hide in damp spots under rocks or logs but may be abroad on cloudy days. Males enter the water in March or April, prior to mating. At this time their skin becomes smooth and the tail develops a fin to aid in swimming. When females arrive the pairs join for mating. Then, crawling on the bottom, the male deposits a gelatinous mass capped with sperm (spermatophore). The female picks this up in her vent, and the sperm serve later to fertilize her eggs. Each egg mass is firm and round, to 1.25 in. in diameter and containing seven to 29 eggs, and is attached to vegetation or other objects in the water. The larvae are pale yellow with two lengthwise blackish stripes, three pairs of gills, and a thin fin along back and tail. When about 2.25 in. long they transform and leave the water. Larvae eat small animals and organic matter on objects in the water; adults feed on worms, insects, and small mollusks. When disturbed, adults elevate their heads and arch their tails up, exposing their bright orange undersides. This is a warning sign to potential predators, who quickly learn if they don't already know that newts have toxins in their skin. These salamanders should not be handled to avoid contact with these toxins.

Lungless Salamanders (Family Plethodontidae)

ENSATINA
Ensatina eschscholtzii

Pl. 353

Length 3 to 6 in.; upper surface dark brown with reddish orange spots; undersurface whitish or gray; limbs orangish at base, but feet dusky; tail constricted at base; eyes large and protruding; 12 to 13 grooves on side of body.

DISTRIBUTION: Mixed Conifer Belt of west slope to around 8,000 ft; prefers conifer stands but found in many habitats from chaparral to oak woodland.

REMARKS: This salamander can be found during damp periods from late April into September but is scarcely seen when there is no moisture. Being one of the lungless salamanders (along with the following salamanders in this section), Ensatina lacks lungs and breathes through thin, moist skin. When its damp hiding place under or in a log is opened, the animal usually is quiet, then crawls away. If molested, it stands on extended legs, arching the tail or sweeping it sideways and occasionally producing a sticky secretion. Its food includes earthworms, insects, spiders, centipedes, and other invertebrates. A female lays eight to 12 eggs about .25 in. in diameter, each in a jelly coat and hidden in moist soil or decaying wood; she remains with them during development. One set, freshly laid, was found in late May, and several near hatching were seen in August and September. A uniformly colored race known as the Yellow-eyed Ensatina (*E. e. xanthoptica*) occurs in the upper foothills of the central Sierra. It is orange brown above and orange-bellied, with a yellow patch on its eye (rather like a California Newt with a constricted tail base).

ARBOREAL SALAMANDER
Aneides lugubris

Length 4.25 to 7.25 in.; body uniformly dark brown (no stripes), often with scattered dots of yellow; belly light gray; head large and muscular, bluntly triangular; 15 grooves on side of body.

DISTRIBUTION: Foothill Belt of west slope from El Dorado County to Madera County to around 5,000 ft; found in blue oak–gray pine woodlands or in ponderosa pine and black oak forests.

REMARKS: This somewhat sturdy animal, with enlarged toe tips and a prehensile tail, can climb better than most salamanders, and individuals or groups may be found to 30 ft above ground in moist cavities in oaks. It also lives on or near the ground in damp logs or wood rat nests and beneath flat rocks or boards. Active adults can be found on the ground anytime during rainy spells. Their food includes beetles, ants, moth larvae, and centipedes. In coastal counties where this species also occurs, eggs have been seen (in trees or at ground level) from July into September. The clutch is 12 to 24 eggs, guarded and kept moist by the female. The egg is attached to a nearby surface by a short stalk. This salamander occasionally makes a mouselike squeak and has tiny sharp teeth that might scratch a captor's hand, although it rarely bites.

SLENDER SALAMANDERS   Genus *Batrachoseps*

Pl. 354

Length 2.75 to 5.5 in.; head tiny; body wormlike with tiny legs and feet; 16 to 21 grooves on side; four toes on hind foot (other salamanders have five toes).

DISTRIBUTION: See below.

REMARKS: During the wet season, logs, boards, or stones may hide one or several of these wormlike creatures, some coiled or looped like diminutive snakes. This salamander crawls feebly with its small legs, or makes lateral sweeps of its body and tail. If picked up it may lash from side to side and the tail may break off at any place beyond its base. This salamander feeds on small ground-dwelling insects or earthworms and sowbugs. Eggs, four to 12 per female, are laid in or under logs, beneath rocks, and probably in small cavities in the earth during the winter months. At hatching the young are about .67 in. long.

Slender salamanders are an extremely complex group whose taxonomy is poorly understood. Analysis of genetic material has detected the presence of several new species in the Sierra Nevada that are impossible or nearly impossible to identify by external characteristics. Some of these new species were first described in 1998 and additional work will surely change the number of species recognized in the Sierra Nevada. Of known species, the California Slender Salamander (*B. attenuatus*) is most familiar. It has tiny legs and a very slim body with a wide red to yellow dorsal stripe; its belly is dark with minute white flecks. It is found below 3,000 ft on the west slope from the American River north to Butte County. The Gregarious Slender Salamander (*B. gregarius*) is virtually indistinguishable from the California Slender Salamander. It occurs in the same habitats from the Merced River south to Kern County on the west slope. The Relictual Slender Salamander (*B. relictus*) ranges from the Tule River drainage (Tulare County) south to the Greenhorn Mountains and lower Kern River Canyon in Kern County. This species is a State and Federal Species of Special Concern. Populations within the lower Kern River Canyon are apparently already extinct, with the last salamander found there in 1971. It occurs in mixed conifer forests and is separated from the Gregarious in having a larger head, longer limbs, a shorter tail, and a dark belly. The Kern Canyon Slender Salamander (*B. simatus*), a State Threatened species, occurs only on the south side of the Kern River Canyon on north-facing slopes of pine, oak, and chaparral. It is distinguished from the Relictual by white flecks on its belly and in having 20 to 21 grooves on the side of its body (Relictual has 16 to 20).

The following species would be very difficult, if not impossible, to separate based on current knowledge: Hell Hollow Slender Salamander (*B. diabolicus*) occurs in the foothills of the west slope from the Merced River Canyon north to the American River, and it may be found together with the California Slender Salamander at some places. Kings River Slender Salamander (*B. regius*) is known only from the Kings River drainage of Fresno County, where it has been found both at low-elevation (1,400 ft) and high-elevation (8,000 ft) sites. Its range probably overlaps that of the Gregarious

Slender Salamander in the Mixed Conifer Belt. Sequoia Slender Salamander (*B. kawia*) occurs within the Kaweah River drainage of Tulare County at elevations of 1,400 to 7,200 ft, where it may be found on moist, north-facing slopes or seepage areas within conifer forest. Kern Plateau Slender Salamander (*B. robustus*) is large and robust with dark spots on a granite-gray body; found on the Kern plateau in forested areas. Resembles Mount Lyell Salamander but with four toes on hind foot.

MOUNT LYELL SALAMANDER   *Hydromantes platycephalus*
Pl. 355

Length 2.75 to 4.5 in.; with speckles of dark chocolate and pale gray above, creating a granitelike pattern; undersurface sooty, flecked with pale gray; head often broader than body; head and body flattened; 12 to 13 grooves on side of body; tail short, blunt at tip; toes partly webbed.

DISTRIBUTION: High Sierra from Sierra County to central Tulare County at 4,000 to 12,000 ft; in moist places under flat granite slabs. State and Federal Species of Special Concern.

REMARKS: In 1915 this exclusively Sierra salamander was discovered by accident when two were caught in a mousetrap. Since then, it has been found in many localities though it is rarely encountered. Elevationally it is recorded from the top of talus slopes above Camp Curry in Yosemite Valley and from the top of Half Dome to above timberline. Its broad flat feet aid the salamander in walking over granite, and it can use its tail as a braking or anchoring device to help climb rock faces. These salamanders are active at temperatures from 30 to 52 degrees F and have been observed walking on snow. Aboveground activity occurs from May to late August. Eggs are probably located in deep fissures but they have not yet been found; young salamanders are observed in June and July. Insects and larvae, spiders, and centipedes serve as food. This rare salamander is protected in California and should not be handled.

Another *Hydromantes* salamander was discovered in 1952 in the Merced River Canyon west of Yosemite National Park. It is found nowhere else in the world and is now protected as a State Threatened species. Named the Limestone Salamander (*H. brunus*), it typically associates with limestone outcrops from 1,200 to 2,500 ft. Uniformly brown above and pale below, otherwise like the Mount Lyell Salamander. Active only during the cool, rainy season from November to March.

Spadefoot Toads (Family Pelobatidae)

WESTERN SPADEFOOT   *Spea hammondii*
Pl. 356

Length 1.5 to 2.5 in.; eye large, pupil vertically elliptical; sole of hind foot with black spur (the "spade") on inner edge; body relatively smooth with minute reddish bumps; dusky green, gray, or brown above with two (or four) broad pale stripes along back and sides; undersurface white (male with black throat).

DISTRIBUTION: On west slope from Sacramento County south; mainly below 1,000 ft in open grasslands. State and Federal Species of Special Concern.

REMARKS: By use of its spades this toad can dig backward in the soil, make a burrow, and soon disappear. It is mostly nocturnal and seldom seen except when spawning. Breeding follows heavy rains that form temporary ponds from February to April. The sexes gather at night, called by notes of the males, a low rasping *a-a-a-ah* or *tirr-r-r-r*. While clasped by a male, a female lays 300 to 500 eggs in loose cylindrical clusters of 10 to 40 eggs each, which are immediately fertilized by the male. Larvae hatch in a few days, and the carnivorous tadpoles may transform into tiny spadefoots within a month to escape drying ponds.

OTHER SPADEFOOTS: The related Great Basin Spadefoot (*S. intermontana*) inhabits high-desert regions just east of the Sierra from the Owens Valley north.

True Toads (Family Bufonidae)

WESTERN TOAD
Bufo boreas

Pl. 357

Length 2.5 to 5 in.; upper surface dull gray or greenish with many large, light-colored warts set in dark blotches; typically with a white stripe down middle of back.

DISTRIBUTION: Occurs throughout the Sierra Nevada except where replaced by the Yosemite Toad (see below); in open valleys or meadows, near water, in woods, and around settlements.

REMARKS: The Western Toad is common over most of California. It is active at dusk and by night—sometimes also in daylight. It finds shelter under rocks, logs, or boards on the ground, and in rodent burrows. Small individuals hop, but the bigger ones walk, dragging their hind feet and leaving imprints of their toes in dusty places. At middle and lower altitudes the species may be active year-round; those in the high mountains hibernate in winter. For mating the toads resort to ponds where the males (having no large vocal pouches) utter low tremulous notes. Breeding in the lowlands is from March to May but is delayed until early summer at high elevations. The male grasps the female in the armpits, and the small black eggs (up to 16,500) emerge in two long gelatinous strings. Fertilization is external. A dozen or more pairs may spawn in one pool. The small black tadpoles grow and transform from June in the lowlands to late August in the High Sierra.

YOSEMITE TOAD
Bufo canorus

Pl. 358

Length 1.75 to 3 in.; resembles Western Toad but space between eyes usually less than width of upper eyelid, and space between large parotoid glands on shoulders less than width of gland. Male: smaller; back and sides olive green, sometimes with minute black spots edged with whitish. Female:

larger; back and sides with irregular, sharp-edged patches of black rimmed with white on olive background; dark brown warts in dark patches. Undersurface whitish in both.

DISTRIBUTION: High Sierra, 4,800 to 12,000 ft (mostly between 8,500 to 10,000 ft), from vicinity of Blue Lakes, Alpine County south to Kaiser Pass, Fresno County; commonly in wet, open meadows. Has disappeared from much of its range over the past 25 years. State and Federal Species of Special Concern.

REMARKS: Being truly a mountain species, this toad does not emerge from hibernation until April or May when snowmelt is coursing through the meadows. Shortly thereafter the males enter pools and begin calling—10 to 20 mellow trilling notes as a prelude to breeding. Short strings or clusters of eggs, 1,000 to 1,500 per female, are laid from May to August. The small tadpoles resemble those of the Western Toad and metamorphose in 40 to 50 days. After spawning, the toads live in damp surface retreats but all disappear by September or October to avoid freezing winter temperatures. Because their mountain meadow habitats are widely separated by bare rocky terrain, it has been suggested that populations may be locally differentiated and uniquely patterned.

Treefrog (Family Hylidae)

PACIFIC TREEFROG
Hyla regilla

Pl. 359

Length .75 to 2 in.; tips of toes with somewhat enlarged pads; hind foot well webbed; conspicuous dark mask extends from nostrils to shoulder; body color variable and changeable—green, brown, reddish, tan, or gray; often with dark T- or Y-shaped mark on head.

DISTRIBUTION: Throughout Sierra Nevada up to about 12,000 ft; found in nearly every habitat.

REMARKS: This widespread frog shelters in rock crevices, under bark, in rodent burrows, on streamside vegetation, under culverts, and around buildings in a wide variety of habitats. It spawns from January to July depending on location. In water (and sometimes from hidden places on land) the male inflates his dusky throat pouch and utters a loud *kreck-ek* at one-second intervals for long periods. When large numbers are present, the chorus is deafening. Females lay loose, irregular clusters of 10 to 70 eggs attached to underwater plants or sticks in shallow, quiet waters. The tadpoles grow and transform in midsummer at lower elevations and late summer at higher elevations. This species sometimes placed in the genus *Pseudacris*.

True Frogs (Family Ranidae)

RED-LEGGED FROG
Rana aurora

Pl. 360

Length 2 to 5.25 in.; upper surface brownish to olive with fuzzy-margined dark spots pale at center (*note:* illustration shows a northern subspecies, not found in the Sierra Nevada, that mostly lacks these pale centers); limbs blotched with black; pale streak on upper jaw from below eye to shoulder; undersurface pale; hind parts, including legs, reddish; low ridge (dorsolateral fold) extends along each side of back from eye to end of body.

DISTRIBUTION: Western foothills north to Butte County below 4,500 ft; in permanent and seasonal ponds or quiet pools along streams. Once found throughout the foothills as far south as Kern County but now nearly extirpated in the Sierra, currently known only at scattered foothill sites from El Dorado County north. Federal Threatened.

REMARKS: Made famous as the jumping frog of Calaveras County in Mark Twain's story, this once common but wary frog is now extremely rare or extirpated over much of its range. Habitat loss and predation by exotic species are probable causes for its precipitous decline. Toward the end of winter Red-legged Frogs deposit about 500 to 1,000 eggs in a soft cantaloupe-sized mass attached to vegetation in shallow water. Each egg is covered by three jelly coats, the outermost being .33 in. in diameter. The males' calls are a stuttering series of guttural *uh* notes, but these are weak and seldom heard. Most of the larvae transform at about 1 in. in length by midsummer. The food consists largely of insects caught in or near the water but adults may consume small mice. This somewhat terrestrial frog may sometimes be found in woodlands far from water.

YELLOW-LEGGED FROGS
Rana boylii, R. muscosa

Pl. 361

Length 1.5 to 3 in.; eardrum inconspicuous, less than diameter of eye; ridges (dorsolateral folds) along back inconspicuous or absent; upper surface with many small rough tubercles; color of upper surface blackish, brownish, grayish, or greenish, with some irregular dark spots; undersurface whitish with yellow on hinder part and hind legs.

DISTRIBUTION: From Foothill Belt into Subalpine Belt; along streams or in lakes. Both are Species of Special Concern.

REMARKS: Two kinds of yellow-legged frogs inhabit the Sierra. The Foothill Yellow-legged Frog (*R. boylii*) lives in foothill streams below 6,000 ft on the west slope north to Butte County. It spawns in streams after the high-water stage is past, from late March to early May. The 100 to 1,200 eggs, about .25 in. in diameter, are in firm jelly, resembling a tiny cluster of grapes, and attached to rocks in shallow, flowing water. They transform into frogs about 1 in. long during July and August. This species has a warty eardrum (making the eardrum hard to see) and a pale triangular patch between its eyes and nostrils.

The somewhat larger Mountain Yellow-legged Frog (*R. muscosa*) has a more pointed nose, shorter hind leg, rather smooth eardrum, and an odor of garlic! It occurs from Plumas County to southern Tulare County, mostly between 4,500 to 12,000 ft. Its smaller egg masses (100 to 350 eggs) are laid in mountain lakes and waters of slow streams during June or July. Because of low water temperatures and a short summer, the larvae commonly overwinter (in water under ice) and transform when about one or two years old.

Both species remain close to water at all times and have disappeared from significant portions of their ranges over the past 25 years. Studies have shown that trout stocked in high mountain lakes consume larval and young Mountain Yellow-legged Frogs. The disappearance of Foothill Yellow-legged Frogs from most of their historical Sierra range has been tentatively linked to the transport by prevailing winds of agricultural chemicals from the Central Valley; interestingly, populations from the Coast Ranges, lying upwind from the sources of pesticides and herbicides, appear to be in much better shape.

BULLFROG   *Rana catesbeiana*

Pl. 362

Length 3.5 to 8 in.; green face, yellow throat; eardrum conspicuous, size of eye (in female) or larger (in male); no ridges (dorsolateral folds) on back; skin rather smooth; upper surface greenish or grayish brown, sometimes with brownish spots; dark crossbars often on hind legs; undersurface whitish to yellowish.

DISTRIBUTION: Central Valley and foothill areas; in lakes, reservoirs, margins of larger streams, and irrigation ditches below 6,500 ft (except higher in Lake Tahoe region).

REMARKS: The Bullfrog of eastern North America was introduced into California in 1896 and is now exceedingly common in many permanent waters, especially those with muddy bottoms. It is highly aquatic and seldom goes far onto the shore, though it may be seen traveling overland on rainy nights. Its food is varied: many kinds of insects, earthworms, snails, small fish, frogs and larvae, small snakes, birds, and mammals. In late spring the loud deep-pitched calls, *jug-o'-rum,* etc., are a prelude to breeding in June or July. The egg mass (10,000 to 20,000 eggs) may be a yard in diameter. The larvae spend a year or more before becoming young frogs about 2 in. long. California fishing regulations require a license to catch Bullfrogs for food but there is no bag limit or season of take. Bullfrogs are commonly thought to be responsible for the decline and disappearance of several native amphibians in parts of the Sierra Nevada, especially Red-legged Frogs.

The Northern Leopard Frog (*Rana pipiens;* length 2 to 4.5 in.) is another exotic frog known in the Sierra Nevada from a population at Lake Tahoe (although its present status there is uncertain). Coloration is either bright green with darker green round spots, or brownish with dark brown round spots; spots always have pale borders. This species may forage at some distance from water but if disturbed makes off rapidly, often in zigzag course by jumps of up to 6 ft.

REPTILES

TURTLES, LIZARDS, and snakes are cold-blooded and must avoid extremes of heat and cold. Their dry, horny skin enables them to live free of moist environments. The shell of a turtle is a set of bony plates covered by a hardened epidermis. Lizards and snakes have many small scales in their skin. Each scale on the back and sides in some species has a low lengthwise keel; those on the undersurface usually are flat and smooth. The undersurface on lizards has many small scales, but on snakes there is a single row of broad scales below on the body and one or two rows beneath the tail. The outer covering of dry skin ordinarily is molted one or more times each year. On most lizards it comes off in pieces, whereas on snakes (and a few lizards) it loosens around the mouth and the animal crawls out of the old covering, leaving the sloughed skin in one piece. Turtles eat some plant material and carrion but lizards and snakes are predatory, taking live prey according to their size. The rattlesnake is the only dangerously venomous Sierra reptile.

Reptiles in the Sierra Nevada are not particularly threatened. Only Western Pond Turtles, an aquatic species impacted by Bullfrogs and habitat disturbance, are known to be declining significantly. Biologists believe that these turtles may at one time have been the most abundant vertebrate, in terms of biomass, in the Central Valley and lower foothills with populations numbering in the millions. Intensely harvested for the food market, and heavily impacted by introduced species, these populations have declined 99.9 percent. There is no sign that the decline is reversing and in fact most turtles seen today are large old adults past their reproductive prime and hatchling turtles are a rare sight.

Taxonomy follows Stebbins (2003).

Water Turtle (Family Emydidae)

WESTERN POND TURTLE   *Clemmys marmorata*
Pl. 363

Length 5 to 7.5 in.; body enclosed in a shell of firmly joined bones covered with a few rows of large horny plates; upper part (carapace) arched, lower part (plastron) flat; head, tail, and legs covered with scales, and all these parts can be drawn into the shell; color olive brown above, yellowish below, variously patterned with dark markings.

DISTRIBUTION: Ponds and quiet streams of Central Valley and the Foothill Belt; introduced elsewhere at higher elevations, but overall its populations have seriously declined. State and Federal Species of Special Concern.

REMARKS: This is the only water-loving turtle native to interior California. It is highly aquatic, basking on rocks or logs in and near water, but submerging at the slightest hint of danger. The food includes aquatic plants, insects, and carrion. At some time from May to August the adult female leaves the water and uses her claws and feet to dig a small hole in a stream bank or hillside often some distance from the home pond or stream. Here she lays one to 13 hard-shelled eggs and covers them with soil. The young hatch in about two months and overwinter in the nest before heading to water the following spring. From about November until February turtles hibernate in mud beneath the water.

Spiny and Horned Lizards
(Family Phrynosomatidae)

WESTERN FENCE LIZARD   *Sceloporus occidentalis*

Pl. 364

Length 6 to 8.5 in.; body and tail rounded; scales on upper surface keeled (each scale having a minute lengthwise ridge) and sharply pointed at tip; scales on undersurface smaller, smooth, overlapping; scales on back of thigh keeled, hind surface of thighs yellow to orange; body above blackish, dark brown, or gray with lengthwise rows of paired blackish spots; undersurface whitish with some dark marks, but throat and sides of belly blue in male, and female with lesser or no blue.

DISTRIBUTION: From Central Valley across Sierra to Great Basin; on rocks, trees, wooden fences, and buildings; mostly below 9,000 ft.

REMARKS: Commonest and most easily seen of all our reptiles is the Western Fence Lizard because when active it lives mostly on surfaces above the ground. From April to October these lizards are abroad during the warmer daylight hours at the lower elevations, and for less time in the High Sierra. The cold season is spent in hibernation within logs or below ground, beyond the reach of frost. Their food includes a variety of insects and spiders. The male often flattens its sides and lowers the skin of the throat, thereby displaying its blue markings, possibly to intimidate another male invading its territory. When courting it does the same, and bobs up and down. Females bury five to 15 soft-shelled eggs (mid-May to mid-July) in damp, well-aerated soil. The young hatch in two months and grow 1 to 2 in. before hibernating.

SAGEBRUSH LIZARD   *Sceloporus graciosus*

Length 4.5 to 6 in.; closely resembles Western Fence Lizard but has a smoother appearance because scales smaller; scales on back of thigh mostly or all smooth (not keeled); brownish gray with striped appearance above; whitish below, but throat and sides of belly pale blue; typically shows rust color behind foreleg or on sides.

DISTRIBUTION: On both slopes mainly in Mixed Conifer and Upper Montane Belts, chiefly on ground near rocks or logs; mostly confined to narrow belt below 8,000 ft.

REMARKS: The little Sagebrush Lizard (not confined to sagebrush in the Sierra) lives mostly on the ground but goes up on boulders or logs and occasionally on trees. It is common around mountain chaparral thickets. In the Yosemite region it is found abroad from late May until mid-October. As food it captures many kinds of small insects, ticks, scorpions, and snails. In late June or July the female lays three to four eggs, which hatch between August and October. Individuals along the east slope are more strongly striped than those along the west slope, and are sometimes considered a distinct subspecies that is a Federal Species of Special Concern.

COAST HORNED LIZARD   *Phrynosoma coronatum*
Pl. 365

Length 2.5 to 6.5 in.; body flattened, broad; head armored and bearing sharp spines ("horns") at rear; similar large, spiny scales along sides of body and tail; undersurface smooth scaled; above yellowish or reddish with about four pairs of large blackish marks bordered behind by white; below yellowish, dusky spotted.

DISTRIBUTION: Scattered locations from Central Valley into Foothill Belt of west slope on open sandy ground; to around 5,000 ft.

REMARKS: This small flat lizard ("horned toad") lives entirely on the ground, where it is well camouflaged and easily overlooked. It takes shelter in burrows or crevices or by burying itself shallowly in sand. Its food is small insects, especially ants. In early summer the female lays six to 16 eggs and the young hatch about two months later, being about 1.13 in. in head-and-body length. A paler and less spiny species (*P. platyrhinos*) inhabits the Great Basin and Mojave Desert along the east side of the Sierra Nevada.

Skinks (Family Scincidae)

GILBERT'S SKINK   *Eumeces gilberti*

Length 7 to 12 in.; body and tail evenly tapered to end; scales smooth, thin, and round edged; legs short, scarcely longer than body diameter. Adult: Head coppery red (except for the subspecies in the southern Sierra); tail pinkish red; body olive brown above, sometimes weakly striped but fading with age; olive yellow on side; pale beneath. Young: head and body dark brown with two sharp pale yellowish stripes along back; undersurface gray; tail blue (red in southern Sierra subspecies).

DISTRIBUTION: West slope from Foothill Belt into open Mixed Conifer Belt, occasionally higher; from Butte County south; on ground in grass or leafy debris.

REMARKS: Both the blue-tailed young and adults are so smooth they can slip through one's finger as if oiled. If a skink is picked up or attacked, the tail breaks off readily and continues to wriggle—a distraction as the animal escapes. This lizard is secretive, finding shelter under logs or rocks and living mostly on the ground amid surface cover, but may forage over logs or on low rock walls. It is most active from March to June. When moving rapidly (to avoid capture) it progresses by snakelike wriggling of the body, but it uses the small legs and feet when stalking prey—mostly insects. In summer, the female lays eight or nine eggs in spaces under rocks or below ground.

OTHER SKINKS: The similar Western Skink (*E. skiltonianus*, pl. 366) occupies comparable habitats on the west slope from the American River drainage north (with isolated populations on east slope just west of Independence and Olancha as well as in the southern Sierra in the Tule River drainage, the

Kern Plateau, and the Piute Mountains). These two skinks can be difficult to tell apart, and juveniles are virtually identical in areas where both species have blue-tailed juveniles. On the Western Skink the dark body stripes extend onto the tail (in Gilbert's Skinks they end just past the hind legs) and the light stripes on body are clean (in Gilbert's Skinks each scale is dark edged). Adult Western Skinks retain hints of the juvenile pattern and bluish tail, while Gilbert's Skinks fade to an unstriped olive yellow color with age.

Whiptail (Family Teiidae)

WESTERN WHIPTAIL   *Cnemidophorus tigris*
Length 8 to 13 in.; body, and especially tail, slender; tail may exceed twice body length; hind legs large and stout; back and sides with fine beadlike scales; undersurface with eight rows of squarish scales; tail ringed with keeled scales. Body blackish with lengthwise pale stripes (young) or small buff to white spots (adult); undersurface white or warm tan, scales dark-edged.

DISTRIBUTION: Edge of Central Valley into Mixed Conifer Belt on west slope; sagebrush or desert flats on east slope; open, dry, sandy, gravelly, or rocky areas.

REMARKS: Swiftest of local lizards is the whiptail, which may be glimpsed as it dashes across a foothill road. It starts suddenly, runs 50 to 100 ft, sometimes on the hind legs, and stops abruptly, often behind a bush or rock. The main power is in the stout hind legs; the long tail being used as a counterbalance and rudder. When foraging, the whiptail makes short jerky advances and often extends its long forked tongue. If pursued it may take shelter in a rodent burrow. The prey is of insects, spiders, and scorpions, sometimes dug out of the ground. Females lay one to two clutches of one to eight eggs during the summer season. One subspecies occurs on the west slope and another on the east slope.

Alligator Lizards (Family Anguidae)

ALLIGATOR LIZARDS   Genus *Elgaria*
Pl. 367

Length 8 to 17 in.; head bluntly triangular, big in old adult; body slender, parallel sided, a flexible fold with granular skin along each side; tail often very long, tapered to tip; legs and feet small; body scales squarish, those on back and sides keeled, in 14 or 16 rows; belly scales flat. Upper surface brown or olive, with dark markings; undersurface gray to yellowish.

DISTRIBUTION: Western foothills to Subalpine Belt (up to 11,000 ft in southern Sierra); on ground in grass, under brush, and around rocks or logs.

REMARKS: These lizards are active by day and dusk and, although essentially terrestrial, they can climb and even swim. The "diamond" head leads many people to infer that the animal is venomous, but it is not. If taken in hand it is aggressive and may twist and pinch a finger, but the fine teeth rarely draw blood; the captor, however, may be smeared with excrement. When undisturbed the lizard walks slowly, but if excited it wriggles the body to aid the small legs and feet in travel. While foraging, the long forked tongue is protruded in search of the insects, spiders, and small lizards or snakes taken for food. The side folds of skin enable the body to swell when filled by a meal or with eggs. The tail breaks easily and often regenerates rather completely; many alligator lizards possess formerly broken tails.

The Southern Alligator Lizard (*E. multicarinata*) of the Foothill Belt usually has 14 rows of scales and dark crossbars on the back. Its eyes are yellow and it has dark stripes down the *centers* of its pale-edged belly scales. The female lays six to 20 eggs between June and early August, and the diminutive young (head and body just over an inch long) hatch in 50 or more days. The Northern Alligator Lizard (*E. coerulea*) lives from the Mixed Conifer Belt into the Subalpine Belt. It is smaller, darker brown, and normally has 16 rows of scales with the dark markings on the back not in distinct crossbars. It has dark brown eyes and dark stripes *between* its rows of belly scales. The female retains her eggs through development and produces two to 15 living young. The ranges of these two species occasionally overlap in the lower reaches of mixed conifer forest.

Boa (Family Boidae)

RUBBER BOA — *Charina bottae*
Pl. 368

Length 14 to 33 in.; body stout, of uniform diameter throughout (no neck); tail short, blunt ended; scales very small, smooth, shiny, 45+ rows around middle of body; top of head with large scale between eyes; a short spine (vestige of leg) projects slightly at each side of vent in males. Color tan to greenish brown above, yellowish below.

DISTRIBUTION: Found in sandy areas near moist montane forests to around 9,000 ft; on east slope south to Mono County, and west slope south to Kern County. Distribution very spotty and localized.

REMARKS: Our small native boa has a blunt tail so it looks like a two-headed snake. It is chiefly active at dusk and night on the ground. It is a good climber, swimmer, and burrower. It shelters in damp places under rocks, logs, or boards on the ground, often near streams. Taken in hand it is docile and may coil in the form of a ball, when the rubbery folds of loose skin become evident. It hunts small mammals and reptiles, which it kills by constriction. The two to eight young are born alive in late summer.

Colubrid Snakes (Colubridae)

RING-NECKED SNAKE — *Diadophis punctatus*
Pl. 369

Length 8 to 30 in.; scales on back small, smooth, in 15 (rarely 17) rows; upper surface uniform olive to slate; ring on neck pale yellow or reddish; undersurface yellow orange tending to red under tail.

DISTRIBUTION: Foothill and Mixed Conifer Belts on west slope, usually in moist forested areas below 6,000 ft; under rocks, logs, or boards, but may be active during day.

REMARKS: When disturbed, this pretty little snake usually coils the tail in a tight spiral and turns it over to reveal the brilliant red underside. Its food includes treefrogs, salamanders, small lizards, snakes, and worms, all of which may be paralyzed by toxic salivary secretions. Females produce one to 10 eggs that hatch in about six weeks. Reportedly lives up to 15 years.

SHARP-TAILED SNAKE   *Contia tenuis*

Length 6 to 16 in.; diminutive, slender snake with small head; scales smooth; gray to reddish brown above; gray sides; underside strikingly barred black and white; sharp spine at tip of tail.

DISTRIBUTION: Foothill and Mixed Conifer Belts of west slope south to Tulare County; in a wide variety of habitat types including broken chaparral, oak woodlands, and forest edges; below 6,500 ft.

REMARKS: Little is known about the life history of this tiny snake, and even its taxonomic relationship to other snakes remains uncertain. Most individuals are less than 10 in. in length and juveniles are as small as 3 in., making them very difficult to spot during the few weeks they are active on the surface. They spend much of their lives hidden underground and only by the chance overturning of logs, rocks, or debris on the ground during the rainy season, is one encountered. Rarely, they are observed crossing roads in the late afternoon on cool overcast days. It is thought that they feed exclusively on slugs, which accounts for their activity during cool rainy periods when other snakes are inactive. Their distribution in the Sierra Nevada and elsewhere is apparently spotty and little studied.

RACER   *Coluber constrictor*

Pl. 370

Length 20 to 75 in.; eyes large; body slender, tail tapered to fine tip; scales on back smooth, 17 rows. Adult uniform olive brown above, greenish or bluish on sides, plain yellow below; young blotched with brown to blackish saddle marks or spots two-thirds down their body length.

DISTRIBUTION: Foothill and Mixed Conifer Belts on west slope, mainly in grassland and open oak woodlands below 6,000 ft; on east slope south to Mono County; most likely encountered north of Lake Tahoe, less common in central and southern Sierra.

REMARKS: Fast-moving Racers often forage with their heads and necks held above the ground, actively looking for prey items to chase down. Mainly terrestrial but climb readily. Despite the species name (*constrictor*), they don't constrict but catch prey and hold it down by a loop of the body. Food includes insects, toads, frogs, reptiles, birds and their eggs, and small rodents. The three to seven white leathery-shelled eggs are laid in June to August under stones or logs or in moist soil. About two months later they hatch, the young being 8 to 12 in. long. No other western snake shows such differences in coloration between young and adults. Young Racers look like Gopher Snakes but have larger eyes, smooth scales, and uniform coloration toward their tails.

STRIPED RACER   *Masticophis lateralis*
Pl. 371

Length 30 to 60 in.; large eyes; slender body, tail tapered to point; scales smooth, 17 rows; upper surface dark brown to black with narrow yellowish line along each side.

DISTRIBUTION: Foothill Belt of west slope, especially in chaparral habitats below 6,000 ft.

REMARKS: This extremely active snake (called California Whipsnake by some authorities) travels very fast on the ground but is also astonishingly adept at climbing over bushes and in trees. When alarmed often ascends into dense shrubs and flees so rapidly it looks like it's falling away. Its prey includes frogs, lizards, snakes (including rattlesnakes), birds, and rodents. When birds are nesting, this racer seeks out nests to swallow the eggs or young. A commotion among small birds in foothill oaks at this season often centers on such robbing. Eggs (six to 11) are laid in May to July.

GOPHER SNAKE   *Pituophis catenifer*
Pl. 372

Length 30 to 84 in., body stout, scales keeled (smooth on lower sides), 29+ rows; tail tapered; ground color buff with large squarish or oval "saddle marks" of black or brown, and smaller dark spots on sides (*note:* the desert subsp. on the east side are generally paler, as illustrated).

DISTRIBUTION: Throughout Sierra Nevada; mainly in grasslands or open areas below 7,000 ft.

REMARKS: The large "bullsnake" often remains motionless when approached, but if aroused it can travel at fair speed. When cornered it will coil the body, draw back, spread the head (somewhat like that of a rattlesnake), fill its lungs, and then lunge and hiss at the intruder. In dry leaves the tail may vibrate, faintly imitating the rattler's warning. A Gopher Snake is immediately distinguishable because it lacks the triangular head and slender neck of a rattlesnake. If held, it may bite a finger but do no other damage. The Gopher Snake can climb trees to hunt bird nests, and it can dig in loose soil in search of rodents. It finds shelter under rocks, logs, or boards and in rodent burrows. Mice, rats, squirrels, pocket gophers, rabbits, birds to the size of quail, and occasionally lizards are eaten. Mating occurs in spring or early summer; the eggs average six to seven per clutch and require about 70 days until hatching. Emerging young are up to 16 in. long.

COMMON KINGSNAKE   *Lampropeltis getula*

Pl. 373

Length 30 to 85 in., body to 1 in. in diameter; scales smooth, 23 (or 25) rows; coloration brownish black, with narrow yellow or creamy white rings encircling body.

DISTRIBUTION: Widely distributed in Sierra Nevada below 7,000 ft.

REMARKS: This strong snake can pursue and capture other snakes, including rattlesnakes, and seems largely immune to the venom of the latter. Besides snakes it also eats lizards, birds and their eggs, mice, and pocket gophers, all of which it kills by constriction. It is active by day and at dusk, and while mainly terrestrial can climb to seek young birds and eggs. When crawling the snake's banded pattern confuses the eye and makes the snake difficult to follow. Its six to 12 eggs are laid in summer and require about 70 days to hatch.

CALIFORNIA MOUNTAIN KINGSNAKE   *Lampropeltis zonata*

Length 20 to 40 in.; scales smooth, 21 to 23 rows; entire snake beautifully patterned with bands of black, white, and red (each white band bordered by two black bands).

DISTRIBUTION: Foothill and Mixed Conifer Belts of west slope; between 1,000 to 6,500 ft; seems to favor forested areas near rocky streams.

REMARKS: The most beautiful Sierra reptile is this snake, which is marked with three contrasting colors. Formerly it was called Coral Kingsnake because its color pattern somewhat resembles that of the venomous Coral Snake (not found in California). It is secretive but not uncommon in good habitat. Its food includes lizards and small rodents, which it kills by constriction. Many aspects of its life history are poorly known.

The Long-nosed Snake (*Rhinocheilus lecontei*, pl. 374) resembles the California Mountain Kingsnake, except that many flecks of contrasting colors somewhat obscure the banded pattern. This is a snake of arid shrub and chaparral habitats with only a few records from the Sierra Nevada foothills from Placer County to Kern County (also on east slope in Inyo and Kern Counties).

Garter Snakes (Genus *Thamnophis*)

Length 18 to 52 in.; neck usually distinct; body slender, tail tapered to sharp tip; scales keeled on back and sides of body and tail; 19 or 21 rows on midbody; upper surface blackish or grayish and with either yellow line along back and pale line on either side, or with many dark spots on back (but no large blotches or crossbands); undersurface pale green or grayish.

DISTRIBUTION: Widespread in Sierra Nevada; in or near water, marshes, or grasslands, some in dry places.

REMARKS: Commonest of serpents in the Sierra are the garter snakes. On open ground they travel slowly, but faster in grassland. Some swim readily by sidewise looping of the body and can dive. They are active by day and at dusk, even later in warm places. At high elevations they are abroad from late May into October and longer in the lowlands. If handled they often discharge foul-smelling fluid from anal scent glands, and also excrement. The young are born alive in broods of 10 to 20, sometimes more. Three species occur in the Sierra.

COMMON GARTER SNAKE   *T. sirtalis*

Usually lives in or near ponds and streams, where it forages primarily for frogs, but may be encountered in drier habitats. It occurs in the Foothill Belt on the west slope below 6,000 ft, and on the east slope from Alpine County north. It usually has seven scales on the upper lip, a yellow dorsal stripe, and red spots along the sides of its body. The underside is plain bluish gray with black on tips of ventral scales. The rear pair of chin scales is usually longer than front pair.

WESTERN TERRESTRIAL GARTER SNAKE   *T. elegans*

Usually has eight scales on the upper lip and the sixth and seventh of these are higher than wide. Lives mainly on land, and eats slugs, salamanders, and mice. Found throughout the Sierra Nevada, south to Kern County, in all habitats from 1,000 to 12,000 ft. The body is typically plain black with sharply edged, yellow to orange back and side stripes, and the belly is pale gray, sometimes with black down the center. Both pairs of chin scales are about equal in length.

SIERRA GARTER SNAKE   *T. couchii*

Highly aquatic and eats fishes, amphibians, and water insects. Found throughout Sierra Nevada along permanent streams and rivers below 9,000 ft (absent on east slope south of Mono County). Its back is pale gray with conspicuous dark checkering, pale stripes absent or weak. Its belly is salmon colored, often heavily marked with black.

SOUTHWESTERN BLACK-HEADED SNAKE   *Tantilla hobartsmithi*

Length 5.5 to 15 in.; tiny snake (most adults under 10 in. long); plain brown above, except for black cap and narrow pale neck ring; reddish stripe down belly.

DISTRIBUTION: Known in Sierra Nevada from the Kings River (Fresno County) south to Kern County; arid and semiarid habitats below 2,000 ft, in grassland, oak woodland, and chaparral.

REMARKS: These snakes may be more widely distributed, but they remain underground much of the time and are rarely observed. Very little is known of their life history. They possess enlarged, grooved rear fangs and mild venom that is thought to aid in subduing small invertebrates.

NIGHT SNAKE   *Hypsiglena torquata*
Pl. 375

Length 12 to 26 in.; body is pale brown with darker brown blotches down center of back and smaller blotches along each side; variously sized and shaped larger blotch behind head on neck, and dark stripe along upper jaw; lustrous white or yellowish on belly; scales smooth.

DISTRIBUTION: Very spotty distribution along entire west slope, typically found in rocky canyons and foothills below 6,000 ft; also occurs on east slope from Alpine County south in arid habitats.

REMARKS: Patterned much like young Racers and Gopher Snakes, the Night Snake is easy to identify by its distinctive brown neck blotch. True to its name, this is a nocturnal or crepuscular snake that spends its day hidden in crevices or undersurface debris. Possesses enlarged rear fangs for injecting venom into its prey, which includes lizards, small snakes, frogs, and salamanders. This snake has vertical pupils like those of a cat. Females lay three to nine eggs around June. Very little is known about the life history or distribution of this highly secretive snake.

Viper (Family Viperidae)

WESTERN RATTLESNAKE   *Crotalus viridis*
Pl. 376

Length 15 to 60 in., girth to 5 in.; body heavy; head broad, bluntly triangular; neck distinct; tail ending in jointed horny rattle; scales on head many and small, but scales on body large and keeled, 23 to 27 rows; pupil of eye vertically elliptical; body yellowish or grayish brown with series of large dark brown or black blotches along back, two rows of small dark spots on sides.

DISTRIBUTION: Lower foothills into Upper Montane Belt on west slope, also on east side (none in Lake Tahoe Basin) south to Inyo County; many records in southern Sierra at 9,000 to 10,000 ft, several at 11,000 ft, commonest in western foothills; found in grasslands, brushy areas, rock outcrops, open woodlands, and along trails.

REMARKS: Our only dangerously venomous reptile, the Western Rattlesnake is the subject of much misinformation and folklore. Its hazard to humans is not great. Of the millions of visitors in the mountains every summer, very few ever see a rattlesnake, but anyone on foot away from settlements *may* meet one. To avoid any danger one should glance occasionally at the trail ahead, look on the other side of a log or rock before jumping over, and not put hands on a ledge above one's head where it is impossible to see over the top.

The rattlesnake, like other cold-blooded animals, has no internal heat regulation; it adjusts its body temperature by moving between warm and cool sites. In cooler weather (October to March) in the foothills it hibernates in frost-free burrows or rock crevices, emerging when the air reaches about 70 degrees F, and is out by day from about April into June. During the heat of summer, however, when exposure to direct sun would be quickly fatal, it is usually abroad between dusk and dawn. At higher elevations hibernation is longer, and the snakes are on the surface mainly during the warmer daytime hours.

Unlike most other snakes the rattlesnake is slow, even lethargic. Often it lies in a warm spot on a rock outcrop or beside a trail, waiting for prey. If come upon quietly it may remain motionless except to flick the slender forked tongue out and back (which assists its sense of smell); often it will glide slowly away. When the snake feels that it is cornered it will coil, in preparation for striking.

The rattlesnake feeds mainly on ground squirrels, other rodents, and smaller rabbits, together with some birds and lizards. As a guide in striking at prey (and enemies) it has on either side of its snout, between the nostril and eye, a small pit containing a delicate heat-sensory structure by which it detects the presence of a warm-blooded mammal or bird. Other prey evidently is located by sight.

The jointed horny rattle on the tail can be vibrated rapidly to buzz, somewhat like a very loud cicada. It is often but not always sounded when the snake is approached. All snakes shed the outer horny covering of the skin at intervals. In other species this slips off the tapered tail, but the end of a rattlesnake's tail is blunt with a constriction. At molt the old horny covering at the end remains loosely attached to the new growth within. Successive molts (commonly two or three per year) result in a chain of loosely attached segments. The number of segments, if the first small "button" is present, indicates the number of molts, not years of age; commonly there are eight to ten, exceptionally up to 22.

Mating occurs in spring. The eggs remain in the female's body until the young are fully developed. They appear late in summer, six to seven (one to 14) in a brood, and are less than 12 in. long when hatched.

The venom apparatus includes two long, sharp, hollow teeth or fangs (like hypodermic needles) hinged inside the roof of the mouth. A small duct from a venom gland connects to each fang. The venom serves to kill prey and to protect against enemies (but when striking in self-defense the snake may not use any venom). When threatened, it places the forepart of its body in an S-shaped curve, holds the tail vertically, and vibrates the rattle. To strike, the mouth opens widely (nearly 180 degrees), the fangs are erected, and the head lunges forward. The fangs penetrate the victim's flesh, the snake's lower jaw rises to grip, and venom is injected. Then the head is pulled backward, withdrawing the fangs. This all happens in an instant. A rattler rarely strikes more than half its total length, usually less, and seldom more than 12 in. above the ground. It cannot jump at prey or enemy. High leather boots usually are adequate protection against snakebite.

In the event someone is bitten, (1) help the victim to lie down and to remain as calm as possible; (2) seek professional assistance immediately; (3) elevate the bitten part above the rest of the body and keep the patient comfortable; and (4) do not make incisions or apply tourniquets or ice, because these "first aid" measures do not work and may make the situation worse. The best treatment is to get to a physician as soon as possible.

BIRDS

BIRDS ARE A conspicuous and ever-present element of the landscape. Not only do they occupy all habitat types from valley floors to alpine peaks but their bright colors, persistent songs, and lively mannerisms make them difficult to overlook. More than any other vertebrate group, they occur in large and diverse numbers in the Sierra Nevada. The one to two million Eared Grebes that gather at Mono Lake each fall are surely the region's greatest wildlife spectacle, and approximately 320 species of bird can be found in the Sierra for all or part of their life cycles.

The most characteristic features of birds are their feathers (fig. 13). These highly complex epidermal structures hold in heat, protect against rain and snow, provide a smooth surface for efficient flight, and serve a wide range of social functions through their coloration and display. Arranged in overlapping layers along armlike limbs (wings), feathers create lift for flight. Elongated tail feathers provide additional rudderlike functions of steering and braking.

Much of a bird's life is spent fueling its metabolic fires for the energetically expensive activities of flying, breeding, molting, and migrating. With high body temperatures, rapid heart rates, supercharged respiratory systems, and fast digestive functions, birds must eat energy-rich foods at rates many times greater than humans. On frigid winter days, small birds such as chickadees have to eat every few seconds merely to stay alive.

The lively and entertaining presence of birds has long made them a favorite object of study. Birds are generally easy to observe, although binoculars are essential for scrutinizing the level of detail necessary to identify

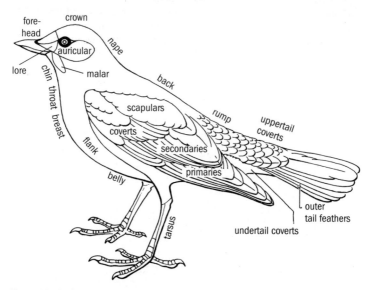

Figure 13. Structure of a bird.

many species. Beginning birders (people who watch birds) focus initially on color patterns but with practice learn to identify birds by their shapes, behaviors, habitats, and calls. All bird study requires patience and a calm approach because birds may flee if disturbed.

Although birds are able to fly when disturbed, they are unable to escape the cumulative and widespread alteration of their habitats by humans. A sizable number of birds have declining populations in the Sierra Nevada but only a handful have been listed as Threatened or Endangered. Two species are known to have become extinct in the Sierra Nevada: The Least Bell's Vireo was a casualty of nest parasitism by Brown-headed Cowbirds. The last Sierra Nevada California Condor was intentionally captured in Kern County in 1987 and placed in a captive breeding program; it is possible that captive-bred birds will one day be returned to their former haunts. Other species, such as the Common Loon and Barrow's Goldeneye, formerly nested in the Sierra Nevada but now occur only as winter visitors.

Roughly half of the 320 species that visit the Sierra Nevada are included here, with an emphasis on regularly occurring species and those that characterize the region in some way. Names and taxonomic order follow the A.O.U. Checklist of North American Birds (7th ed.).

Loon (Family Gaviidae)

COMMON LOON   *Gavia immer*
Pl. 377

Length 32 in., wing span 46 in.; head, neck, and back black, streaked and spotted with white; underparts white. Smudgy brownish gray appearance in winter. **CALL** is a long *oo-ah'-ii* and laughterlike notes; seldom vocalizes in winter.
DISTRIBUTION: Visits larger lakes and reservoirs; rare in summer but fairly common in fall, winter, and spring. Formerly nested just north of the Sierra.
REMARKS: In the water this loon sits low, mostly submerged. It dives frequently to capture fish with its long, stout bill. Easily frightened by the presence of humans and often swims away under the water's surface. Helpless on land because its legs are set far back and are specialized for swimming. It mainly winters on the seacoast and is less common inland.

Grebes (Family Podicipedidae)

PIED-BILLED GREBE   *Podilymbus podiceps*
Pl. 378

Length 13 in., wing span 16 in. In breeding season, dark gray above with brownish sides and mottled dusky underparts, conspicuous black patch on their throats; rather stout bill is pale, with a band of black. In nonbreeding season, they are brownish overall and lose the black on their throats and bills. Young birds have reddish caps and are striped vividly black and white, like a zebra with longitudinal stripes. **CALL** is a cuckoolike *cuck-cuck-cuck... cow-cow;* alarm call, *coot, coot.* **NEST** is near tules, a floating pile of decayed plants; eggs five to eight, dull bluish white.

DISTRIBUTION: Fairly common birds on quiet waters of lower elevations, rare above 5,000 ft (west slope) or 7,000 ft (east slope). Some wander briefly up to Upper Montane and Alpine Belts in late summer.

REMARKS: This familiar little grebe shows a narrow head and thick arched neck. It lunges forward to dive but can disappear quietly by sinking. Its food includes small fishes and aquatic insects and plants. Generally solitary and easily overlooked, especially on its favorite haunts of ponds rimmed in dense vegetation.

EARED GREBE   *Podiceps nigricollis*
Pl. 379

Length 13 in., wing span 16 in.; body plump, neck and bill slender, tail not evident. The breasts and necks of summer adults are slate black and these birds develop conspicuous fans of orange feathers on each side of their faces; winter birds are duller and plain faced (as illustrated). All birds show an intense red eye. **CALL** is a squeaky whistle, *ooEEK.* **NEST** is a hollowed out mound of decaying vegetation on the ground or floating; eggs three to four, whitish.

DISTRIBUTION: Nests sparingly at some east side lakes. By midsummer, grebes from across western North America begin to gather at Mono Lake, eventually peaking at over one million birds in September and staying until temperatures drop to freezing. In late summer, rare on subalpine and alpine lakes.

REMARKS: Riding rather high in the water with necks held vertically, Eared Grebes dive frequently to feed or when disturbed. They feed on a wide variety of insects, crustaceans, or mollusks, but at Mono Lake they feed most heavily on brine shrimp and brine flies. The gathering of grebes at Mono Lake is one of North America's foremost wildlife spectacles.

OTHER GREBES: The Western Grebe (*Aechmophorus occidentalis,* length 25 in.; pl. 380) is a large and long-necked grebe that is common on many large lakes and reservoirs in the Sierra; it has black upper parts and sparkling white underparts, with a long, sharp greenish yellow bill. Nearly identical in appearance is the Clark's Grebe (*A. clarkii*), which has an orangish bill and typically shows white above the eye.

Pelican (Family Pelecanidae)

AMERICAN WHITE PELICAN   *Pelecanus erythrorhynchos*
Pl. 381

Length to 70 in., wing span to 96 in.; huge, ungainly bird with large orange bill and throat pouch; body all white, wing primaries black.

DISTRIBUTION: Summer visitor to large bodies of water, often seen crossing in groups over the Sierra to and from nesting colonies in the Great Basin.

REMARKS: The pelican rides high in the water, its great bill held close to the breast. It fishes with quick thrusts of the bill while floating alone or in groups that cooperate to improve their fishing success. When startled they rise noisily, striking the water with both wings and feet. Once aloft they alternate several slow wing beats with long glides. Flocks fly in line or irregular V-formation, spiraling to rise over high ridges.

Cormorant (Family Phalacrocoracidae)

DOUBLE-CRESTED CORMORANT   *Phalacrocorax auritus*
Pl. 382

Length 33 in., wing span 52 in.; bill, head, neck, and body slender; plumage black; throat pouch orange. **CALL** is an odd grunting, generally silent. **NEST** is a large, bulky stick structure placed in trees; in colonies with other cormorants or with herons or egrets.

DISTRIBUTION: Once a rare visitor to the Sierra but now fairly common at large lakes and reservoirs, especially during the nonbreeding season. In recent years it has begun nesting at several low-elevation lakes. California Species of Special Concern (nesting).

REMARKS: On the water, fish-seeking cormorants ride low, their necks upright and bills tilted slightly upward. Frequently observed perched on pilings, logs, or bare snags drying out their wings in the sun. In flight their wings beat rapidly, their tail is evident, and their neck is crooked.

Herons (Family Ardeidae)

GREAT BLUE HERON   *Ardea herodias*
Pl. 383

Length 48 in., wing span 72 in.; head white on top, with black plumes; back, wings, and tail grayish blue; neck pale gray; underparts streaked black and white; legs long and bare. **CALL** is a loud, harsh croak, repeated. **NEST** occurs mostly in colonies; a crude platform of sticks, usually high in an open tree near water; eggs three to six, dull greenish blue.

DISTRIBUTION: Common resident in lower open foothill areas up to the Mixed Conifer Belt. Wanders higher into the mountains in late summer, especially along the larger rivers.

REMARKS: In flight the blue color, slow flapping of the large broad wings, and trailing long legs make identification of this heron easy. Either standing or flying, the neck is crooked (whereas that of a crane is extended). The Great Blue Heron may appear along any open water, marsh, or meadow, wading in the shallows or stalking slowly over grassland in search of food. The stout, yellowish bill, 4.5 to 6 in. long, is an effective pincer to grasp a fish in water, a frog on the bank, or even a mouse in dry grassland—all of which serve as food.

OTHER HERONS: Several other wading birds may be found at the edges of the Sierra Nevada. The Great Egret (*Ardea alba,* length 39 in.; pl. 384) is a slightly smaller, all white version of the Great Blue Heron. Common around marshes, wet meadows, and pastures at low elevations; rare above the Mixed Conifer Belt. The Green Heron (*Butorides virescens,* length 18 in.; pl. 385) is a small, short-necked heron that lives and nests in willow thickets bordering the slow-moving west-slope streams or ponds of the foothill region (also rare on the east slope). The head is black topped, the back and wings grayish green, the neck and shoulders reddish brown, and the undersurface grayish.

New World Vultures (Family Cathartidae)

TURKEY VULTURE *Cathartes aura*
Pl. 386

Length 30 in., wing span 72 in.; plumage dull black, flight feathers silvery and translucent; head lacks feathers and is red. **CALL** is a loud hiss if disturbed at nest, but generally silent. **NEST** is in the hole of a cliff, no lining; eggs two, white, brown-blotched.

DISTRIBUTION: Common on lower elevations of both slopes, some being present year-round; rare above Mixed Conifer Belt and then only in migration or in late summer and fall when they wander upslope.

REMARKS: Turkey "buzzards" soar overhead with their long wings tilted upward. Whenever the air is warm they circle and spiral on upwelling currents with little change in the set of wings or tail. Their teetering flight with wings held in a V-posture is a diagnostic feature. Individual birds are usually spaced out, perhaps one per square mile, scanning the ground for any dead animals—ground squirrel, rabbit, horse, or cow. When one sees such food it glides down. Other vultures are attracted by this signal and soon converge toward the site. A large carcass may bring a dozen or more to tear off and devour the carrion. In morning and evening and on overcast days vultures perch on open trees in hunched postures with their heads between their shoulders. During migration they may be seen in loose flocks.

OTHER VULTURES: The huge California Condor (*Gymnogyps californianus,* pl. 387) nested historically in the Sequoia National Park region but is now State and Federal Endangered and no longer occurs in the Sierra Nevada. Hinging on the success of captive breeding programs this mighty bird may be seen once again in its former haunts. Its wings have large white areas below at the front; the wing span is nearly 10 ft.

Goose and Ducks (Family Anatidae)

CANADA GOOSE *Branta canadensis*
Pl. 388

Length 35 to 43 in., wing span 50 to 60 in.; head and neck black with broad white chin band; back brown, undersurface gray, tail black, area under tail white. **CALL** is a deep two-part *ka-honk.* **NEST** is on ground (some on hay piles), made of grass and twigs lined with down; eggs four to ten, dull white.

DISTRIBUTION: Locally common resident on both slopes of the Sierra, especially at lakes and parks around human activity.

REMARKS: Depending on their contact with humans, these wild geese can range from extremely wary to completely complacent about the presence of humans. They are often seen swimming on large lakes or streams or feeding on short grasses in lush meadows. Young gray goslings swim under care of the parents until they are able to fly. By the end of summer, adults and immatures band together and migrate in V-shaped flocks. In winter, geese of this and other species are abundant on grasslands and grainfields of the Central Valley.

WOOD DUCK   *Aix sponsa*
Pl. 389

Length 18 in., wing span 30 in. Adult male: top of head shiny green with violet crest; patch on chin white; back brown; wings black, purple, and white; breast chestnut; flanks golden buff. Adult female: eye patch teardrop shaped and white, upper parts brownish, underparts speckled white, blue wing patch may be hidden. **CALL** in female is a rising *wher-eek;* male gives an upslurred whistle. **NEST** is in a tree hole at 6 to 30 ft, lined with down; eggs 10 to 15, ivory.

DISTRIBUTION: Resident in Foothill and lower Mixed Conifer Belts along quiet tree-bordered waters; may wander upslope after breeding. Generally rare along the east slope.

REMARKS: Unlike its relatives, the Wood Duck lives at all times on ponds or slow-moving streams that are well screened or arched over by willows, cottonwoods, oaks, and waterside vines where it is hidden from view. It nests in a rotted-out cavity or woodpecker hole in a tree, usually one over water, and it readily uses artificial nest boxes. The young, within hours or a day of hatching, flutter down and join their mother on the water. Acorns are common food items, but Wood Ducks also eat many aquatic insects.

MALLARD   *Anas platyrhynchos*
Pl. 390

Length 20 to 25 in., wing span 35 in.; legs and feet orange red; wing patch blue, edged with white. Adult male: head and neck glossy green with narrow white neck ring; breast chestnut; back and belly pale gray; tail with upcurled feathers; bill greenish yellow. Adult female: mottled brown, lighter below, feathers pale edged; a dark line through eye; bill orange and dusky. **CALL** in female is a loud *quack quack* call, in male a nasal whistle. **NEST** is on ground near water, made of grasses, reeds, and down; eggs eight to 12, greenish or grayish buff.

DISTRIBUTION: Common on quiet waters on both slopes of Sierra up to midelevations.

REMARKS: The common Mallard may appear at times on almost any lake or smooth stream, particularly those margined with aquatic plants. Some of these birds nest in secluded sites on such waters on either side of the mountains. Like other so-called puddle ducks, they are surface feeders—tipping "bottom up" to reach food plants under shallow water.

COMMON MERGANSER
Mergus merganser

Pl. 391

Length 21 to 27 in., wing span 34 in.; bill long, slender, bright red; back of head with short crest; feet reddish. Adult male: head and neck glossy green; upper back black; lower back and tail gray; neck, much of wings, and undersurface white. Adult female and immature: head and neck reddish brown, but throat white; back and tail gray; underparts scaled faintly white. CALL is a deep hoarse croaking. NEST is in hollow tree or on ground, lined with grasses, roots, and down; eggs six to 17, ivory.

DISTRIBUTION: Breeds on forest-margined lakes or swift streams from upper Kern River north. Occurs from Mixed Conifer Belt down into foothills, but may wander higher after breeding season. Numbers increase in many areas during migration. Small groups may overwinter on ice-free waters.

REMARKS: This low-slung duck bears horny "teeth" and a hooked tip, useful for catching the various kinds of fishes taken for food. It dives and swims readily under the surface when searching for prey. While sometimes accused of harming trout fisheries, they actually have a negligible impact. Groups of females and young mergansers are frequently observed along rivers or secluded lakeshores; they are always nervous and swim quickly away from humans.

OTHER DUCKS: The small Harlequin Duck (*Histrionicus histrionicus,* length 16 in.) has nested rarely on swift streams of the Mixed Conifer Belt and higher in the central Sierra; it is a State and Federal Species of Special Concern. There are no recent nesting records, but scattered sightings keep hope alive that this bird may still nest in remote sites. The adult male is dark slate blue with white patches on head, body, and wings and a white collar; the female is dull dark brown with a white patch on each cheek and ear region. The species winters on the central California seacoast.

Besides those discussed in detail in this subsection, at least twelve ducks are regularly observed in the Sierra Nevada, most occurring during migration and winter. Three of the most common species are the Gadwall (male is rich gray with a black rump, female is similar to the Mallard), the Ring-necked Duck (male is jet black above, gray below, with conspicuous white and black rings around bill; female is uniformly brown with same bill markings), and the Bufflehead (a small, active duck; male is strikingly white with black face and back; female is dingy gray brown with large white cheek patch).

Osprey, Hawks, and Eagles (Family Accipitridae)

OSPREY
Pandion haliaetus

Pl. 392

Length 21 to 25 in., wing span to 65 in.; blackish brown above; most of head white except for dark mask behind eye; white under; long wings with dark spot at the wrist; tail banded. CALL is a shrill *kee kee* and a low *kak kak.* NEST is near water in tall, broken-topped trees, sometimes on artificial structures, large and bulky, made of sticks; eggs three, creamy with brown blotches.

DISTRIBUTION: Typically observed near sizable bodies of water; nests at scattered locations but widespread during migration. California Species of Special Concern (nesting).

REMARKS: In flight, the "Fish Hawk" has a characteristic crook in its wing, giving it a gull-like appearance that is different from other raptors. When seeking food the bird often hovers high over water with feet dangling, then plunges feet first to capture fish. An array of tiny spikes on each footpad helps the bird carry slippery, struggling fish to distant dining perches.

BALD EAGLE *Haliaeetus leucocephalus*
Pl. 393

Length 31 to 40 in., wing span 80 to 96 in.; body blackish brown; head and tail pure white in adults. Immature birds show mottled white under. **CALL** is a short, chirping whistle. **NEST** is a massive stick structure high in trees, rarely on cliffs.

DISTRIBUTION: Uncommon but widespread migrant, nests in secluded areas near large bodies of water. Locally common in winter around some reservoirs. State Endangered, Federal Threatened.

REMARKS: This big, white-headed eagle, emblem of the United States and a familiar image, was until recently a scarce bird in the Sierra. They are now relatively common about lakes and large rivers as their populations continue to rebound from the disastrous effects of DDT. Fish are the primary component of their diet, being captured in shallow swoops over the water's surface or discovered as carrion. Also forage on deer or waterfowl carcasses and steal fish from Ospreys.

NORTHERN HARRIER *Circus cyaneus*
Pl. 394

Length 18 to 24 in., wing span 38 to 48 in.; a slim, agile hawk with long, slender cross-barred tail and narrow but round-ended wings; rump white. Adult male: pale bluish gray above; white below; black-tipped wings. Adult female and immature: dark brown above, paler and streaked below; female is vividly brown streaked below, while young birds have a cinnamon cast. **CALL** is a piercing whistle by females and young, or rapid barking notes by males. **NEST** is on ground, made of dried grasses and stems; eggs five, dull bluish white.

DISTRIBUTION: Uncommon resident on lower west slope. Common on east slope in breeding season, irregular in winter. Regularly wanders upslope into Alpine Belt in late summer and fall. California Species of Special Concern (nesting).

REMARKS: Except in migration, when they may fly extremely high, Northern Harriers are usually seen skimming perilously low over grasslands and marsh vegetation as they hunt for small rodents, birds, and insects. They fly with wings tilted up in a V, constantly stalling, readjusting, hovering, somersaulting in midair, and diving abruptly into tall grasses. Like owls, they have flattened facial disks that funnel the sounds of hidden prey to their ears with pinpoint accuracy.

SHARP-SHINNED HAWK — *Accipiter striatus*

Length 10 to 14 in., wing span 20 to 28 in.; between robin and pigeon in size; spread wings short and rounded; tail long and narrow, square ended, banded. Adult: above dark bluish gray; below finely barred with white and cinnamon. Immature: brown above; white below with smudgy brown streaks. **CALL** at nest is a series of short, sharp *kee-ki-ki* calls. **NEST** is in trees from 10 to 40 ft, a flat platform of twigs; eggs four to five, bluish white, brown-blotched.

DISTRIBUTION: Rarely nests in the Sierra. Winters in woodlands below heavy snow. Widespread and abundant during migration. California Species of Special Concern (nesting).

REMARKS: With short, powerful wings and long, rudderlike tails, the three *Accipiter* hawks specialize at speeding through densely forested areas and capturing small birds unawares. So fast are these hawks in flight that often all an observer sees is a gray blur amid the shrill calls of alarmed songbirds. Being the smallest of the three, Sharp-shinneds target small, finch-sized birds. In all three *Accipiter* hawks, females are larger than males.

COOPER'S HAWK — *Accipiter cooperii*
Pl. 395

Length 14 to 20 in., wing span 29 to 37 in.; slightly smaller than crow; resembles Sharp-shinned Hawk but about twice the bulk, and tail rounded at end. **CALL** in adult, is a harsh, nasal *kluk, kluk, kluk;* in juveniles it is a rapid, high-pitched begging call. **NEST** is a stick platform well up in trees; eggs four to five, bluish white, buff spotted.

DISTRIBUTION: Resident mostly in Foothill and Mixed Conifer Belts, in open woodland, often near streams. Califonia Species of Special Concern (nesting).

REMARKS: This midsized *Accipiter* is marked by a round-ended tail and other subtle marks that cannot always be detected, making it readily confused with Sharp-shinned Hawks. It circles in the open more often than the Sharp-shinned, yet it can be secretive. Like other hawks and owls, it tears and swallows large pieces of prey. After digestion of a meal, the bones, feathers, and hair are formed into a pellet and regurgitated. Pellets from below a nest in Yosemite Valley had remains of chipmunk, Northern Flicker, Steller's Jay, American Robin, Western Tanager, warblers, and towhees.

NORTHERN GOSHAWK — *Accipiter gentilis*

Length 21 to 26 in., wing span 40 to 46 in.; size of Red-tailed Hawk but more slender, wings shorter, rounded, tail longer, narrower. Adult: dark slate above, white below with very fine dark crossbars; at close range shows a distinct white eyebrow and red eye. Immature: dark brown above, white below with dark brown streaks. CALL is a loud, cackling *kak, kak, kak*. NEST is in trees at 20 to 60 ft, and it is a shallow twig platform; eggs three to four, bluish white.

DISTRIBUTION: Uncommon resident in Mixed Conifer and Upper Montane Belts, may wander downslope in winter. State and Federal Species of Special Concern (nesting).

REMARKS: This bird is a highly secretive specter of mature conifer forests. Rarely is it seen in its dense forest home, and its true numbers are difficult to estimate, though surveys suggest that logging of older forests has significantly impacted its population. It is extremely aggressive in defense of its nests and will launch fierce attacks even at humans, but excessive human activity still causes it to abandon nest sites. Feeds on grouse, other birds, squirrels, and chipmunks.

RED-TAILED HAWK   *Buteo jamaicensis*
Pl. 396
Length 19 to 25 in., wing span 48 to 56 in.; wings broad; tail broad, short, fan shaped in flight. Above dark brown, tail bright reddish in adults (finely banded brown in immature birds); highly variable patterning below, ranging from dark brown to white in different individuals. CALL is a shrill long whistle, *squee-oo.* NEST is a bulky twig platform well up in trees or on cliffs; eggs two to three, dull white, brown-spotted.

DISTRIBUTION: Common resident over most of Sierra, roams in summer up to 12,000 ft. The most frequently observed hawk in the Sierra.

REMARKS: Singly or in pairs, Red-tails circle and glide high in open air as they watch for squirrels or rabbits on the ground. When prey is sighted, the hawk swoops and strikes with its sturdy sharp claws. Larger animals are torn apart and eaten where killed, but smaller ones are carried off to a tree perch. Like other flesh-eating birds, a Red-tail may gorge a large meal that will suffice for several days. When not hunting, the hawk will perch high in a dead or live tree where it has a wide view. If disturbed it leaps off, beats strongly with its big wings, and soon begins to soar.

GOLDEN EAGLE   *Aquila chrysaetos*
Pl. 397
Length 30 to 40 in., wing span 80 to 90 in.; plumage dark brown, paler (golden brown) on head; immature birds show white patches at their tail bases and on their wings. CALL is a single loud cry, sometimes repeated, but generally silent. NEST is high in large trees or on cliffs, made of a massive pile of sticks and twigs, and lined with grass; eggs two, dull creamy white with brown spots.

DISTRIBUTION: Resident at low to midelevations on both slopes, but lives and nests at nearly all elevations. Lower elevation birds may wander upslope as the snows melt. California Species of Special Concern.

REMARKS: Golden Eagles are massive and powerful predators. They soar skillfully with their wings stretched horizontally and at times circle so high they become mere specks in the sky despite their 7-ft wing spans. Because of their size they have huge territories that keep them widely dispersed over vast landscapes. Their principal food items are ground squirrels and rabbits, but they are capable of killing much larger prey.

Falcons (Family Falconidae)

AMERICAN KESTREL
Falco sparverius

Pl. 398

Length 9 to 12 in., wing span 23 in.; our smallest raptor, body only slightly bigger than a robin; wings pointed and long; tail slender; two vertical black bars on side of head below eye; top of head, back, and most of tail rusty red; undersurface white. Adult male: wings blue gray, tail with one black band and white tip. Adult female: wings rusty brown, tail with several narrow black bars. **CALL** is a repeated shrill *kill-y kill-y*. **NEST** is in holes in trees or rock ledges; eggs four to five, creamy, brown-dotted.

DISTRIBUTION: Resident, commonest at lower elevations and valleys but after breeding found up to the Subalpine Belt; chiefly about grasslands and exposed ridgelines.

REMARKS: This little falcon is an active and agile hunter, flicking over meadows with quick wing beats or stopping to hover for several seconds and scan for prey. When perching they constantly bob their tails. Occasionally a pair will pester a shrike or a large hawk, perhaps in defense of their forage area. Small rodents and grasshoppers are the principal food; a few small birds are eaten.

OTHER FALCONS: The similarly sized but much darker Merlin (*Falco columbarius*, length 10 in.; pl. 399) is a rare winter visitor to the Sierra (a California Species of Special Concern), while two larger falcons, the Peregrine Falcon (*F. peregrinus*, length 16 in.; pl. 400) and the Prairie Falcon (*F. mexicanus*, length 16 in.; pl. 401), are uncommon residents and migrants (former is State Endangered, and latter is a California Species of Special Concern on nesting grounds). The Peregrine is dark slate with a single black bar on its face, and the Prairie is sandy brown with dark "armpits." All falcons are identifiable by their long wings that taper evenly down to sharp tips.

Fowllike Birds (Family Phasianidae)

BLUE GROUSE
Dendragapus obscurus

Pl. 402

Length 20 to 23 in., wing span 26 in.; form fowllike, larger than quail; plumage dark bluish gray with fine lighter markings; tail square ended with pale band across dark tip. **CALL** of male in nesting season is deep wooden *unt, wunt, wunt, tu-wunt, wunt, wunt* so low in pitch that some people cannot hear them; females nervously cluck in alarm when their chicks are threatened. **NEST** is on ground, a slight depression lined slightly with grasses, leaves, and feathers; eggs seven to 10, pinkish buff, brown spotted.

DISTRIBUTION: Resident, mostly in upper Mixed Conifer and Upper Montane Belts.

REMARKS: This grouse lives year-round in conifer forests where its main food, needle tips of pines and firs, is always available. Its dense body plumage and feathered legs protect against the cold of winter. In spring and early summer males perch solitarily on high tree limbs and boom at short intervals for hours; inflated neck sacs covered by bare yellow skin serve as resonators to make a far-carrying sound. The females, on the ground, incubate and raise their broods of chicks in June or early July. Males move upslope in small groups, followed later by hens and young. The summer diet includes several kinds of berries and insects. Blue Grouse return downslope before winter. Goshawks and martens are their chief enemies.

OTHER FOWLLIKE BIRDS: Two introduced game birds have established themselves in the Sierra after repeated releases by California Fish and Game personnel. The White-tailed Ptarmigan (*Lagopus leucurus,* length 12 in.; pl. 403), similar in shape to the Blue Grouse but with large areas of white feathers, occurs in alpine areas of the Yosemite area. The Wild Turkey (*Meleagris gallopavo,* length 36 to 46 in.; pl. 404) is a huge iridescent green and copper bird that is now abundant in low- to midelevation oak woodlands. Such introductions have been made with blatant disregard for native flora and fauna and the impact of their presence is little studied.

Quail (Family Odontophoridae)

MOUNTAIN QUAIL   *Oreortyx pictus*

Pl. 405

Length 10.5 to 12 in., wing span 16 in.; has long, slender, black plume on head; throat and side of head chestnut; white vertical streak below eye; head, upper back, and breast bluish gray; rest of back, tail, and wings brown; flanks chestnut with white and black bars. **CALL**, of male, is a single *quee-ark* or *wook,* at intervals; alarm call, *ca-ca-ca-ca* or *gup-gup* repeated. **NEST** is on ground under brush, lined with pine needles or grasses; eggs 10 to 12, buff, no spots.

DISTRIBUTION: Resident from lower Subalpine down into Mixed Conifer Belt; many breed at higher elevations then descend to below winter snows. Found in brushy, forested, and steep, rocky areas.

REMARKS: The picturesque Mountain Quail is seldom easy to find or see, though its loud calls are often heard. The birds forage quietly in sheltered places and when disturbed scurry quickly into dense brush, rather than flying off or posting a watchful scout as do California Quail. Pairing begins by early April, and the nesting season is from mid-May into July. When downy broods are out the parents utter various low clucking and whining notes and some harsher calls. A few insects are eaten early in summer, but seeds of grasses and herbs and berries of various shrubs are the staple foods. By early fall the quail gather in small flocks and begin to move downslope until the following spring.

CALIFORNIA QUAIL
Callipepla californica
Pl. 406

Length 9.5 to 11 in., wing span 14 in.; crown of head with short black top-knot curving forward; body plump; back, tail, and wings plain grayish brown; breast clear blue gray; belly white or buff with dark scaly marks; flanks chestnut with broad white streaks; face of male black, rimmed with white, top-knot more pronounced. **CALL** differs among assembly call, *chi-ca'-go*; disturbance call, an explosive *whit, whit,* repeated; or that of a lone male, a loud *kyark.* **NEST** is on ground in slight depression with sparse grass lining; eggs 12 to 16, ivory with light brown spots.

DISTRIBUTION: Common resident of lower grasslands and foothill forests in streamside thickets or open chaparral areas.

REMARKS: Interrupted shrubby cover, margined by scattered herbaceous plants, is preferred habitat for this common lowland quail. Only in nesting season are the birds in pairs, the male on guard while the female incubates. The downy chicks leave the nest at once, in care of both parents, and within two weeks have grown enough to fly. Later in summer family groups merge into larger flocks that forage and live together, roosting at night in oaks or in other dense-foliaged trees or shrubs. Quail run rapidly on the ground. When frightened they flush with whirring wings and sail into escape cover. Their food is mostly of seeds and some leafy materials with a few berries and insects. Cooper's Hawks, Bobcats, Foxes, Coyotes, and domestic cats are common enemies.

Coot (Family Rallidae)

AMERICAN COOT
Fulica americana
Pl. 407

Length 13 to 16 in., wing span 24 in.; bill narrow, white; feet webbed like a duck except that each toe has a separate web; head and neck black, rest of body dark slate; white patch under tail sometimes prominently displayed. **CALL** is an explosive *pulque, pulque,* repeated; also a harsh *kerk.* **NEST** is in marshes, often exposed, a mound of tules or sedges; eggs eight to 12, buff with dark dots.

DISTRIBUTION: Common resident on slower waters at lower elevations, abundant in some areas during migration and winter. Rare above foothill habitats.

REMARKS: The familiar, dark-colored coot may appear on any quiet lowland stream or pond margined with aquatic vegetation. When swimming, coots jerk their heads fore-and-aft in keeping with strokes of their lobed feet. If disturbed they paddle toward open water. When forced to fly they run on the surface with much splashing of wings and feet before rising into the air. Coots eat both plant and animal materials. They variously reach for plants on the water surface, dive for deeper morsels, or go ashore to nip off vegetation there. The downy young take to the water soon after hatching; they are black with patches of crinkly hairlike feathers of bright orange. In winter, coots gather in large flocks.

Plover (Family Charadriidae)

KILLDEER *Charadrius vociferus*

Pl. 408

Length 9.5 to 10.5 in., wing span 20 in.; pale brown above; rump tawny orange; forehead and undersurface white, two black bands on breast. **CALL** is a loud, plaintive *kill-dee,* often repeated. **NEST** is on dry ground or gravel, sometimes near water, shallow, bare or scantily lined; eggs four, pear shaped, buff, dark blotched.

DISTRIBUTION: Common resident in valleys and lower elevations, but nests sparingly up to Subalpine Belt; numbers increase during migration and may remain common in mild winters. Found at wet grasslands, water margins, or even in dry open areas, often seen in towns and parks.

REMARKS: Singly or in small groups the Killdeer is the most widespread shorebird. It is a very active hunter that runs in quick dashes and stops frequently to catch insects or small aquatic animals. It has the distinctive habit of bobbing its foreparts upward at steady intervals. When startled it flies off to circle and call noisily. The speckled eggs and scant nest lining are difficult to see against most backgrounds. The same is true of the downy chicks marked with broken patterns of black, brown, and white. When approached, a parent will run away from the nest or young before flying, and if particularly disturbed will cry desperately and flail as if broken winged to distract a predator's attention.

Sandpipers (Family Scolopacidae)

SPOTTED SANDPIPER *Actitis macularia*

Pl. 409

Length 7 to 8 in., wing span 15 in.; pale brown above; white below with round black spots in summer, spots absent in winter; spread wing shows a narrow white bar. **CALL** is a loud, clear *peet-tweet-tweet.* **NEST** is on wet meadow or gravel, scant lining of grasses or none; eggs four, pear shaped, buff, darkly blotched.

DISTRIBUTION: Breeds at any elevation on open sandy or pebbly lake or stream shores, retreats to low elevations in winter.

REMARKS: The pale brown and white body, inch-long bill, and incessant bobbing of the hind parts mark this small freshwater sandpiper. As it walks the head moves fore-and-aft in unison with the feet. On taking to flight it makes an arc over the water to some more distant shore; after the first few strokes the wings are held spread, curving downward and moving only at the tips, creating a curious stiff-winged flight. The bird forages in the shallows or on the shore close to water, picking up small aquatic animals or insects for food. It is seen singly or in pairs and does not flock. Females are aggressive and dominant, often mating with several males and defending large territories where the males raise their chicks.

WILSON'S SNIPE   *Gallinago delicata*
Pl. 410

Length 10.5 in., wing span 18 in.; complexly patterned black, buff, and white above; strong brown stripes on head; large eye and extremely long bill; tail tipped rufous. **CALL** when flushed, is a harsh *scri-ape;* loud *wheet* or *TIKa* calls from display perches; most familiar are the hollow *whuwhuwhuwhu* sounds made by their flight feathers during evening display flights. **NEST** is shallow, grass-lined hollow on ground in wet grassy or marshy areas, well concealed; eggs three to four, pear shaped, rich brown with darker brown splotches.

DISTRIBUTION: Resident and breeds up to Mixed Conifer Belt, much more common at lower elevations. Optimum habitat is moist valley meadows and marshes on east side of Sierra where they are a familiar bird; less common on west slope. Widespread below snow level during migration and winter.

REMARKS: This extremely well-camouflaged shorebird of dense grassy areas is often not seen until it flushes with a loud cry from underfoot. During the breeding season they fill the air over lush valleys with their strange "winnowing" display flights. Flying so high that they are hard to spot, they swoop and climb sending air through fanned wing and tail feathers and creating a hollow quavering sound. In soft muddy areas they use their long bills to probe deeply for worms and insect larvae. Their eyes are set so far back on their skulls that they can see to the rear when their heads are down feeding.

WILSON'S PHALAROPE   *Phalaropus tricolor*
Pl. 411

Length 9.25 in., wing span 17 in.; head, neck, and bill slender; legs black in breeding season. Adult female (spring): top of head, hind neck, and back pale gray; sides of head and neck black and cinnamon; breast tawny; chin and belly white. Adult male (spring): duller, black and cinnamon subdued. Adults (fall) and immatures: upper surface uniform pale gray; legs yellow. **CALL** is low nasal *wurk.* **NEST** is in marsh or grass, shallow, sparse grass lining; eggs four, pear shaped, buff with dark blotches.

DISTRIBUTION: Common migrant and sparse breeder (May to late September) along east base of Sierra south to Bishop, numbers increase dramatically in late June as migrants from northern breeding areas gather in marshes and on lakes on their way south.

REMARKS: In spring and fall many of these small slender birds appear on Mono Lake. They forage along the shore or ride on the water and turn from side to side, using their needlelike bills to pick food from the surface. Among phalaropes the differences between sexes are reversed, with females aggressively and actively courting males. While the sexes in most shorebirds are identically colored, in phalaropes the female is larger and more brightly colored than the inconspicuous male, who cares for the eggs and young while the female prepares to migrate south.

OTHER SHOREBIRDS: Besides the four shorebirds described above, an additional 25 species regularly visit the Sierra region during migration. Most stop at low-elevation marshlands, especially on the east slope, but a few visit high-elevation lakeshores. Many are extremely difficult to identify, requiring use of specialized field guides.

Gulls and Terns (Family Laridae)

CALIFORNIA GULL   *Larus californicus*
Pl. 412

Length 20 to 23 in., wing span 54 in. Adult: head, neck, tail, and undersurface white; back pale gray; wing tips black; bill yellow with a black and red spot near tip; legs and feet yellow (*note:* illustration is of California Gull in winter plumage). Immature: mixed dark and light browns; dark tail and wing tips; pink-based blackish bill. **CALL** is a high *kyarr* or a repeated *kee-kee-kee.* **NEST** is on ground of islands in lakes, scant lining of grasses, twigs, or feathers; eggs three, buff gray, blotched with dark brown.

DISTRIBUTION: Visits a variety of mountain lakes in summer, most abundant in the Mono Lake region; sparse at low elevations in winter. California Species of Special Concern (nesting).

REMARKS: Great Basin lakes are the summer home of the California Gull. In some years up to 65,000 pairs have nested on islands in Mono Lake, and there are smaller colonies on other lakes at the east base of the Sierra. Adults often visit Lake Tahoe (perhaps from Nevada's Pyramid Lake), and a few are seen around other Sierra lakes up to 10,000 ft. On the water the gull rides high, with wing tips crossed over the back; in the air the long pointed wings sweep in graceful arcs or are spread as the bird circles and glides.

OTHER GULLS AND TERNS: The smaller Ring-billed Gull (*L. delawarensis;* length 17.5 in.), distinguished by its paler gray back and broad black ring on its bill, is uncommon throughout the Sierra.

Five species of terns also appear on lakes of the Sierra in summer or during migration. They are gull-like but slender with long, narrow wings and forked tails. Terns fly gracefully, change direction quickly, often hover, and plunge into the water to catch small fish. The Caspian Tern (*Sterna caspia,* length 21 in.) is white with a black crown and pale gray back and wings and has a stout red-orange bill. The smaller Black Tern (*Chlidonias niger,* length 10 in.; pl. 413) is black on the head, neck, and undersurface; silvery gray on the back, wings, and tail; State and Federal Species of Special Concern (nesting).

Pigeons and Dove (Family Columbidae)

BAND-TAILED PIGEON   *Columba fasciata*
Pl. 414

Length 15 to 16 in., wing span 26 in.; above bluish gray, below pinkish brown; tail with pale gray band across tip, square ended; back of neck with white collar. **CALL** is a deep *wuh'-woo*, repeated. **NEST** is usually in oaks at 8 to 40 ft; a loose, bulky stick platform; eggs one (seldom two) pointed, white.

DISTRIBUTION: Common breeder in forests of Foothill and Mixed Conifer Belts where oaks are abundant. May wander to higher elevations after breeding but descends into foothills for winter. Primarily a bird of the west slope.

REMARKS: Our native pigeon of the West usually lives in flocks. Pairs often nest close together and join others while feeding. Their general behavior is much like that of the domestic bird, clapping their wings when starting to fly and cooing intermittently while perched. Flocks tend to remain hidden in foliage but may sun themselves on bare branches or rocks. Acorns are a staple food, together with berries of manzanita, toyon, chokecherry and coffee-berry; grain in fields is eaten when little else is available. Acorns are swallowed whole and the thick shells cracked open in the bird's powerful gizzard.

OTHER PIGEONS: Around towns and human developments the introduced Rock Dove (*C. livia,* length 12.5 in.) can be abundant; usually distinguished by its dark head and lack of white collar, but large Rock Dove groups nearly always contain individuals with a wide mix of colors and patterns.

MOURNING DOVE   *Zenaida macroura*
Pl. 415

Length 11 to 13 in., wing span 18 in.; above olive brown with black spots on wings; brown pale below; breast pink hued; tail long and finely tapered with white edge. **CALL** is a mellow *ah-coo', roo, coo.* **NEST** is on tree branch, bush, or ground; a very simple twig platform; eggs two, white.

DISTRIBUTION: Common resident at low elevations; in open woodland or chaparral mixed with grassland. May range into Mixed Conifer Belt where there is suitable habitat.

REMARKS: Mourning Doves in swift whistling flight are common over valleys and foothills near areas with water. They perch on fences, overhead wires, or open-branched trees, feed on the ground, and seek drinking water in the morning and evening. When walking, their gait is slightly angular and the head bobs to and fro with each step. The food consists entirely of seeds gleaned on the ground. Doves nest through a long season, from March to July or later, and may raise as many as six broods. The young are fed a special material (pigeon milk) formed in the parent's gullet. Through much of the year the birds occur in pairs, but in winter they live in loose flocks ranging widely in search of food.

Roadrunner (Family Cuculidae)

GREATER ROADRUNNER   *Geococcyx californianus*
Pl. 416

Length 20 to 24 in., wing span 22 in.; body is size of small chicken but tail is very long; legs and feet stout; plumage pale brown, feathers of back dark centered, tail mostly black with white tip on each feather, head blackish with a slight crest. **CALL** is a series of about six low *coo* notes descending in pitch; bill is clicked when excited. **NEST** is a stick platform in bushes or low trees; eggs three to five, white.

DISTRIBUTION: Sparse resident in lowest foothills; found in open chaparral.

REMARKS: The running "ground cuckoo" of the arid West must be sought around dry shrubby cover of the foothills or valley edges. When flushed it will run, then hop or fly to a low perch and stand while raising and lowering both the head, crest, and tail. It is a skillful, aggressive hunter and has a varied diet—lizards, snakes, tarantulas, crickets, grasshoppers, mice, and small birds. Wary and easy to overlook, but population seems to be declining due to habitat alterations and fragmentation.

Barn Owl (Family Tytonidae)

BARN OWL   *Tyto alba*
Pl. 417

Length 15 to 16 in., wing span 42 in.; glaring white heart-shaped face, no ear tufts; eyes dark; upper surface light golden brown; undersurface white, lightly speckled. **CALL** is a single, long rasping *sksch;* also a rapid *click, click, click* made with bill. **NEST** is in the hole of a tree, cliff, or earth bank, unlined; eggs five to seven, white.

DISTRIBUTION: Widespread resident near fields and grasslands on west slope from Central Valley into foothills and lower edge of Mixed Conifer Belt. On east side uncommon in low-lying agricultural areas of northern Sierra.

REMARKS: Originally, this owl roosted and nested in cavities of cliffs, gullies, or large trees. Now it also uses barns, attics, and old-fashioned steeples. Dense-foliaged trees often serve for daytime shelter. If disturbed it will fly off, even in strong sunlight, and find another retreat. The flight of this and other owls is silent because of their very soft feathers. At dusk the Barn Owl goes hunting over grasslands or alfalfa fields inhabited by its prey—small rodents. These are grasped and killed by the sharp claws, torn into a few small pieces, and swallowed. Digestion removes the flesh, and then the leftover hair and bones are regurgitated as an oblong pellet. By gathering pellets below a roost and identifying their contents (skulls, teeth, and bones), we learn the owl's diet. Besides small mice, many pocket gophers and insects are taken. This owl's diet is of great benefit to farmers and gardeners.

Typical Owls (Family Strigidae)

WESTERN SCREECH-OWL   *Otus kennicottii*
Pl. 418

Length 9 in., wing span 20 in.; head flat topped, with ear tufts; plumage streaked with dark and light gray, resembling oak tree bark (*note:* illustrated screech-owl shows more brown tones than typical for those found in Sierra Nevada); eyes yellow. CALL is of low-toned quavering notes in rapid accelerating trill; single clucking notes when adults and young forage together. NEST is in tree cavities; eggs four to five, white.

DISTRIBUTION: Common resident on west slope from Mixed Conifer Belt down into the Central Valley, prefers habitats with oaks or trees along rivers.

REMARKS: The "bouncing ball" call of this small owl is a characteristic night sound in the foothill oak region. Calls heard year-round but are most pronounced in the breeding season. After breeding, some move upslope into the Mixed Conifer Belt. Feeds largely on insects, but also takes small mammals.

Poorly known because of its secretive behavior and infrequent calling is the diminutive Flammulated Owl (*O. flammeolus,* length 7 in.), which is a surprisingly common, though local, summer visitor to ponderosa and Jeffrey pine forests. It has a soft ventriloquial hoot and is the only small owl with dark eyes.

GREAT HORNED OWL   *Bubo virginianus*
Pl. 419

Length 20 to 22 in., wing span 44 in. or larger; head flat topped with large ear tufts; facial disk reddish; eyes yellow; wings and back finely marbled dark and light brown; underside with horizontal barring. CALL is a deep *whuh-whoodo, whoo-whoo.* NEST is in a hole in a cliff or in a deserted nest of hawk, crow, or magpie; eggs two to three, white.

DISTRIBUTION: Widespread resident on both slopes up to Subalpine Belt. Resides in wooded areas, frequently found in human-altered landscapes.

REMARKS: This large fierce owl is the feared predator of the avian world. Its melancholy nighttime calls announce its presence to competitors and prey alike. Great Horneds are notoriously intolerant of other owls or raptors in their territory, chasing or killing any smaller than an eagle. Their diet verges on the astonishing, ranging from scorpions to skunks, crayfish to large snakes, although the majority of their prey consists of rabbits, wood rats, and rodents. They are one of the earliest breeding animals in the Sierra, laying eggs as early as January in some areas. This ensures that juvenile Great Horneds are already proficient hunters by the time other young birds and mammals are setting out on their own.

NORTHERN PYGMY-OWL   *Glaucidium gnoma*

Length 7 in., wing span 14.5 in.; head round (no tufts); eyes yellow; plumage grayish brown above with small white spots; undersurface white with distinct brownish streaks; bill pale yellow. **CALL** is a mellow whistled *whoot* or *whoot-whoot,* repeated at intervals; also, a long trill followed by one to three distinct hoots. **NEST** is at 6 to 75 ft usually in old woodpecker holes near meadows; eggs three to four, white.

DISTRIBUTION: Probably common and widespread in Foothill and Mixed Conifer Belts of west slope, and uncommon to rare on east slope. Even in areas where they are resident, however, they can remain silent and undetectable for months at a stretch then enter periods of daily activity, making it hard to determine their actual status.

REMARKS: Unlike most other owls, the Northern Pygmy-owl calls and is active by day. It lives mainly amid dense foliage where it can hide when not foraging, but when hunting it may be spotted sitting on exposed perches. Small birds recognize this sparrow-sized owl as an enemy; if one is located they congregate in frenzied mobs, uttering distress notes. These mobs seem to attract every small bird in the forest. A person's whistled imitation of the owl's voice may attract a pygmy-owl—and also small birds. The young are fed lizards, plucked small birds, and mice; later they catch grasshoppers. Adults take chipmunks and smaller rodents and, in summer, birds. After a meal the owl may perch high in the open while grooming.

SPOTTED OWL   *Strix occidentalis*

Pl. 420

Length 19 in., wing span 40 in.; head rounded, no ear tufts; eyes dark; bill pale yellow; plumage soft brown with many white spots in crosswise rows. **CALL** is a series of barking notes in characteristic cadence, *whup, whoo-hoo, hoooo.* Contact call, given mostly by female, is an upslurred whistle *coooweep.* **NEST** is in the cavity of a cliff or tree; eggs two to three, white.

DISTRIBUTION: Uncommon resident in Mixed Conifer Belt of west slope. Found mainly in mature conifer forests, but also in oak woodlands. State and Federal Species of Special Concern.

REMARKS: Walking in the woods at dusk one may hear the barking calls of this owl and occasionally glimpse its rounded head. In daytime the repeated insistent calls of a gray squirrel, or of kinglets, warblers, and jays, may lead an observer to a Spotted Owl perched motionless in the dense forest. One foothill rancher enjoyed a pair of Spotted Owls near his home because of their varied calls in the early evening. Continued cutting of mature conifer stands has led to a serious decline in numbers of this gentle and confiding owl. Wood rats, white-footed mice, and flying squirrels are primary food items.

GREAT GRAY OWL   *Strix nebulosa*

Pl. 421

Length 27 in., wing span to 54 in.; head big, round, no ear tufts; eyes and bill yellow; plumage grayish brown, dully streaked with white. **CALL** is a single deep *whoo* at irregular intervals. **NEST** is nearly always in the top of a large, broken-off snag; eggs three, dull white, simply laid on bare wood.

DISTRIBUTION: Sparse resident on west slope south to Madera County; at 3,200 to 7,900 ft in coniferous forests interspersed with large meadow systems. State Endangered.

REMARKS: This big owl of the Eurasian and American Arctic occurs sparingly in the northern Rockies and Sierra Nevada. Most Sierra records are from the Mixed Conifer and Upper Montane Belts of the Yosemite region, where there is a small population. Scattered records come from other northern Sierra locations. It seems to be most active in early morning and late afternoon, so bird students should watch and listen in deep woods for a large, dark, round-headed owl with a deep voice and penetrating yellow eyes.

LONG-EARED OWL
Asio otus

Pl. 422

Length 16 in., wing span 36 in.; head and face round, tall ear tufts above eyes; brownish black above, mottled; pale brown below with darker vertical stripes; eyes yellow. **CALL** is a long mellow *hoot,* repeated; also catlike calls. **NEST** is old nest of crow, magpie, or hawk, in tree; eggs four to five, white, oval.

DISTRIBUTION: Uncommon on both slopes below Upper Montane Belt, usually found in dense riparian and oak thickets. California Species of Special Concern (nesting).

REMARKS: A smaller and slimmer version of a Great Horned Owl, best distinguished by the vertical striping on its underside (compared to the Great Horned's horizontal bars). Meadow mice and deer mice, some other rodents, and a few birds are taken for food. Nesting is in late April or May, and by June family groups may be found by day in willow thickets. This is a secretive, rarely observed, and poorly known owl in the Sierra.

NORTHERN SAW-WHET OWL
Aegolius acadicus

Pl. 423

Length 8.5 in., wing span 17 in.; head round, no tufts; eyes yellow; above cinnamon brown with white spots; below white with reddish brown streaks. **CALL** is a fast, monotonously repeated single-note whistle; also, a raspy call, like a saw being sharpened. **NEST** is in a variety of tree cavities; eggs four to five, white, oval to round.

DISTRIBUTION: Uncommon on both slopes in conifer forests.

REMARKS: With only scattered records of this species in the Sierra, its true distribution and abundance remain poorly understood. It is known to nest in old woodpecker holes and to feed mostly on small rodents. The call is heard mainly in the nesting season and roosting birds are occasionally observed on low branches in dense coniferous forests.

Nightjars (Family Caprimulgidae)

COMMON NIGHTHAWK   *Chordeiles minor*
Pl. 424

Length 9.5 in., wing span 24 in.; wings long and slender, reaching beyond tail when folded; plumage complexly barred or spotted with brown, gray, black, and white; in flight a white bar across outerpart of each wing shows prominently. **CALL** is nasal *pee'-nt* or *pee'-ark,* one- or two-syllabled. **NEST** is just bare ground or rock; eggs two, creamy.

DISTRIBUTION: Summer visitor and breeder from Mixed Conifer Belt into Subalpine Belt, also in Sagebrush Belt on east side.

REMARKS: Nighthawks begin to hunt flying insects at sundown, do some foraging at night, and continue into the morning on cloudy days or when the young need food. Generally, they fly high with agile, batlike wing beats. They call repeatedly while flying and also produce an odd booming "whoof" by diving and sending air through their wing tips. By day the nighthawk perches lengthwise on a tree limb or log and is well camouflaged by its plumage.

OTHER NIGHTHAWKS: The Lesser Nighthawk (*C. acutipennis,* length 8.5 in.) occurs in summer at the edge of the Central Valley, has a low and purring call but is silent in flight, and forages close to the ground.

COMMON POORWILL   *Phalaenoptilus nuttallii*

Length 8 in., wing span 17 in.; head broad and oversized for the body; eyes huge and deep black; bill and feet small; feathers soft, owllike; throat and corners of tail white; plumage otherwise mixed black, gray, and brown. **CALL** is a mellow, *poor-will,* repeated; a soft *quirt* in flight. **NEST** is just bare ground, eggs two, pinkish.

DISTRIBUTION: Fairly common summer visitor in chaparral of Foothill Belt, also along east base of Sierra in Sagebrush Belt. Wanders higher into mountains in late summer.

REMARKS: When darkness falls the poorwill takes wing and weaves in irregular course close above the ground and shrubbery. Its mouth is as broad as the head and fringed with bristles, a gaping trap that serves to gather the flying insects consumed as food. By day the bird rests quietly on the ground under a bush, its variegated plumage blending with surface objects, making it difficult to see. The young remain on the site where hatched until they are able to fly.

Swifts (Family Apodidae)

WHITE-THROATED SWIFT   *Aeronautes saxatalis*
Pl. 425

Length 6.75 in., wing span 15 in.; swallowlike but wings longer, slender, tail longer; black except for white on throat, midbreast, and sides of rump.

CALL is rapid shrill twittering notes. **NEST** is in cliff cavities; saucer shaped, made of feathers or twigs glued to rock with sticky saliva; eggs three to six, white.

DISTRIBUTION: Summer visitor locally on west slope up into Upper Montane Belt. Rarely encountered on east slope. Most often seen about high ridges and rock faces in river canyons.

REMARKS: Swifts forage high in the air, often in loose companies, alternately on level course, climbing by rapid fluttering flight, or diving at tremendous speed as they pursue flying insects. They differ from swallows in having a crossbow outline because of their backward-curving wings. Swifts are abroad from early morning until dusk. They never alight on the ground or a perch but roost and nest in crevices of cliffs that are inaccessible to other animals.

OTHER SWIFTS: Two other swifts occur primarily on the west slope, but range widely while feeding or migrating; both are California Species of Special Concern (nesting). The large Black Swift (*Cypseloides niger,* length 7.25 in.) is all black, and it has a broad tail and a more leisurely, swallowlike flight. The smaller Vaux's Swift (*Chaetura vauxi,* length 4.75 in.) is sooty gray with noticeably paler throat and rump patches; recognized by its high-intensity quicksilver wing beats.

Hummingbirds (Family Trochilidae)

ANNA'S HUMMINGBIRD   *Calypte anna*
Pl. 426

Length 4 in.; back and rump metallic green; below dusky, green tinged; male with entire head, chin, and throat iridescent rose red. **CALL** of perched male is a squeaky and buzzy *zeezy-zeezy,* often given in a long series; the feeding female gives a low *tsup.* **NEST** is a cup 1.75 in. in diameter, well hidden in trees or shrubs, made of spider webs, mosses, and lichens, and lined with plant down; eggs two, white.

DISTRIBUTION: Year-round in western foothills, mostly in mixed woodland and chaparral; moves upslope in summer. Scarce on east side.

REMARKS: This largest of local hummingbirds uses both wild and garden flowers for nectar. On occasion it visits sapsucker drillings to take the tree sap. Such foods are supplemented with a steady supply of small insects and spiders. Nesting begins as early as December, and it is not uncommon to see males performing their vigorous courtship displays while snow lies on the ground. In summer some individuals move upslope to feed on flowers that blossom at that season. Males are particularly fierce in defense of their feeding territories, attacking nesting females, other males, and any bird or mammal that dares to trespass.

CALLIOPE HUMMINGBIRD   *Stellula calliope*
Pl. 427

Length 3.25 in. Adult male: throat streaked with long, slender, iridescent lavender feathers; light green above; white below; sides dusky green. Adult female and immature: green above; finely speckled throat; sides washed in buff. **CALL** in pursuit a faint *tweez-e-zeet-zee;* otherwise, thin whistles and chirps. **NEST** is in trees at 9 to 75 ft, on twigs, diameter about 1.25 in., of plant down and lichens; eggs two, white.

DISTRIBUTION: Migrate in small numbers through foothills. Breeds on both slopes from Mixed Conifer Belt nearly to treeline, favoring flower-laden meadows along forest edges.

REMARKS: The diminutive Calliope Hummingbird arrives in April or May, probably along the lower slopes, nests in the main forest belt, and departs southward in July or August by way of the higher mountains. It thus takes advantage of the seasonal shift in blossoming flowers by moving upslope as the year advances. Both coniferous and deciduous trees serve for roosting and nesting. Flowers of currant, gooseberry, manzanita, paintbrush, and penstemon are commonly visited for nectar.

RUFOUS HUMMINGBIRD   *Selasphorus rufus*
Pl. 428

Length 3.75 in. Adult male: bright reddish brown above; chin and throat iridescent coppery red, bordered below by white; undersurface rufous brown. Adult female: back bronzy green; throat speckled with small red feathers; sides of body and base of tail rufous-tinged (*note:* illustrated bird is an immature, which closely resembles female in appearance). **CALL** is a high *zee,* often repeated.

DISTRIBUTION: Migrates along lower west slope in spring, and at higher elevations of both slopes during summer and fall.

REMARKS: The Rufous Hummingbird moves north in spring along the foothills when flowers there are blossoming and afford nectar for its food. It nests north of California, but returning males appear at higher elevations by early July. Later in that month females and immatures arrive. From then into September the species outnumbers all other hummingbirds around any area with mountain flowers, even well above timberline. Individuals often defend specific feeding patches.

Kingfisher (Family Alcedinidae)

BELTED KINGFISHER   *Ceryle alcyon*

Length 11 to 14.5 in., wing span 20 in.; head oversized with shaggy crest; bill stout; blue above, finely spotted white; white below with blue breast band, females have an additional rusty brown belly band. **CALL** is a loud rattle. **NEST** is near water on vertical sand or clay bank in 3- to 6-ft tunnel; eggs three to six, white.
DISTRIBUTION: Found by streams and lakes

throughout much of Sierra, most common in foothills, withdrawing from higher frozen waters in winter.

REMARKS: Sooner or later the kingfisher's rattling call may be heard around most waters. The bird perches briefly on some bare branch or snag then moves on to scan another stretch of water. Its prey of large aquatic insects and small fishes is caught by sudden plunges into water; sometimes the bird hovers on beating wings while scanning the water below. One of the main requirements is for clear water where it can readily spot prey items. Solitary except during the breeding season, when pairs cooperate to spend up to three weeks digging a nest hole in a sandy bank.

Woodpeckers (Family Picidae)

LEWIS'S WOODPECKER   *Melanerpes lewis*
Pl. 429

Length 11 in., wing span 21 in.; iridescent greenish black above; belly and face rose red; breast and neck collar grayish white. **CALL** is a series of harsh *chur* calls, but this species is generally silent. **NEST** is in tree holes; eggs five to nine, white.

DISTRIBUTION: Of irregular occurrence, seasonally and elevationally; in open forested areas, especially in recently burned stands.

REMARKS: These birds are wanderers, apt to be seen anywhere in the Sierra except in dense conifer forests. They may nest in a locality one year, or be only a winter visitant, or else be entirely absent. If they have any pattern it would be that they generally nest at lower elevations east of the crest and winter in the low western foothills. In winter their staple food is acorns and much of their time is spent guarding acorn caches. They also flycatch for large flying insects from high exposed perches, making long acrobatic flights. In sustained flight the long wings beat continuously, making them look more like crows than woodpeckers from a distance. This mannerism and their distinctive coloration make identification easy.

ACORN WOODPECKER   *Melanerpes formicivorus*
Pl. 430

Length 9 in., wing span 17 in.; chin, back, and wings shiny black; forehead, rump, belly, and patch on wings (in flight) white; crown red; throat and sides of head yellowish; red crown on female reduced in size. **CALL** is a nasal *ya'-kup, ya'-kup, ya'-kup;* also *krra'-ka, krra'-ka.* **NEST** is in a hole in a tree or pole, at 10 to 30 ft; eggs four to five, white.

DISTRIBUTION: Common resident in foothills of west slope up into lower Mixed Conifer Belt; on east slope only in the very north, and a small colony near Lone Pine. Favors open oak woodlands.

REMARKS: Unlike their shy forest-dwelling relatives, Acorn Woodpeckers are easy to see and hear, almost always in or near oaks, and mainly in groups of two or more birds. Acorns are their habitual food, the stout shells pecked off to uncover the nutrient-rich meats inside. During the season of plenty, huge numbers of acorns are stored for future use. Acorn Woodpeckers drill many holes in trees or posts and tamp an acorn into each hole. Specific trees are used as granaries, essentially pantries that hold up to 50,000 acorns. Because it takes so much work to store and guard this many acorns, Acorn Woodpeckers live in cooperative social groups that also work together to raise the dominant pair's youngsters.

WILLIAMSON'S SAPSUCKER   *Sphyrapicus thyroideus*

Length 9 in., wing span 17 in. Adult male: mostly black; rump and large patch on wing white; small white stripes behind eye and bill; chin red; belly yellow. Adult female: head and throat brown; breast black; belly yellow; rump white; rest of plumage barred with black, white, and pale brown. **CALL** is a strong *queeah*. **NEST** is in a hole in a conifer trunk; eggs five to six, white.

DISTRIBUTION: Uncommon resident in Upper Montane and Subalpine forests of both slopes, especially where lodgepole pines dominate; appears to migrate down into Mixed Conifer forests in winter, but there are few records.

REMARKS: Male and female Williamson's Sapsuckers are so markedly different in color that they were at one time thought to be separate species. They summer in the higher coniferous forests, foraging mostly on lodgepole pine but also on firs, Jeffrey pine, hemlock, and occasionally aspen. They excavate tiny pits into bark to obtain sap that they drink; these pits are arranged in irregularly horizontal rows but never completely encircle the trunk. One 60-ft lodgepole pine had 26 rows of punctures all made in one season. Many trees react to the drilling by later producing a swollen ring in the wood beneath each row; the resulting scarlike growths can be seen on many living and dead lodgepoles. In winter, when sap movement is scant, the Williamson's Sapsucker probably finds dormant insects or larvae hidden in bark crevices.

RED-BREASTED SAPSUCKER   *Sphyrapicus ruber*

Pl. 431

Length 9 in., wing span 16 in.; whole head, throat, and breast crimson red; back and wings black, with white spots; prominent white stripe along edge of wing; belly yellowish. **CALL** is a single low *churr*. **NEST** is in a hole dug in a tree; eggs five to six, pinkish white.

DISTRIBUTION: Common summer bird in Mixed Conifer Belt up into the lower Upper Montane Belt, found on both slopes. After breeding, wanders both up and down slope before retreating to lower elevations for winter. Inhabits mixed woodlands and forests.

REMARKS: Sapsuckers are woodpeckers that feed on tree sap and cambium (the soft nutrient-rich tissue under tree bark). This species works mainly on deciduous trees—willow, cottonwood, aspen, oak, and apple—but sometimes on pines or incense-cedar. It drills small holes, wider than high, in horizontal rows on trunks or limbs. The pits extend through the bark into the cambium. Sap flows from the wounds, and the bird revisits the site at intervals, using its brushlike tongue to take the sticky fluid and any insects caught in it. (Other birds may also visit the drillings for the same reasons.) Repeated rows of holes are drilled below the first series, sometimes in subsequent years, yielding grill-like patterns. Occasional trees are completely girdled, attacked by insects or fungus, and eventually killed. This sapsucker seldom calls, pecks only quietly, and is best detected by its sap wells.

NUTTALL'S WOODPECKER   *Picoides nuttallii*

Length 7 in., wing span 13 in.; head black with two white stripes on side; wings and back black with white bars; flanks and outer tail feathers white with black bars; male with red on back of head. **CALL** is a short rattling trill. **NEST** is a hole in a tree; eggs three to six, white.

DISTRIBUTION: Common resident in Foothill Belt, mainly in oaks. Rare visitor on east slope.

REMARKS: Among the foothill oaks one often hears a brief rattling call that draws attention to its maker, this lively little woodpecker. In the air its wings beat a few strokes and then close, whereupon the bird swoops downward; its course is deeply undulating when going between trees. In foraging it hitches upward on dry or dead limbs, pecking and digging out boring insects for food. Besides oak trees it also gives attention to gray pines, streamside cottonwoods, and even apple trees in orchards. In the latter places, Nuttall's and Downy Woodpeckers may be near one another.

DOWNY WOODPECKER   *Picoides pubescens*

Length 6.5 in., wing span 12 in.; above black, but wings white-dotted and middle of back white; side of head with two white bars; below white; outer tail feathers white with small black bars; male with red on head. **CALL** is a soft *pik*. **NEST** is in a hole in a tree at 10 to 25 ft; eggs four to five, white.

DISTRIBUTION: Uncommon resident from Central Valley into lower Mixed Conifer Belt; rare on lower east slope. Prefers willow, cottonwood, or hardwood groves near streams, but can be found in adjacent oak and pine forests.

REMARKS: The smallest Sierra woodpecker is the Downy, looking like a diminutive version of the Hairy Woodpecker. It is not common, seldom calls, and seems to have a restricted range. Once a bird is located it can usually be found repeatedly in the same forage area. The Downy makes small irregularly placed pits in bark when digging out insects for food. Larger holes excavated in trees or branches that are well advanced in decay are used for nesting or night shelter.

HAIRY WOODPECKER   *Picoides villosus*
Pl. 432

Length 9.25 in., wing span 15 in.; patterned like Downy Woodpecker except that outer tail feathers are pure white; male has red on back of head. **CALL** is a single sharp *speenk*. **NEST** is in a hole dug in a tree; eggs three to six, white.

DISTRIBUTION: Resident from foothill woodlands into the Subalpine Belt; widespread on east slope at least south to northern Inyo County. Inhabits partly open conifer forests and also deciduous trees along streams and meadow edges.

REMARKS: The Hairy Woodpecker occurs widely in forests. It digs or flakes off bark to find insect larvae, more often in dying or dead trees where these are common. In spring when courting, the male frequently utters a staccato run of notes, *spenk-ter-ter-ter,* and drums on a resonant tree. Young just out of the nest may call noisily, but in other seasons this species is rather quiet.

WHITE-HEADED WOODPECKER   *Picoides albolarvatus*
Pl. 433

Length 9.25 in., wing span 16 in.; plumage all black except white forehead and throat and white patch on wing (best seen in flight); male with red arc on back of head. **CALL** is a high sharp *wi-ek,* repeated when excited. **NEST** is in a hole, often in a dead tree stub at 5 to 15 ft; eggs three to seven, white.

DISTRIBUTION: Common from Mixed Conifer Belt into the lower Upper Montane Belt, found on both slopes but more common on west side; in conifer forests.

REMARKS: No woodpecker is so readily identified as the one with the conspicuous white head, which often perches within easy view and in some places is fairly common. It forages mostly on living pines and firs, feeding on both insects and conifer seeds. For nesting it uses upright stubs of dead trees that are hard on the outside but soft within. By pecking out innumerable short splinters a gourd-shaped cavity is dug, the entrance 1.5 to 2 in. in diameter and the interior 3 to 4 in. across by 12 to 16 in. deep. Mountain cabins are sometimes the targets of this excavating. The eggs and later the young, naked at hatching, rest on a lining of chips or rotted wood, which is kept clean by the parents. Both adults forage and bring food at short intervals so that the young become fledged and ready to emerge within a couple of weeks. Over the years the many holes of this and other woodpeckers serve chickadees, nuthatches, and perhaps pygmy-owls and flying squirrels for nests or shelters.

BLACK-BACKED WOODPECKER   *Picoides arcticus*
Pl. 434

Length 9.5 to 10 in., wing span 16 in.; above black; below white, barred with black on the flanks; one white bar on side of head; male has golden yellow crown. **CALL** is a single low *week* or *tup*. **NEST** is in a hole in a tree or stump; eggs four, white.

DISTRIBUTION: Sparse resident in Upper Montane and Subalpine Belts; may descend to lower elevations during cold winters. Shows a preference for lodgepole pines, especially in burned areas, but is nowhere predictable.

REMARKS: This woodpecker of northern boreal forests extends south down the spine of the Sierra Nevada, where it resides in high-elevation coniferous forests. Except when drilling for food or drumming during the courting season, it is quiet and may escape notice, making it a bird that birders treasure finding. It is one of few woodpeckers in the world that has only three toes on each foot (instead of the usual four).

NORTHERN FLICKER *Colaptes auratus*
Pl. 435

Length 13 in., wing span 20 in.; above brown, narrowly barred with black; below pale gray with many black dots and a black bar on breast; rump prominently white; wings and tail show dull red in flight (caused by red shaft on each feather); male shows red malar stripe. **CALL** is varied; a loud *claip* or *klee-ap;* in spring a rolling monotonous *kuk, kuk, kuk;* when two flickers meet, *yuck-a, yuck-a*. **NEST** is an excavated hole 2 in. in diameter, in a tree or stub often at 8 to 25 ft; eggs five to 12, shiny white.

DISTRIBUTION: Common in summer throughout the Sierra, absent only from higher alpine areas; in winter moves below level of heavy snow because they obtain much of their food on the ground. Prefer open forests with large scattered trees but are possible anywhere.

REMARKS: Unlike other woodpeckers, flickers forage on the ground for ants or grasshoppers and seek berries on various kinds of bushes in addition to foraging on tree trunks. Up to 45 percent of their diet consists of ants, especially large black carpenter ants (*Camponotus*) that are common on the forest floor. Their flight is strong and direct, with infrequent wing beats; upon alighting they may perch on a branch, bow deeply several times, and utter their explosive *klee-ap*. In winter, flickers typically occur in loose groups, probably a combination of local birds and birds that have migrated from the high mountains and from the north. Like other woodpeckers, flickers sleep in holes at night, and in winter they often drill under the eaves of buildings for such shelter.

PILEATED WOODPECKER *Dryocopus pileatus*

Length 16.5 to 18 in., wing span 29 in.; body black; pointed crest on head bright red; wing with large white patch under and smaller white patch above; long white stripe extending from bill down neck and onto sides of body; male has red malar. **CALL** is a loud series of low-pitched *kuk* notes in slow and irregular series, much like the Northern Flicker. **NEST** is in a hole well up in a tree; eggs three to four, white.

DISTRIBUTION: Common resident in Mixed Conifer Belt of west slope; uncommon at midelevations on east slope from Mono County north. Found in sizable tracts of mature coniferous forest.

REMARKS: These large woodpeckers with wild cries and flaming red crests are declining as mature forests of the Sierra Nevada are increasingly logged. They live mainly on conifers, digging carpenter ants and large beetle larvae from dead wood for food. When at work the noise is like that of someone pounding with an ax; its head can sweep an 8 in. arc and chips may be thrown fully 2 ft. The excavations often are several inches wide and some are as long as a person's forearm. The nest cavity is 6 in. in diameter by 18 in. deep and the entrance is 3 to 4 in. across. In flight the head is drawn back, the wings beat continuously, and the course is direct.

Tyrant Flycatchers (Family Tyrannidae)

OLIVE-SIDED FLYCATCHER   *Contopus cooperi*

Length 7.5 in., wing span 13 in.; large headed and short tailed; plumage olive brown above with two white tufts on sides of rump (occasionally hidden by wings); white under with dingy flanks, creating a dark-vested appearance.

CALL is a soft *puck,* two or three times, mostly at evening; the song is a loud *wher, wheé, whew.*

NEST is usually in conifers at 60 to 70 ft, made of twigs, leaflets, and moss; eggs three to four, creamy with brown blotches.

DISTRIBUTION: Fairly common summer visitor to coniferous forests at nearly all elevations except the very highest; often seen at lower elevations during migration. Favors areas where tall conifers give sweeping views of open areas.

REMARKS: In mid-May these flycatchers may be noted migrating along both sides of the Sierra to their summer homes in the main coniferous forest belt. When finally settled on breeding grounds they perch on treetops, greeting the earliest dawn with a three-syllabled song that sounds like *what peeves you,* and giving at dusk the softer call note. From treetops they also actively circle out to capture large insects in the highest airspace used by any of the Sierra flycatchers. At summer's end they depart quickly and are gone by late August.

WESTERN WOOD-PEWEE   *Contopus sordidulus*
Pl. 436

Length 6.5 in., wing span 10.5 in.; overall dingy gray brown, slightly paler throat and belly. Very similar to the Willow Flycatcher in appearance but has longer wing tips that reach halfway down the tail on a perched bird. **CALL** is a rough, slightly melancholy *peeer;* song mixes this distinctive call with *tswee-tee-teet* phrases. **NEST** is on a horizontal limb at 15 to 40 ft, made of a well-formed cup of plant fibers and grasses; eggs three, white, brown-blotched.

DISTRIBUTION: Common summer visitor from Foothill Belt up to Subalpine Belt of both slopes; in open forest or woodland.

REMARKS: The Western Wood-pewee is the commonest and most widely distributed of Sierra flycatchers and is the plainest in garb, with no special white markings. Plaintive wood-pewee calls are one of the Sierra's characteristic sounds during the lazy days of summer, extending from before daybreak to the final evening chorus. During May they migrate in numbers through the lower elevations and are soon settled for the summer. Their main haunt is the airspace 15 to 40 ft high where they feed on a wide variety of small flying insects. Nesting begins in May and continues until the end of July. By mid-September all have gone southward.

Small Flycatchers (Genus *Empidonax*)
Pl. 437

Length 5 to 6 in., wing span 8 to 8.75 in.; bill small, flattish; most with a white ring around eye and two dull white bars on wing; different species are olive green to ashy gray above, and yellowish to gray below.

REMARKS: Five species of these little flycatchers visit the Sierra for the summer. They are similar in size, with only minor differences in color. Each has rather different calls, and for nesting each occupies a particular habitat (see following accounts). In late summer, however, some stray elsewhere, even to high elevations, before migrating southward; this is an especially tricky time to identify these difficult species. All these species have the usual habits of perching in rather upright postures while watching for passing prey, flicking their tails and wings at intervals, and darting on short circling flights to capture insects.

WILLOW FLYCATCHER　　　　　　　　　　　　　　　　*E. traillii*

Brownish above, more so than other *Empidonax* in the Sierra, also the only one lacking eyerings and distinct wing bars; pale gray to whitish below, with white throat; lower mandible all orange. **CALL** is a soft but distinct *whit,'* sometimes repeated two or three times; song is sneezy *fitz-bew* often repeated. **NEST** is low in dense willow thickets; cuplike, made of grasses and plant fibers; always over water or damp ground.

DISTRIBUTION: Formerly common in lower foothills, now very rare and localized, found primarily around Lake Isabella on the Kern River and in scattered mountain meadows throughout the rest of the Sierra Nevada. Widespread during migration, especially in riparian zones. State Endangered (nesting).

HAMMOND'S FLYCATCHER   *E. hammondii*

Grayish with olive tinge, paler below; lower mandible orange with dusky tip. **CALL** is a sharp *peek;* song *see'wit, see-vrk, grr-vik;* slightly rougher than the very similar Dusky song. **NEST** is on horizontal limb at 15 ft or higher, made of plant fibers.

DISTRIBUTION: Summer visitor in Mixed Conifer and Upper Montane Belts, mostly on west slope; less common at higher and lower elevations; found in dense, shady coniferous forests; perches at 20 to 100 ft.

GRAY FLYCATCHER   *E. wrightii*

Silvery gray with faint hints of olive tinge; longish bill, lower mandible orange with sharply demarcated blackish tip. Easily identified by behavior of dipping its tail downward while perched. **CALL** is a sharp *whit;* song of two phrases, a strong *chi-wip* and liquid *whilp* in varied combination. **NEST** is in tall sagebrush, a deep cup of grasses, and other materials.

DISTRIBUTION: Summer visitor on east slope from Inyo County north in Sagebrush Belt, occurs locally on the Kern Plateau; sometimes near forest edges.

DUSKY FLYCATCHER   *E. oberholseri*

Virtually identical to Hammond's; wing tips slightly shorter; lores noticeably paler. **CALL** is a *pit,* or *swee'pit;* song lisping, *see'pit, ggrrreep, see'pit, psuweet.* **NEST** is low in small trees or shrubs at 15 ft or less, made of plant and bark fibers.

DISTRIBUTION: Common summer visitor on both slopes from lower Mixed Conifer Belt into Subalpine Belt; a bird of sunny open woodlands, rocky outcrops, and brush habitats; perching at 10 to 30 ft in nearby trees.

PACIFIC-SLOPE FLYCATCHER   *E. difficilis*

Above olive green; below yellowish; prominent almond-shaped pale eyering; lower mandible mainly orange. **CALL** is a clear whistled *swee'p;* song is a thin, high-pitched *see'rip, sip, see'rip,* repeated. **NEST** is in low trees or stumps or on ledges, a cup of rootlets, moss, and other materials.

DISTRIBUTION: Summer visitor in Mixed Conifer Belt on west slope, less common at slightly higher and lower elevations; prefers lush streamside forests of mixed tree species.

BLACK PHOEBE   *Sayornis nigricans*

Pl. 438

Length 6.75 in., wing span 11 in.; solid jet black except for crisp white belly. **CALL** is a single plaintive *pser;* the song has two pairs of similar notes, with alternate rising and falling inflection. **NEST** is on ledge of rock or flat surface on a building, a cup made of mud pellets mixed with grass; eggs three to five, white.

DISTRIBUTION: Common resident on west slope up to lower edge of Mixed Conifer Belt; summer visitor in Owens Valley; in open woodlands, especially along rock-bordered streams or around old buildings and under bridges near water.

REMARKS: The Black Phoebe is able to find insect food at all seasons and to live year-round in the Sierra. In spring it lives near water to obtain mud for nest making. Then it forages over a stream or pool and even takes insects from the water surface in low swooping flights. In winter the bird occurs more widely, being the only flycatcher to brave cold winter above the low foothills. This phoebe commonly sits in exposed places, on streamside rocks, on bare branches or twigs, and on the roofs of small buildings, but in the heat of summer it seeks shady perches. Because of its special nesting needs it is of less uniform occurrence than many other birds, although bridges and buildings have increased the places where it can live.

SAY'S PHOEBE   *Sayornis saya*

Length 7.5 in., wing span 13 in.; size and form of Black Phoebe; top of head dark brown; back grayish brown; tail blackish; throat and breast gray, belly cinnamon. **CALL** is a long plaintive *pee-ur;* song is fast *pit-tse-ar.* **NEST** is on shallow ledge on rock faces or human structures, a bulky shallow cup of grass stems lined with hair; eggs four to five, white, pear shaped.

DISTRIBUTION: Summer visitor locally in low foothills of west slope and along east base of Sierra; nests on east slope but wanders after nesting season; some winter in Foothill Belt. Dry open areas in sagebrush, grasslands, or forest edges.

REMARKS: This brownish phoebe nests and forages in dry areas largely devoid of trees and shrubs. Here it uses the few elevated perches as lookout points to scan for insects, but it will hover in midair if a perch is not present. In winter it appears in the low western foothills, perching on rocky outcrops and earthen bluffs. Arrives on breeding grounds as early as late February and moves to wintering areas in October.

ASH-THROATED FLYCATCHER   *Myiarchus cinerascens*

Length 8.25 in., wing span 12 in.; head with small bushy crest, body slender, tail long; head and back grayish brown; closed wing with two dull white bars; breast light gray; belly white, yellow tinged; spread wings and tail show reddish brown. **CALL** is a throaty *ker* or *ker-cherr'* of descending pitch, sounding like a referee's whistle; song a loud burry *ka-brick,* often repeated at short intervals. **NEST** is in holes of trees or stumps, lined with grass, rootlets, feathers, and often cast snakeskins; eggs four to five, creamy, with fine dark lines or spots.

DISTRIBUTION: Fairly common summer visitor at lower elevations of west slope, rare on east slope; in a wide variety of scrub and open woodland habitats.

REMARKS: The slender form, slight crest, long tail, and rather upright posture make the Ash-throated easy to recognize. It is the only flycatcher that regularly patrols chaparral areas, where it forages low over the vegetation. Unlike others of its kind, the bird makes frequent changes of position and hunts over a relatively large area, as opposed to returning repeatedly to the same perch. Being a cavity nester, it must live in places having trees with decay cavities or abandoned woodpecker holes where the eggs can be incubated and the young reared.

WESTERN KINGBIRD
Tyrannus verticalis

Length 8 to 9.5 in., wing span 15.5 in.; head large; upper surface and breast light gray, throat paler; belly yellow; wings dark brown; tail black with white margin on outermost feathers; crown of male with concealed red. **CALL** is a sharp *whit,* and loud harsh bickering notes that also form the basis of a hard, squeaky song. **NEST** is of a diameter to 6 in., made of grasses and weed stems, in trees or bushes, even on fence posts; eggs three to five, creamy, brown blotched.

DISTRIBUTION: Summer visitor along both sides of Sierra (more numerous on west slope) in dry open grasslands and woodlands with scattered trees, poles, or posts for lookouts. Makes rare appearances as high as treeline during both spring and fall migration.

REMARKS: The kingbird, like any flycatcher, sits on exposed perches and watches for flying insects with frequent turns of the head. When one passes nearby, the bird darts out and snaps it in the bill, then resumes watching from the same or another perch. This species also catches grasshoppers on the ground. Kingbirds arrive in April or May and live in more open areas than other flycatchers. They resent intrusion of their territories and will take after an approaching crow, heron, or owl, hovering and pecking at the larger bird while uttering harsh cries. If a person approaches a kingbird nest, the parents, sometimes joined by other pairs, will flutter overhead, voicing their protest, and the male may flash his red crown feathers. After the nesting season some kingbirds wander into the mountains for a while, but all depart southward by August or September.

Shrike (Family Laniidae)

LOGGERHEAD SHRIKE
Lanius ludovicianus

Pl. 439

Length 8 to 10 in., wing span 12 in.; dark gray above; pale gray below; black mask; wing black but shows broad white patch in flight; tail black centrally but tip and margins white. **CALL** is a harsh *skree,* often repeated; spring song is somewhat varied, consisting of harsh squeaks and warbles. **NEST** is in trees at moderate height, bulky but compact, of twigs and other materials, felted with hair or feathers; eggs five to seven, grayish or greenish white, brown-speckled.

DISTRIBUTION: Formerly common resident at low elevations throughout the Sierra region; occasionally wanders to Upper Montane Belt in late summer; in large mountain meadows and other open areas where exposed perches are available. State and Federal Species of Special Concern.

REMARKS: Shrikes are stocky songbirds with sharply hooked bills that hunt down prey like small raptors. They feed on grasshoppers, crickets, ground beetles and similar insects, some mice, and occasionally small songbirds. Because they lack talons for holding prey, they impale food on spines to hold it in place while they tear off bite-size pieces. Except when nesting, they live solitarily and widely dispersed. Favor perches at 4 to 15 ft on exposed tree limbs, wires, or posts where they can watch the open ground beneath for prey. When changing position they fly low over the ground, then up onto a new lookout.

Vireos (Family Vireonidae)

CASSIN'S VIREO   *Vireo cassinii*

Length 5 to 5.5 in., wing span 9.5 in.; grayish green above; whitish below with dingy yellow flanks; strong white eyering that extends over bill; two vague white bars on wing. **CALL** is a harsh *chee,* repeated; song is a burry *suweet, seeoo, seeoowip,* cadence often transcribed as *question, answer, so what!* **NEST** is in oak or conifer at 5 to 30 ft, a basket lashed in twig crotch, made of plant fibers, exterior decorated with petals, spider web, and other materials; eggs three to five, white, few dark spots.

DISTRIBUTION: Common summer visitor at middle elevations on both slopes; in oak and conifer forests; widespread during migration.

REMARKS: During April and May, these vireos are migrants through foothill woodlands before they settle down to nest in the main conifer belt. At the end of summer some wander higher before departing southward. In the nesting period they inhabit oaks and conifers on rather dry slopes but may also live in mature cottonwoods or alders. These vireos keep to open places under the canopy, and their movements are rather deliberate as they forage. May continue singing until late July and leave the Sierra by October. All vireos are characterized in having rather stout bills with tiny hooked tips.

HUTTON'S VIREO   *Vireo huttoni*

Length 5 in., wing span 8 in.; plumage brown olive, slightly paler below; diffuse eyering but lacks strong spectacles of Cassin's Vireo; two vague white bars on wing. **CALL** is a low, harsh squeal; song is monotonously repeated *zree* notes. **NEST** is in oak, hung from small forked branch, mainly of moss; eggs four, white, brown dotted.

DISTRIBUTION: Fairly common resident in Foothill and lower Mixed Conifer Belts on west slope; in oaks, especially live oaks.

REMARKS: This vireo resembles a Ruby-crowned Kinglet in coloration but is more deliberate in movements and has a stout bill with a tiny hooked tip. This vireo lives and nests in the evergreen oaks of the lower west slope but may wander into the Mixed Conifer Belt during winter.

WARBLING VIREO   *Vireo gilvus*
Pl. 440

Length 5 to 5.5 in., wing span 8.5 in.; grayish above, slightly paler below, with faint greenish yellow tones; best recognized by broad, diffuse white eyeline. **CALL** is a throaty *zree;* song is a bright, sustained warbling with continued repetition. **NEST** is in a tree, hung in small crotch, made of plant fibers and bark strips; eggs three to five, white, with dark brown dots.

DISTRIBUTION: Common summer visitor throughout the Sierra below the Upper Montane Belt; found mostly in deciduous trees near streams but also in conifer forests.

REMARKS: In spring and early summer the voluble warbling songs of these vireos are a major part of the bird chorus along many stream borders, but until you know their songs they are not conspicuous. They are likely to be heard in midday, when other species are quiet, and the male even sings when sitting on eggs. These are the commonest of local vireos, but nest parasitism by Brown-headed Cowbirds has greatly impacted their populations (as well as those of other vireos, especially Least Bell's Vireo, which has been extirpated from the Sierra). They usually forage and sing well up in the trees, although the nest may be lower.

Jays and Crows (Family Corvidae)

STELLER'S JAY   *Cyanocitta stelleri*
Pl. 441

Length 12 in., wing span 19 in.; sooty black head and crest; rest of body dark blue, wings and tail show narrow black bars. **CALL** extremely variable, includes a loud harsh *ksch, kschak,* or *glook,* each in threes; a whistled *skwee-oo;* a low crackling *ker-r-r-r-r;* a "squeaky wheelbarrow" note; rarely a faint whisper song. In addition to this varied repertoire, also an accomplished mimic that imitates the calls of many other Sierra birds. **NEST** is in conifers at 8 to 40 ft, diameter to 12 in., made of twigs with mud, lined with needles or grass; eggs three to five, greenish with olive brown spots.

DISTRIBUTION: Common resident throughout the Sierra from Mixed Conifer Belt into Upper Montane Belt, occurs even higher in areas of human activity; less numerous on east slope; many move to lower levels in winter; mainly in coniferous woods.

REMARKS: Noisy, pompously crested Steller's Jays are mostly solitary, or in pairs while nesting, but gather in numbers to vocalize around an owl or another unusual subject. In winter they forage in large loose flocks. Much of their time is spent in trees, where they ascend from branch to branch as if going up a staircase, perch momentarily at a high lookout, then glide on spread wings and tail to the base of another tree. They also forage on the ground. These jays are quiet and stealthy while nesting but return to their noisy habits once their broods fledge. Their diet is varied: seeds, nuts, and acorns; insects and other small animals, and food gleaned at camps and resorts. In nesting season they often eat the eggs or young of small birds; a jay or two near such a nest may bring complaining calls from various smaller birds nearby.

WESTERN SCRUB-JAY   *Aphelocoma californica*
Pl. 442

Length 12 in., wing span 15.5 in.; tail and upper parts bright blue, with gray back; thin white eyeline; white under except for blue half collar. **CALL** is varied; includes a familiar raspy *shreep*, in a short series. **NEST** is in low trees or shrubs at 3 to 40 ft, made of long twigs, lined with rootlets or hair; eggs four to six, green with darker green dots or buff with red dots.

DISTRIBUTION: Abundant resident in Foothill Belt up into lower edge of Mixed Conifer Belt where oaks are present; sparse resident on east slope in pinyon pines and junipers; seldom wanders to high elevations in late summer as many other low-elevation birds do.

REMARKS: This avian busybody of foothill woodlands is easy to see and hear. Often it stands alertly with feet spread, head up, and tail level or tilted upward; again it will perch motionless for minutes with the tail hanging vertically. Being bold and curious, it watches all local events and is quick to dash off in noisy flight and investigate. If an owl or another predator is sighted, the bird's excited calls promptly bring other jays to the spot. The varied vocabulary evidently is meaningful to others of the species. In the spring season, however, the pairs are silent and secretive within their nesting areas. Then they eat insects and the eggs or young of small birds. Otherwise acorns are their staple diet. Besides those eaten, the jays bury many acorns singly in the soil; some are later recovered and eaten, but others remain to sprout and grow.

PINYON JAY   *Gymnorhinus cyanocephalus*

Length 10 to 11.75 in., wing span 19 in.; above dull blue, somewhat lighter blue below; no crest or special markings. **CALL** is a high nasal *kä'-e,* singly or repeated. **NEST** is in pinyon pines or junipers, at 10 to 50 ft, made of twigs, with deep felted cup; eggs four to five, bluish white with fine dots or streaks.

DISTRIBUTION: Locally fairly common residents along entire east base of Sierra; in pinyon pines or junipers and sagebrush; casual visitor on west slope.

REMARKS: Pinyon Jays, unlike other jays, are gregarious and even nest in loose colonies. At all seasons the birds live and forage in loose flocks of four to 40 or more. Nuts of pinyon and other pines are preferred food throughout the year, supplemented with grasshoppers and other insects while feeding young. The flocks are prone to wander in late summer and fall, and if the pine nut crops fail these flocks may cross over onto the west slope. Members of a feeding flock indulge in much conversational calling.

CLARK'S NUTCRACKER   *Nucifraga columbiana*
Pl. 443

Length 12 to 13 in., wing span 24 in.; head and body light gray; wings black with large white patch at rear margin; tail white except black central feathers. **CALL** is a harsh nasal cawing, *kayr* or *kra-a,* often prolonged, repeated irregularly; softer calls by young. **NEST** is in conifers at 8 to 40 ft, of twigs and bark; eggs two to three, pale green, sparingly flecked.

DISTRIBUTION: Common resident of high mountain forests (mostly above 9,000 ft), mostly nesting on east slope; occasionally wanders to lower elevations in winter; in treetops of open forest and on ground.

REMARKS: Nutcrackers are a familiar and conspicuous bird of upper sun-drenched slopes. They seek prominent lookouts in the tops of conifers, do much restless flying, call loudly and often, and hang out around campgrounds where they have earned the nickname "camp robbers." Nesting begins in snowbound March, nestlings are fed in April or May, and fully fledged young accompany their parents by June. Thereafter nutcrackers live in loose, straggling companies. The staple diet is of pine nuts picked or pried out of cones, each bird burying as many as 98,000 surplus nuts in the soil as a safeguard against winter shortages. Other food includes seeds, carrion, and insects. Nutcrackers take some flying insects in the manner of a flycatcher. The birds also glean tidbits of food in camps or at high mountain resorts.

BLACK-BILLED MAGPIE   *Pica hudsonia*
Pl. 444

Length 16 to 20 in., wing span 24 to 25 in.; plumage iridescent black showing beautiful green and purple tones in the sunlight; belly and shoulder patches sharply white. **CALL** is varied, harsh or soft; *qua, qua,* two to six times. **NEST** is in trees at up to 50 ft, bulky ball of twigs up to 24 in. diameter, with side entrance; eggs five to eight, grayish green with olive brown spots.

DISTRIBUTION: Common resident locally along base of east slope.

REMARKS: Magpies are gregarious, living where trees (or bushes) for roosting and nesting are near open grasslands or fields and the birds can find insects or seeds for food. On the ground they either walk or hop, the tail being held horizontally. The relatively quiet Black-billed Magpie occurs in the Great Basin and lower east slope in open valleys with trees or large bushes.

OTHER MAGPIES: The talkative Yellow-billed Magpie (*P. nuttalli*) lives in the Central Valley and some open spots in the western foothills. Physically the two differ only in the color of bill.

AMERICAN CROW   *Corvus brachyrhynchos*
Pl. 445

Length 17 to 20 in., wing span 39 in.; plumage glossy black; tail is square tipped. **CALL** is a loud harsh *caw* or *karr.* **NEST** is in trees, often hidden, a large cup of twigs lined with bark strips or grasses; eggs five to six, green, brown-blotched.

DISTRIBUTION: Common resident locally in Central Valley and lower edge of western foothills, seen rarely at higher elevations during spring and fall; uncommon on east slope in small pockets but absent over large areas.

REMARKS: Crows are not of uniform occurrence. Flocks live in certain areas over the years, but other places that seem of equal character are unoccupied. While foraging, the birds range over open flat country where both insects and various plant foods are available. For nesting, and roosting at night, they seek substantial trees fairly resistant to swaying by wind. In winter they use groves of densely spaced trees, often in residential areas, where members of a large flock can roost close together.

COMMON RAVEN   *Corvus corax*
Pl. 446

Length 24 in., wing span 53 in.; plumage glossy black; tail wedge shaped. **CALL** is a deep throaty *croak.* **NEST** is on cliffs, made of sticks with lined depression; eggs five to six, green, brown spotted.

DISTRIBUTION: Rather uncertain because expanding into new areas. Formerly restricted mainly to open foothills in the southern Sierra but now widespread.

REMARKS: The rapid spread of ravens in the Sierra is illustrated by the fact that in 1950 they had never been reported in Yosemite National Park; today they are conspicuous and regularly encountered. Elsewhere, they have become increasingly common in the foothills of the northern Sierra since 1990. Ravens seem particularly adept at monopolizing human-altered landscapes, following roads into new landscapes and finding a steady supply of food in birds and mammals killed along those roads. Intelligent and playful, ravens are often seen engaging in acrobatic chases and dives.

Lark (Family Alaudidae)

HORNED LARK   *Eremophila alpestris*
Pl. 447

Length 6.5 to 7 in., wing span 12 in.; sandy brown above with faint dark gray streaks; whitish below, tinged yellow and rufous; black collar on throat; face yellow with black mask; tail blackish with white outer edge; male has short black "horn" (of feathers) above each eye. **CALL** is a faint high *see* or *see-tle;* song is a tinkling *teet, toot, teet-teetle-eetle-ettle* when bird circles in air. **NEST** is on open ground in scant cover, a depression lined with grasses; eggs two to five, gray green, with brown blotches.

DISTRIBUTION: On open areas of lower west and east slopes of Sierra and more rarely at high elevations above treeline; inhabits open, sparse grassland and brushland.

REMARKS: Wide, open areas with sparse surface vegetation are the home of these larks. Here their pale feathering blends closely with the ground color. They walk with a slight sidewise swaying of the body and fore-and-aft movement of the head. Horned larks are commonly found in loose flocks, even in the nesting season when several pairs will often mingle during their daily activities. On taking flight the birds may scatter in low undulating flight, then wheel about and come together again near the place from which they started. Their food is mostly seeds picked from the ground, a little green vegetation, and some insects.

Swallows (Family Hirundinidae)

TREE SWALLOW · *Tachycineta bicolor*
Pl. 448

Length 5 to 6.25 in., wing span 14.5 in.; blackish above with steel blue iridescence; white below; females duller than males. **CALL** is a faint *seet,* sometimes repeated as a twitter. **NEST** is in holes in trees or buildings, lined with grasses and feathers; eggs four to six, white.

DISTRIBUTION: Summer visitor on both slopes of Sierra, breeding as high as Upper Montane Belt; often near standing water and mountain meadows.

REMARKS: These fairly common and widespread swallows lack the white rump marks of the similar Violet-green. They live near quiet water, perching on exposed twigs of the tree in which their nest cavities are located. Arriving early in March and staying through September, these hardy swallows sometimes winter in the Central Valley. Unlike other swallows, they can feed on berries and seeds if insects are not available.

VIOLET-GREEN SWALLOW · *Tachycineta thalassina*
Pl. 449

Length 4.75 to 5.5 in., wing span 13.5 in.; bronzy or emerald green above, violet on rump; white below, extending up onto sides of head and rump; female slightly duller. **CALL** is a plaintive *tsee,* sometimes repeated. **NEST** is in cavities of trees, cliffs, or buildings, lined with grasses and feathers; eggs four to five, white.

DISTRIBUTION: Common summer visitor throughout the Sierra, less common at higher elevations. Seen in huge numbers during fall migration, when thousands may be seen streaming overhead or perching on telephone wires and fences.

REMARKS: Often forages much higher in the air than other swallows but is sometimes seen with Tree Swallows and White-throated Swifts, when the differences in form and manner of flight between swallow and swift are evident. For nesting the Violet-green uses either natural cavities or woodpecker holes in trees or small crevices in cliffs. The species is present from mid-February to mid-October, though they are most common from April to early September.

NORTHERN ROUGH-WINGED SWALLOW *Stelgidopteryx serripennis*
Pl. 450

Length 5 to 5.75 in., wing span 14 in.; drab gray brown above; paler below, tending toward white near tail. **CALL** is a repeated rough *prrit*. **NEST** is solitary, or in loose groups at suitable sites, burrows dug into earth or sand banks, occasionally in crevices or holes in human structures; eggs six to seven, white.

DISTRIBUTION: Fairly common on both slopes at low elevations, ranging up to lower Mixed Conifer Belt on west slope.

REMARKS: These modestly colored birds are noted for their ability to skim low over the ground, seldom climbing higher into the sky, as do other swallows. Rather solitary, they rarely flock and spend most of their time working marshy areas near their nest sites. Because they mainly use earthen banks for nest sites, this somewhat limits their distribution. A late migrant compared to other swallows, they don't arrive in numbers until mid-April then quickly leave once their young are raised.

CLIFF SWALLOW   *Petrochelidon pyrrhonota*

Length 5 to 6 in., wing span 13.5 in.; dark bluish brown above except for orange rump and creamy white forehead; light gray under; dusky red on sides of face. **CALL** while feeding, is a low *shurr;* when disturbed at nest, a plaintive *kleer,* repeated; song of squeaky notes. **NEST** is in colonies on rough cliffs or under bridges and the eaves of buildings; spherical gourd with narrow-necked opening, made of mud pellets; eggs three to six, creamy with brown spots.

DISTRIBUTION: Common summer visitor at lower elevations on both eastern and western sides of the Sierra crest, locally abundant around nest colonies; forages in open.

REMARKS: These highly colonial swallows originally made nests on cliffs but now commonly use the spaces under building eaves or bridges, crowding dozens to hundreds of nests together at favorable sites. Each nest is made of thousands of mud pellets gathered singly at some water margin. The narrowed roundish entrance at the top leads into an expanded chamber provided with slight fibrous lining. Nests are safe from most enemies, but the birds will fly about and utter complaining cries if a person approaches a colony. On the west slope adults arrive in March but nesting is delayed until early May. By then flying insects are more abundant, so that the swallows can alternate feeding with nest building, incubation, and caring for the young.

BARN SWALLOW
Pl. 451
Hirundo rustica

Length 7 in., wing span 15 in.; shiny dark blue above; forehead and under-surface reddish brown; breast with bluish half collar; tail long, slender, and deeply forked. **CALL** is a series of twittering notes, both musical and throaty. **NEST** is on flat beams or ledges in buildings or under bridges; an open cup of mud, grass, and feathers; eggs four to five, white with brown spots.

DISTRIBUTION: Common summer visitor locally on west slope into Mixed Conifer Belt, occasionally higher; uncommon along east base of Sierra; near water where nesting sites are present.

REMARKS: Barn Swallows are immediately recognizable by their long, needlelike tails that are often fanned out during dexterous flying maneuvers. When one perches on a twig or wire, the pointed tips of the two wings and the two long, outermost tail feathers are evident. Apparently, their nesting range has expanded upslope in response to abundant nesting sites available around human structures. The species is present from March until mid-September but some stay later than other swallows.

Chickadees and Titmice (Family Paridae)

MOUNTAIN CHICKADEE
Pls. 452, 455
Poecile gambeli

Length 5 to 5.5 in., wing span 8.5 in.; cap, eyeline, and throat black; face and eyebrow white; body gray. **CALL** is a wheezy *chick-a-dee-dee,* or *chee-chee-chee;* song, *tee-tee, too-too;* alarm, a sharp *tsik-a.* **NEST** is in tree cavities or old woodpecker holes; eggs five to eight, white.

DISTRIBUTION: Resident from Mixed Conifer Belt to Subalpine Belt, found on both slopes; some descend to lower elevations in winter but they are the most common bird in subalpine forests during winter; mainly in open woods.

REMARKS: Ever active and acrobatic, little chickadees spend most daylight hours scanning the outer foliage and twigs of conifers and oaks for their minute insect food, often hanging inverted to do so. Their foraging is mostly within 50 ft of the ground, sometimes in shrubs or in tree cavities, but rarely on the ground. In April or May each pair chooses a small territory, looks into many recesses, and usually selects a nest hole 2 to 10 ft above ground, often one dug by a woodpecker. The bottom is felted with mammal hair or feathers. The female incubates persistently, being fed by the male. After the broods are abroad, chickadees form loose bands of their own kind or with other small birds. During the winter they drift slowly through the trees, feeding and calling often to keep in touch with one another. Suet, bacon, or peanut butter hung up near a cabin will often attract chickadees.

OTHER CHICKADEES: The Chestnut-backed Chickadee (*P. rufescens,* length 4.75 in.) is a very recent arrival in the Sierra Nevada, invading the region from the Cascade Mountains of Oregon. It is now common in middle elevation forests on the west slope south to Madera County and apparently still expanding southward. Lacks the white eyebrow of Mountain Chickadees, but is more readily recognized by its bright rufous back and flanks.

OAK TITMOUSE   *Baeolophus inornatus*

Length 5 to 5.5 in., wing span 9 in.; plain grayish brown above, paler below; head with erect tapered crest. **CALL** is wheezy and chickadee-like; song is a sharp, *peet'-o*, three to five times in quick succession. **NEST** is in natural cavities or woodpecker holes in trees; eggs six to eight, white, sometimes reddish spotted.

DISTRIBUTION: Common resident in Foothill Belt on west slope; in oak woodlands.

REMARKS: These somber-garbed relatives of the chickadees are lively and highly inquisitive. While their crests are habitually erect, they can be raised or lowered according to the bird's mood. They forage, upright or inverted, mainly in the outer foliage of oaks, sometimes in pines, and occasionally in brush or on the ground. The male's shrill repeated song is a feature of foothill woodlands at nesting time. Broods accompany the parents for a few weeks after emerging; thereafter titmice live mostly in pairs, apparently mating for life. The food, minute insects, is gleaned from twigs, leaves, and crevices; they also peck open acorns with their stout little bills.

OTHER TITMICE: The closely related Juniper Titmouse (*B. griseus*), only recently elevated to species status, is a bird of Great Basin pinyon pine and juniper woodlands. Its exact range is still being worked out but it lives within eyesight of the Sierra Nevada and may wander onto its slopes at times. Recognized as being a grayer bird that lacks the brownish tones of the Oak Titmouse.

Bushtit (Family Aegithalidae)

BUSHTIT   *Psaltriparus minimus*
Pl. 453

Length 4 to 4.5 in., wing span 6 in.; plain gray above, paler below; cap brownish; tiny blackish bill; noticeably long tail for such a small bird. **CALL** is a low *pst, pst,* variously inflected, and often insistently given. **NEST** is usually in oaks; a gourdlike sac 8 to 9 in. long, entrance at side near top, woven of spider web, mosses, lichens, plant down, and other materials; eggs five to seven, white.

DISTRIBUTION: Common resident in Foothill Belt, mostly below ponderosa pines on the west slope and Jeffrey pines on the east slope; sometimes nests in higher forests; many wander upslope after nesting and may even remain at higher elevations through winter; inhabits foliage of oaks and tall shrubs.

REMARKS: This tiny mite of a bird is hardly larger than a hummingbird. Except when nesting, Bushtits live in loose flocks of 10 to 50, forming noisy roving bands that work slowly through the foliage calling almost constantly to keep in touch with each other. The birds perch upright or inverted while scanning leaves for the minute insects taken as food. If a hawk or other enemy is sighted, all the birds freeze motionless and utter a special "confusion chorus" note. Unlike related chickadees and titmice, Bushtits build their own nest, a gray socklike structure hung from a small branch. Even after the young birds fledge, the entire family may return to sleep at night in the warm nest.

Nuthatches (Family Sittidae)

RED-BREASTED NUTHATCH **Sitta canadensis**

Pls. 454, 455

Length 4 to 4.75 in., wing span 8.5 in.; bluish gray above; reddish brown under (verging on bright orange red in males); cap and eyeline black; white eyebrow and face. **CALL** is a high nasal *yank,* singly at intervals, but repeated quickly when disturbed. **NEST** is in a hole of a tree at 5 to 40 ft, with soft lining; eggs four to seven, white, brown spotted.

DISTRIBUTION: Common resident of midelevation conifer forests; most abundant in Mixed Conifer and Upper Montane Belts of west slope, but nest at both higher and lower elevations and in comparable forests on east slope; after nesting season wanders unpredictably to nearly all habitats, many wintering at lower elevations on west slope and sometimes also on east slope.

REMARKS: In summer these nuthatches are primarily restricted to tall shady conifer forests. Their clear, far-carrying calls suggest children's trumpets or elfin horns. If disturbed by the presence of a jay or other marauder, they launch into excited calls, sometimes for several minutes. Their food consists of small insects gleaned from bark as well as conifer seeds and acorns. They excavate a new nest hole each year in soft decayed wood and sometimes smear pitch around the entrance to ward off predators.

WHITE-BREASTED NUTHATCH **Sitta carolinensis**

Pls. 455, 456

Length 5 to 6 in., wing span 11 in.; cap and back of neck black; back and tail bluish gray; face and underparts white. **CALL** of west slope subspecies is a nasal *keer,* while subspecies on east slope give a series of high-pitched notes *yidididididi.* **NEST** is in old woodpecker hole or decayed cavity, lined with hair, feathers, or leaves; eggs five to nine, white, brown spotted at large end.

DISTRIBUTION: Common resident on both slopes; west-slope subspecies ranges from Central Valley up to Mixed Conifer Belt, east-slope subspecies ranges up and over the crest into Upper Montane Belt on west slope; prefers open forests with well-spaced trees.

REMARKS: These nuthatches are the largest of our three species. They usually forage within 20 ft of the ground, on rough-barked trees, most commonly on oaks but also on some conifers. By use of their stout, curved claws they hitch either upward or downward, not using their tails for support. Their sturdy bills serve variously to probe for insects, to open nuts on occasion, and to enlarge nest holes. They scan crevices and holes for food, exceptionally catching insects in flight, calling softly at irregular intervals. For nesting this species often uses a hole within 10 or 15 ft of the ground.

PYGMY NUTHATCH *Sitta pygmaea*

Length 3.8 to 4.5 in., wing span 7.75 in.; dull blackish cap; blue gray above; whitish below with buff tinge. **CALL** is a high rapid series of *peep* notes by members of flock. **NEST** is in a hole of a tree, lined with hair, feathers, and other materials; eggs four to nine, white, brown dotted.

DISTRIBUTION: Sparse resident of Mixed Conifer Belt on west slope and in Jeffrey pines of east slope; in open, parklike stands of large pines.

REMARKS: These diminutive nuthatches are of irregular and rather unpredictable occurrence. Save when nesting, they roam widely in small flocks that forage among the conifer needles and on the small outermost twigs in the manner of chickadees. When a flock is moving they create a babble of small voices, but while foraging the notes are few. The little birds commonly work at 75 ft or more above ground. Flocks often roost together in cavities to tolerate freezing cold nights.

Creeper (Family Certhiidae)

BROWN CREEPER *Certhia americana*
Pl. 455

Length 5.25 in., wing span 7.75 in.; dark brown above, streaked white and buff; dull white below; tail reddish, long stiff tips; bill longish and curved. **CALL** is a thin sibilant *see*; song is *see', see', se-teetle-te, see',* commonly transcribed as *trees, trees, beautiful trees.* **NEST** is behind loosened pieces of tree bark within 15 ft of ground, made of bark strips, twigs, feathers, and other materials; eggs four to eight, white, reddish dots at large end.

DISTRIBUTION: Common resident almost everywhere there are conifers in the Sierra; may use other forest types, especially in fall and winter when it occurs at lower elevations; large numbers regularly winter in the higher mountains.

REMARKS: The little brown-streaked creeper is so perfectly camouflaged that it is not easy to find on the trunk of a large tree unless the observer is guided by its wiry call note. The bird clings to the rough bark surface with its delicate curved claws and presses the pointed tail feathers inward for support. From the base of a tree it hitches upward for some distance, then flits to another tree and starts a new ascent. It always moves upward or in spiral course, never turning sideways or heading downward like a nuthatch. A creeper seems to forage without rest, scanning bark crevices for the tiny insects and spiders used as food. In spring a nest often may be found by observing a parent fly directly to the site.

Wrens (Family Troglodytidae)

ROCK WREN *Salpinctes obsoletus*

Length 5 to 6 in., wing span 9 in.; light grayish brown above, finely speckled white; whitish below; reddish tail with light tip and black subterminal bar; pale line over eye. **CALL** is a clear tinkling trill, also a buzzy *ti-keer;* song is of clear and burred notes varied in pitch, *chr, chr, chr, ter, ter, ter, eche,*

eche. **NEST** is in a cliff cranny or rodent burrow, made of twigs or grasses with approach runway of rock scrap or pebbles; eggs five to six, white, brown dotted.

DISTRIBUTION: Uncommon but widespread resident across the entire Sierra except for the very highest peaks; scarce at midelevations on west slope; in winter below heavy snow; lives on rock outcrops or rock slides, also around dry earth walls of gullies.

REMARKS: These large, pale-colored wrens live among bare broken rocks or on earthen bluffs anywhere from lowlands to high summits, a wider range than nearly all other Sierra birds. They often appear on highland granite domes or rock slides. Their long bills and claws, short legs, and flattish heads and bodies allow them to prowl into crevices when searching for food. Ever active, they turn from side to side, bob frequently, and utter trilled calls at regular intervals. Their varied songs can be heard during the spring months.

CANYON WREN *Catherpes mexicanus*

Length 5.5 to 5.75 in., wing span 7.5 in.; overall color rich reddish brown with fine black and white dots; throat and breast pure white; tail with four or five narrow black bars. **CALL** is a short *bzert;* song is about 10 loud clear notes, descending in pitch and slowing at end. **NEST** is near stream in rock crevices, made of twigs felted over with moss or other soft materials; eggs five to six, white with brown dots.

DISTRIBUTION: Fairly common resident from Foothill Belt into Mixed Conifer Belt on west slope, and low elevations on east slope; about crannies in rock walls or rockslides, often near water.

REMARKS: Anyone who visits a rock-walled foothill canyon during the spring is likely to hear the loud clear songs of these wrens, but the birds may not be easy to find. Typically they inhabit rather remote canyons but sometimes live about wooden cabins where they can be watched at close range. Their color is striking—pure white throats and reddish backs. Hopping in zigzag paths on bent legs, they slowly raise and quickly lower their bodies every few seconds. When foraging they prowl into all manner of crevices in search of insects. Unlike Rock Wrens, they favor areas near shade and water.

BEWICK'S WREN *Thryomanes bewickii*

Length 5 to 5.5 in., wing span 7 in.; above warm brown; below ashy white; conspicuous white line over eye; outer tail feathers tipped with grayish white. **CALL** is a hoarse *tserk,* also a *chee chee;* song is mixed and lively, two or more quick notes followed by lower burry notes and closing with a fine trill. **NEST** is in cavity of tree or trash pile mostly filled with twigs or plant stems, lined with hair, feathers, or grasses; eggs five to seven, white, brown spotted.

DISTRIBUTION: Common resident below Mixed Conifer Belt on west slope, rare in summer and uncommon in winter at low elevations on east slope; lives in mixed brush rather than trees.

REMARKS: Chaparral and shrubby hillside vegetation is the home of the Bewick's Wren. A foraging bird on the ground holds its tail up, but a singing male lets it droop. Both songs and calls are varied, so that an observer must study at length to learn them. With a long tail and active manners, these wrens closely resemble House Wrens but are recognized by their conspicuous white eyeline.

HOUSE WREN   *Troglodytes aedon*
Pl. 457

Length 4.5 to 5.25 in., wing span 6 in.; gray brown above, paler below; finely barred with black on wings and tail; vague white line through eye. **CALL** is a scolding *schee;* song is a rapid, bubbling mix of notes. **NEST** is in a hole of a tree or building, large for the bird, made of twigs lined with soft materials; eggs six to eight, white, thickly brown dotted.

DISTRIBUTION: Common summer visitor in Foothill Belt of west slope, abundant in valley bottoms on lower east slope; travel upslope after breeding; favors streamside thickets and brushy meadow edges.

REMARKS: House Wrens arrive in mid-April and for a month or so the bubbling song of males is one of the most frequent of avian voices. The birds usually forage low in thickets or chaparral but need a tree cavity, a space in some building, or a box in which to nest. Any extra interior space is filled with coarse twigs until the entrance is small, then a smoother lining is added. Males often build a number of rough nests to attract females to their territories, and females signal their acceptance of a male by finishing one of the nests with finer materials. After the broods are fully fledged some of these wrens wander upslope, occasionally toward timberline.

WINTER WREN   *Troglodytes troglodytes*

Length 4 in., wing span 5.5 in.; plumage dark reddish brown with many faint dark bars; pale line over eye; tail short and cocked. **CALL** is *tschep,* often in quick pairs; song is extended melodious trill. **NEST** is usually near water in cranny of stump or root tangle; made of twigs and moss; eggs four to seven, white, brown dotted.

DISTRIBUTION: Uncommon resident on west slope in Mixed Conifer Belt, in coniferous forests on east slope of northern Sierra; in damp canyons amid exposed tree roots and woody debris.

REMARKS: Smallest of North American wrens, this dark reddish species must be sought in moist, shady sites. It twists about, bobbing frequently, and skips from perch to perch, holding its diminutive tail cocked up at a sharp angle. It favors dark recesses under overhanging banks or logs, and amid downed branches. In consequence an observer usually has only glimpses of the bird. Its long, complex song is sometimes heard in winter as well as in the spring nesting season.

Dipper (Family Cinclidae)

AMERICAN DIPPER *Cinclus mexicanus*

Pl. 458

Length 7 to 8.5 in., wing span 11 in.; plumage entirely slate gray; translucent eyelid shows up as blinking white spot over eye. **CALL** is a short *bzeet,* singly or in rapid series; the elaborate, varied song is of whistled and trilled phrases, clear and ringing but sometimes scarcely heard over the rush of streams. **NEST** is on rocks near or over rushing water, made of moss, entrance on side; eggs three to six, white.

DISTRIBUTION: Common throughout main forest belt on both slopes at 2,000 to 11,000 ft; lives along cold, swift, permanent streams, occasionally on lake shores.

REMARKS: This is our only songbird that lives solely on perennial cascading streams. The dense feathering that sheds water is an adaptation to its aquatic life. When perched on a midstream rock, the dipper bobs down and up every few seconds. It flies along a winding stream course, keeping close over the water and uttering the short call repeatedly. To feed, the bird forages in the shallows or plunges right into the water, where it can walk on the bottom while searching for aquatic insects. The dipper is a yearlong resident wherever streams remain unfrozen during winter. Its song may be heard at almost any season, being most impressive in winter when other bird voices are few. The nest is usually placed where moistened by spray, even behind a waterfall, so that its mossy exterior remains green as long as it is used.

Kinglets (Family Regulidae)

GOLDEN-CROWNED KINGLET *Regulus satrapa*

Pl. 455

Length 4 in., wing span 7 in.; olive green above; whitish below; a white stripe over eye with black border above; crown orange and yellow (male) or simply yellow (female); one or two light bars on wing. **CALL** is a high-pitched, wiry *tse, tse-tse* series; song is a series of calls turning into a chickadee-like chatter. **NEST** is hidden in fir foliage, a cup of mosses, lichens, spider web, and other materials; eggs eight to nine, creamy with brown spots.

DISTRIBUTION: Abundant resident from Mixed Conifer Belt to Upper Montane Belt on the west slope, more localized and uncommon on east slope; some descend onto lower slopes during winter; inhabits dense foliage in conifer forests.

REMARKS: Faint lisping calls from among the highest tufts of needles or leaves are sometimes the only clues for locating these kinglets. Save when pairs are nesting, they travel in small groups, hopping and fluttering as they glean little insects from twigs and leaves. Their color matches the foliage except when a favorable view permits one to see the brilliant crown patch. Their excited series of calls closely resemble those given by Brown Creepers, whose notes are given mostly in clear pairs.

RUBY-CROWNED KINGLET *Regulus calendula*

Length 4 to 4.5 in., wing span 7.5 in.; grayish green above; buffy white below; eyering dull white; wing with one or two light bars; male has concealed red crown, exposed occasionally. **CALL** is a ratchety *che,* given two to many times; summer distress call *yer-rup,* repeated; song resembling *see, see, see, oh, oh, oh, cheerily, cheerily, cheerily,* the last three notes loudly whistled. **NEST** is on conifer branch, often high, a bulky cup of soft material; eggs five to 11, white, brown spotted.

DISTRIBUTION: Uncommon summer visitor in Upper Montane and Subalpine Belts; abundant winter visitor in trees of foothills and lowlands, these wintering birds being perhaps a combination of birds who have moved downslope and those migrating from northern regions.

REMARKS: The Ruby-crowned Kinglet, although of small size, has a clear, far-carrying song. This song may be heard in the lowlands during late spring, as Ruby-crowneds prepare to move upslope and begin nesting in higher elevation conifer forests. Ruby-crowneds forage acrobatically in the terminal foliage of conifers and in oaks, and may dart out to catch flying insects. In winter they hunt in leafless willows or alders and occasionally drop down to search plants on the ground. When one of these birds discovers an owl perched in a tree, its repeated insistent calls often attract others of the species to flutter about and join in a complaining chorus. Their summer *yer-rup* call often announces jays prowling near a kinglet nest.

Gnatcatcher (Family Sylviidae)

BLUE-GRAY GNATCATCHER *Polioptila caerulea*

Length 4.5 to 5 in., wing span 6 in.; bluish gray above; below pale gray; distinct white eyering; tail black, with white edges; forehead of male blackish. **CALL** is a weak *chee-e;* song is a high-pitched, wheezy *cheu, chee, chree,* of three to six notes. **NEST** is in oaks at about 10 ft, a small cup of grass covered with lichens or spider web; eggs four to five, pale greenish or bluish, brown spotted.

DISTRIBUTION: Uncommon summer visitor in foothills of both slopes; arid scrub and open woodlands with tangled thickets.

REMARKS: From April until early fall, Blue-gray Gnatcatchers prowl about dense thickets and chaparral, twitching their long tails as they hunt among foliage and small twigs for insects. At nesting time each pair lives within a hundred-yard radius of their nest tree, but when the young are fledged family parties range more widely. Some stray upslope in late summer before migrating southward.

Thrushes (Family Turdidae)

WESTERN BLUEBIRD   *Sialia mexicana*
Pl. 459

Length 6.5 to 7 in., wing span 13.5 in. Adult male: head, wings, and back mostly dark blue; breast and sides of body rich chestnut; belly grayish. Adult female: like male but colors much subdued; upper parts with bluish tinge; underparts with chestnut tinge. **CALL** is a soft *kew,* also a harsh *che-check;* song (uncommon) is repeated soft calls. **NEST** is in tree cavities and woodpecker holes (or in nest boxes); eggs three to eight, pale bluish green.

DISTRIBUTION: Common resident in open woodlands and meadows in coniferous forests from Foothill Belt into Mixed Conifer Belt; more common on west slope; favor meadows and dry grassy hillsides.

REMARKS: In spring and early summer pairs of these bluebirds live about oak trees over grasslands. While watching for insects, they occupy open perches offering a wide view. Some prey is caught in flight and some, including grasshoppers, are taken on the ground. After nesting, the birds stay in loose flocks of varying size. When disturbed they fly off scattering high into the air, calling frequently. Until the next spring season they wander widely, concentrating wherever their favorite foods—mistletoes and other berries—can be found.

MOUNTAIN BLUEBIRD   *Sialia currucoides*
Pl. 460

Length 7.25 in., wing span 14 in. Adult male: clear sky blue above, lighter on breast, belly pale gray. Adult female: grayish with hints of blue in wings and back. **CALL** is a weak *few;* song is a short, subdued warble. **NEST** is in woodpecker hole or other tree cavity; eggs four to eight, bluish white.

DISTRIBUTION: Common summer visitor across Sierra mostly from Upper Montane Belt to above treeline; widespread on east slope.

REMARKS: This stunning blue bluebird summers in the High Sierra about meadows, grass patches, and open ridgelines. Perches on rocks or tree stubs are used when watching for insects. In areas lacking perches they will hover on beating wings at 10 to 20 ft in the air while scanning the ground for food. The species arrives in May on west slope (early March on east slope) and has been seen until late September at high elevations. As a migrant, they make rare appearances at midelevations on west slope. They winter at the very lowest edges of the Sierra Nevada with sparse records from higher elevations.

TOWNSEND'S SOLITAIRE   *Myadestes townsendi*

Length 8 to 8.5 in., wing span 14.5 in.; plumage gray, slightly paler below; long white-edged tail; middle of wing shows pale buff flash in flight; white eyering gives it a wide-eyed appearance. **CALL** is a metallic *clink,* occasionally a harsh *chack*; song is an elaborate musical warbling. **NEST** is at the base of a tree or in a crevice of an earthen bank, also on rocky outcrops near streams; of twigs and needles; eggs three to five, bluish white, brown spotted.

DISTRIBUTION: Summer visitor from Mixed Conifer Belt into Subalpine Belt on west slope, in various forests on east slope; uncommon winter visitor on lower west slope, common in juniper woodlands on east slope; favor open dry areas, both vegetated and rocky.

REMARKS: This solitaire has a varied, intermittent song of clear full notes, some suggestive of a mockingbird or thrasher. Summer songs, morning or evening, come from high in the conifers, but in fall or early winter the birds sing from lower in junipers or oaks and during midday. Winter songs function to protect feeding territories. While singing a bird may flutter upward several feet, then drop back to its perch. Their bell-like calls resemble the whistled notes of the Northern Pygmy-owl. In warm weather solitaires eat insects, catching many in flight, but in fall and winter they seek berries of juniper, mistletoe, toyon, manzanita, and the like.

HERMIT THRUSH
Catharus guttatus

Length 6.75 in., wing span 11.5 in.; plain brown above but tail reddish; breast buffy with round blackish spots; belly whitish with dingy flanks; eyering and band on wing (seen in flight) buff. **CALL** is a soft *tup* or *chuck* one or two times, occasionally a harsh *tschee;* song is ethereal and flutelike, of musical phrases. **NEST** is in a low tree, made of twigs, bark shreds, and grasses, scantily lined; eggs three to five, blue with brown spots.

DISTRIBUTION: Fairly common summer visitor on both slopes, from Mixed Conifer Belt to treeline on west slope and comparable habitats on east slope; common winter visitor on west slope below heavy snow; inhabits glades and ravines under shady cover.

Hermit Thrush

REMARKS: This quiet, reclusive relative of the robin lives on or near the ground under dense canopy. Every few seconds it twitches its wings, then the tail is raised and slowly lowered. These mannerisms and the rufous tail distinguish this thrush from the Swainson's Thrush. In foraging, the Hermit hops a few steps, quickly flicks pieces of leafy debris aside

Swainson's Thrush

BIRDS AND MAMMALS

Birds (pls. 377–488)

Mammals (pls. 489–536)

Plate 377. Common Loon

Plate 378. Pied-billed Grebe

Plate 379. Eared Grebe

Plate 380. Western Grebe

Plate 381. American White Pelican

Plate 382. Double-crested Cormorant

Plate 383. Great Blue Heron

Plate 384. Great Egret

Plate 385. Green Heron

Plate 386. Turkey Vulture

Plate 387. California Condor

Plate 388. Canada Goose

Plate 389. Wood Duck

Plate 390. Mallard

Plate 391. Common Merganser

Plate 392. Osprey

Plate 393. Bald Eagle

Plate 394. Northern Harrier

Plate 396. Red-tailed Hawk

Plate 395. Cooper's Hawk

Plate 397. Golden Eagle

Plate 398. American Kestrel

Plate 399. Merlin

Plate 400. Peregrine Falcon

Plate 401. Prairie Falcon

Plate 402. Blue Grouse

Plate 403. White-tailed Ptarmigan

Plate 404. Wild Turkey

Plate 405. Mountain Quail

Plate 406. California Quail

Plate 407. American Coot

Plate 408. Killdeer

Plate 409. Spotted Sandpiper

Plate 410. Wilson's Snipe

Plate 411. Wilson's Phalarope

Plate 412. California Gull

Plate 413. Black Tern

Plate 414. Band-tailed Pigeon

Plate 415. Mourning Dove

Plate 416. Greater Roadrunner

Plate 417. Barn Owl

Plate 418. Western Screech-Owl

Plate 419. Great Horned Owl

Plate 420. Spotted Owl

Plate 421. Great Gray Owl

Plate 422. Long-eared Owl

Plate 423. Northern Saw-whet Owl

Plate 424. Common Nighthawk

Plate 425. White-throated Swift

Plate 426. Anna's Hummingbird

Plate 427. Calliope Hummingbird

Plate 428. Rufous Hummingbird

Plate 429. Lewis's Woodpecker

Plate 430. Acorn Woodpecker

Plate 432. Hairy Woodpecker

Plate 431. Red-breasted Sapsucker

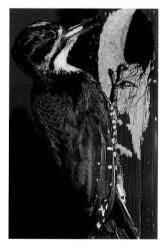

Plate 434. Black-backed
Woodpecker

Plate 433. White-headed Woodpecker

Plate 435. Northern Flicker

Plate 436. Western Wood-Pewee

Plate 437. Hammond's Flycatcher

Plate 438. Black Phoebe

Plate 439. Loggerhead Shrike

Plate 440. Warbling Vireo

Plate 441. Steller's Jay

Plate 442. Western Scrub-Jay

Plate 443. Clark's Nutcracker

Plate 444. Black-billed Magpie

Plate 445. American Crow

Plate 446. Common Raven

Plate 447. Horned Lark

Plate 448. Tree Swallow

Plate 449. Violet-green Swallow

Plate 450. Northern Rough-winged Swallow

Plate 451. Barn Swallow

Plate 452. Mountain Chickadee

Plate 453. Bushtit

Plate 454. Red-breasted Nuthatch

Mountain
Chickadee

White-breasted
Nuthatch

Brown
Creeper

Golden-crowned
Anglet

Red-breasted
Nuthatch

Plate 455. Small forest birds

Plate 456. White-breasted Nuthatch

Plate 457. House Wren

Plate 458. American Dipper

Plate 459. Western Bluebird

Plate 460. Mountain Bluebird

Plate 461. American Robin

Plate 462. Northern Mockingbird

Plate 463. California Thrasher

Plate 464. European Starling

Plate 465. Cedar Waxwing

Plate 466. Yellow-rumped Warbler

Plate 467. Wilson's Warbler

Plate 468. Western Tanager

MacGillivray's
Warbler

Black-throated
Gray Warbler

Yellow-rumped
Warbler

Common Yellowthroat

Nashville Warbler

Townsend's Warbler

Hermit Warbler

Wilson's
Warbler

Orange-crowned
Warbler

Yellow
Warbler

Plate 469. Wood warblers

Plate 470. Green-tailed Towhee

Plate 471. Rufous-crowned Sparrow

Plate 472. Chipping Sparrow

Plate 473. Savannah Sparrow

Plate 474. Fox Sparrow

Green-tailed Towhee   Spotted Towhee   California Towhee

Chipping Sparrow   Lark Sparrow

Fox Sparrow   Song Sparrow   Lincoln's Sparrow

Golden-crowned
Sparrow   White-crowned
Sparrow   Dark-eyed
Junco

Plate 475. Miscellaneous sparrows

Plate 476. Song Sparrow

Plate 477. White-crowned Sparrow

Plate 478. Golden-crowned Sparrow

Plate 479. Dark-eyed Junco

Plate 480. Red-winged Blackbird

Plate 481. Western Meadowlark

Plate 482. Yellow-headed Blackbird

Plate 483. Bullock's Oriole

Plate 484. House Finch

Plate 485. Lesser Goldfinch

Plate 487. House Sparrow

Plate 486. American Goldfinch

Gray-crowned Rosy-Finch

Evening Grosbeak

Pine Grosbeak

Purple Finch

Cassin's Finch

House Finch

Red Crossbill

Pine Siskin

Lesser
Goldfinch

Lawrence's
Goldfinch

American
Goldfinch

Plate 488. Finches of the Sierra

Plate 489. Virginia Opossum

Plate 490. Water Shrew

Plate 491. Broad-footed Mole

Plate 492. Shrew-mole

Plate 493. Coyote

Plate 494. Gray Fox

Plate 495. Red Fox

Plate 496. Black Bear

Plate 497. Ringtail

Plate 498. Raccoon

Plate 499. Wolverine

Plate 500. River Otter

Plate 501. American Marten

Plate 502. Striped Skunk

Plate 503. Western Spotted Skunk

Mountain Lion

River Otter

Badger

Coyote

Black
Bear

Brian Maebius

Plate 504. Notable carnivores of the Sierra

Plate 505. Short-tailed Weasel

Plate 506. Long-tailed Weasel

Plate 507. Mink

Plate 508. American Badger

Plate 509. Mountain Lion

Plate 510. Bobcat

Plate 511. Mule Deer

Plate 512. Bighorn Sheep

Plate 513. Porcupine

Plate 514. Mountain Beaver

Plate 515. California Ground Squirrel

Plate 516. Belding's Ground Squirrel

Plate 517. Golden-mantled Ground Squirrel

Plate 518. Northern Flying Squirrel

Plate 519. Yellow-bellied Marmot

Plate 520. Western Gray Squirrel

Plate 521. Yellow-pine Chipmunk

Plate 522. Shadow Chipmunk

Plate 523. Lodgepole Chipmunk

Plate 524. Beaver

Plate 525. Beaver dam

Plate 526. Muskrat

Plate 527. Mountain Pocket Gopher

Plate 528. Heermann's Kangaroo Rat

Plate 529. Great Basin Pocket Mouse

Plate 530. Deer Mouse

Plate 531. Long-tailed Vole

Plate 532. Mountain Vole

Plate 533. Pika

Plate 534. Brush Rabbit

Plate 535. Desert Cottontail

Plate 536. Snowshoe Hare

with its bill, and gazes intently at the cleared spot to find insects for food. The nesting season song is exalted music to human ears—slow cadenced, rising and falling in pitch, varied, and not continuous. The summer birds are present from May into August; others from the Northwest and Alaska are winter visitants from mid-October into April.

OTHER THRUSHES: The once common but now quite rare Swainson's Thrush (*C. ustulatus*, length 7 in.) has inexplicably disappeared from many of its former haunts. Formerly an inhabitant of the same forests as Hermit Thrushes, it is best detected by a haunting song that seems to spiral off into infinity.

AMERICAN ROBIN   *Turdus migratorius*

Pl. 461

Length 10 to 11 in., wing span 17 in.; dark grayish brown above, head and tail blackish; rich reddish brown below; chin and area under tail white. **CALL** of various notes: *tuk, tuk,* one or several times, shrill when excited; also a squealing *wi'eh;* song is of four or more loud caroling notes on same pitch with rising and falling inflection. **NEST** is in trees at four to 75 ft usually on horizontal branch (or shelf in building) to 4 in. high and 6 to 7 in. diameter, made of grass stems, pine needles, and other materials, mixed with mud; eggs four to five, deep blue.

DISTRIBUTION: Abundant summer visitor throughout the Sierra; winters below heavy snows; favors open coniferous forests but found in many habitats.

REMARKS: The familiar, red-breasted robin is common and widespread. Males average slightly darker and larger than females; their bills are almost clear yellow in summer. From late April through summer the birds remain in pairs, busy with nesting. Then the male's song is heard, especially from dawn into early morning and toward sundown. The nest is formed of grasses and needles with many pellets of mud gathered singly and pressed into the structure to make a rigid cup. When the mud has dried, the eggs are laid and incubation begins. In this season and while feeding young, the adults forage singly in damp grassland. Each stands, watches, and listens. If nothing is detected it runs a few steps and stands again. When a larva, insect, or worm is located, the bird bends over and grasps the prey. The spotted young emerge from late May until the end of July, being later in high elevations, and some parents may rear second broods. Later, adults and young gather in large flocks that roam together and winter at lower elevations. When grassland invertebrates become scarce or unavailable in fall and winter, robins feed on berries of many plants—elderberry, juniper, chokecherry, toyon, mistletoe, and others. With the development of lawns and irrigated farms, robins have adapted to nesting around human habitations.

In winter, American Robins are joined by Varied Thrushes (*Ixoreus naevius*, length 9.5 in.), who breed in Canada and Alaska. These large thrushes resemble robins but have orangish wing bars and a dark collar across their throat.

Babbler (Family Timaliidae)

WRENTIT
Chamaea fasciata

Length 6.5 in., wing span 7 in.; grayish brown above; paler below; throat with faint dusky streaks; distinctive cream-colored eye. **CALL** is a subdued ratchety *krrr;* song is clear whistled, on one pitch, *pit, pit, pit-tr-r-r-r-r,* of uniform cadence in female but speeding into a trill in the male. **NEST** is in shrubs at 18 to 24 in. or trees to 15 ft, a deep cup of cobweb and bark fibers with incurved edge and fine lining; eggs four, pale greenish.

DISTRIBUTION: Common resident of Foothill Belt in chaparral or low trees.

REMARKS: This unique bird has no close relatives in North America and has generated a bit of controversy as to which family it belongs. Currently it is considered one of the Old World insectivores known as babblers. With their slender tails cocked up, pairs feed secretively within the depths of dense chaparral and shrubs, rarely in the open and seldom in trees. Pairs are spaced out and resident on their territories of .5 to 2.5 acres, which they defend noisily and probably never leave in their lifetime. Adults eat insects and berries. The parents alternate in incubating and feeding the young.

Mockingbird and Thrasher (Mimidae)

NORTHERN MOCKINGBIRD
Mimus polyglottos

Pl. 462

Length 9 to 11 in., wing span 14 in.; plain dark gray above; white below; in flight shows large white patch on wing and white margin on tail. **CALL** is a harsh *chuck;* song is highly varied, often mimicking calls of other birds. **NEST** is in thick bushes or trees, bulky, made of twigs, with soft lining; eggs three to six, bluish or greenish white, brown blotched.

DISTRIBUTION: Fairly common resident at low elevations on west slope and around some lower foothill towns; rare on east slope; live in scattered trees, often near towns and farms.

REMARKS: The mockingbird appears to have moved northward and up into the foothills with the arrival of European settlers and their farms, orchards, and gardens. These birds are now a conspicuous resident in some lowland areas. Except at the end of summer when they are molting, mockingbirds are vocal and persistent songsters, even singing far into the night. Their vocabulary includes modified songs and calls of finches, meadowlarks, shrikes, scrub-jays, titmice, and other local associates. Young are fed a protein-rich diet of invertebrates, but the rest of the year mockingbirds search out a diet of fruits and berries.

CALIFORNIA THRASHER   *Toxostoma redivivum*
Pl. 463

Length 11.5 to 13 in., wing span 12.5 in.; plumage plain brown, slightly paler beneath; chin whitish; base under tail is orangish; bill 1 in. long and curved. **CALL** is a low *chuck;* song is lengthy, of chuckling notes, whistles, and other sounds, in irregular sequence. **NEST** is in shrubs or low trees, a rough bowl of twigs with smooth lining; eggs two to four, blue with brown dots.

DISTRIBUTION: Fairly common resident of Foothill Belt in mixed chaparral and riparian areas.

REMARKS: Thrashers are adapted by structure and habits for life in dense brush. Their short, round wings and long tail are suited to brief flights with agile turns, and their plain brown plumage is inconspicuous. With stout legs and feet, and tail cocked up for balance, the bird can run and dodge about under brush cover to escape observation and enemies. Only for singing does it emerge to perch on a tall shrub or small tree, mostly in morning and toward evening in the spring. No two songs seem alike, being a varied array of notes, deep and rich, whistled, or chuckling. The population is never large, perhaps a pair or two per quarter section.

Starling (Sturnidae)

EUROPEAN STARLING   *Sturnus vulgaris*
Pl. 464

Length 7.5 to 8.5 in., wing span 16 in. Adult (spring): black with green and purple gloss; bill yellow. Adult (winter): black, finely speckled with buff or white; bill black. **CALL** is a clear whistle; several guttural and chattering notes; song is varied, including notes of other birds. **NEST** is in cavities of trees, cliffs, or buildings, irregular, of grasses, and other materials; eggs five to seven, slightly glossy, pale blue to whitish.

DISTRIBUTION: Introduced 1872 to 1896 in eastern states and now spread across North America; widespread on lower slopes throughout the Sierra; inhabits farms, pastures, lawns, and open wild areas.

REMARKS: The starling, an undesirable alien, began appearing in California during the 1940s and is still increasing in numbers as it moves aggressively into sites modified by humans. Unlike native blackbirds it has a short tail and zigzag walk and flies by alternately flapping and sailing, often with great speed. One of its worst impacts lies in taking over tree cavities needed by nesting bluebirds, titmice, chickadees, and other birds. It feeds on insects, wild and cultivated fruits, and grains.

Waxwing (Family Bombycillidae)

CEDAR WAXWING   *Bombycilla cedrorum*
Pl. 465

Length 6.5 to 7.5 in., wing span 12 in.; grayish brown above; belly yellowish; tail yellow tipped; conspicuous crest and black mask; waxy red tips on some shorter wing feathers. **CALL** is a faint high-pitched *zee,* often repeated.

DISTRIBUTION: Nonbreeding visitor (September to June) on both slopes at lower elevations; flocks spend time in berry-producing trees or shrubs.

REMARKS: Compact flocks of 15 to 50 Cedar Waxwings can be seen flying low overhead and perching close together in the upper parts of trees. These flocks wander nomadically in the Sierra searching for crops of berries and are unpredictable in any area from year to year. When feeding, the birds flutter and cling to small branches and occasionally voice their shrill, rattling notes. Their diet is of berries on mistletoe, madrone, toyon, and ornamental shrubs. Absent during summer when they fly north to breed from Oregon to Canada.

Warblers (Family Parulidae)

ORANGE-CROWNED WARBLER   *Vermivora celata*
Pl. 469

Length 5 in., wing span 7.25 in.; dull greenish above, greenish yellow below with vague streaking; faint yellowish eyeline. **CALL** is *chit* or *tsip;* song is rapid, a weak tinny trill rising and then falling in pitch at end. **NEST** is on ground of shaded hillside, made of grasses and plant fibers; eggs three to six, white, heavily speckled with dark brown.

DISTRIBUTION: Common migrant and spring breeder on west slope up to lower Mixed Conifer Belt, uncommon migrant along east base of Sierra; common at higher elevations after breeding; lives in shaded inner foliage of trees and shrubs or chaparral.

REMARKS: Orange-crowned Warblers are the first warblers to arrive each spring in the foothills, appearing almost overnight as soon as oaks open their flowers. They quickly reach numbers that verge on abundant, filling the woodlands with their rapid, trilling songs and feasting on numerous insect larvae. Once their young have hatched and can fend for themselves, they disappear within days, leaving before many other songbirds have even begun nesting. One need only travel upslope to rediscover these same birds feeding actively in meadows up into the Subalpine Belt, where they remain common until early September.

NASHVILLE WARBLER   *Vermivora ruficapilla*
Pl. 469

Length 4.75 in., wing span 7.5 in.; olive green above; yellow below; head and nape gray; prominent white eyering; crown of male is chestnut but usually concealed. **CALL** is *tseep* or *tsip;* song is four or five rapid shrill notes, then three or four lower, *tsirp, tsirp, tsirp, tsirp, sup, sup, sup.* **NEST** is on ground, well made of bark strips and grasses with fine lining; eggs four to five, cream, with small or large spots of reddish brown.

DISTRIBUTION: Common summer visitor in Foothill and Mixed Conifer Belts of west slope, rare on east slope of northern Sierra; moves into Upper

Montane and Subalpine Belts after breeding; forages mostly in oaks or other broadleaved trees, commonly at 25 to 40 ft.

REMARKS: The light grayish head, white eyering, and yellow underparts distinguish this species from other tree-foraging warblers in the Sierra. The birds are not always easy to see against the light green foliage of early summer, and they occasionally forage up to 70 ft above ground. They may feed in conifers, but their overwhelming association seems to be with black oaks and other broadleaf trees. They arrive in May and after nesting may linger at higher elevations until mid-September.

YELLOW WARBLER   *Dendroica petechia*
Pl. 469

Length 5 in., wing span 8 in.; greenish yellow above; lemon yellow below; male streaked below with chestnut. **CALL** is a loud *tsip;* song is high, shrill *swee swee swee ti ti ti swee*, often transcribed as *sweet sweet sweet I'm so sweet.* **NEST** is in bushes or low trees, a compact woven cup of grayish weed fibers and fine grasses with soft lining; eggs three to four, white to pale green or gray with largish spots of dark brown.

DISTRIBUTION: Summer visitor on both slopes from valley bottoms into Mixed Conifer Belt; in streamside deciduous trees and montane chaparral. California Species of Special Concern (nesting).

REMARKS: These attractive yellow birds were once common but are now declining in many areas. Dam constructions and other human impacts on nesting habitats have certainly had a significant impact, as has nest parasitism by Brown-headed Cowbirds. Their clear, sharp songs can be heard from late April to early July in waterside willows, cottonwoods, and alders. The species forages and sings at up to 40 ft above ground, but usually places its nest below 15 ft.

YELLOW-RUMPED WARBLER   *Dendroica coronata*
Pls. 466, 469

Length 5.5 in., wing span 9.25 in.; rump always yellow (except young), chin usually yellow. Adult male (summer): back bluish gray, streaked with black; breast black; crown, chin, and flanks yellow. Adult female (summer): like male but breast mottled gray and black. Adult (winter) and immature: brownish above and below, little or no black on breast; smudgy and streaky appearance. **CALL** is a sharp *tsip;* song is a mellow, tinkling, *turly, urly, urly, urly, urly, i-ci.* **NEST** is usually in conifers, at 9 to 50 ft, bulky, made of bark and needles, lined with feathers; eggs three to five, greenish white with black, brown, or lilac spots.

DISTRIBUTION: Common summer visitor from Mixed Conifer Belt to treeline on both slopes, remains at high elevations late into fall; common winter visitor at lower elevations; breeds chiefly in conifers, but occurs in virtually every habitat during migration.

REMARKS: Yellow-rumped Warblers are the commonest and most widespread of Sierra warblers. From fall until spring these hardy birds can be found below the snow line in broadleaf trees of town and country, even foraging on the ground. During the breeding season they occupy conifer forests above the foothills. In trees they hunt small insects in the outer foliage, changing locations by short semicircular flights out beyond the leaves, and catching flying insects there. In winter they may supplement their diet with small fruits, which enables them to overwinter in the Sierra. Except when pairs are nesting, these warblers typically occur in groups, sometimes numbering in the hundreds and mixing with bluebirds, juncos, or other small birds. The Yellow-rumped has seven or eight different plumages according to age, sex, or season, making it a challenge to identify if the yellow rump is not seen.

BLACK-THROATED GRAY WARBLER   *Dendroica nigrescens*
Pl. 469

Length 5 in., wing span 7.75 in.; grayish black overall above, grading to black on head; throat black (in male); belly white with thick black streaks; conspicuous white eyeline and cheek stripe; female has a reduced streaky patch on a white throat. **CALL** is a low *chit*; song is a drawling *wee'zy, wee'zy, wee'zy, wee'zy, wer.* **NEST** is low in bush or at 15 to 50 ft in conifers, a deep loose cup of plant fibers, grass, and moss; eggs three to five, creamy, brown-blotched.

DISTRIBUTION: Fairly common summer visitor on west slope in upper foothills and lower Mixed Conifer Belt, sparse on east slope of northern Sierra; mainly in dry canyon live oak and black oak woodlands.

REMARKS: The crown and upper foliage of canyon live oaks are the usual foraging areas for this rather slow-moving warbler. Although strikingly patterned, its coloration blends with sun-dappled leaves so that the bird is not always easy to see. It arrives in April, and young may be out of the nest early in June; may wander to Upper Montane Belt in late summer and some individuals remain until September.

HERMIT WARBLER   *Dendroica occidentalis*
Pl. 469

Length 5 in., wing span 8 in.; head lemon yellow; blue gray above; white below except for black throat; females and immatures have a much smaller black patch on throat. **CALL** is a moderate *tchip*; song is *ter'ley, ter'ley, ter'ley, sic', sic'.* **NEST** is in fir on branch, at 15 ft or much higher, compact, made of twigs, moss, and plant down; eggs three to five, white, heavily brown and gray spotted.

DISTRIBUTION: Uncommon summer visitor in same forest belts as Black-throated Gray Warblers but favors shaded pine and fir forests at slightly higher elevations.

REMARKS: This bird occupies coniferous forests at middle elevations, moving to higher elevations after breeding then quickly migrating south. The song is more rapid than that of the Black-throated Gray and not so clear as that of the Yellow-rumped Warbler. Its yellow head is conspicuous as the bird forages at 20 ft or more above ground on flat spreading branches of firs and pines.

Townsend's Warblers (*D. townsendi,* length 5 in.), looking like Hermit Warblers with blackish masks, are commonly observed during migration but they nest to the north of the Sierra Nevada.

MACGILLIVRAY'S WARBLER
Oporornis tolmiei

Pl. 469

Length 5.25 in., wing span 7.5 in.; head, neck, and throat gray (darker in male); plain dull green above; yellow below; white crescents above and below eye. **CALL** is a loud *tchip;* song is three to five clear separate notes, then several shorter ones close together, *sir-pit,' sir-pit,' sir-pit,' syr, sip, sip.* **NEST** is low in a bush, made of coarse and fine grass; eggs three to five, dull white blotched with dark brown.

DISTRIBUTION: Fairly common summer visitor on both slopes from midelevations up to the Upper Montane Belt; around dense, low shrubbery over damp ground.

REMARKS: Unlike the tree-dwelling warblers, this species lives in thickets of cherry, thimbleberry, bracken, and similar plants, but seldom invades chaparral. The birds forage within about 4 ft of the ground and stay within shrub cover, being more often heard than seen and making them seem far less common than they really are. Some males go up into low trees to sing, but others sing and forage within thickets. Nests are commonly within 30 in. of the ground. Moves upslope after breeding and continues feeding in moist thickets until migrating south in August.

WILSON'S WARBLER
Wilsonia pusilla

Pls. 467, 469

Length 4.75 in., wing span 7 in.; yellowish green above, forehead and undersurface yellow; black cap (reduced or absent in female). **CALL** is a throaty *tchep;* song is flat toned, *chi, chi, chi, . . . chit, chit,* louder and faster at end. **NEST** is in low bushes or on ground, rather bulky, made of mosses or grasses with small lined cup; eggs four to six, white, with reddish brown spots.

DISTRIBUTION: Common migrants throughout Sierra, locally common while nesting from Mixed Conifer Belt to treeline on both slopes; mostly in thickets over damp ground near streams or lakes, but more widespread in migration.

REMARKS: This black-capped warbler forages mostly within 6 ft of the ground in thickets of willows, alders, dogwoods, and other moisture-loving plants. In summer up to eight pairs per mile may be found in the plant cover along some streams. This warbler often captures flying insects. Its song is sharp and staccato. One northern subspecies migrates northward along both bases of the mountains in May. The subspecies that nests in the Sierra arrives early in May, nests in June, and visits the higher elevations until mid-September.

YELLOW-BREASTED CHAT   *Icteria virens*

Length 7 to 8 in., wing span 9.75 in.; plain greenish brown above; throat and breast yellow; belly white; broken eyering and white malar. **CALL** and song both varied, whistles and chuckling notes, some imitations of other birds. **NEST** is in bush or small tree, 6 to 7 in. diameter, loosely woven of grasses and plant stems; eggs three to five, white, spotted with reddish brown and gray.

DISTRIBUTION: Local summer visitor along west base of Sierra, rare east of crest; in dense streamside thickets. California Species of Special Concern (nesting).

REMARKS: Largest, and sometimes the most vocal, of Sierra warblers is the Yellow-breasted Chat, which summers in lowland riparian growths. It is rather slow of movement, and its calls and songs are varied, unlike the set phrases of other warblers. The songs may be heard before daybreak and after dusk and even when other birds are quiet in the afternoon heat or at midnight. When singing it often jumps into the air and then flutters down with drooping wings and tail, but this bird is otherwise very difficult to observe.

Tanager (Family Thraupidae)

WESTERN TANAGER   *Piranga ludoviciana*
Pl. 468

Length 7.25 in., wing span 11.5 in. Adult male: head fluorescent reddish orange; wings, upper back, and tail black; rest of body yellow. Adult female: dull yellowish olive above, with dusky gray back and wings; dull yellow below. **CALL** is a hoarse *cher'tig* or *chee'-tik,* repeated; song is a drawling *cher'-wer,* three to many times, similar to song of American Robins but hoarser. **NEST** is on horizontal branch of pine or fir, in foliage, made of needles, twigs, or plant stems, lined; eggs three to five, blue, brown spotted.

DISTRIBUTION: Common summer visitor in Mixed Conifer Belt of west slope, scarcer on east slope; in open forest.

REMARKS: Tanagers migrate through the foothills in May and settle for summer in open forest areas above, where they remain until mid-September. The birds are deliberate in movement and not shy, sometimes coming to the ground or tables in a camp. Although brightly colored, the male is not always easy to see when in foliage. The female builds the nest and incubates, but both parents feed the young. Early in the summer, insects are the chief food, but later berry crops attract the birds, sometimes in small flocks, before they migrate.

Towhees, Sparrows, and Junco (Family Emberizidae)

GREEN-TAILED TOWHEE
Pipilo chlorurus

Pls. 470, 475

Length 7.25 in., wing span 9.75 in.; gray brown above; wings and tail dull yellowish green; throat white, bordered by black stripes; breast ashy; crown bright chestnut. **CALL** is catlike, *me-u* or a longer *mee-a-yew;* song is wheezy, *eet-ter-te-te-te-si-si-si-seur.* **NEST** is low in shrub, bulky, made of needles, twigs, grasses well lined; eggs three to four, bluish white, with red and gray spots.

DISTRIBUTION: Uncommon summer visitor in Mixed Conifer and Upper Montane Belts on both slopes, lower on east side where it is more common; in shrubs, usually ceanothus, sagebrush, or bitterbrush.

REMARKS: The sprightly Green-tailed Towhee, with its catlike call, shares many habitats with Fox Sparrows whose song is remarkably similar. It arrives early in May and may remain until early October. Nesting occurs in late May and June, and by late July the streaked-breasted young are much in evidence. It forages like a Fox Sparrow under shrubby cover and takes shelter there when disturbed.

SPOTTED TOWHEE
Pipilo maculatus

Pl. 475

Length 8.5 in., wing span 10.5 in. Adult male: upper surface and forepart of body black; small white spots on wings and larger ones at end of tail; flanks reddish brown; tail long and uniformly dark; belly white; iris red. Adult female: like male but head brownish black. Immature: light brown and buff overall, with dark brown streaks. **CALL** is catlike, a long *zuee,* slightly varied; song trilled, *tu-wheeze.* **NEST** is usually on ground, made of grasses and bark strips, lined; eggs three to four, white or tinted, finely marked with reddish brown.

DISTRIBUTION: Common resident mainly below Mixed Conifer Belt on west slope, also along east base of Sierra; on ground under or near brush.

REMARKS: Brushy thickets are the home of this brightly marked towhee. It scratches industriously in the ground litter, kicking backward with both feet as it searches for seeds and insects. The tail is usually cocked up at a jaunty angle. In spring the males, toward evening, go into the tops of bushes or low trees and repeat their short, explosively trilled songs. The streaked young are abroad by July, and in late summer and fall some Spotted Towhees range upslope into the Mixed Conifer Belt but return as snow and cold weather arrive.

CALIFORNIA TOWHEE
Pipilo crissalis

Pl. 475

Length 8.5 to 10 in., wing span 11.5 in.; mostly gray brown; undertail coverts bright reddish brown; throat pale orange with dusky streaks. **CALL** is a loud *chink,* also squealing notes by a pair; song is a quick series of *chink* notes, more rapid at end. **NEST** is in bush or tree at 3 to 8 ft, a bulky well-made cup of plant fibers finely lined; eggs three to four, pale bluish green sparingly spotted.

DISTRIBUTION: Common resident in lower foothills of west slope; in thickets around open areas.

REMARKS: California Towhees forage on open areas of sparse grassland, about foothill gardens, and on road margins, always near shrubs or small trees into which they can fly to safety. When startled into flight they may give their sharp call repeatedly. The long tail is closed and straight out while on the ground but widely spread for steering when the bird dodges around shrubs or trees. Nesting begins in April and finishes by the end of June. Unlike many other foothill birds this towhee is resident throughout the year, never wandering upslope. It is notorious for the persistence with which it attacks its own image in reflective surfaces such as car hubcaps or sideview mirrors.

RUFOUS-CROWNED SPARROW
Aimophila ruficeps

Pl. 471

Length 6 in., wing span 7.75 in.; grayish brown above with rufous streaks; light grayish below; crown and eyeline rufous; malar whitish with narrow black border on each side. **CALL** is a slow, nasal *dear, dear, dear*; song is weak, but somewhat like that of Lazuli Bunting. **NEST** is on ground, made of stems and grasses, lined; eggs four to five, white.

DISTRIBUTION: Local resident in Foothill Belt of west slope; on dry rocky hillsides with scattered small shrubs.

REMARKS: Open shrubby areas mixed with grass are the haunts of this little sparrow. It avoids broad expanses of chaparral. Never a common bird because it seems to be such a habitat specialist. The male's song is seldom heard, but the plaintive calls are given rather frequently.

CHIPPING SPARROW
Spizella passerina

Pls. 472, 475

Length 5.5 in.; wing span 8.5 in.; light brown above with darker streaks; plain ashy white below (streaked in juveniles); crown bright rufous; a black line through eye and white line above eye. **CALL** is a weak *tseet*; song is a mechanical trill of dry chips, much like the song of the Dark-eyed Junco. **NEST** is in shrubs or low trees at 2 to 12 ft; made of plant stems, grasses, and rootlets, finely lined with hair; eggs three to five, bluish green, with brownish black marks.

DISTRIBUTION: Fairly common summer visitor from the lower slopes nearly to timberline throughout the Sierra; usually in clear areas near small trees.

REMARKS: Chipping Sparrows may be present from April to late September, at any elevation, wherever smooth bare or grassy ground is close to small trees. This is the niche that hikers seek for their camps so these rather fearless little birds are often close about human visitors. They are active from dawn to dusk, even in midday heat, scanning the surface for their food of seeds and insects. Their nesting begins late in April at lower elevations and continues into July in the higher mountains. Then family groups are in evidence until migration in late September.

BREWER'S SPARROW   *Spizella breweri*

Length 5.5 in., wing span 7.5 in.; resembles Chipping Sparrow but paler and lacking reddish tones, crown finely streaked and no white line over eye. **CALL** is a weak *tseet;* song is a series of buzzy trills on different pitches. **NEST** is low in sage or other bushes; compact, made of twigs, stems, and rootlets, lined; eggs three to four, pale bluish green, reddish spotted.

DISTRIBUTION: Common summer visitor on east slope in Sagebrush Belt; rare spring migrant on west slope.

REMARKS: This dull-garbed relative of the Chipping Sparrow matches in coloration the Great Basin sagebrush, in which it is perhaps the most common bird. Some wander into sagebrush high on the east slope. In early fall, before the southward migration, they are abundant about Mono Lake.

The Black-chinned Sparrow (*S. atrogularis,* length 5.75 in.) is a very localized summer visitor in dense arid foothill chaparral on the west slope. It has a black chin and rusty brown back; rest of body is plain dark gray; bill is bright pink.

VESPER SPARROW   *Pooecetes gramineus*

Length 6.25 in., wing span 10 in.; streaked above with brown and black, whitish below with narrow brown streaks on breast and flanks; outermost tail feather on each side mostly white; bend of wing chestnut. **CALL** is sharp chip, also buzzy, rising *seeet;* song is two to three clear notes, then two higher notes followed by buzzy trills. **NEST** is in depression on ground, made of grasses, rootlets, and other materials; eggs four to five, white with reddish brown marks.

DISTRIBUTION: Uncommon summer visitor along east base of Sierra and in southern High Sierra; another subspecies is a rare winter visitor in Foothill Belt of the west slope; frequents open grasslands with scattered shrubs.

REMARKS: Unless the diagnostic chestnut shoulder of the Vesper Sparrow is seen, this bird simply looks streaky and is difficult to identify. Its white-edged tail is best seen when the bird takes flight. The males perch on scattered shrubs to sing, but otherwise the species stays mostly on the ground. Highly adapted to living in arid conditions, these sparrows can survive on dry seeds without water.

LARK SPARROW   *Chondestes grammacus*
Pl. 475

Length 6.5 in., wing span 11 in.; head has vivid pattern of chestnut, white, and black patches; back is brown streaked; below is very pale gray; black dot in center of breast; tail dark with prominent white corners. **CALL** is a weak *seep;* song begins with two loud notes and continues into series of trills and buzzes. **NEST** is on ground under grass clump (loosely formed) or in a bush or tree, a cup of grasses and twigs, lined; eggs four to five, whitish, with dark lines.

DISTRIBUTION: Common resident on west slope mainly in Foothill Belt; local summer visitor east of mountains; in grasslands with scattered small trees.
REMARKS: Grasslands with fences, poles, or scattered oaks are the Lark Sparrow's domain. Its rounded, white-margined tail is spread when the bird rises from the ground and sometimes while perched. The varied, wheezy song may last for a minute or more and is heard throughout the day in spring. Nesting begins late in May. During fall and winter small flocks roam the countryside, foraging on the ground, going into trees if disturbed, and then sometimes flying off in the open to more distant perches.

SAGE SPARROW   *Amphispiza belli*

Length 6 in., wing span 8.25 in.; overall faintly streaked appearance, brownish above and whitish below; head is grayish and contrasts with brownish body; dark breast spot. **CALL** is a faint *seet;* song is tinkling, *inksely-inksely-inksely-ser.* **NEST** is 1 to 2.5 ft up in a shrub, a cup of plant stems lined with flower heads; eggs three to four, pale bluish with reddish brown marks.

DISTRIBUTION: Sparse resident on west slope in Foothill Belt, Eldorado County to Mariposa County, in chamise chaparral; summer visitor on east slope in Sierra County, and from Mono Lake south, in Sagebrush Belt. West slope race (Bell's Sparrow) is a State and Federal Species of Special Concern (nesting).
REMARKS: Two races of this sparrow inhabit opposite sides of the Sierra, a darker race (often referred to as the Bell's Sparrow) with richer browns and grays occurs on the west slope in chamise chaparral; and a sandy gray form (known as the Sage Sparrow) occurs amid sagebrush on the east slope (extending onto west slope in Tulare and Kern Counties). The birds seldom

appear outside the shrubby cover except when males ascend onto high branches to sing in spring.

SAVANNAH SPARROW   *Passerculus sandwichensis*
Pl. 473

Length 5.5 in., wing span 6.75 in.; streaked above with black and brown; white below, narrowly streaked with dark brown across breast and along flanks; a pale stripe over each eye; yellowish spot in front of eye. **CALL** is a weak *seet;* song is two or three short chirps followed by a buzzing insectlike trill. **NEST** is in grassland or pasture, on ground, made of grasses and horsehair; eggs four to five, greenish or bluish white, spotted with brown.

DISTRIBUTION: Common summer visitor in Great Basin and larger valleys of northern Sierra (subsp. *nevadensis*); also winter visitor (of several northern races) in lower foothills of both slopes; inhabits grassland.

REMARKS: Savannah Sparrows live in grassland or on open ground at all times, finding their food and nesting there. Individuals sometimes perch on bushes, rocks, or low fences, but then drop down and disappear into sheltering grasses or low plants. Much of the time they are inconspicuous until they fly out from dense grasses when disturbed. The birds summering on the east side are present from late April until mid-September.

FOX SPARROW   *Passerella iliaca*
Pls. 474, 475

Length 7 in., wing span 10.5 in.; bill much stouter than in other sparrows; wintering subspecies uniform dark brown above; summer visitors have gray head and back, contrasting with reddish wings and tail; both are white below with bold triangular black spots (*note*: with several subspecies possible in the Sierra, not all will appear exactly like illustrated bird). **CALL** is a single loud *chink;* song is clear, melodious, two loud notes, *wee chee,* and a trill. **NEST** is at 8 to 24 in. or higher in snowbrush or other shrub, a loose exterior of twigs lined with pine needles and hair; eggs three to four, pale greenish marked with reddish brown.

DISTRIBUTION: Common summer visitor in montane chaparral habitats from Mixed Conifer Belt to Subalpine Belt on both slopes (two subspecies); also migrant and winter visitor in Foothill and Mixed Conifer Belts (other subspecies); in and near thick shrubs.

REMARKS: The sprightly Fox Sparrow summers in thickets of ceanothus, manzanita, and other mountain chaparral, often in close association with Green-tailed Towhees. The birds live and forage on the ground, near or under brush. They jump and scratch backward with both feet, showering debris and making holes 2 or 3 in. wide to obtain seeds for food. When an observer approaches they are adept at circling within the shrubbery or flying off near the ground to hide in another bush. Males perch on high twigs of bushes or low branches of trees to sing their clear lay. The nests are well hidden. Summer birds arrive in May and depart by September but are replaced by members of several northern races that come as winter visitants. Some of these winter birds travel well up into the mountains until snow drives them downslope. Summer birds have gray heads that contrast with their reddish wings and tails, while most winter birds are a darker rich brown.

SONG SPARROW
Melospiza melodia
Pls. 475, 476

Length 5 to 6.5 in., wing span 8.25 in.; dark brown and gray above, whitish below, all surfaces have dark smudgy streaks; a pale stripe over crown and one over each eye; a dark spot on breast. **CALL** is a low, blurred *chimp;* song is variable, usually three short notes, *cheet, cheet, cheet,* a longer note, then a trill. **NEST** is on ground, in bush or low tree; made of slender twigs, plant stems, and grasses; eggs three to four, greenish white, spotted with reddish brown.

DISTRIBUTION: Local resident at low to midelevations on both slopes; in meadows or shrubbery near water.

REMARKS: The streaky Song Sparrow carries its tail up at an angle with the back. It is active and moves easily within brushy thickets, much like a wren. It lives in pairs or singly, never in flocks, in damp places or near water. The song may be heard beyond the nesting season. A grayish race nests on the east slope in summer, and some individuals of that race winter on the lower west slope. Two resident dark-colored races of the Central Valley occur in the foothills, and still other subspecies from the north appear in winter.

LINCOLN'S SPARROW
Melospiza lincolnii
Pl. 475

Length 5.5 in., wing span 7.5 in.; brown and gray above streaked with black; chin and belly white; buffy flanks and chest band are narrowly black streaked. **CALL** is a low *sip;* song is rapid, gurgling, *zee, zee, zee, ti-ter-r-r-r-r.* **NEST** is on grass tuft in swampy ground, a cup woven of grasses; eggs four to five, pale, bluish green with reddish brown marks.

DISTRIBUTION: Locally common summer visitor throughout much of Sierra below the Alpine Belt; also winter visitor on lower west slope, mainly in Foothill Belt; in wet meadows or tall grass with willows.

REMARKS: Looking remarkably similar to the Song Sparrow, the Lincoln's Sparrow shows more gray in its face and has sharp blackish streaks over an orangish band on its breast. In summer this sparrow lives in mountain willow thickets shared by White-crowned Sparrows but is reclusive, keeping under cover of damp vegetation when foraging or singing. The nesting population arrives by mid-May but by the end of July is no longer seen or heard. Birds of a northern race winter on the west slope.

WHITE-CROWNED SPARROW — *Zonotrichia leucophrys*
Pls. 475, 477

Length 7 in., wing span 9.5 in.; crown with three white and four black stripes alternating (light and dark browns on young birds); gray above, streaked with brown; tail plain brown; two rows of white spots on closed wing; below grayish white, unstreaked. **CALL** is a sharp *peenk* or faint *seep;* song is clear, plaintive *we chee' ah we-e-e-e ah.* **NEST** is on ground or up to 3 ft in shrub, made of plant stems, bark shreds, and other materials, lined with fine grass; eggs three to five, pale bluish green, brown spotted.

DISTRIBUTION: Two different races in the Sierra: Mountain White-crown (*Z. l. oriantha*) is a common summer visitor in Upper Montane and Subalpine Belts on both slopes; Gambel's White-crown (*Z. l. gambelii*) is a common winter visitor below heavy snow on both slopes. Area between eye and bill (the lores) is black in Mountain race and white in the Gambel's race.

REMARKS: White-crowned Sparrows are present somewhere in the Sierra at all seasons, the Mountain race from May through September at high elevations and the Gambel's from mid-September until early May on the lower slopes, both eastern and western. The birds forage on level grasslands near bushes, into which they dart when frightened. The summer population lives in montane meadows near shrubby willow thickets that serve as escape cover, song perches, and nesting sites.

GOLDEN-CROWNED SPARROW — *Zonotrichia atricapilla*
Pls. 475, 478

Length 7.5 in., wing span 9.5 in.; dull brown above, black-streaked; pale grayish brown below; two rows of white spots on wing; crown of adult golden yellow, margined with black (dull brown in young birds). **CALL** is one-syllabled *tsick;* while song is three clear whistled notes descending in pitch, like *oh dear me.*

DISTRIBUTION: Common winter visitors on west slope in Foothill Belt, rarer on the east slope; in or near thickets.

REMARKS: The slightly larger Golden-crowneds share lowland and foothill thickets with Gambel's White-crowns from October to May. On their arrival in fall, Golden-crowneds are possible almost anywhere in the Sierra Nevada but all end up downslope when the snows begin. Much of their time is spent feeding on open ground adjacent to dense thickets where they retreat when alarmed.

DARK-EYED JUNCO — *Junco hyemalis*
Pls. 475, 479

Length 6 in., wingspan 9.25 in.; head, neck, and breast black (dark in male, grayish in female and immature); back, wings, and flanks reddish brown; tail black except two outer feathers on each side white; belly white; bill pinkish. **CALL** is a weak *seep* or sharp *tsick;* song is a rapid, quavering metallic trill of one to three seconds, *eetle, eetle, eetle*. **NEST** is sunk in ground, about 3 in. by 3 in., thick walled, of stems, dried grass, and moss, finely lined; eggs three to five, pinkish to bluish white, marked with reddish brown and gray.

DISTRIBUTION: Abundant summer visitor on both slopes in open conifer woods at nearly all elevations; also common winter visitor on west slope below heavy snow (sparse on east slope).

REMARKS: By all appearances Dark-eyed Juncos are the commonest summer birds in the Sierra Nevada. They glean seeds on the ground under open forest, hopping in zigzag course and flashing their conspicuous white tail margins. Nesting begins in May when males perch above ground to sing. Young emerge from late June into August, indicating that some pairs may renest or rear second broods. Nests are often near meadow margins or open creek banks, sometimes beside logs, occasionally in the open. The juvenile birds are streaked above and below, but by fall these immature birds develop a dark cowl and unstreaked body. Family parties of late summer merge into the loose flocks that wander until the next spring. Some remain in the lower forest where snow does not persist, while others move to the foothills and lowlands.

Grosbeak and Bunting (Family Cardinalidae)

BLACK-HEADED GROSBEAK   *Pheucticus melanocephalus*

Length 8.25 in., wing span 12.5 in. Adult male: mostly black above; neck collar, rump, and undersurface orange brown; wing with two bars and large patch of white. Adult female: dull brown above, streaked with black; a light stripe over crown and one above each eye; wing with two white bars; breast light brown, belly whitish. **CALL** is a sharp *spick;* song is a rolling, musical, rapid warble of ascending and descending notes, very robinlike in quality. **NEST** is usually near streams in low trees or bushes, bulky, loose woven, shallow, made of twigs or plant stems; eggs three to four, bluish green, brown spotted.

DISTRIBUTION: Abundant summer visitor on west slope, in Foothill and Mixed Conifer Belts; uncommon on east slope; in streamside trees and open forest, especially wherever oaks are present.

REMARKS: The rich warbling songs of Black-headed Grosbeaks are a prominent and insistent element of the spring bird chorus, and when the birds are seen they are immediately recognizable by their stout, oversized bills. Males begin singing on arrival in April and continue into July, sometimes on the wing, and also when incubating the nest. Singing "females" may be either males not yet in adult plumage or females (who also sing in this species). Grosbeaks prefer open woods, usually near water, and forage much in crown foliage. Nests are commonly within

12 ft of the ground. Most broods emerge in late May and June, but a few do late in July.

LAZULI BUNTING · *Passerina amoena*

Length 5.5 in., wing span 8.75 in. Adult male: head, throat, back, and rump sky blue; breast tawny; rest of underparts white; tail and wings blackish brown; one (or two) white wing bars. Adult female and immature: tawny brown above, with hints of light blue; pale brown below; belly whitish. **CALL** is a weak *tsip;* song is bright, rapid, of short phrases high, low, then high in pitch. **NEST** is at 4 ft or less, usually in weeds or bushes, made of leafy grasses, finely lined, and lashed to a support stem or crotch; eggs three to four, pale bluish green, rarely speckled.

DISTRIBUTION: Common summer visitor at lower elevations on both slopes, but occasionally occurs at midelevations such as in the Mixed Conifer Belt; in a wide variety of shrub and meadow habitats, especially near water.

REMARKS: The bright blue male of this species finds perches on tall bushes or treetops to sing, which it does persistently through much of the day. The dull-colored female remains more in tangled undergrowth. Both forage within weedy or shrubby cover, and the nest is in that sort of shelter. Males on productive territories may succeed in attracting several mates. The birds begin arriving by mid-May and the last depart late in September.

Blackbirds, Meadowlark, and Oriole (Family Icteridae)

RED-WINGED BLACKBIRD · *Agelaius phoeniceus*

Pl. 480

Length 8.5 to 9 in., wing span 13 in. Adult male: all black except for red shoulder patch (epaulet). Adult female: reddish-brown and black streaks above; a light stripe over each eye; heavily streaked with dark brown below. **CALL** in flocks is a sharp *chack,* of male near nest *tee'-urr;* song is *tong-leur'-lee,* slightly trilled at end. **NEST** is in cattails or tules near water or in dense moist weeds, a woven cup of reeds, grasses, or plant bark, lashed to upright stems; eggs four to five, bluish green, brown blotched.

DISTRIBUTION: Common summer visitor up to Subalpine Belt on both slopes; retreats to lower elevations in winter or leaves some areas altogether; breeds locally around marshy areas, winters in a wide variety of wetland and grassland habitats, often around farms, fields, or towns.

REMARKS: In spring Red-winged Blackbirds occupy marshes or wet swales, each male defending a small territory that may house as many as five females. The male in courting display has his feathers fluffed out, tail spread, wings drooping, and the red epaulets conspicuously raised. Commonly he clings to an upright stem, giving the on-guard call *tee'urr* at intervals. Meanwhile the smaller and duller females are busy close by their nests, maintaining constant vigilance against attack by Marsh Wrens (who destroy eggs and nestlings of other birds). On the west slope, nesting is spread from April into June. At other seasons Red-wingeds gather into flocks of up to several hundred and range widely over pastures and grasslands. During this time, males generally hide their red epaulets and look much like other blackbirds.

OTHER BLACKBIRDS: The very similar Tricolored Blackbird (*A. tricolor*, length 8.75 in.), with a white lower border on the red epaulet, nests in the Kern River Valley and perhaps elsewhere; State and Federal Species of Special Concern (nesting).

WESTERN MEADOWLARK
Pl. 481

Sturnella neglecta

Length 9.5 in., wing span 14.5 in.; brown above, with tiny black bars; head with three pale stripes; tail short and white-margined; brilliant yellow below; breast with black crescent. **CALL** is a clear whistle, a short *chuck,'* or a throaty *chr-r-r-r-r;* song is clear, rolling, melodious, eight to 12 notes. **NEST** is on weedy ground, made of dried grasses, often with scant "dome," and approach runway; eggs three to seven, white with brown and gray spots.

DISTRIBUTION: Common resident in clearings of Foothill Belt; summer visitor along east base of Sierra; wanders regularly to higher elevations after breeding; in grasslands and open areas.

REMARKS: The melodious voice of the Western Meadowlark at nesting time is a pleasing element in open areas on both sides of the Sierra. Males sing while perched on trees, rocks, wires, or posts, and sometimes on the wing. When foraging the birds walk on the ground, taking both insects and seeds. In fall and winter, meadowlarks live in loose roving flocks of 10 to 75 birds that are less closely knit than those of blackbirds.

YELLOW-HEADED BLACKBIRD
Pl. 482

Xanthocephalus xanthocephalus

Length 9.5 in., wing span 15 in. Adult male: head, neck, and breast yellow; wing patch white; plumage otherwise black. Adult female: slightly smaller; head, chin, and breast dull yellow; body dark brown, unstreaked. **CALL** is low-pitched *kluck* or *cack,* varied; song is a series of low harsh notes. **NEST** is in tules or cattails at 1 to 3 ft over water, a tall woven basket of reeds or grasses; eggs three to five, grayish or greenish white, heavily brown-spotted. **DISTRIBUTION:** Local summer visitor along east base of Sierra; in cattail or tule marshes.

REMARKS: Nesting Yellow-headed Blackbirds utter an amazing array of calls sounding like *gurrl, yewi,* or *cut-that-out,* and the song has been compared to the noise of a rusty gate hinge. Nests are placed scatteringly in marsh vegetation with enough water below to discourage land predators. Some pairs begin nesting early while others wait until summer. In migration and winter the birds sometimes occur in flocks with other kinds of blackbirds.

BREWER'S BLACKBIRD   *Euphagus cyanocephalus*

Length 9 in., wing span 15.5 in. Adult male: shiny iridescent black, iris pale yellow. Adult female and immature: dull brownish black, iris dark brown. **CALL** is a harsh *tchick;* "song" is a wheezy *tseur* or *tshee.* **NEST** is usually in a tree at moderate height (often in colonies); made of twigs and grasses firmed with mud; eggs three to seven, greenish gray, brown spotted.

DISTRIBUTION: Common resident at lower elevations on both slopes, nests to 8,000 ft and invades mountains to timberline during summer; in grasslands, marshes, or other open areas.

REMARKS: The Brewer's is the commonest and most wide ranging of our blackbirds and is one species that readily adjusts to human activity. The females and young are not streaked like those of other species. The nests are usually in trees but occasionally close to the ground or even in bushes, and noisily defended against invaders. Both parents feed the brood, often walking close together over grassland when seeking insects or worms then flying directly to the nest. Most nesting is below 4,000 ft but after the broods are fledged the adults and young, in small groups, move up to forage on mountain meadows, and some remain there into October. Lowland winter flocks may include hundreds of individuals.

BROWN-HEADED COWBIRD   *Molothrus ater*

Length 7.5 in., wing span 12 in. Adult male: shiny black except head and breast matte brown. Adult female: dull brown, paler and faintly streaked below. **CALL** is a series of chattering notes, of male a sharp whistle; song is a liquid gurgling *glu-glu-glee.*

DISTRIBUTION: Summer resident throughout the Sierra; winters at lower elevations on west slope; in streamside vegetation and pastures.

REMARKS: Bird students dislike the Brown-headed Cowbird because it does not build its own nest but lays its eggs singly in the nests of other songbirds.

After hatching, the young Brown-headed Cowbird takes a major share of the food brought by the foster parents and may evict one or more of the rightful nestlings. When grown the young "alien" departs to join other Brown-headed Cowbirds. Brown-headed Cowbirds are closely wedded to humans in the Sierra Nevada, favoring areas with stocks and stables, where they frequently mingle with Brewer's Blackbirds. Their numbers have increased exponentially in the region since their arrival in the early 1900s, and in most areas they have detrimentally impacted native songbird populations.

BULLOCK'S ORIOLE   *Icterus bullockii*
Pl. 483

Length 8 to 9 in., wing span 12 in. Adult male: black above except for large white wing patch; fluorescent orange below; tail black with outer feathers orange. Adult female and immature: grayish brown above; sides of head and breast yellow; belly whitish; wing with two white bars; tail yellowish when spread. **CALL** is a harsh *cha-cha-cha* chatter; song is rapid, accented *hip'-kip-y-ty-hoy'-hoy*. This is one of few species where the female also sings. **NEST** is in trees at 6 to 40 ft; a hanging pouch to 9 in. long of woven plant fibers or horsehair; eggs three to six, gray white, with scrawling blackish lines.

DISTRIBUTION: Common summer visitor at lower elevations on both slopes; very rarely wanders upslope after breeding; in oaks, cottonwoods, and other deciduous hardwoods.

REMARKS: No foothill bird is more brilliant than the male of this colorful oriole—orange, black, and white—as it is glimpsed in flight or in the trees. The birds arrive in late March or early April. Soon they are building their airy, hanging nests (which often survive into the next winter and are conspicuous after the leaves fall). They forage for insects and fruits in the trees and take others on the ground. Males precede the females in both arrival and departure.

Finches (Family Fringillidae)

GRAY-CROWNED ROSY-FINCH   *Leucosticte tephrocotis*
Pl. 488

Length 5.75 in., wing span 13 in.; body deep brown, feathers rosy hued on forepart of wing, rump, tail, and flanks; forehead black but back of head gray; female duller than male. **CALL** is *zee'o, hootititeet;* song is high pitched, chirping, varied. **NEST** is in niche of cliff or under a rock, thick walled, of mosses and dried grasses; eggs four to five, white.

DISTRIBUTION: Locally fairly common resident in Alpine Belt from peaks west of Lake Tahoe to Olancha Peak, Tulare County, at 9,500 to 14,000+ ft; about cliffs and talus near snowbanks and alpine turf; in winter some descend to east-slope Sagebrush Belt.

REMARKS: The alpine bird of the Sierra Nevada is the rosy-finch that inhabits bleak places above timberline. In summer it finds seeds of sedges and some frozen insects at the melting edges of snowbanks and takes similar food from small patches of green turf near lakes. It also catches flying insects, a diet that is possible even in winter because winds continuously deposit lowland insects on mountain peaks. Adults eat mostly plant materials, but young receive a high proportion of animal food. They have a protective "snow mask" of specialized feathers over their nostrils. These rosy-finches live in small talkative flocks, up to a dozen or more, which fly and wheel in the open over their rugged homeland. Little is known of their winter habits because few people venture into the Alpine Belt during winter, but it is thought that they retreat eastward and downslope during severe weather.

PINE GROSBEAK · *Pinicola enucleator*

Pl. 488

Length 9 in., wing span 14.5 in.; large, plump, long tailed; wings and tail dark gray; males otherwise pinkish red, females and immatures gray-bodied with dull yellow on crown and rump. CALL is a loud clear *woit-leek,* repeated; song is short, musical warble. NEST is in conifer at 16 to 35 ft out on a branch; a frail twig platform, grass lined; eggs three, greenish blue, with dark spots.

DISTRIBUTION: Sparse resident in Upper Montane and Subalpine Belts on both slopes, Plumas County to Fresno County, at 4,700 to 10,000 ft; in open forests near meadows.

REMARKS: These relatively uncommon boreal finches are strict residents of the High Sierra, where they have resided in isolation from northern populations since the Ice Age. Pine Grosbeaks are always unpredictable because they wander nomadically in search of food, a quest that on rare occasions takes them to lower elevations. Needle buds, fir and hemlock seeds, and berries of high-elevation shrubs are included in their diet. When observed, they seem quite tame and may allow close approach.

PURPLE FINCH · *Carpodacus purpureus*

Pl. 488

Length 6 in., wing span 10 in. Adult male: back and wings dark brown, tinged with red; head and breast red; belly white. Adult female: grayish brown (olive-tinged) above streaked with dusky brown; whitish below, broadly streaked with dark brown; a dark patch behind eye. CALL is a sharp *pert;* song is a short rapid rolling warble. NEST is in tree at 5 to 40 ft on a branch out from the trunk, a well-made cup of twigs, mosses, and grasses; eggs four to five, pale bluish green, with gray or black streaks.

DISTRIBUTION: Common resident mainly in Foothill and Mixed Conifer Belts of west slope, sparse summer visitor on east slope south through Mono County; common winter visitor in Foothill Belt; in conifers and oaks.

REMARKS: There are three tree-dwelling finches in the Sierra Nevada in which the males are reddish on crown, breast, and rump but the females are streaked and without red. In general, the Cassin's Finch inhabits the higher forests, the Purple Finch the Mixed Conifer Belt, and the House Finch the foothills and lowland valleys. The Purple Finch's song is short and rolling without the squeals of the House Finch's song, but their sharp *pert* call is most diagnostic. This species forages in terminal foliage of trees and bushes, sometimes on the ground, eating buds, catkins, and berries. When wintering at lower elevations they may gather in flocks of up to 15 birds.

CASSIN'S FINCH   *Carpodacus cassinii*
Pl. 488

Length 6.25 in., wing span 11.5 in. Both sexes very like their counterparts in the Purple Finch, but patterning is crisp, especially on back and wings, with cold gray appearance overall and finer streaking; on perched birds wing tips are noticeably longer than in the similar Purple Finch. **CALL** is two- or three-syllable *kee-up* or *chidilip;* song resembles that of Purple Finch but livelier and more complex. **NEST** is in pine at 10 to 80 ft among needles at end of branch; made of twigs, grasses, and bark strips; eggs four to five, bluish green, gray to black spots.

DISTRIBUTION: Common summer visitor from Mixed Conifer Belt to Sub-alpine Belt on both slopes, favors lodgepole pine forests; in winter descends to lower elevations and may mingle with Purple Finches; in open forests and about meadows.

REMARKS: The Cassin's Finch, largest of the red finches, has a song that is more varied than that of the Purple Finch, with both well-rounded notes and some House Finch–like squeals. They also appear to mimic the songs of several other forest birds. In both Purple and Cassin's Finches, one-year-old males with femalelike appearances will sing, giving the impression that female finches also sing. Cassin's Finches spend time both on the ground and in treetops, feeding on a variety of conifer seeds, berries, and insects. When not nesting these finches occur in small flocks of up to a dozen.

HOUSE FINCH   *Carpodacus mexicanus*
Pls. 484, 488

Length 6 in., wing span 9.5 in. Both sexes are very similar to their counter-parts in the Purple Finch, but red on male limited to more discrete patches and streaking on female is more diffuse and indistinct; bill is distinctly short and curved. **CALL** is *chee-ep,* rising in pitch at end; song varied, bubbling, and long, with squeaking notes. **NEST** is usually low, in tree, bush, cliff crevice, or vine on a house, a sturdy cup of grasses or other stringy material; eggs four to five, pale bluish green, few dark spots at large end.

DISTRIBUTION: Abundant resident in Central Valley and Foothill Belt (locally higher) on west slope and summer visitor along base of east slope; in scattered trees amid grassland and near water.

REMARKS: Of all native birds the House Finch is perhaps best adapted to human presence. Pairs often nest in vines on dwellings, and feed around towns and houses. At other seasons the birds live in small or large flocks that frequent fields and grasslands. When frightened, they take off in the open on high circling flights before descending again. They eat seeds of grasses and small herbaceous plants, thistles, and some wild berries. In new plumage the red feathers on males are white edged, but these margins wear off over winter so that the birds become brighter colored by nesting time.

RED CROSSBILL
Loxia curvirostra

Pl. 488

Length 6.25 in., wing span 11 in.; bill heavy, mandibles curved, crossed near tip. Adult male: wings and tail dusky brown, plumage otherwise red. Adult female: like male except color is olive yellow instead of red. **CALL** is *kip, kip, kip;* song is a mix of warbling notes. **NEST** is in pine among needles near end of a limb, made of twigs, grass, and moss; eggs three to four, greenish white, few spots.

DISTRIBUTION: Highly nomadic resident from Mixed Conifer Belt to Subalpine Belt on both slopes; in conifers.

REMARKS: The Red Crossbill's peculiar mandibles serve to pry between the scales of a cone and extract the seeds that are almost their only food source. On the ground, the birds can also glean food by spreading the jaws and using the tongue. Males vary in color from greenish yellow or orange to bright red. Most often Red Crossbills stay high in the trees, where frequent calls give indication of their presence as they forage or fly. Small flocks may visit lowland localities in winter, and at all seasons they wander widely in search of food.

PINE SISKIN
Carduelis pinus

Pl. 488

Length 5 in., wing span 9 in.; plumage streaked brown and dull white, middle of wing and whole base of tail show yellow in flight; tail short and deeply notched. **CALL** is a plaintive *swe-ah,'* higher pitched at end; also a throaty "watch-winding" *zwe-e-e-e-et*, ending strongly and abruptly; song twittering, goldfinchlike. **NEST** is usually in conifer on a spreading branch, made of twigs, plant fibers, and moss; eggs three to four, pale bluish green, lightly dotted at large end.

DISTRIBUTION: Nomadic resident from Mixed Conifer Belt to Subalpine Belt on both slopes, some descending to lower elevations in winter; mostly in conifers but more widespread in winter.

REMARKS: This duller, high-mountain relative of the goldfinches lives from spring to fall in the mountain coniferous forest but winters at lower levels. Much of the year the birds are in noisy flocks of several to over one hundred birds. In flight each member rises and drops independently, yet the flock remains compact. Often these siskins leave high perches to fly in wide circles, then return almost to the same places. The food includes tender buds of conifers and black oak and the catkins of alders and willows. In late summer they seek ripening seeds of sunflower like plants near the ground.

LESSER GOLDFINCH
Carduelis psaltria

Pls. 485, 488

Length 4.5 in., wing span 8 in.; dull olive and faintly streaked above; wings and tail blackish with white patches; males show black cap that females lack. **CALL** is plaintive and kittenlike *tee-yee;* song lively series of trills and twitters. **NEST** is in tree or shrub at 5 to 15 ft, lashed in a crotch, made of plant fibers, compact; eggs four to five, pale bluish green.

DISTRIBUTION: Common resident in Foothill Belt of west slope, uncommon on lower east slope; may wander upslope briefly in late summer; in diverse woodland, chaparral, and grassland habitats.

REMARKS: Three species of goldfinches live in the lower edges of the Sierra. Save when paired for nesting they are commonly in small flocks. Their flight is undulating—a few wing strokes and the bird rises, then swoops down with wings closed; members of a flock rise and fall independently of one another. The Lesser Goldfinch is the most widespread species. It forages widely for buds and seeds in treetops but also drops down to seek seeds of thistles and other composites.

OTHER GOLDFINCHES: The Lawrence's Goldfinch (*C. lawrencei*, length 4.75 in.) is a scarce, local summer visitor on the lowest edges of the west slope. Dry, rocky hillsides near oak woodlands and streams are its typical haunts. The male has a black face and chin; and yellow on its breast, rump, and wing bars. The female lacks the black but has yellow on the wing.

The American Goldfinch (*C. tristis,* length 5 in., pl. 486) is a slightly larger and more familiar goldfinch. Males in breeding plumage have black caps, wings, and tail that contrast sharply with a brilliant yellow body; females and winter birds are a duller mix of grays, olives, and yellows, but all show buff or white wing bars. Resident in Foothill Belt grasslands on west slope, uncommon-to-rare winter visitor at base of east slope.

EVENING GROSBEAK
Coccothraustes vespertinus

Pl. 488

Length 8 in., wing span 14 in.; large chunky bird with stout, pale green bill. Adult male: body brownish yellow; crown, wings, and tail black; a large white wing patch; forehead and stripe over eye yellow. Adult female and immature: brownish gray, darkest on head; belly whitish; wings and tail black, with white patches and spots. **CALL** is a shrill *plee-ek;* song is three loud high notes given slowly, *zer-r-p, zir-r-p, prili-p.* **NEST** is in trees at moderate height, made of twigs and rootlets, lined; eggs three to four, pale greenish blue, sparse dark marks.

DISTRIBUTION: Nomadic residents on both slopes from Mixed Conifer Belt to Upper Montane Belt, mainly wanders in flocks; mostly in dense pine or fir forests.

REMARKS: The Evening Grosbeak is a large finch, sharply attired but a poor songster. Their loud calls are unmistakable. The birds are variable in occurrence—sometimes locally common, in small groups, again scarce or absent. They forage both high in trees and on the ground. Buds of various trees and some berries are included in their diet.

Old World Sparrow (Family Passeridae)

HOUSE SPARROW   *Passer domesticus*
Pl. 487

Length 6.25 in., wing span 9.5 in. Adult male: crown gray; upper surface chestnut brown, streaked with black; black "bib" on throat and much of breast; grayish white below. Adult female and immature: head grayish brown; no black chin or throat, otherwise like dull male. **CALL** is a harsh *chissick;* song is irregular, not melodious. **NEST** is in branches of a tree or stuffed into a cavity, a bulky sphere of grass, and other materials, lined with feathers, entrance on side; eggs three to seven, white, heavy with gray brown marks.

DISTRIBUTION: Introduced from Europe, in California since 1871; most common in towns and settlements at low elevations.

REMARKS: The introduced English, or House, Sparrow became abundant during horse-and-buggy days in the Central Valley and probably followed stock and rail traffic into the mountains. Feeds largely on seeds, commonly finding these foods in waste grains or in manure around stables. Seldom ventures above the foothill country. At all seasons lives in loose flocks. Males in fresh fall plumage are white on the chin; the black appears over winter with wear of the feathers. Takes possession of cavities that could be used by native nesting songbirds and has thus impacted some songbird populations.

MAMMALS

MAMMALS—THE FURRED and four-footed animals (quadrupeds)—are warm-blooded and have a regulated body temperature about that of humans. In consequence they can be rather independent of environmental temperatures although many species avoid temperature extremes by finding shelter in caves, hollow trees, or the ground, often within a nest of plant fibers. The body is insulated by the *pelage,* or covering of hair. Commonly this is of two types: longer and stouter *guard hairs* that resist wear, and softer and shorter *underfur* that protects against heat loss. Pigments in the hair provide the external color, and a number of species change their color seasonally. All species nourish their young after birth with milk from the female's mammary glands. At birth the young are either naked, blind, and helpless (e.g., rabbits, squirrels, rodents, carnivores) or fully haired with eyes open and able to move about (e.g., Porcupines, hares, deer). Mammals have acute senses of smell, hearing, and sight; many species have sensory hairs on the head (*vibrissae,* or whiskers) that provide touch sensations from objects in the environment as the animal moves about. Most mammals are active only by night, but their presence is marked by tracks (fig.14), droppings, nests, and other "signs." To overcome the winter food shortage some species migrate (e.g., bats, deer), others hibernate in a long winter sleep at reduced body temperature (e.g., bats, ground squirrels, chipmunks), and still others cache food in large storehouses to feed on during the winter months (e.g., tree squirrels, Pikas, Beavers).

The Sierra Nevada is especially rich in mammalian species and the eastern front of the range has a greater diversity of species than any part of the Western Hemisphere north of Central America. At least 115 species find a home in the Sierra Nevada, including at least 70 species in montane and alpine environments. These numbers include several species that are endemic or nearly endemic to the area: Alpine Chipmunk, Long-eared Chipmunk, Lodgepole Chipmunk, Panamint Chipmunk, Mountain Pocket Gopher, and Mt. Lyell Shrew.

Perhaps the Sierra Nevada's most conspicuous extinction is the final extermination of Grizzly Bears in 1924. These large, and formerly common, carnivores undoubtedly played a significant role in shaping the ecosystems where they roamed. Today, Wolverines and Sierra Red Foxes apparently hover on the edge of extinction in the Sierra Nevada but are so rarely observed that next to nothing is known about their populations. A handful of other species have small or declining populations.

Taxonomy follows Jameson and Peeters (2003) and Wilson and Ruff (1999).

Marsupial (Order Marsupialia)

VIRGINIA OPOSSUM   *Didelphis virginiana*
Pl. 489
Length 25 to 40 in.; about the size of a house cat but heavier bodied (weighing 8 to 13 lb.); body gray with grizzled appearance (due to long white hairs

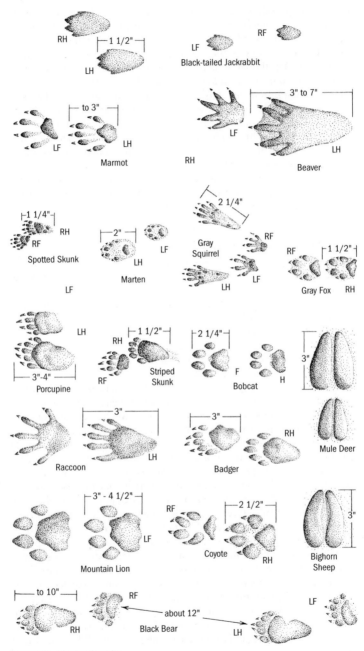

RH
1 1/2"
LH
Black-tailed Jackrabbit
LF
RF

to 3"
LF
LH
Marmot

3" to 7"
LF
RH
LH
Beaver

1 1/4"
RH
RF
Spotted Skunk
LF

2"
LH
LF
Marten

2 1/4"
Gray Squirrel
RF
LH
LF

RF
1 1/2"
Gray Fox
RH

LH
3"-4"
Porcupine

1 1/2"
RH
RF
Striped Skunk

2 1/4"
F
H
Bobcat

3"
Mule Deer

Raccoon
LH

3"
RH
Badger

3" - 4 1/2"
LF
Mountain Lion

RF
2 1/2"
Coyote
RH

3"
Bighorn Sheep

to 10"
RH
RF
about 12"
Black Bear
LH
LF

Figure 14. Mammal tracks.

over blackish woolly underfur); white face; long snout; large, naked blackish ears that may appear white tipped; long, scaly, prehensile tail; first toe on the hind foot is opposable to the others, creating a distinct track.

DISTRIBUTION: On west slope generally below level of winter freezing (roughly 3,000 ft) though sometimes seen up to 6,000 ft; occurs in all habitats but most abundant around human habitations and near water.

REMARKS: First introduced into California in 1910s, this awkward looking mammal has steadily spread across much of the state west of the Sierra Nevada. They are poorly suited to cold weather and it is common to see ones with portions of their thin ears missing due to frostbite. The only marsupial living north of Mexico, females raise their litters of five to 13 young in external abdominal pouches. Opossums may breed when only six months old, have two litters per year, and have a breeding season that extends from January to October—all reasons for their prolific spread in California. Just about anything edible, plant or animal, will be consumed.

Insectivores (Order Insectivora)

SHREWS
Genus *Sorex*

Pl. 490

Length 3.5 to 6 in.; smaller than a house mouse; snout distinctly long and tapered with long whiskers; teeth pointed, red tipped; eyes and ears tiny; feet delicate; pelage short, dense, smooth, uniform blackish, brownish or grayish above, lighter (to whitish) below.

DISTRIBUTION: Throughout the Sierra Nevada; some in wet places near streams or in meadows, others in drier sites.

REMARKS: Shrews, among the smallest of the mammals, are secretive, rarely being seen and leaving little evidence of their presence. They forage with ceaseless energy in moist places, amid grass or leaves, under logs or stones, and in burrows of mice or moles. Some venture into dry chaparral or among rocks. Between short bouts of profound slumber they dart about rapidly, twitching their noses and hunting mainly by scent or touch, occasionally giving high-pitched squeaks. Like their relatives, the moles, they feed on insects, worms, carrion, and various plant materials. One of these voracious "microcarnivores" will eat the equivalent of its weight each day. Mice captured in traps set by naturalists often are consumed overnight by shrews, leaving only skin and bones. Little is known about shrew home life. In the Sierra, young are produced from May to August, two to six (or more) per litter, naked and minute at birth but maturing rapidly. Few shrews survive a second winter. Six or more species inhabit the Sierra Nevada, some of local occurrence and others of wide distribution there and elsewhere. Precise identification requires study of skins and skulls by a trained mammalogist.

The Water Shrew (*Sorex palustris*), largest and most unusual of the local species, has a tail as long as its body (3 in.). The hind toes are closely fringed with stiff hairs, and the pelage is water resistant. It lives in or near rapid mountain streams, is abroad by day, and is often seen by hikers and fishermen. It not only swims and dives but can walk on the bottom and skitter a short distance across water surfaces (supported by air bubbles trapped under hairs on its feet).

BROAD-FOOTED MOLE
Scapanus latimanus

Pl. 491

Length 5.5 to 7 in., weight 2 oz. Body stocky; nose long, very flexible, and snoutlike; forefeet disproportionately large and flat with broad fleshy palms and heavy claws; no eyes or ears visible; pelage short, velvety, silvery black or grayish; tail scantily haired and short. **SIGN** includes low ridges (mole runs) on surface and irregularly conical mounds (mole hills).

DISTRIBUTION: All of Sierra below 9,500 ft; in loose soils of meadows, open forests, and streamside areas.

REMARKS: The mole lives entirely underground and is only rarely observed on the surface (though young moles travel above ground while dispersing in spring). When hunting food it pushes through soft soil an inch or so below the surface by use of its broad forefeet and claws. This makes a low rounded ridge over the animal's temporary shallow subway. These irregular runs, often yards in length, may be revisited after a few hours or days as the mole searches for food: earthworms, insects or their larvae, other small animals, and some seeds. Even though they lack external ears, moles have excellent hearing and unerringly track down living food by following sound waves conducted through the soil. They also have specialized receptors called Eimer's organs on their snouts that confer a higher degree of touch sensitivity than is found in most other mammals. Deeper permanent burrows also are dug, with an enlarged nest chamber. The excavated soil is pushed up in frequent short vertical tunnels onto the surface to become conical mole hills (fig. 15). Moles are active throughout the year and their young, two to four per litter, are born in spring. Because moles have very narrow hips (which enable them to turn around in tunnels) females bear their young from reproductive organs located anterior to the hips so the young can be born without having to squeeze through the tiny pelvic gap.

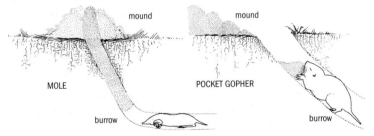

Figure 15. Burrowing methods of mole and pocket gopher. The mole pushes excavated soil up through a mound, but the pocket gopher pushes the soil out through a hole temporarily opened on the surface.

The Shrew-mole (*Neurotrichus gibbsii*, pl. 492) is a small (length 3.5 to 4.5 in.) mole of humid coastal forests that ranges south at least into Nevala County. It looks much like a shrew except that its front feet are somewhat large and its tail is hairy. Unlike other moles, this species is active on the surface during the day.

Bats (Order Chiroptera)

Length 3 to 5.5 in., wing span 8 to 15.5 in.; body mouselike; wings formed of thin webs of skin between bones of arm and second to fifth fingers on each "hand"; first finger free, with claw; also a web between hind legs and tail; mouth wide; ears large, paper thin; hind toes with sharp curved claws; pelage dense, uniformly colored, usually brownish.

DISTRIBUTION: Sierra-wide in numerous habitats. The range of many species is poorly known.

REMARKS: Our only flying mammals are bats that emerge at dusk to catch night-flying insects for food. Their seemingly erratic flights are purposeful, mainly in pursuit of prey. When hunting, bats emit short bursts of high-frequency calls (up to 50 bursts per second at frequencies of 50,000 cycles or higher); these echo back from the diminutive prey to the bats' highly sensitive ears, somewhat in the manner of human radar. By this guidance insects are precisely located and caught, often within milliseconds.

Of roughly 17 species of bats inhabiting the Sierra Nevada, some hunt close to the ground between trees and shrubs, over water, over clearings, and others at heights of 25 to 50 ft within the forest, while free-tailed bats of the foothills forage out in the open. Seven of the species in the Sierra belong to the genus of very small bats (*Myotis*); there is usually one or more species of this genus in most locations. During the day, bats hang singly or in groups by their hind claws in dark crevices in trees or rocks, some in caves, and some in buildings. Several species, such as Townsend's Long-eared Bat (*Corynorhinus townsendii*), mate in fall then females store sperm over winter and become pregnant in early spring—a reproductive strategy of some hibernating bat species. Young bats, one or two per female, are born in early summer. When small they may cling to the mother while she forages but later remain in the roost until they can fly. In winter, when insects are scarce, some species hibernate and others migrate to warmer places. Bat populations have been in decline generally and some species are threatened; Townsend's Long-eared Bat is a State and Federal Species of Special Concern. Identification of bats is difficult and often requires specimens in hand to compare with detailed technical descriptions.

Carnivores (Order Carnivora)

COYOTE
Canis latrans

Pls. 493, 504

Length 42 to 52 in., weight 20 to 30 lb. or more. Size and form of large collie dog; ears to 4.5 in. long, pointed, held erect; tail bushy, diameter 4 in., dark at tip; pelage long, gray to grayish brown, dark stripe along back, underparts white; nose, ears, back, and legs reddish. **SIGN** is doglike; tracks longer than wide, 2.5 in. by 2 in., hind foot smaller, marks of claws show in soft soil; droppings to .75 in. in diameter. **VOCALIZATIONS** are loud high-pitched barking and wailing, mainly at night.

DISTRIBUTION: Throughout the Sierra; some from high mountains winter at lower levels; live and hunt in open, usually singly.

REMARKS: Coyotes, our native "wild dogs," remain fairly common despite persistent efforts to reduce their numbers. People in remote high camps are often entertained by Coyotes singing at dawn or dusk—one animal sometimes sounding like a chorus—and by occasional daytime glimpses of the animals. Coyotes are opportunists as to food. They dig out ground squirrels or pocket gophers, catch rabbits, mice, and grasshoppers, take occasional birds, and sometimes scavenge deer killed by Mountain Lions; they also eat carrion. Berries of manzanita, juniper, or other plants are eaten. For shelter they use a rock den, enlarge a rodent burrow, or dig their own. The young, six or seven (three to 11), are furred at birth and fed at the den by both parents, but by fall scatter for independent life.

In the western lowlands and foothills they show a paler, less furry coat, larger ears, more slender snout, and smaller teeth than those in the mountains. Large Coyotes closely resemble wolves, of which there are two old, unverified reports from the Sierra.

GRAY FOX
Urocyon cinereoargenteus

Pl. 494

Length 40 in., weight 7 to 10 lb. Form and size of small collie dog; body and tail iron gray with black stripe along middle; tail black tipped; back of ears, sides, and legs yellowish brown; chin and belly white; ears and legs relatively short compared to the Red Fox. **SIGN** includes tracks about 1 in., claw marks showing in soft soil;

droppings doglike, diameter .5 in. **VOCALIZATIONS** are a sharp bark and growling notes.

DISTRIBUTION: Foothill and Mixed Conifer Belts, in brushy areas of many habitats; solitary.

REMARKS: The principal home of this fox is the west slope, where it is the commonest carnivore; some individuals roam into midelevation forests above the foothills. It is active by day or by night, trotting briskly under the shrubbery, across roadways, and into rocky places; it also climbs trees and may even den there. From August to early winter it may feed largely on the berries of manzanita or coffeeberry; other plant material is also consumed. Animal food includes pocket gophers, mice, other rodents, rabbits, and some birds (even as large as quail). The young, averaging four per litter, are born in spring and remain under parental care about two months before becoming independent.

RED FOX   *Vulpes vulpes*
Pl. 495

Length 42 in., weight 7 to 15 lb. Size of small collie; ear 4 in., pointed, black tipped; coat rich reddish, underparts whitish; front legs blackish; "cross" phase is more brownish with dark streak down back and shoulders; other color phases rare; all have very large and bushy white-tipped tail. **VOCALIZATION** is a bark, louder than that of the Gray Fox.

DISTRIBUTION: Only in higher mountains; occasionally down to about 6,000 ft in winter. State Threatened and Federal Species of Special Concern (for High Sierra Population).

REMARKS: These native foxes (Sierra Nevada Red Fox, *V. v. necator*) are extremely scarce and poorly known in the High Sierra with very few records. Here they travel in and out of sparse forest in search of White-tailed Jackrabbits, squirrels, chipmunks, mice, and some birds. In winter, dense fur grows out between their toes, for easier travel on snow. Rocky dens presumably are used as shelter, where the young (three to nine) are born about April.

Red Foxes of an eastern subspecies have been introduced and now occur in the Central Valley and adjacent foothills.

BLACK BEAR   *Ursus americanus*
Pls. 496, 504

Large, to 5 ft. long and 40 in. high at shoulder (males being larger and heavier than females); tail 6 in. or less; weight usually under 300 lb.; front foot squarish (to 6.5 in. by 4 in.), hind foot triangular (to 9 in. by 4.5 in.); all five toes and claws of each foot usually show in tracks; pelage long, heavy, either glossy black or cinnamon brown. **SIGN** includes irregular, large blackish droppings; tracks in dusty places; scratches on trees. **VOCALIZATIONS** include sniffs or snorts; a loud growl or bawl when scared or injured.

DISTRIBUTION: Mainly in Mixed Conifer and Upper Montane Belts at 1,200 to 8,500 ft, more common on west slope; inhabits forested areas or thickets, sheltering in caves, rock piles, or hollow trees.

REMARKS: This bear is the largest living Sierra carnivore. Footprints in dusty places, large and irregular blackish droppings, and claw marks on trees are common evidence of its presence during summer and fall. The bears themselves are often near campgrounds or mountain resorts. Almost anything its paws can reach serves as food—small mammals or insects in nests, any flesh or carrion, garbage, grasses, leaves, fruits, berries, and nuts. Bears usually acquire much fat in fall, and some time after snow arrives they den up for a midwinter sleep that is less profound than the true hibernation of ground squirrels. In mid- or late winter the cubs are born, two or three of diminutive size (8 oz. or less), which are nursed in the den until they are able to go foraging with the mother. Both young and adults are adept climbers and may take to trees when disturbed. Some bears near summer homes or campgrounds become nuisances by learning to raid food supplies and garbage cans. *Do not feed bears as they can inflict severe injuries.*

OTHER BEARS: The Grizzly Bear (*Ursus arctos*), emblem of California, originally inhabited the foothill oaks and chaparral and the lower forests of the Sierra. It is distinguished from the Black Bear by its long front claws, shoulder hump, grizzled coat, and larger size. Once abundant, California's grizzlies were mercilessly hunted until the last living individual was seen during 1924 in Sequoia National Park. The word *Yosemite* is apparently derived from the Miwok word for this bear.

RINGTAIL   *Bassariscus astutus*
Pl. 497

Length 27 to 31 in., weight 2 to 2.5 lb. Ears 1.75 in., conspicuous, rounded; body slender; legs short; tail long, bushy, with alternate black and white rings; body drab brown, paler below; face masked with large white "spectacles." **SIGN** includes roundish track, diameter 1 in., droppings slender, irregular. **VOCALIZATION** is a bark for adults; young make squeaking noises.

DISTRIBUTION: Foothill and lower Mixed Conifer Belts (rarely to 7,200 ft) in rocks or brush near water.

REMARKS: The Ringtail, relative of the Raccoon, is nocturnal and hence rarely seen, and its tracks are seldom in evidence. For daytime shelter it uses holes in oaks or other trees, small caves, spaces within rock piles, or old cabins. The long tail serves for balance in climbing and leaping on trees or rocks, at which the animal is agile. Its food includes white-footed mice, wood rats, other rodents, sparrows, and berries of manzanita, madrone, and other plants. The annual litter of three or four is born in May or June. Early settlers often made it a pet to roam their cabins and keep down the mouse population, so it has been called the Miner's Cat.

RACCOON   *Procyon lotor*
Pl. 498

Length 24 to 40 in., weight 9 to 18+ lb. Body robust, face with black mask bordered by white; ear 2 to 2.25 in., rounded, white edged; pelage dense,

1 in. long, yellowish or grayish brown with black-tipped guard hairs, paler beneath; tail bushy, four to six black rings alternating with yellowish white. SIGN includes handlike tracks, front 1.75 in. long, hind 3 in. long.

DISTRIBUTION: Widespread except at high elevations, mostly near water.

REMARKS: Raccoons typically sleep by day in rotted-out cavities of trees, then descend at night to forage on the ground or in shallow water. Others den in rock piles or large burrows. Their tracks often show in streamside mud or sand, those of the front and hind foot commonly in pairs. Raccoons exceed bears in their varied diet—rodents and rabbits, birds, frogs, fishes, insects, other invertebrates, acorns, wild and cultivated fruits, berries, and grapes, besides carrion and cultivated grain and melons. They seem to be intelligent and highly curious animals, stopping repeatedly to probe into matters that catch their interest. The young, averaging four (three to seven) are born in April or May and remain with their mother until late summer.

WOLVERINE — *Gulo gulo*

Pl. 499

Length 35 to 40 in., weight 30 to 60 lb. It has a bearlike head, heavy forelegs, arched back, and bushy tail. The body is dark brown with a broad yellowish stripe on each side from shoulder to rump; the face, feet, undersurface, and end of tail are blackish, with the forehead and edges of the ears buff. Its food includes various rodents and sometimes larger prey taken from bears or Coyotes.

DISTRIBUTION: The Wolverine formerly roamed throughout the High Sierra, chiefly above 8,000 ft; never common, it is now extremely rare and seen few times per decade if at all. State Threatened and Federal Species of Special Concern.

RIVER OTTER — *Lutra canadensis*

Pls. 500, 504

Weasel-like in appearance and aquatic in habits; a scarce resident of some west slope rivers to elevations of 9,000 ft. It also occurs on the east slope in rivers from Lake Tahoe south to Inyo County. Otters are dark brown with a sleek silvery sheen when wet; they also have webbed feet and a thick-based tail. They are much larger than Minks, being 33 to 52 in. long and weighing up to 6 lb. SIGN is a latrine on the bank of a stream or river, where feces mixed with fish scales accumulate.

AMERICAN MARTEN — *Martes americana*

Pl. 501

Length 24 to 27 in., weight 2 to 3 lb. Size of a small domestic cat but slender with a weasel-like body; ears 1.5 in., rounded; tail black tipped and bushy, diameter to 3 in.; above yellow brown grading to dark brown on tail; paler below with patch of orange or buff on throat.

DISTRIBUTION: Mainly in Upper Montane and Subalpine Belts to southern Tulare County, at 7,000 to 10,300 ft; about rockslides in summer and fall, otherwise prefers mature red fir stands.

REMARKS: This medium-sized member of the weasel family is mostly solitary and seldom seen. Loss of its preferred habitats through logging appears to have impacted its numbers and made it even more difficult to find. It is an agile climber, taking shelter in tree cavities well above ground, and it hunts some food among high branches. In winter the undersurface of its feet becomes densely furred, facilitating travel on snow. During warmer months the marten hunts Pikas and rodents in rockslides but also captures ground squirrels, chipmunks, and sometimes grasshoppers. It also takes Chickarees and birds, more often in winter. Mating occurs in summer but development of the embryos is suspended until late December, and the three young (one to five) are born in spring.

FISHER   *Martes pennanti*

Length 35 to 40 in., weight 4 to 12 lb. Now very rare in the Sierra due to logging and human activity, it has the form of a heavy, oversized weasel. The nose, lower legs and feet, hind part of the body, and all of the tail are black; the body otherwise is drab brown, becoming grayish on head and shoulders. In these mountains it lives in the upper Mixed Conifer and Upper Montane Belts at about 5,000 to 8,000 ft, feeding on squirrels, other rodents, and birds. Solitary and apparently needing large areas of mature forests free of human disturbance, this species is rarely seen. State and Federal Species of Special Concern.

STRIPED SKUNK   *Mephitis mephitis*

Pl. 502

Length 24 to 28 in., tail 10 to 13 in., weight to 8+ lb. About size of a house cat; head small, body stout, legs short; pelage long, black except for narrow white line up forehead and large white area from back of head to shoulders, continuing as two white stripes to base of tail; tail bushy (hairs to 5 in. long). **SIGN** includes odor; tracks of five toes and claw marks on each foot, hind foot 1.5 in. long.

DISTRIBUTION: Widespread and found in nearly all habitats in the Sierra, absent only above timberline.

REMARKS: The skunk goes foraging at dusk without fear of human or beast. It is "armed" with a defensive nauseating scent that can be sprayed from glands below the tail to a distance of 6 ft. The plumelike tail is somewhat of an indicator: if raised upright, an intruder should retire. May also stamp its front feet on the ground as a display of irritation. The long foreclaws aid in turning over stones when searching for food and in digging out insects in the ground, leaving small forage pits as evidence of such work. About half the food includes grasshoppers, beetles, and other surface-dwelling insects. This is supplemented by mice, pocket gophers, wood rats and squirrels, occasional reptiles and amphibians, berries of shrubs, and other plant materials. For shelter the skunk may take over a ground squirrel or badger burrow, or use a hollow log, a hole under a stump, a rock crevice, or a space under some deserted building. The young, about five per litter, are born in spring. The Striped Skunk differs from its spotted cousin in being more cosmopolitan in its habitat choices, less strictly nocturnal, and less apt to climb.

WESTERN SPOTTED SKUNK   *Spilogale gracilis*
Pl. 503
Length 15 to 18 in., tail 5 to 6.5 in., weight to 1.5 lb. Size of a medium ground squirrel; neck distinct, legs short; black with white spot on forehead, one below each ear, and four broken stripes on neck, back, and sides; tail bushy, with long white hairs at tip. SIGN includes odor; tracks of hind foot to 1.25 in. long, with marks of five toes and pads.

DISTRIBUTION: Widespread in most habitats except high mountains, may be more common at lower elevations; in dry brushy or rocky outcrops and canyons.

REMARKS: This little creature is nocturnal, nimble, and a fair climber on fence posts, trees, and beams. At times it upends to stand and walk on the forefeet—in play, in anger, or before discharging scent. For shelter it uses hollow logs, crevices in rock heaps, burrows of other animals, and crannies under or in houses or farm buildings. The long, stout front claws are used in digging. The spotted skunk has a varied diet of many crickets and other insects, small rodents, birds, carrion, eggs, and some plant materials. Mating is in fall and the litter of about four is born in April or May, with the young becoming full sized in about three months. Much remains to be learned about the life history of this animal in the western United States, where it is tentatively separated from the Eastern Spotted Skunk (*S. putorius*), pending further taxonomic study.

SHORT-TAILED WEASEL   *Mustela erminea*
Pl. 505
Length 7 to 12 in., weight 2 to 5 oz. Our smallest carnivore, this weasel is the size of a medium chipmunk, with slim body and short legs. In summer it is chocolate brown above and white below but becomes all white in winter except the black tail tip. It is a smaller version of the Long-tailed, best identified by its shorter tail of 2.5 to 3.5 in. (tail is 4.5 to 6.25 in. in Long-tailed). It lives in higher elevation coniferous forests and subalpine habitats south to southern Tulare County, but, being uncommon, neither its full range nor local habits are well known. Preys on voles in alpine meadows.

LONG-TAILED WEASEL   *Mustela frenata*
Pl. 506
Length 12 to 22 in., weight 4 to 11 oz. Head short and tapered; neck, body, and tail long and slender, limbs short; in summer, upper parts including

legs brown, undersurface creamy yellow; in winter, white above and below; end of tail black at all seasons.

DISTRIBUTION: Widespread throughout the Sierra and possible in nearly all habitats; in old logs and under rock piles, sometimes under buildings.

REMARKS: The weasel is a fearless little carnivore, active at all seasons, and often abroad in daytime. Having a slender body it can seek squirrels or pocket gophers in their burrows and find other rodents in rock crevices. It can run up and down trees almost as easily as a tree squirrel. Rodents (especially voles) and small birds are usual prey, these animals recognizing the weasel as an enemy and giving voice when one appears. Weasels breed in summer but embryo development is suspended until about March, and the four to nine young are born a month later. The change to a white coat in winter makes the weasel almost invisible on snow.

MINK *Mustela vison*
Pl. 507

Mainly a lowland animal, but some live in the central and northern Sierra up to 9,000 ft. It has the contours of a weasel but is larger (up to 28 in. long and over 2 lb.). The coat is dark brown, blackish at the end of the tail. It is highly aquatic and finds much of its food in water, but can travel and hunt on land, being mainly nocturnal. As food it takes fishes, frogs, aquatic invertebrates, and some small mammals and birds.

AMERICAN BADGER *Taxidea taxus*
Pls. 504, 508

Length 2 to 2.5 ft, weight 12 to 24 lb. Body robust, broad, flattish; legs short, stout; front claws stout and long (1 to 1.5 in.); head with black cap extending down onto snout, and white checks; body grayish yellow grizzled with white; narrow white stripe from nose over crown and along back; pelage long on sides; tail bushy; legs black. **SIGN** includes flattish holes about 12 in. in diameter in ground; tracks 2 in. long, "toed in"; droppings 1 in. diameter, scarce.

DISTRIBUTION: In dry open country, irrespective of elevation, from Central Valley over the Sierra and into the Great Basin; solitary, partly diurnal.

REMARKS: The American Badger in structure and habits is preeminently a digger with stoutly muscled foreparts, short sturdy legs, and heavy foreclaws. These enable it to dig so efficiently that it seems to swim into the soil. Other carnivores hunt by sight and stealth, but the American Badger often senses (smells?) its prey—commonly ground squirrels or pocket gophers—in underground nests and rapidly digs them out. Other small animals and carrion are eaten. This badger also digs to escape a pursuing dog or human, to bury larger prey such as a rabbit until consumed, to make a sleeping place or nest chamber, and to bury its droppings. On the surface it can run with deceptive speed. Usually silent, it can hiss, growl, and grunt. If cornered it bites fiercely and may emit a strong scent from glands near the anus. The young, usually two (one to five), are born fully furred early in April and cared for by the mother until late summer.

MOUNTAIN LION   *Puma concolor*
Pls. 504, 509

Length 6 to 8 ft, weight 80 to 200 lb. Form catlike, but easily mistaken for a large dog such as a Golden Retriever if seen briefly; rich tawny to reddish brown above; chin, throat, and middle of undersurface white; tail long and slender, black-tipped. **SIGN** includes tracks, catlike, wider than long, 3 to 4.5 in., hind edge of heel pad with two indentations.

DISTRIBUTION: Wide-ranging and possible in any habitat in the Sierra; not common but possibly growing in numbers in the foothills.

REMARKS: Among local carnivores, the Mountain Lion (also called Cougar, Panther, or Puma) is second in size only to the Black Bear. Being quiet and secretive, it is very rarely seen, even by people who live within its range. It is most active at the twilight hours of dawn and dusk. Mule Deer are its favorite and principal food. The lion creeps stealthily within a short distance of a deer and then with a few quick bounds jumps on the quarry and strikes it down. Leaps of over 25 ft are possible. Deer killed by Mountain Lions show characteristic opening of the chest cavity, with ribs on one side "sawed" away; lungs, heart, and liver eaten first; then the carcass is covered with sticks and leaves. Sometimes they eat much of the carcass, or only a small part and cover the remainder. The dusky-spotted kittens, usually two or three, may be born at any season and live with the mother for much of their first year. Home ranges of males are a minimum of 64 square miles and don't overlap with other males, the boundaries being marked by urine or excretions from anal scent glands. Females stake out smaller territories and young lions wander nomadically in search of vacant territories. Encounters with this big cat seldom result in injury or death to humans but extreme caution is advised because of the potential risk.

BOBCAT   *Lynx rufus*
Pl. 510

Length 30 to 45 in., weight 12 to 25+ lb. Size and form of a large house cat with a very short tail (5 to 6 in. long); pelage soft, deep; light reddish brown above in summer, gray in winter; undersurface and inner sides of legs white, spotted or barred with black; ears black tufted, black at tip and base; tail black tipped, white below. **SIGN** includes tracks, round, about 2 in. in diameter, heel pad notched behind.

DISTRIBUTION: Widespread and common to uncommon in nearly all habitats and successional stages.

REMARKS: The common name of Bobcat refers to its short tail. Less shy than the Mountain Lion and often active by day, a Bobcat may be glimpsed as it bounds across a road and disappears in the brush or as it intently stalks some small prey item. Usually silent, it can scream and yowl during the mating season, a noise like the one house cats make but louder. Bobcats can climb trees readily when in need of safety or when stalking the nest of some large bird. Rabbits and rodents make up most of the food, especially ground squirrels, wood rats, and pocket gophers. Some small birds and a few quail are eaten. A Bobcat may kill deer that are impeded by deep snow. The young, commonly three (two to four), are born in spring in a den among rocks or at hollowed tree bases.

Hoofed Animals (Order Artiodactyla)

WILD PIG   *Sus scrofa*

Length up to 5 ft, height 2 to 3 ft, weight up to 600 lb. Piglike in form but covered with blackish brown bristly hair and body compressed from side to side; snout fleshy; may show protruding canine tusks.

DISTRIBUTION: Scattered local populations throughout foothills of west slope; favors oak woodlands at lower elevations.

REMARKS: Both feral hogs and wild boars are present in California's wildlands (the latter being introduced in 1924), freely interbreeding and producing mixed stock of various colors. Wild Pigs have poor eyesight but an excellent sense of smell that allows them to detect predators and to find food. Evidence of their presence is often conspicuous, for they leave large swaths of overturned soil where they have scoured the ground for acorns and plant bulbs. Actually seeing the animals is another thing altogether, for they are exceedingly wary and reclusive. Because they consume such a large number of acorns, a key food item for many native species, and disrupt much of the forest floor, they may have a detrimental impact on local ecosystems.

MULE DEER   *Odocoileus hemionus*

Pl. 511

Adults 32 to 42 in. high at shoulder, 5 to 6 ft. long; males may weigh 200 lb. Ears large, 8 to 9 in. long to 4 in. wide; tail blackish above, white beneath; adults uniform bright reddish brown in summer, grayish brown in winter; rump and throat whitish; young fawns reddish brown, spotted with white; antlers only in males, spikelike in second summer, branched in older deer. **SIGN** includes sheeplike tracks, sharply pointed, varying with sex and age; droppings black elliptical pellets or small masses depending on diet and season.

DISTRIBUTION: Occurs throughout the Sierra in summer; in winter, migrates to below heavy snow.

REMARKS: The millions of people who visit the Sierra see only a few of the countless deer living there, so adept are these animals at hiding in brushy cover. Some deer live yearlong in the foothills and lower forests, but many migrate upslope with advancing spring greenery and later a few continue almost to the crest. Their downslope return begins with the first heavy snows, commonly by mid-November. In winter large numbers of deer may concentrate on the west slope near the lower border of ponderosa pine forests where the snow is 18 in. deep or less. Deer forage mostly in morning, late afternoon, and early evening; by day they bed down, often under sheltering bushes where there is a clear view of surroundings. The bed is a slight depression, 2 or 3 ft in diameter, sometimes scraped free of surface litter. The animals drink regularly, often traveling far in late summer when water is scarce. Deer eat a great variety of plants, browsing on shrubs and grazing on grass and herbs in meadows. Many bushes of ceanothus and other shrubs are trimmed of terminal branchlets and leaves. If local deer numbers are large the bushes may show excessive use and be pruned in peculiar shapes by overbrowsing. Antlers begin growth on bucks in April and become mature by late summer, and the dried velvet (covering skin) is rubbed off by September. Bucks use their antlers contending with other males during the mating season or rut in early winter; the antlers are dropped by March. Fawns, commonly two per birth, appear in June; by early fall their spots disappear with molt into the winter coat. Does and fawns commonly keep together until the next young are due. Native enemies are the Mountain Lion, which can kill deer of any age, and the Coyote, which kills fawns and the occasional older deer hampered by snow. Hunters shoot many deer annually under legal control, and an unknown number are removed by poachers. Some deer die of starvation, many are killed along highways, and nearly all populations have been significantly impacted by human development cutting off their traditional migration routes between the high and low country.

BIGHORN SHEEP   *Ovis canadensis*
Pl. 512

Height at shoulder 3 to 3.5 ft, body length 4 to 6 ft, weight to 160 lb. Sturdy and well muscled; coat gray or buffy brown with large whitish rump patch; hairs stiff, dense; horns permanent—on old males massive, spiraled back and outward often to full circle, on females small, erect, with slight backward curve. SIGN includes tracks to 3 in. long; droppings cylindrical to .5 in. long, slightly pointed at one end.

DISTRIBUTION: Originally from near Sonora Pass south to Mt. Langley and the Kaweah Range, now limited to a few herds from Yosemite National Park to Mt. Langley; in Alpine and Subalpine Belts near crest on open areas. Migrate downslope in winter along the east slope. State and Federal Endangered.

REMARKS: Early travelers found bands of Bighorn Sheep rather often along the Sierra crest, but meat hunters and herders of domestic sheep soon reduced the numbers. There are currently five subpopulations in the Sierra, three of which (including the population on the east side of Yosemite National Park) were initiated by reintroduction of sheep into historically occupied areas. The total population of Sierra Bighorn Sheep declined in the late 1990s to about 100 individuals and they were given an emergency listing as Endangered in 1999. Numbers have since rebounded slightly. Bighorn require rocky, steep escape terrain near suitable feeding and bedding sites. Grasses, herbs, and browse (twigs and leaves of shrubs and trees) are eaten. In winter, Bighorn Sheep move downslope or occupy windswept ridges; migration routes are an important habitat requirement. The combination of these requirements results in small, isolated populations. The sheep are gregarious, with group size and composition varying by season. During the mating season most older males are found living apart from females and young. Ewes generally remain for life in the band in which they were born. Mating is in late fall, when rams fight by kicking and butting. Gestation is about 180 days, and lambs appear in May or June. Later they play much with one another and with their mothers. The principal losses are in winter when both young and adults become isolated by deep soft snow. Mountain Lions may also hunt them in some areas.

Rodents (Order Rodentia)

PORCUPINE   *Erethizon dorsatum*
Pl. 513

Length 26 to 37 in., weight 8 to 15 lb. (up to 40 lb.). Upper surface and sides of body and tail densely armed with pointed hollow quills up to 3 in. long; yellow hairs between quills to 7 in. long; winter fur black, 4 in. long. SIGN includes paired incisor marks .25 in. wide on peeled trunks, mainly conifers; droppings bean shaped, to 1 in. by .63 in., of undigested bark pulp, resembling compressed sawdust; tracks to 3 in. long, toed-in.

DISTRIBUTION: Mainly in Mixed Conifer and Upper Montane Belts in open forests at 4,000 to 11,000 ft south to Tulare County; occasionally in lower valleys of west slope and on sagebrush plains of northeast.

REMARKS: This largest of terrestrial rodents is well protected. When alarmed it turns away, erects its quills, humps its body, and swings its stout tail laterally. If any quills touch an inquiring dog or person, the barbed tips lodge in the "enemy's" skin. Nevertheless, Porcupines are still taken as food by Fishers and Mountain Lions. The Porcupine is active mainly at night and is a slow-moving methodical animal. It climbs readily to eat the succulent inner bark of trees, mostly conifers, but in spring takes some herbaceous plants on the ground. Its voice is a grunting or groaning *unh*. Individuals may rest or sleep aloft in trees but often shelter in rock slides. The single young is born in late spring, well haired, with its eyes open; its soft quills soon harden. Forest damage is slight with few "porkies" present, but moderate numbers may girdle and top many forest trees.

MOUNTAIN BEAVER   *Aplodontia rufa*
Pl. 514

Length 11 to 14 in., tail 1 to 1.5 in., weight 2 to 3 lb. Body stocky, limbs short, front claws long; head blunt, eyes and ears small; white spot at base of each ear; long stiff whiskers; pelage dense, short, erect, blackish brown above, grayish below. SIGN includes surface runways and underground tunnels 6 to 7 in. (to 10 in.) in diameter, with many openings, under shrubbery near small streams; much fresh cut vegetation or bark on ground, also nearby bushes or trees pruned of small twigs. VOCALIZATIONS range from soft whining and sobbing to a booming noise that gives them the nickname "boomer"; most common is a harsh chattering when irritated.

DISTRIBUTION: Locally in Upper Montane and Subalpine Belts on both slopes at about 5,000 to 11,000 ft; favors riparian habitats; mostly nocturnal, some activity on cloudy days. State and Federal Species of Special Concern for Sierra Nevada populations (*A. r. californica*).

REMARKS: The Mountain Beaver, or Aplodontia, looks like an oversized tailless meadow mouse. It is a relict rodent, of wider occurrence in the geological past, now living only from southern British Columbia to Sequoia National Park. Although it is no beaver, it was given this name by miners for its habit of gnawing off bark and cutting limbs. Most of the population inhabits coastal lowlands (south to Marin County). In the Sierra its burrows and runways are near small streams bordered by willow, dogwood, fern thickets, and other riparian plants. The burrows are extensive with many entrances, often damp, and kept clean. Most kinds of plants near the burrows are cut for food, often in excess amount, and piles of this green fodder may be seen near or in the damp or wet tunnels. Mountain Beavers sometimes climb shrubs or small trees to cut small twigs for food or nest making. The animals seem sociable but not gregarious. The young, usually three or four, are born in spring and become full sized by late summer.

CALIFORNIA GROUND SQUIRREL or BEECHEY GROUND SQUIRREL

Spermophilus beecheyi

Pl. 515

Length 15 to 18 in., weight 1 to 1.5 lb. Body dull brownish gray, mottled with white scallops and black crosslines, sides of neck and shoulders grizzled white with dark brown patch between shoulders; plain buff below; tail long and somewhat bushy. **SIGN** includes burrows to 4.5 in. in diameter; also runways about 3 in. wide through grass. **VOCALIZATION** is a sharp metallic clink.

DISTRIBUTION: Widespread in open or early successional habitats mainly below 8,000 ft (though as high as 10,000 ft in southern Sierra); commonest on plains and open foothills, fewer in Mixed Conifer Belt.

REMARKS: These lowland ground squirrels, once enormously abundant, have been far reduced to protect crops and pastures even though they play an enormously important role in ecosystems. Their burrows, in hillsides where possible, extend many feet and may be two yards or more in depth. These serve for safety retreats, hibernation, food storage, and the rearing of young. The tunnels also afford shelter for toads, various snakes, burrowing owls, skunks, and other animals and influence soil moisture and other ecological processes. Grasslands often show trails where the squirrels travel repeatedly between their burrows and feeding places. This species, like other ground squirrels and the chipmunks (but not the tree squirrels or marmot), has thin inner cheek pouches for carrying food or nest material. In spring the squirrels eat some green vegetation, but most of the year they depend on seeds of grasses and low herbs. They may dig bulbs and at times climb into oaks for acorns. The annual brood, averaging five or six, appears from April into June, and the young become independent by late summer. Individuals living above the snow line hibernate in winter, while some in the lowlands hibernate from late summer until about January or February.

BELDING'S GROUND SQUIRREL — *Spermophilus beldingi*
Pl. 516

Length 10 to 12 in., weight 7 to 10 oz. Body light yellowish gray, with broad streak of bright reddish brown down back; tail short, reddish under. SIGN includes burrows, usually in flat ground, about 2 in. in diameter. VOCALIZATIONS include a call of five to eight shrill, short whistles, *seek,* in quick succession; female with young utters a single note, *e-chert!*

DISTRIBUTION: High mountain meadows south to southern Tulare County, as high as 11,500 ft and as low as 6,000 ft (west slope) or 4,900 ft (east slope); mainly in meadows, also on dry slopes and sagebrush flats.

REMARKS: This ground squirrel of the higher Sierra meadows is often locally abundant. People hiking through meadows where these ground squirrels live get used to being announced by repeated shrill piping whistles relayed from one squirrel to another. Any Belding's Ground Squirrels that are out in the open run toward their burrows, then stand straight upright on their hind feet to look about for the impending danger—this familiar posture gives them their common nickname "picket pin." The species feeds mainly on herbs and grasses and does not climb. Adults emerge in March, possibly earlier, while there is still much snow. The young, averaging about eight, appear from mid-May onward according to elevation. When half-grown they emerge to live about the mouth of the parent burrow, gradually learning to forage for themselves. By late August or early October, all the population is in hibernation.

GOLDEN-MANTLED GROUND SQUIRREL — *Spermophilus lateralis*
Pl. 517

Length 9 to 11 in., weight 4 to 8 oz. Head and neck all yellowish or coppery red; back grizzled brown; each side with a broad white stripe bordered with black; undersurface pale gray to whitish; tail with black centrally, buffy at margin. SIGN includes burrows 2 to 2.5 in. in diameter, usually near rocks or logs.

DISTRIBUTION: Mainly in Upper Montane and Subalpine Belts, lower on east slope, at 6,000 to 11,800 ft; lives on forest floor, around chaparral and meadow margins, and on steep rocky slopes.

REMARKS: The "Copperhead" is the commonest and often the tamest of the Sierra ground squirrels, easily mistaken for a large chipmunk except that its stripes don't extend onto its head and neck. It rarely stands up on its hind feet and only occasionally gives a sharp warning call. It will often gather food until its cheek pouches bulge with the load. This material may be eaten, carried into the burrow, or quickly buried in a shallow surface excavation. Only occasionally are burrow entrances seen, and the tunnels probably do not extend far into the ground. The food is mostly a mixture of plant materials. Leaves and seeds on the ground and fungi make up a large portion of the diet, thus enabling Golden-mantled Ground Squirrels to avoid competing with their chipmunk neighbors who specialize more in seeds that are still on branches. Adults may emerge from hibernation by early April, and the young, two to six per litter, are born in June and July, appearing above ground at about six weeks of age. Some do not enter hibernation until mid-October; at lower elevations occasional adults may be abroad in winter. Enemies include weasels, Coyotes, and hawks.

NORTHERN FLYING SQUIRREL · *Glaucomys sabrinus*

Pl. 518

Length 10 to 13 in., weight 3 to 6 oz. A small squirrel with a fur-covered membrane along each side between the legs; head rounded; eyes large; tail broad, flat, heavily furred; pelage dense, silky, brownish gray above, dull white below. **VOCALIZATION** is a low *whurr*.

DISTRIBUTION: Mixed Conifer and Upper Montane Belts of west slope (extending onto east slope in Lake Tahoe and Mammoth Lakes regions) at 3,000 to 8,100 ft; in black oak woodlands and conifer forests (especially mature fir stands with open understories).

REMARKS: This nocturnal squirrel runs up a tree, spreads its legs with their connecting skin webs, and silently glides down through the air for as much as 100 ft. Just before alighting it bends the broad tail upward to act like a rudder, so that the squirrel lands upright on its feet on the trunk of another tree—with a faint thump. The instant it lands it immediately runs around to the backside of the trunk just in case an owl has been following close behind. It does not fly. The silky pelage makes for silent gliding to help avoid hunting owls, and the big eyes are efficient for nighttime vision. Some foraging is done on the ground, where they seek hypogeous fungi. By day this squirrel shelters in cavities of black oaks or firs, sometimes in woodpecker holes, using shredded bark to form an insulated nest. Litters vary from two to six and are born mainly in June and July, but half-grown young have been found late in October. It is said that flying squirrels may be nearly as abundant as Chickarees or ground squirrels in many areas but that they are very rarely seen even where common. Their food includes lichens, fungi, nuts, seeds, tree buds, insects, and some animal flesh (as these squirrels are often caught in meat-baited traps set for carnivores). In turn they are an important item in the diet of Spotted Owls.

YELLOW-BELLIED MARMOT · *Marmota flaviventris*

Pl. 519

Length 18 to 28 in. weight 5 to 10 lb. Body stout, legs and feet small, tail medium length and bushy; upper surface yellowish brown grizzled with white; face blackish; a narrow white band before eyes; sides of neck and undersurface buffy. **SIGN** includes burrows 5 to 6 in. in diameter under large rocks or at bases of trees; blackish droppings to .5 in. in diameter, long, pointed at one end. **VOCALIZATION** is a loud sharp whistle, *sirk,* sometimes repeated.

DISTRIBUTION: Length of Sierra to southern Tulare County; Upper Montane Belt to above timberline at 6,200 to 12,000 ft; in or near meadows with rock outcrops or boulders for shelter.

REMARKS: Largest of the squirrel tribe are the marmots, which include the mountain-dwelling marmots of the west as well as the eastern Woodchuck. Marmots prefer meadows with nearby escape cover in the form of rock outcrops or talus. They emerge lean in spring—April or May—when snow is still present and feed avidly by day on grasses or other meadow vegetation, becoming thickly layered with fat (to half their body weight) by September or October before returning to hibernation. During the warmer daylight hours they alternate foraging with resting on a rock that commands a wide view. Such lookouts are marked by many droppings. When danger threatens, their loud whistles are sounded and the animals run for their burrows or flatten themselves against some rocks. Dens are located under rock piles or tree roots where neither humans nor carnivores can dig; hence the tunnels and nest places are poorly known. The three to eight young are born early in spring and able to go about on the surface by July.

WESTERN GRAY SQUIRREL   *Sciurus griseus*
Pl. 520

Length 19 to 22 in., weight 1.5 to 2 lb. Body uniform gray with slight salt-and-pepper effect; undersurface white; tail gray, margined with white, large and bushy. **SIGN** includes remains of pine cones cut open to obtain seeds; bulky, rounded nests conspicuous among high branches of trees. **VOCALIZATION** is a hoarse rough coughing, usually in slow series.

DISTRIBUTION: Foothill and Mixed Conifer Belts of west slope; from 400 to 6,000 ft in conifer forests or mixed woodlands; also on east slope in Sierra County, Alpine County and adjacent counties.

REMARKS: The gray squirrel is slender but strong muscled with a long, broadly haired tail that serves as counterbalance and rudder. Sharp claws on all toes help in clinging to irregularities in tree bark when climbing. Its gait is bounding, using the fore- and hind legs in pairs; on a flat area it can leap up to 4 ft at each jump. It runs easily on overhead branches and crosses between adjacent trees where branches overlap. The animal is active throughout the year, remaining hidden only during bad weather. It builds outdoor globular stick nests to 18 in. in diameter with a central lined cavity; they are placed at heights up to 75 ft, mainly in conifers. Rotted holes in oaks also are lined to serve for shelter. The principal food is pine seeds, walnuts, and acorns, available over a long season. Pine cones are cut and sometimes opened on a convenient branch above ground. Otherwise the cone is allowed to drop; then the squirrel descends and cuts off the scales one by one to get at the seeds. Many seeds are buried in small caches; the squirrels later locate and eat them when food is scarce. Those not recovered may sprout and start new trees. The young number two to four per brood and are born in spring, appearing in early summer when about half-grown. The gray squirrel population fluctuates from year to year for unknown reasons, possibly in response to changing acorn crops.

CHICKAREE or DOUGLAS' SQUIRREL   *Tamiasciurus douglasii*

Length 11 to 12 in., weight 7 to 10 oz. Upper surface dark brown with reddish tinge along back and black line low on each side; undersurface white or buffy; tail blackish with silvery hair tips. **SIGN** includes green fir or pine cones, or remains of these cones with scales removed, scattered or in small heaps on forest floor or on logs. **VOCALIZATIONS** include a prolonged whinnying of high notes, four to five per second; also a short explosive *quer'-o,* often repeated.

DISTRIBUTION: Throughout Upper Montane and Subalpine Belts, at 5,000 to 11,000 ft; some in Mixed Conifer Belt, especially in winter, but otherwise in dense mature conifer forests at higher elevations.

REMARKS: This sprightly talkative squirrel of the higher forests is less active on the ground than its gray counterpart. It gallops when moving up tree trunks or on the ground; but moves the feet separately when on branches or descending. A person who sits quietly and "squeaks" can often attract a Chickaree for a close view, when it will call repeatedly, jump, and flick its tail. This squirrel is active all winter, save in severe storms, and bounds readily over the snow. From fall until spring it eats seeds of firs, pines, and even giant sequoias. It cuts and drops many green cones, then descends to cache them beside logs or rocks near its home trees; one squirrel had nearly 500 stowed in a 50 by 50 ft area. Chilled under winter snow, the seeds remain palatable until eaten. When feeding, the squirrel sits on the ground, a log, or a rock where it can watch for enemies. Holding a cone in its "hands," it cuts off the scales, one by one, and shucks and eats the seeds, leaving only the ragged core. The Chickaree's nest is usually hidden in a pine or fir tree cavity some feet above ground and lined with grass, small twigs, or other soft materials. The young, born mainly in June and July, average about five per litter. Hawks and weasels are the principal enemies.

Chipmunks (Genus *Tamias*)

Small, marked with alternate dark and light stripes, nine along back, five on each cheek; a pale spot behind each ear; sides yellowish to reddish brown, undersurface whitish, tail flat, brushlike, with hairs on sides. Nine species of chipmunk live in the Sierra Nevada, generally separated into distinct elevational ranges, but in some areas up to five species are found within short distances of each other. Identification of individuals is sometimes possible by carefully noting the animal's size, color, area of occurrence, kind of environment occupied, and voice; but in other cases identification is difficult or impossible except for experts.

The colorful little chipmunks are busy every sunny day from spring until early fall. Much of their activity centers on finding food during the summer's plenty to store against times of scarcity. Unlike most ground squirrels, chipmunks store little fat for an extended hibernation; instead they stockpile large caches of food to nibble on until the snows melt in spring. Like the related ground squirrels, however, chipmunks have pairs of thin internal cheek pouches used to carry seeds, nuts, or berries. Their forefeet serve well as hands to gather and manipulate food and for digging. Some food is eaten when found, some taken into their underground burrows, and some buried on the surface. The chipmunk digs a small pit as deep as its head, discharges the contents of the pouches, fills the excavation, and pats down the surface. In springtime there are many "pugholes" where buried food has been removed. Besides getting food and caring for young, chipmunks find time for much that seems like play, when one pursues another round and about over logs and stumps. The burrow serves for escape shelter, for sleeping, for rearing the young, and, in the higher elevations, for winter dormancy. Chipmunk burrows, unlike those of ground squirrels, are usually hidden; few have been found and excavated by naturalists. Some nests have been discovered in decaying stumps. The foods have been learned by examining the contents of cheek pouches of chipmunks taken as scientific specimens. They include seeds of pines and other conifers, shrubs such as ceanothus, many wildflowers, grasses, and sedges, and occasionally fungi (particularly the hypogeous fungi, the "false truffles"). The pouches of one chipmunk were loaded with 20 Jeffrey pine seeds, and another had 1,169 mixed small seeds. Insects are also eaten but are devoured immediately. At lower elevations young are born by May or earlier, but higher up they arrive into July. Broods commonly are three to six, and young are abroad within a month. Chipmunks are the prey of snakes, hawks, weasels, martens, and other carnivores.

ALPINE CHIPMUNK   *T. alpinus*

Length 6.5 to 8 in.; smallest and palest have pale buff sides (reddish in other species); black tip on tail .75 in. or more in length, tail bright orange yellow on underside, flat and broad in appearance; stripes not strongly contrasting, dark stripes reddish or brownish (never blackish), light stripes grayish. **VOCALIZATIONS** include a low wiry *sweet,* repeated; a slow *whit;* a low chuckle. **DISTRIBUTION:** Mt. Conness, Tuolumne County, to Olancha Peak, Tulare County, 7,600 to 12,600 ft; Subalpine and Alpine Belts; among rocks or fallen timber, essentially terrestrial (rarely in trees).

YELLOW-PINE CHIPMUNK   *T. amoenus*

Pl. 521

Length 7.5 to 8.5 in.; sides bright reddish; tail edged with buffy-tipped hairs that are pale yellow on their shafts (versus deep orange in the Lodgepole

Chipmunk); dark stripes on body often blackish (outermost stripe conspicuous compared to other species), light stripes red tinged (inner pair on body grayish and broad, outer pair whitish and narrow). **VOCALIZATIONS** are the same as those of Lodgepole Chipmunk.

DISTRIBUTION: East slope south to Mammoth Pass, west slope south to Donner Pass, Nevada County, 5,000 to 9,400 ft; in open conifer forests around chaparral, logs, and rocks, mostly terrestrial.

MERRIAM'S CHIPMUNK   *T. merriami*

Length 8.5 to 11 in.; large, dullest colored, stripes not contrasting; head and sides grayish; tail long and bushy, edged white; light stripes on body grayish. **VOCALIZATIONS** include a high *whisk;* a low *bock,* repeated; also sputtering notes.

DISTRIBUTION: West slope from Tuolumne County south, mostly below 4,500 ft (but occasionally higher); in chaparral or foothill woodlands around brush, climbs trees readily.

LEAST CHIPMUNK   *T. minimus*

Length 7 to 8.5 in.; small, pale, grayish; sides lightly washed with red; rump grayish (brownish in Yellow-pine Chipmunk); tail long, narrow, round, grayish yellow under, carried straight up when running; stripes well defined, inner ones on body extend to base of tail, dark stripes blackish and wider than light ones. **VOCALIZATIONS** include a high *tsew;* also a rapid *chip,* repeated.

DISTRIBUTION: Only on east side in Sagebrush Belt, 6,400 to 10,500 ft; on ground or among bushes.

PANAMINT CHIPMUNK   *T. panamintinus*

Length 7.5 to 9 in.; medium sized, brightly colored, reddish overall but back of head and rump conspicuously grayish; tail buffy edged and with black tip; dark cheek stripe and outermost dark stripe on body inconspicuous or absent.

DISTRIBUTION: On east slope in narrow elevational band (5,500 to 9,000 ft) of Inyo County; restricted to pinyon pine woodlands, found amid rocks.

LONG-EARED CHIPMUNK   *T. quadrimaculatus*

Length 8 to 10 in.; ruddy brown, bright white patch at base of conspicuously long, pointed ears; stripes on face more sharply contrasting than on body (dark stripe on cheek very distinct); tail hairs white-tipped, underside of tail reddish brown. **VOCALIZATIONS** include a sharp *psst,* usually single; a hollow *bock,* at intervals.

DISTRIBUTION: Plumas County south to Bass Lake, Madera County, on both slopes, 3,200 to 7,500 ft; mostly in Mixed Conifer Belt, around brush patches or logs, in open forest, rarely a few feet up in trees.

SHADOW CHIPMUNK   *T. senex*
Pl. 522

Length 9 to 10 in.; large, dull colored; sides reddish; ears two toned (blackish with gray rim on trailing edge); tail blackish, frosted reddish above, rusty brown on underside, tail hairs white tipped; stripes on body not strongly contrasting. VOCALIZATIONS are the same as those of Long-eared Chipmunk.

DISTRIBUTION: On both slopes south to Shaver Lake, Fresno County, at 3,300 to 9,000 ft; mainly in Upper Montane Belt, in thickets and around logs; freely climbs in trees, occasionally to 50 ft.

LODGEPOLE CHIPMUNK   *T. speciosus*
Pl. 523

Length 8 to 9 in.; brightest colored; sides bright reddish brown; white stripes on head and back; ears two toned (black with whitish trailing edge); tail edged with buffy-tipped hairs that are deep orange on their shafts; outermost dark stripe on body inconspicuous or absent, outermost light stripe broader than inner light stripe. VOCALIZATIONS include a high *whisk,* repeated; a shrill *tsew;* a rapid *pst-pst-pst-a-ku* when frightened and retreating.

DISTRIBUTION: On both slopes from Lake Tahoe south to southern Tulare County, 5,200 to 8,500 ft (in the north) to 5,000 to 11,000 ft (in the south); Upper Montane and Subalpine Belts, on ground about logs or rocks but near trees which it climbs (to 40+ ft) to escape.

UINTA CHIPMUNK   *T. umbrinus*

Length 8.5 to 9 in.; head, rump, and sides grayish with reddish hue; tail edging buffy; dark cheek stripe weak; outermost dark stripe on body absent, outermost light stripe pure white and equal in width to innermost light stripe (innermost is wider in Yellow-pine Chipmunk).

DISTRIBUTION: Along Sierra crest from Mammoth Pass, Mono County south to Cirque Peak, Inyo and Tulare Counties, 7,500 to 10,500 ft; open subalpine forests (restricted to stands of trees, while Alpine Chipmunk occupies adjacent rocky areas).

BEAVER   *Castor canadensis*
Pl. 524

Length 34 to 40 in., weight 34 to 50 lb. Body stout, head blunt, tail flat, paddlelike and scaly; hind feet webbed; pelage dense with long overhairs and plush underfur; rich golden brown, tail blackish. SIGN includes dams of brush and mud backing up water on streams to form ponds; "houses" of logs, twigs, and brush in ponds; toothmarks of gnawing on trees; burrows about 15 in. in diameter in stream banks.

DISTRIBUTION: Local along some large rivers at the edge of Central Valley and introduced at a few places higher in the Sierra on both slopes; lives on slow-moving streams and some lakes.

REMARKS: Beavers were native in waters of the Central Valley before the arrival of European settlers, but trapping soon decreased the population and numbers remain low. This largest of our rodents lives beside and in water. It builds dams to form ponds where it can avoid attack by large carnivores. The dams are made of logs and brush (pl. 525), and the spaces between are filled with mud. In the pond or on the bank the animal constructs a house (lodge), often 4 or 5 ft in diameter, with nest chambers inside reached by a tunnel from below the water surface. Beavers subsist mostly on the inner bark (cambium) of cottonwoods, aspens, and willows. These trees are cut by gnawing with the big incisor teeth. Some bark is removed in place, and smaller sections of the tree are dragged or floated to the pond and consumed there, after which the peeled wood is added to the dam. In the lowlands Beavers often complicate farming practices by damming irrigation ditches. There is no shortage of food for them in these warm, flooded lowland locations. In the higher Sierra, however, limited supplies of aspens and willows at some locations could lead Beavers to shift their home ranges every couple of years.

Another aquatic mammal that could be confused with the Beaver is the much smaller Muskrat (*Ondatra zibethicus;* length 15 to 24 in., weight under 4 lb; pl. 526). This large vole relative was introduced into the Central Valley, where it has proliferated and spread into slow-moving waters at the very base of the Sierra Nevada (mostly on the west slope, but also on east slope from Mono County north). Muskrats are immediately recognizable by their narrow tails that are higher than wide.

WESTERN JUMPING MOUSE   *Zapus princeps*

Length 9.5 in., weight .67 to .88 oz. Small mouse with long tail and strong jumping hind legs; a groove on front of each incisor tooth; front legs short, hind legs and feet long and narrow (unlike wider feet of kangaroo rats); tail fully one-third again the length of head and body, scaly, few hairs and lacks crested look of pocket mice and kangaroo rats; middle of back dark, sides bright straw yellow; below pure white; tail and feet dusky.

DISTRIBUTION: Upper Montane and Subalpine Belts on both slopes south to northeastern Tulare County, 5,500 to 10,000 ft; in wet meadows and grassy stream borders.

REMARKS: Like a kangaroo rat, the jumping mouse bounds on its long hind feet, covering 2 to 3 ft at each leap, and uses the tail for support and balance. Among streamside willows it makes zigzag jumps to avoid obstructions and seek shelter. It takes readily to water and swims well. Small grass seeds, fruits, and insects serve as food. The mouse digs inconspicuous burrows but in summer makes nests hidden in surface vegetation. These are spherical, about 5 in. in diameter, of long, dry grass blades. One or two litters of five or six are born in summer. In other areas they are known to hibernate 8 to 9.5 months, an extraordinary period of time.

MOUNTAIN POCKET GOPHER *Thomomys monticola*
Pl. 527

Length 8 to 9 in., weight 3 to 6 oz. Body stocky with rather blunt head; long front teeth (incisors) project prominently from the mouth; a large external fur-lined cheek pouch at each side of mouth; eyes and ears small; foreclaws long, slender; tail short, slender, sparsely haired; pelage short, smooth, light to dark brown, paler below; dark patch behind ear; fur on feet whitish. SIGN includes scattered low, rounded mounds of loose earth.

DISTRIBUTION: Common south to northern Tulare County, from 5,000 ft to timberline; most often in deep soils around moist meadows and in soft soil of open forest but not in dense woods or bare rocky areas.

REMARKS: Signs of pocket gophers—their surface mounds and earthen cores—are common, but the animals are seldom seen. Only a quiet observer, standing still, may observe the cautious gopher poke its head out of its burrow then dart over to snip off some part of a green plant, usually in the early morning or late afternoon. Each pocket gopher lives separately in an extensive tunnel system about 2 in. in diameter at 6 to 18 in. underground, and rarely emerges. To extend a main tunnel, a short lateral is dug to the surface, excavated soil is pushed out, and then the opening is closed; farther on, another lateral and mound are made. The gopher digs with its forefeet, cuts roots with its incisor teeth, and scrapes the loosened material backward (a flap of skin behind the incisors keeps dirt out of the mouth). Then it turns about in place (a feat that is possible because pocket gophers have narrow hips) and pushes the soil out the lateral by using the forefeet and chin. The loose dirt forms a fanlike mound because successive loads are pushed in radiating pattern from the tunnel mouth. At one side, a circular earthen plug marks the last earth from the lateral that closed the entrance. Mole hills by contrast, arise in volcano-like mounds from below and are composed of lumpy soil (see fig. 15).

When winter snow covers the land at higher elevations, the gopher tunnels through the snow along the ground surface, packing excavated soil into these tunnels. Spring thaw reveals these filled tunnels as long, branched "gopher cores" lying on the ground and over small rocks or low bushes. Cores persist until washed apart by heavy rains. In high elevations some gophers in fall move into drying meadows, but with the spring thaw they tunnel upslope to drier sites.

From spring to fall a gopher makes short vertical holes, crops vegetation around the edge, and then fills the hole level with the surface. At dusk or at night gophers will occasionally come on top of the ground and may go 100 ft from the opened burrow in search of food. The food is primarily roots and bulbs, supplemented with stems and leaves of green plants during spring and summer. Some is stored in enlarged chambers of the tunnel system for use in times of scarcity. The nest cavity, 6 to 8 in. in diameter, is filled with shredded plant fibers, crinkled like excelsior. This makes an insulated sleeping compartment and serves to shelter the annual brood of five or six young. Weasels and snakes kill gophers in the tunnels, American Badgers and Coyotes dig them out of the nests, and owls catch some abroad at night. On cultivated lands gophers damage useful plants but on the wild lands of the Sierra their burrowing is an important agency of soil formation and erosion, helping to make meadows. The tunnels also serve as shelter for many small mammals, amphibians, and insects.

OTHER POCKET GOPHERS: The Botta's Pocket Gopher (*T. bottae*) inhabits foothill lowlands below 5,000 ft along the entire west slope and in high Sierra meadows south of Yosemite. It is of variable size and color, being best recognized by its range, although the Mountain Pocket Gopher also has much longer and almost pointed ears with a distinctive black patch behind the ear. The Northern Pocket Gopher (*T. talpoides*) is found along the east slope of the Sierra south through Mono County. It may be found in pinyon-juniper woodlands, sagebrush scrub, and riparian and meadow habitats to 9,000 ft.

HEERMANN'S KANGAROO RAT *Dipodomys heermanni*
Pl. 528

Length 10 to 13 in., weight 1.5 to 3 oz. Large strong kangaroo-like legs and feet; tail as much as twice length of body, with tuft at end; pelage silky, above dark sandy brown, with white stripe across each thigh, undersurface white. **SIGN** includes burrows about 2 in. in diameter in loose soil near bases of bushes, entrance filled by day with soft earth; tracks show paired impressions of hind feet with long heel print, in series 7 to 36 in. apart, tail track interrupted.

DISTRIBUTION: Low western foothills from southern El Dorado County to Fresno County; annual grassland and open shrub and woodland habitats.

REMARKS: The kangaroo rat makes strong leaps with its long hind legs and feet, using its tail as a stabilizer and support. When frightened it makes repeated jumps of 3 ft or more and disappears so rapidly that it is difficult for an observer to figure what transpired. The bounds are shorter when foraging at night. It feeds selectively on seeds of certain plants, using the small forefeet to stuff them into its fur-lined cheek pouches. When a load is accumulated, the animal takes its food into the burrow for later use. Some seeds are buried in shallow surface pits and covered. Burrows are dug in loose soil at the bases of shrubs and may be complex, on more than one level; enlarged chambers serve for the nest and for food storage. The young, two to four per brood, are born in spring.

OTHER KANGAROO RATS: The California Kangaroo Rat (*D. californicus*) resembles the Heerman's but has four toes on its hind foot instead of five and has a white-tipped tail. It occurs on the west slope in mixed chaparral habitats below 1,300 ft from El Dorado County north. The Panamint Kangaroo Rat (*D. panamintinus*) inhabits pinyon-juniper woodlands and sagebrush scrub habitats along the east side of the Sierra. It may be found in these habitats up to 8,000 ft elevation.

CALIFORNIA POCKET MOUSE   *Chaetodipus californicus*

Length 7.5 to 9 in., weight to 1 oz. Body the size of a House Mouse; a fur-lined pouch at each side of the mouth; forelegs and forefeet small, hind feet and tail long; pelage olive brown flecked with blackish above, white beneath; strong white spinelike hairs on sides and rump. **SIGN** includes holes .75 to 1.25 in. in diameter, closed by day, under bushes.

DISTRIBUTION: Foothill Belt of west slope from El Dorado County south, prefers blue oak–gray pine woodlands and chaparral habitats.

REMARKS: Pocket mice, like the related kangaroo rats, spend the day in their burrows and forage at night. They are quadrupedal hoppers, moving in a loping stride, with all four feet touching the ground at each stride (unlike kangaroo rats that are bipedal hoppers with only their hind feet touching the ground). When undisturbed their jumps are short, but if alarmed they bound rapidly in 3-ft leaps. Their food is of small seeds, gathered by the little front feet and carried in the cheek pouches. In addition to caching food, pocket mice can undergo short periods of dormancy, called torpor, during winter months. The annual brood of two to six is born in May or June. Pocket mice look very much like other mice but are recognized by their fur-lined mouth pouches, the naked soles on their feet, and their long and distinctly crested tails.

OTHER POCKET MICE: Great Basin Pocket Mouse (*Perognathus parvus*, pl. 529) inhabits pinyon-juniper woodlands and sagebrush scrub along the east side of the Sierra. It lacks the spinelike white hairs of the California Pocket Mouse and has an olive gray, silky pelage.

BUSHY-TAILED WOOD RAT   *Neotoma cinerea*

Length 14 to 19 in., weight 9.5 to 16.25 oz. Larger bodied than Dusky-footed Wood Rat and with a bushy tail; pelage long, dense, and soft, sandy brown above, darker on tail; feet and undersurface of body and tail white; long hairs on sides of tail form a flat brush to 1 in. wide. **SIGN** includes sparse accumulations of sticks and woody debris in rock crevices; droppings black, cylindrical, .5 in. by .17 in.; also leave stains of brown sheen over white wash on prominent rock outcrops.

DISTRIBUTION: Mountain slopes, 5,000 to 13,000 ft on both sides of crest; often in talus slides or rocky outcrops associated with coniferous forests or montane chaparral; mostly nocturnal.

REMARKS: This big wood rat lives near Pikas in the rugged high country and evidently is active throughout the year. Its abode often has a musky odor from secretions of glands on the wood rat's chest. These elongated glands are most pronounced in males and exude a waxy substance that is rubbed onto rock surfaces along with urine. Together, the gland secretions and urine form a very distinctive whitewash on rock edges that marks the presence of this animal—this whitewash often has a patch of lichen growing underneath and can be seen at long distances. Like the Dusky-footed Wood Rat, it trades and packs, sometimes to the dismay of campers and cabin dwellers in its territory. Its building tendencies are limited to casual accumulations of woody scraps, but there is likely a hidden insulated nest to offset the chill of winter. The food is of fruits, nuts, and seeds, even bark, of local plants. From three to five young are produced in July; they grow rapidly, soon becoming full sized.

DUSKY-FOOTED WOOD RAT   *Neotoma fuscipes*

Length 16 to 19 in., weight 7.25 to 8.75 oz. Size and form of house rat, but tail shorter than body, round and well haired (not scaly or bushy); ears large, rounded, finely haired; body pelage dense, soft, brownish gray with black hair tips; undersurface of body and tail and top of feet white, top of feet dusky.

SIGN includes nests 2 to 3 ft high (occasionally to 5 ft), rounded or conical, made of twigs, leaves, wood scraps, and other materials on ground under trees or brush, also in oaks at several feet above ground, or in rock crevices; droppings cylindrical, .38 in. by .13 in., on runways or about houses.

DISTRIBUTION: Foothill Belt into lower Mixed Conifer Belt (200 to 4,600 ft) on west slope, amid trees or brush or among rocks. Those occurring south of Lake Tahoe may be assigned to a new species (*N. macrotis*) separable only by DNA and skull characteristics.

REMARKS: The "trade rat" or "pack rat" carries various articles about, sometimes into cabins or camps, where it may exchange them for table utensils or other shiny objects. It is mainly nocturnal, and hence rarely seen, but active throughout the year. The nests, one or more per rat, vary in form and composition, according to materials close by. Each contains one or more chambers connecting to runways that lead out onto or into the ground or nearby logs. The inhabitant usually forages within 25 yards of its home on the ground or climbing onto trees and rock faces, eating fruits, berries, seeds, bark, leaves, herbs, and grasses. The young, two to four in a litter are born mostly from March to May and weaned in about two months.

OTHER RATS: Introduced Black Rats (*Rattus rattus;* length 13 to 18 in.) are similar in appearance but have tails that are longer than their bodies and are scaly with few hairs. Their distribution is spotty in the low western foothills, nearly always associated with buildings.

White-footed Mice (Genus *Peromyscus*)

Medium-sized mice; upper surface brown, light or dark (bluish gray in young); pale gray to pure white under; eyes large, black; ears thin, relatively large; tail slender, well haired. Four species occur in Sierra Nevada.

White-footed mice are some of the commonest and most widespread of North American mammals and there are many species within this group. The four Sierra species are graded in size (see measurements), especially as to the ear and hind foot. The Deer Mouse is less than half the weight of the largest, the California Mouse. All four are in the Foothill Belt, to which the Pinyon and California Mice are restricted; the Brush Mouse continues through the Mixed Conifer Belt; and the Deer Mouse lives almost everywhere (even above timberline). Being nocturnal and making no obvious trails or burrows, these little animals leave scant evidence, but when naturalists set lines of traps they usually catch more white-footed mice than all other kinds. Once in June on the east slope 30 traps in four nights took 66 Deer Mice and 10 other small rodents, evidence of a peak population. White-footed mice are most active in early hours of the night, but some retire only at dawn; they do not hibernate. Mostly they run on the ground while searching for their food, which includes seeds of grasses, herbs, and conifers, larvae or adult insects, and some fungi. The Pinyon Mouse and Brush Mouse are excellent climbers, and may forage and seek shelter by climbing. Deer Mice are naked when born but soon become fully haired and mature rapidly. The total life span is short and females may begin bearing young when only five weeks old. The California Mouse is a monogamous species, with long-term pair bonds and male caring for female and young (one of very few species within mammals showing this trait). Unoccupied and inadequately screened mountain cabins are often invaded by these mice; bedding and other fabrics are chewed to obtain nest material, and cereal foods are eaten. Because of their abundance, white-footed mice are common prey for snakes, owls, and mammalian carnivores.

BRUSH MOUSE   *P. boylii*
Head and body 3.5 to 4 in., tail 3.75 to 4.33 in., hind foot .88 in., ear .75 in., weight .75 to 1.25 oz. Tail equals head and body.

DISTRIBUTION: West slope along entire Sierra, 200 to 8,100 ft, Foothill and Mixed Conifer Belts; also on east slope from Alpine County north and Inyo County south; on wooded or brushy slopes with access to water; climbs rocks and trees; breeds April to June, young two to five.

CALIFORNIA MOUSE or PARASITIC MOUSE   *P. californicus*

Head and body 4 to 5 in., tail 4.63 to 5.33 in., hind foot 1 to 1.13 in., ear .8 to .88 in., weight 1.5 to 1.75 oz. Largest; tail longer than head and body.

DISTRIBUTION: West slope, Mariposa County to Tulare County in Foothill Belt, among oaks or dense chaparral, closely associated with wood rats (whose nests they use) and California bay trees (whose seeds are a major food); the least common species.

DEER MOUSE   *P. maniculatus*
Pl. 530

Head and body 3 to 4.13 in., tail 2 to 3 in., hind foot .75 in., ear .63 in., weight .5 to .67 oz. Smallest; tail shorter than head and body.

DISTRIBUTION: Widespread and in nearly all environments; mostly on ground; commonest Sierra mammal (in fact, the most abundant and widespread mammal in California and North America); breeds April to October, young usually three to four.

PINYON MOUSE   *P. truei*

Head and body 3.25 to 4.33 in., tail 3.67 to 4.33 in., hind foot .88 to 1 in., ear .8 to 1 in., weight .83 to 1.4 oz. Tail equals head and body, two toned (dark above and light below) with a characteristic buffy stripe separating dorsal and ventral colors; ear large (equal to or greater than length of hind foot).

DISTRIBUTION: West slope along Sierra to 2,000 ft in Foothill Belt and on east slope at higher elevations amid pinyon pines; in brushy and rocky places; breeds May to June, young three to four.

WESTERN HARVEST MOUSE   *Reithrodontomys megalotis*

Length 5 to 6 in., weight .25 to .5 oz. Size and form of a House Mouse; each upper incisor tooth with lengthwise groove; tail equal to body length; pelage above blackish with buffy sides, below dull white; ear tawny-haired and large.

DISTRIBUTION: Widespread but avoids high elevations, mostly in grasslands, meadows, or early successional stages of other habitats.

REMARKS: This little mouse is common in grassy or weedy places, often near water but sometimes on rocky slopes. It feeds on small seeds of local plants. The spherical nest is woven of shredded plant fibers, lined with fine grasses or down from willow or cottonwood. Elsewhere the nest is elevated in grass or bushes, but locally it is hidden in leafy ground debris. When disturbed the mouse utters a series of high-pitched squeals. Young are produced from April to October, usually four per litter. Superficially, this species resembles the House Mouse, which has a scaly tail with few hairs and lacks grooves on its incisors, and the Western Jumping Mouse, which has a tail 1.5 times its body length.

Voles (Genus *Microtus*)

Length 6 to 9 in., weight 1 to 3 oz. Body cylindrical with truncated snout, short legs and tail; eyes small, ear buried in fur; pelage long, dense, and soft, above dark brown, below dark gray. **SIGN** includes runways 1 to 1.5 in. wide cut in grass, with open holes to underground tunnels; droppings blackish, .38 in. by .06 in. There are three species in the Sierra Nevada plus the closely related Sagebrush Vole, all being similarly colored and difficult to separate.

The other common name for voles, meadow mice, indicates that these small rodents usually live in damp green grassland. Here they make small runways by clipping the vegetation close to the surface. In tall dense grass these paths are shielded from view above. The runways, with neat piles of grass cuttings and droppings, connect to holes, always open, leading to underground tunnels. An enlarged chamber, below ground, contains the globular nest of shredded plant fibers felted into a warm shelter. Voles are active day and night and do not hibernate. They consume large amounts of green watery vegetation, which is low in nutritive value. In the lowlands there are repeated broods, often at short intervals, through much of the year. At higher elevations voles breed from April or May into September, usually having three to seven per litter. Mountain Voles can breed within three weeks of birth, giving them about the highest reproductive potential of any mammal. Voles are known to undergo extreme variation in numbers. When population densities are very high, they may impact their own food supplies. Because of their abundance, voles are caught by snakes, hawks, owls, herons, and many carnivorous mammals, such as weasels, in the simple grass mouse predator food chain. The Long-tailed Vole does not regularly make and live in runways. It seems to range freely in damp streamside locations or dry woodlands.

SAGEBRUSH VOLE   *Lemmiscus curtatus*

A small, grayish vole with very short tail (about 1 in.).
DISTRIBUTION: Occurs in pinyon-juniper woodlands and sagebrush scrub on the east side of the Sierra.

CALIFORNIA VOLE   *M. californicus*

Tail (1.56 to 2.69 in.) more than twice length of hind foot (.81 to 1 in.) but less than 32 percent of body length (4.75 to 5.75 in.).
DISTRIBUTION: Lives in grasslands and wet meadows from the Central Valley through the western Foothill Belt (up to 4,500 ft) and also on the east slope in Mono and Inyo Counties.

LONG-TAILED VOLE   *M. longicaudus*
Pl. 531
Tail (2 to 3.75 in.) more than twice length of hind foot (.81 to 1 in.) and more than 33 percent of body length (4.25 to 5.13 in.).

DISTRIBUTION: Occurs in rather dry grass patches within forested areas in parts of the Mixed Conifer Belt but more commonly at higher elevations to 10,700 ft on both slopes.

MOUNTAIN VOLE   *M. montanus*
Pl. 532
Tail (1.63 to 2.13 in.) less than twice length of hind foot (.81 to 1.73 in.).
DISTRIBUTION: Occupies wet meadows from the Mixed Conifer Belt (5,000 ft) up to 11,000 ft at timberline, on both slopes south to Tulare County.

HEATHER VOLE   *Phenacomys intermedius*
Length 5 to 6 in., weight to 1.5 oz. Resembles voles but differs in having short tail (just over 1 in.); pelage gray, brown tinged above, whitish below; tail distinctly two toned (dark above and light below).
DISTRIBUTION: Sierra County to Humphrey Basin, Fresno County, chiefly in Subalpine Belt, 7,400 to 10,800 ft; in meadows and heather patches or in adjacent forest edges.
REMARKS: Only continued trapping will reveal the presence of this scarce, poorly known animal, which lives solitarily near red heather amid scattered lodgepole pines. Piles of droppings suggest places where the mice have wintered under the snow. Near these are cut twigs, 1.5 to 3 in. long, of heather, willow, and other plants from which the leaves have been eaten. During summer, young are born in underground nests made of grasses and mosses.

HOUSE MOUSE   *Mus musculus*
Length 5.5 to 8 in., weight .5 to 1 oz. Small; tail slender, nearly hairless, scaly; body uniform dark grayish or yellowish brown above, plain dusky brown below (white-footed mice are similar in appearance but white below); has an unpleasant odor. **SIGN** includes holes to 1 in. in diameter in woodwork or food packages; irregular chewing on clothing or fabrics; droppings spindle shaped, blackish, .06 in. by .25 in.
DISTRIBUTION: Ubiquitous below 7,000 ft, but may be higher where inadvertently introduced; in all types of buildings, sometimes spilling over into adjacent grasslands.
REMARKS: The plain little House Mouse, an Old World alien, invaded America and California along with European settlers and has long resided in settlements and on farms on the lower slopes of the Sierra. It is often unknowingly carried in baled hay, household goods, or bundles of clothing to new locations. While usually thought of as an inhabitant of buildings, in the lowlands it has reverted to a wild state and lives successfully year-round in grasslands a mile or more from dwellings. Sometimes its numbers there equal the common native white-footed mice and voles. Very little is known

about its possible distribution in the higher Sierra. Indoors it is a nuisance, eating many kinds of human food, scattering its droppings, and gnawing into packages, clothing, furniture, or cabinets. It begins breeding as early as 35 days of age and may have five broods averaging five or six young in a single year. The young mature quickly, and the life span is short.

Rabbits and Their Allies (Order Lagomorpha)

PIKA *Ochotona princeps*

Pl. 533

Length 6.5 to 8 in., weight 5 to 6.5 oz. Body short; face and ears rounded; fore- and hind legs small, about equal; tail not evident; pelage pale gray with reddish overcast; soles haired except ends of toes. **SIGN** includes piles of vegetation cut green and cured as hay in shelter under rocks; droppings small flat pellets, diameter .13 in., in groups on lookouts; also whitish urine stains on rocks.

VOICE: A high nasal *peek* or *check-ick,* uttered once or repeated for 10 to 15 seconds.

DISTRIBUTION: Mainly in Subalpine Belt, occasionally higher or lower, 7,700 to 12,000 ft; lives in rock slides.

REMARKS: Resembling a small guinea pig, the Pika (pronounced *pie-ka*), Cony, or Rock Rabbit, is in fact a distant alpine relative of the true rabbits. They live solitarily in high mountain talus and rock slides, sometimes in a density of six per acre. Hikers in the mountains often hear the Pika's nasal bleating during the day and by careful searching may see one or more. The animal's day begins when the air is well warmed and ends before the chill of evening. But it is even active in winter under the snow blanketing its domain. When not foraging the Pika perches on a backward-slanting rock with a good outlook and overhead protection, from where it can scramble to safety. These lookout posts are dotted with the diminutive droppings and whitened by urine stains. For food the Pika makes numerous trips to cut stems, up to 3 ft long, of plants growing near rockslides and carries these in its mouth into shelters under overhanging rocks, where they become dried. Sometimes a cubic yard of this "hay" is gathered and stored for winter. Marmots, Bushy-tailed Wood Rats, ground squirrels, and chipmunks are associates of the Pika, and its main enemies are weasels, martens, and hawks. The three or four young are born between May and September.

BRUSH RABBIT *Sylvilagus bachmani*

Pl. 534

Length 11 to 14 in., ears 2.5 to 3 in.; weight 1 to 1.5 lb. Ear shorter than head, half as broad as long, moderately pointed, sparsely haired on inner surface; body dark brown above, heavily washed with black giving deep gray effect; nape has patch of reddish brown; grayish white below; tail small and inconspicuous, underside partly white. **SIGN** includes droppings, flattened spheres, diameter .25 in.; runways (habitual trails about 4.5 in. wide) under brushy cover.

DISTRIBUTION: Foothill Belt of west slope to 4,000 ft, mostly under chaparral. **REMARKS:** The little bluish Brush Rabbit, about half the weight of a cottontail, is abroad in early morning and toward dusk. It seldom ventures far from sheltering shrubs, and each individual has a restricted home range, generally under one acre in size. Sometimes, when come upon, the animal will "freeze" immobile. Then, if it senses danger, it takes a few quick hops and disappears into the chaparral, with which its coat blends in color. Its food is composed of grasses and herbs during spring but includes stems of ceanothus and other shrubs. Breeding can occur from January through July depending on elevation, and Brush Rabbits may have multiple litters per year.

COTTONTAILS
Pl. 535

Sylvilagus audubonii, S. nuttallii

Length 12 to 15 in., ears 2.5 to 4 in., weight 1.5 to 3 lb. Smaller than a jackrabbit or domestic rabbit; ears rounded, about length of head; upper surface of body yellowish brown with blackish overwash; undersurface and tops of hind feet white; tail moderately sized and cottony white beneath. **SIGN** includes droppings flattened spheres, diameter .25 in.

DISTRIBUTION: See below.

REMARKS: Cottontails are common where areas of grassy forage are bordered by shrub and vine tangles that afford escape shelter. Less often they live on open grassy hillsides and use remodeled ground squirrel burrows for hiding and nesting. They forage in the early morning, disappear during midday, and are abroad again toward evening or even late afternoon in glades shaded from direct sunshine. In favorable pasturage two, three, or more may be seen close together, and they sometimes venture out 25 ft or so from the sheltering thickets. At a hint of danger they head for safety, displaying the cottony white tail at each bound. The blind, nearly naked young, about six per litter, are born in spring and early summer. The nest is lined with fur from the female's body and placed in a short burrow or in a secluded surface depression.

Two species of cottontails occur in the Sierra Nevada. The Desert, or Audubon's, Cottontail (*S. audubonii*) lives in grasslands and open shrub or forest areas of the Foothill Belt of the west slope and on the east slope north to northern Inyo County. Its coloration is grayish above; its ears are relatively long, pointed and sparsely furred on the inner surface; and its whiskers are black. The Mountain, or Nuttall's, Cottontail (*S. nuttallii*) lives among rocky, sagebrush-covered hills and canyons on the east slope south to northern Inyo County (where the two species potentially overlap). Its coloration is brownish; its ears are relatively short, rounded, and heavily furred on the inner surface; and its whiskers are partly white.

SNOWSHOE HARE

Lepus americanus

Pl. 536

Length 14 to 17 in., ears 3 in., weight 2 to 4 lb. Of rabbit form, bigger than cottontail; feet large (4.5 to 5.5 in.); upper surface darkish cinnamon brown in summer, all white in winter (ear tips dusky); underparts and lower surface of tail pale dusky. **SIGN** includes prints of hind feet in snow, over 3.5 in. wide; browsed stems cleanly snipped off at a 45-degree angle (true for all hares and rabbits; compared to tattered or squared-off look of stems browsed by deer).

DISTRIBUTION: Coniferous forests 3,000 to 7,500 ft, south to southern Tulare County; favors dense streamside vegetation. State and Federal Species of Special Concern for Sierra Nevada populations (*L. a. tahoensis*).

REMARKS: The Snowshoe, or Varying, Hare (so named because its color changes from white in winter to brown in summer) ranges from the Arctic south into the Rocky Mountains and the Sierra Nevada. Here it lives amid streamside alders and willows, in dense thickets of young conifers, and under ceanothus-manzanita chaparral—plant cover equivalent to that occupied by the Brush Rabbit at lower elevations. The Snowshoe Hare is seldom seen because it shelters by day in a shallow form under protective vegetation, going out to forage at dusk, by night, or in early morning. It eats grasses, herbs, and shrubs, together with bark of some deciduous trees in winter. The young, average three to four per litter, are born in spring and able to forage when about two weeks old.

BLACK-TAILED JACKRABBIT

Lepus californicus

Length 17 to 21 in., ears 4 to 6.5 in., weight 3 to 7 lb. A long-legged rabbit with enormous ears; feet large like Snowshoe Hare; body pale yellowish brown above, ticked with black; undersurface pale buff to white; tail long (2 to 4.5 in.), upper surface of tail black and extending onto rump. **SIGN** includes oval tracks, each set of four prints separated by up to 10 ft when animal running; droppings flattened spheres, diameter .38 in.; forms (resting places) on ground under bushes; trails straight, narrow, through grass in open.

DISTRIBUTION: Central Valley and Foothill Belt on west side, mainly in unobstructed grassland but some in openings amid chaparral; also in flatter open areas east of the Sierra.

REMARKS: The long-eared hare of the American West was named "jackass rabbit" by the pioneers, in contrast to the shorter eared cottontails. Unlike cottontails, this animal lives in the open, makes off overland if alarmed (never hiding in shrubbery or burrows), and bears fully formed young. When foraging it makes short hops, keeping the soles of the hind feet on the ground and the ears erect. If frightened, it lays the ears back and leaps two to three yards at a bound, touching only the toes. Jackrabbits are active toward dusk, at night, and in the earlier morning. During midday each rests in a sheltered form under a bush, where there is a clear view all about to watch for enemies—Coyotes, eagles, or large hawks, and also dogs and hunters. Food includes grasses, herbs, and stems and leaves of shrubs. Alfalfa, grains, and other crops also are relished and often damaged. In consequence, there has been unending destruction of "jacks," so that the population today is a small fraction of that around 1900. Jackrabbits carry a disease, tularemia, transmissible to humans. Young, four or five per litter, are produced through most of the year. The newborn are about 6 in. long, fully haired with eyes open and 2-in. ears.

WHITE-TAILED JACKRABBIT *Lepus townsendii*

Length 18 to 22 in., ear to 6 in., weight 5 to 8 lb. A relative of the Black-tailed Jackrabbit but larger and heavier, its snout is broad with parallel sides (narrow and tapered in Black-tailed); brownish gray in summer, all white in winter except black ear tips; feet and tail well furred, always white; tail white both above and below. **SIGN** includes flattened spherical droppings, diameter .5 in.

DISTRIBUTION: High Sierra crest and upper east slope from Mt. Whitney region north; to 12,000 ft in sagebrush, subalpine conifers, alpine dwarf-shrub, and grasslands; also on flat areas east of the mountains, especially in winter. State Species of Special Concern.

REMARKS: Largest of the hares, the White-tailed is uncommon in the Sierra. Populations are now fragmented and apparently in drastic decline. It lives in open or semiopen places (particularly where there is a cover of trees, shrubs, or krummholz) but is active at late dusk and into the night, hence it is rarely seen. Its "eye shine" to a flashlight or headlight is fiery red, more brilliant than that of the Black-tailed. Groups of droppings under bushy mats of whitebark pine and similar cover indicate that these sites serve for shelter by day or during winter storms. The young, two or three per litter, are born from late spring into summer.

REFERENCES

General

Browning, P. 1992. *Place Names of the Sierra Nevada.* Berkeley, CA: Wilderness Press.

Duane, T. P. 1999. *Shaping the Sierra: Nature, Culture, and Conflict in the Changing West.* Berkeley and Los Angeles: University of California Press.

Farquhar, F. P. 1965. *History of the Sierra Nevada.* Berkeley and Los Angeles: University of California Press.

Gilligan, D. 2000. *The Secret Sierra: The Alpine World above the Trees.* Bishop, CA: Spotted Dog Press.

Grinnell, J., and T. I. Storer. 1924. *Animal Life in the Yosemite.* Berkeley and Los Angeles: University of California Press.

Irwin, S. 1991. *California's Eastern Sierra.* Los Olivos, CA: Cachuma Press.

Johnston, V. R. 1998. *Sierra Nevada: The Naturalist's Companion.* Rev. ed. Berkeley and Los Angeles: University of California Press.

Schaffer, J. P. 1998. *The Tahoe Sierra.* 4th ed. Berkeley, CA: Wilderness Press.

Schoenherr, A. A. 1993. *A Natural History of California.* California Natural History Guides, no. 56. Berkeley and Los Angeles: University of California Press.

"Sierra Nevada Ecosystem Project (SNEP) Report." 1996. Davis: Centers for Water and Wildland Resources, University of California, Davis.

Smith, G., ed. 2000. *Sierra East.* California Natural History Guides, no. 60. Berkeley and Los Angeles: University of California Press.

Sumner, L., and J. S. Dixon. 1953. *Birds and Mammals of the Sierra Nevada.* Berkeley and Los Angeles: University of California Press.

Whitney, S. 1979. *A Sierra Club Naturalist's Guide to the Sierra Nevada.* San Francisco: Sierra Club Books.

Geology

Alt, D., and D. W. Hyndman. 2000. *Roadside Geology of Northern and Central California.* Missoula, MT: Mountain Press Publishing.

Hill, M. 1975. *Geology of the Sierra Nevada.* California Natural History Guides, no. 37. Berkeley and Los Angeles: University of California Press.

Huber, N. K. 1987. *The Geologic Story of Yosemite National Park.* U.S. Geological Survey Bulletin 1595. Washington, D.C.: U.S. Geological Survey. Reprint by Yosemite Association, 1989.

Matthes, F. E. 1950. *The Incomparable Valley: A Geological Interpretation of the Yosemite.* Edited by Fritiof Fryxell. Berkeley and Los Angeles: University of California Press.

Moore, J. G. 2000. *Exploring the Highest Sierra.* Stanford, CA: Stanford University Press.

Fungi

Arora, D. 1986. *Mushrooms Demystified: A Comprehensive Guide to the Fleshy Fungi.* 2d ed. Berkeley, CA: Ten Speed Press.

Arora, D. 1991. *All That the Rain Promises and More. . . .* Berkeley, CA: Ten Speed Press.

McKenny, M., and D. E. Stuntz. 1987. *The New Savory Wild Mushroom.* Revised and enlarged by Joseph Ammirati. Seattle: University of Washington Press.

Orr, R. T., and D. B. Orr. 1979. *Mushrooms of Western North America.* California Natural History Guides, no. 42. Berkeley and Los Angeles: University of California Press.

Lichens and Mosses

Brodo, I., S. D. Sharnoff, and S. Sharnoff. 2001. *Lichens of North America.* New Haven, CT: Yale University Press.

Fink, B. 1935. *The Lichen Flora of the United States.* Ann Arbor: University of Michigan Press.

Hale, M. E., and M. Cole. 1988. *Lichens of California.* Berkeley and Los Angeles: University of California Press.

Vitt, D. H., J. E. Marsh, and R. B. Borey. 1988. *Mosses, Lichens & Ferns of Northwest North America.* Edmonton, Alberta: Lone Pine Publishing.

Ferns

Grillos, S. J. 1966. *Ferns and Fern Allies of California.* California Natural History Guides, no. 16. Berkeley and Los Angeles: University of California Press.

Howell, J. T., and R. J. Long. 1970. The ferns and fern allies of the Sierra Nevada in California and Nevada. *Four Seasons* 3(3): 1–18.

Lellinger, D. B. 1985. *A Field Manual to Ferns & Fern-Allies of the United States & Canada.* Washington D.C.: Smithsonian Institution Press.

Wildflowers, Shrubs, and Trees

Arno, S. 1973. *Discovering Sierra Trees.* Three Rivers, CA: Yosemite and Sequoia Natural History Associations.

Blackwell, L. 1997. *Wildflowers of the Tahoe Sierra.* Renton, WA: Lone Pine Publishing.

Blackwell, L. 1999. *Wildflowers of the Sierra Nevada and the Central Valley.* Renton, WA: Lone Pine Publishing.

Botti, S. J. 2001. *An Illustrated Flora of Yosemite National Park.* El Portal, CA: Yosemite Association.

Carville, J. S. 1997. *Hiking Tahoe's Wildflower Trails.* Renton, WA: Lone Pine Publishing.

Chabot, B., and W. Billings. 1972. Origins and ecology of the Sierran alpine flora and vegetation. *Ecol. Monogr.* 42: 163–199.

Fauver, T. 1998. *Wildflower Walks and Roads of the Sierra Gold Country.* Grass Valley, CA: Comstock Bonanza Press.

Graf, M. 1999. *Plants of the Tahoe Basin: Flowering Plants, Trees, and Ferns.* Berkeley and Los Angeles: University of California Press.

Griffin, J. R., and W. B. Critchfield. 1972. *The Distribution of Forest Trees of California.* Research paper PSW-82. Berkeley, CA: USDA Forest Service.

Hickman, J., Ed. 1993. *The Jepson Manual of Higher Plants of California.* Berkeley and Los Angeles: University of California Press.

Lanner, R. M. 1984. *Trees of the Great Basin.* Reno: University of Nevada Press.

Lanner, R. M. 1999. *Conifers of California.* Los Olivos, CA: Cachuma Press.

Niehaus, T. F. 1974. *Sierra Wildflowers: Mt. Lassen to Kern Canyon.* California Natural History Guides, no. 32. Berkeley and Los Angeles: University of California Press.

Pavlik, B. M., P. Muick, S. Johnson, and M. Popper. 1991. *Oaks of California.* Los Olivos, CA: Cachuma Press.

Peterson, P. V., and P. V. Peterson, Jr. 1975. *Native Trees of the Sierra Nevada.* California Natural History Guides, no. 36. Berkeley and Los Angeles: University of California Press.

Smiley, F. J. 1921. A report on the boreal flora of the Sierra Nevada of California. *Univ. Calif. Publ. Botany* 9: 1–423.

Stuart, J. D., and J. O. Sawyer. 2001. *Trees and Shrubs of California.* California Natural History Guides, no. 62. Berkeley and Los Angeles: University of California Press.

Thomas, J. H., and D. R. Parnell. 1974. *Native Shrubs of the Sierra Nevada.* California Natural History Guides, no. 34. Berkeley and Los Angeles: University of California Press.

Weeden, N. 1981. *Sierra Nevada Flora.* Berkeley, CA: Wilderness Press.

Insects

Biggs, K. 2000. *Common Dragonflies of California.* Sebastopol, CA: Azalea Creek Publishing.

Borror, D. J., and R. E. White. 1970. *A Field Guide to Insects of America North of Mexico.* Boston: Houghton Mifflin.

Borror, D. J., C. A. Triplehorn, and N. F. Johnson. 1989. *An Introduction to the Study of Insects.* 6th ed. New York: Holl, Rinchartz and Winston.

Garth, J. S., and J. W. Tilden. 1986. *California Butterflies.* California Natural History Guides, no. 51. Berkeley and Los Angeles: University of California Press.

Manolis, T. 2003. *Dragonflies and Damselflies of California.* California Natural History Guides, no. 72. Berkeley and Los Angeles: University of California Press.

Opler, P. A. 1999. *A Field Guide to Western Butterflies.* Boston: Houghton Mifflin.

Powell, J. A., and C. L. Hogue. 1979. *California Insects.* California Natural History Guides, no. 44. Berkeley and Los Angeles: University of California Press.

Fish

McGinnis, S. M. 1984. *Freshwater Fishes of California.* California Natural History Guides, no. 49. Berkeley and Los Angeles: University of California Press.

Moyle, P. B. 1993. *Fish: An Enthusiast's Guide.* Berkeley and Los Angeles: University of California Press.

Moyle, P. B. 2002. *Inland Fishes of California.* 2d ed. Berkeley and Los Angeles: University of California Press.

Sigler, W. F., and J. W. Sigler. 1987. *Fishes of the Great Basin.* Reno: University of Nevada Press.

Amphibians and Reptiles

Basey, H. E. 1976. *Discovering Sierra Reptiles and Amphibians.* Three Rivers, CA: Yosemite and Sequoia Natural History Associations.

Behler, J. L., and F. W. King. 1979. *The Audubon Society Field Guide to North American Reptiles and Amphibians.* New York: A. A. Knopf.

Brown, P. R. 1997. *A Field Guide to Snakes of California.* Houston: Gulf Publishing.

Stebbins, R. C. 2003. *A Field Guide to Western Reptiles and Amphibians.* 3d ed. Boston: Houghton Mifflin.

Birds

Beedy, E. C., and S. L. Granholm. 1985. *Discovering Sierra Birds.* Three Rivers, CA: Yosemite and Sequoia Natural History Associations.

Ehrlich, P. R., D. S. Dobkin, and D. Wheye. 1988. *The Birder's Handbook: A Field Guide to the Natural History of North American Birds.* New York: Simon & Schuster.

Gaines, D. 1992. *Birds of Yosemite and the East Slope.* Lee Vining, CA: Artemisia Press.

National Geographic Society. 2002. *Field Guide to the Birds of North America.* 4th ed. Washington D.C.: National Geographic Society.

Ryser, F. A. 1985. *Birds of the Great Basin.* Reno: University of Nevada Press.

Small, A. 1994. *California Birds: Their Status and Distribution.* Vista, CA: Ibis Publishing.

Sibley, D. A. 2003. *The Sibley Field Guide to Birds of Western North America.*

Mammals

Burt, W. H., and R. P. Grossenheider. 1976. *A Field Guide to the Mammals.* 3d ed. Boston: Houghton Mifflin.

Grater, R. K. 1978. *Discovering Sierra Mammals.* Three Rivers, CA: Yosemite and Sequoia Natural History Associations.

Halfpenny, J. 1986. *A Field Guide to Mammal Tracking in Western America.* Boulder, CO: Johnson Books.

Hall, E. R. 1995. *Mammals of Nevada.* Reno: University of Nevada Press.

Ingles, L. G. 1965. *Mammals of the Pacific States.* Stanford, CA: Stanford University Press.

Jameson, E. W., Jr., and H. J. Peeters. 2004. *Mammals of California.* 2d ed. Berkeley and Los Angeles: University of California Press.

Wilson, D. E., and S. Ruff, Eds. 1999. *The Smithsonian Book of North American Mammals.* Washington, D.C.: Smithsonian Institution Press, in association with the American Society of Mammalogists.

PLATE CREDITS

Except as noted below in italics, drawings are credited in general terms in the acknowledgments for the first edition.

MRS. MERREL (ALICE) ACKLEY 195

SHERRY BALLARD 51

ERWIN & PEGGY BAUER 423, 452, 497

ROBERT BEHRSTOCK / AZALEA CREEK PUBLISHING 235, 243

LINDA H. BEIDLEMAN 118

DAVID BIGGS / AZALEA CREEK PUBLISHING 238

TOM BRAKEFIELD 496, 521, 530

BROTHER ALFRED BROUSSEAU, ST. MARY'S COLLEGE 66, 89, 93, 107, 111, 129, 150, 159, 176, 211, 213

CALIFORNIA ACADEMY OF SCIENCES 16, 19, 20, 21, 28, 51, 62, 80, 95, 195, 224, 403, 411, 424, 426, 427, 430, 432, 433, 434, 454, 457, 467, 473, 478, 483, 484, 489, 490, 492, 494, 495, 496, 498, 499, 500, 501, 502, 503, 507, 508, 509, 510, 512, 513, 514, 518, 520, 521, 523, 524, 525, 526, 527, 528, 530, 532, 535

SCOTT CAMAZINE 325

CHRISTOPHER CHRISTIE 67

JACK KELLY CLARK, COURTESY UNIVERSITY OF CALIFORNIA STATEWIDE IPM PROGRAM 233, 234, 251, 252, 261, 318

ROBERT CLAYPOLE 71, 125, 139, 244, 366, 369

GERALD AND BUFF CORSI 95, 403, 430, 495, 499, 501, 507, 508, 509, 510, 512, 513, 525

ROBERT CURTIS 222, 491

MIKE DANZENBAKER 437

JOSEPH W. DOUGHERTY 43, 48, 59, 65, 68, 70, 74, 75, 79, 84, 85, 88, 94, 97, 99, 103, 109, 112, 117, 123, 133, 135, 137, 142, 151, 226, 227, 367

A.V. EVANS 228, 229, 230, 231, 245, 246, 249, 253, 256, 260, 263, 264, 265, 267, 268, 269, 272, 273, 278, 291, 303, 305, 317, 322, 323, 324, 326

WILLIAM C. FLAXINGTON 350, 355, 365, 370, 371, 372, 373, 374, 375

WILLIAM FOLLETTE 45, 46, 54, 56, 61, 63, 64, 69, 72, 76, 77, 90, 91, 101, 102, 104, 110, 115, 121, 122, 130, 140, 155, 156, 157, 164, 169, 172, 177, 178, 179, 184, 192, 194, 197, 201, 202, 203, 205, 208, 216, 217, 218

RICHARD FORBES 360, 505, 522, 529, 531, 534, 536

WILL FUNK 442, 493, 515, 519

PETER GAEDE 455, 469, 475, 488; *also drawings on pages 36, 37, 40, 66, 80*

JOHN GAME 47, 58, 81, 83, 87, 92, 100, 114, 124, 127, 132

WILLIAM GRENFELL 404, 431, 440, 465, 466, 471, 472

JOYCE GROSS 356, 357, 359

P. HAGGARD 232, 236, 237, 250, 257, 258, 262, 266, 270, 271, 276, 277, 279, 281, 282, 283, 284, 285, 287, 288, 289, 290, 292, 293, 294, 295, 297, 298, 300, 301, 302, 304, 306, 307, 308, 309, 310, 311, 313, 314, 320, 321

CHRIS HEAIVILIN / AZALEA CREEK PUBLISHING 240, 242

JAMES HOGUE 247, 248, 275, 315, 316

JANET HORTON 480

DR. LLOYD GLENN INGLES 411, 424, 426, 427, 432, 433, 434, 454, 457, 467, 478, 483, 484, 490, 492, 500, 502, 514, 518, 520, 523, 526, 527, 528, 532, 535

STEPHEN INGRAM 1, 2, 3, 4, 5, 6, 7, 8, 9, 10, 11, 14, 27, 60, 116, 143, 144, 145, 146, 147, 148, 149, 152, 154, 162, 167, 170, 171, 173, 174, 180, 181, 183, 185, 186, 187, 188, 190, 191, 196, 198, 199, 206, 207, 209, 212, 214, 215, 358, 361, 443, 449, 458, 511

JEANNE R. JANISH *drawings on pages 83, 85, 98*

ALDEN M. JOHNSON 489, 494, 503

STEVE JUNAK 44, 49, 50, 52, 53, 55, 78, 82, 98, 105, 108, 113, 119, 126, 134, 141, 158, 161, 163, 165, 166, 168, 175, 182, 193, 200, 204, 210

RUSS KERR / MAJESTYOFBIRDS.COM 377, 378, 379, 380, 381, 382, 383, 384, 385, 386, 387, 388, 389, 390, 391, 392, 393, 394, 395, 396, 397, 398, 399, 400, 401, 406, 407, 408, 412, 413, 415, 416, 417, 420, 422, 425, 429, 435, 436, 438, 439, 444, 445, 446, 447, 448, 450, 451, 453, 456, 462, 463, 464, 476, 477, 481, 485, 486, 487

PETER KNAPP 73, 86, 96, 106, 120, 131, 136, 138, 352, 402, 405, 409, 414, 419, 421, 428, 441, 460, 461, 470, 474, 506, 517, 533

PAUL KOSNIK 353, 354

INDEX

metallic wood borers, **204,** pl. 266
Metal Mark, 209
Metalmark, Mormon, **218,** pl. 297
Mezira, 196
Micropterus
    coosae, 246
    dolomieu, **246,** pl. 348
    punctulatus, **246,** pl. 349
    salmoides, **246,** pl. 347
Microtus
    californicus, 379
    longicaudus, **379**–380, pl. 531
    montanus, **380,** pl. 532
midges
    dixid, **224**–225
    midges, **225**
    mountain, **225**
    phantom, **224**–225
    See also flies; mosquitoes
Milbert's Tortoiseshell, 220
Milkweed Beetle, 206
Milkweed Bug, 196
milkweeds
    purple, **70**–71, pl. 62
    showy, 71
millipedes, **183,** pl. 227
mimicry, by butterflies, 71, 213
Mimidae, **322**–323, pls. 462–463
Mimulus
    aurantiacus, 130–131
    guttatus, **103**–104, pl. 137
    lewisii, 104
    primuloides, 104
Mimus polyglottos, **322,** pl. 462
Miner's Cat. *See* Ringtail
miner's lettuce, **98,** pl. 126
mining, for gold, 25
mining bees, **233**
mining of leaves
    by fruit flies, 227
    by leafminers, 208–209
Mink, **359,** pl. 507
minnows
    California Roach, **238**–239, pl. 330
    Hardhead, **239,** pl. 331
    Hitch, **238**
    Lahontan Redside, **238,** pl. 329
    Sacramento Pikeminnow, **239**
    Speckled Dace, **239**–240, pl. 332
    Tui Chub, **237**–238, pl. 328
mints
    giant hyssop (horsemint), **86,** pl. 97

    gray-leaved skullcap, **87**
    mountain pennyroyal (coyote mint),
        86, pl. 98
    mustang, 86
    self-heal, **86**–87, pl. 99
minute pirate bugs, **197,** pl. 252
Miridae, **197**
mistletoes
    on cottonwoods, 165
    oak mistletoe, **106,** pl. 141
    western dwarf, 106
Misumena, 178
mites
    eriophyid, 154
    red-spider, **182**
    See also ticks
Mixed Conifer Belt, 21
mock orange, wild, **122,** pl. 159
Mockingbird, Northern, **322,** pl. 462
    See also Thrasher
Moina, 176
mole
    Broad-footed, **351,** pl. 491
    Shrew-, **352**
mole salamanders
    California Tiger Salamander, **248,**
        pl. 350
    Long-toed Salamander, **248**–249,
        pl. 351
Mollusca, **172**–176
mollusks
    amber snails, 174
    chaparral snails, 173
    Ear Snail, **174**–175
    Forest Disc, 174
    hesperian snails, 173
    Keel Shell, 175
    land and aquatic forms, 172
    Pacific Banana Slug, 174
    Philippine clams, 175
    Quick Gloss, **173**–174
    shoulderband snails, 173
    sideband snails, 173
    Tadpole Physella, 175
    Ubiquitous Peaclam, 175
    Western Glass-snail, 174
    Western Pearlshell, **175**–176
Molothrus ater, **339**–340
Monadenia, 173
Monarch, 213, **222,** pl. 311
Monardella
    lanceolata, 86

ABOUT THE AUTHORS

Tracy I. Storer was professor of zoology at the University of California, Berkeley, coauthored *California Grizzly* with Lloyd P. Tevis, Jr. (California, revised edition 1996), and wrote many other books and articles. Robert L. Usinger was professor of zoology at the University of California, Berkeley, and author of *Aquatic Insects of California* (California, 1959) among other publications. David Lukas is a professional naturalist and author of *Wild Birds of California* (2000) and *Watchable Birds of the Great Basin* (1999).

Series Design: Barbara Jellow
Design Enhancements: Beth Hansen
Design Development: Jane Tenenbaum
Illustrator/Cartographer: Bill Nelson
Composition: TechBooks
Text: 9/10.5 Minion
Display: ITC Franklin Gothic Book and Demi
Printer and Binder: Everbest Printing Company